EXPANDING HORIZONS
IN AFRICAN STUDIES

Proceedings of the

Twentieth Anniversary Conference, 1968

EXPANDING HORIZONS
IN AFRICAN STUDIES

Program of African Studies,
Northwestern University

Edited by

Gwendolen M. Carter & Ann Paden

Evanston   Northwestern University Press   1969

CONTENTS

Contents

PREFACE

The title of this volume, *Expanding Horizons in African Studies,* is appropriate not only to the participants' contributions to the Twentieth Anniversary Conference of the Program of African Studies at Northwestern University, but also to the Program's activities since its inception. This was the first formally organized program of African studies in the United States, and under the stimulus and leadership of Melville J. Herskovits it sought to broaden and deepen knowledge, experience, and insight regarding the vast and significant continent of Africa. It seemed especially fitting, therefore, that the conference recognizing the twentieth anniversary of the formal establishment of the Program of African Studies should concentrate on evaluating the current state of African studies and on anticipating the methods and directions which will characterize African studies in the coming decades.

A further objective was to bring back to Northwestern University as many as possible of those scholars who had combined their advanced training here with a concern for African studies. This objective complemented the primary purpose of the conference since so many of the creative leaders in specialized aspects of African studies are among the seventy-eight Ph.D. recipients who had been enrolled in the Program.

The papers presented in this volume are drawn primarily

from our own Ph.D.'s, with additional contributions from members of our staff, current and past, and from African colleagues who through their association with the Program have shared their knowledge and wisdom with us. Several members of the group preferred to contribute informally in the conference sessions. Where texts were available, remarks of discussants have been included in the volume; these unfortunately are not inclusive, but they are suggestive of the lively and productive interaction that occurred throughout the conference among those presenting papers and the discussants and other participants in the several sessions.

The Program's close working relations with African institutions remain a constant source of stimulus and enrichment. It was a particular satisfaction that, through the support of the Carnegie Corporation, it was possible to bring a number of outstanding African scholars to participate in the conference. Drs. S. Joshua L. Zake, Isaria Kimambo, Victor Uchendu, and Abeodu Jones hold Northwestern Ph.D.'s; and Drs. Mabogunje, Nketia, Mazrui, Ansre, Demoz, El-Dabh, and Bentsi-Enchill have particular links with the Program. Much of the success of the conference was due to the willingness of these participants to bring their special experience and insights into all its sessions.

The conference was opened by President Roscoe Miller, who presented greetings and congratulations on behalf of the university. At the first dinner short speeches were given also by several of those most closely associated with the Program over a long period of time. Mrs. Frances Herskovits, who recalled the early days of the Program, received a rising tribute of respect and affection. Joseph Greenberg, who has made such pioneer and creative contributions to the study of linguistics, spoke with humor and force of early interdisciplinary interactions, and subsequently in an unrecorded Dialogue on Sociolinguistics demonstrated his continued mastery in his field. Equally stirring was Akin Mabogunje's enunciation of the theme so well realized in the conference itself: the contributions, past, present, and future, of mutual enterprise between African and American scholars.

At the concluding dinner Vice-President Payson Wild affirmed the university's commitment to the Program of African Studies, and many of the participants spoke of the stimulation they had received by meeting with scholars from many disciplines and from many countries and of the value of such exchanges of ideas within free-ranging yet directed discussions. African and American participants alike affirmed their determination to maintain the new links of cooperation which had been established through the conference. Previously, graduate students enrolled in the Program had presented syntheses of the sessions for which they had served as rapporteurs. It seemed particularly appropriate that this forward-looking conference should be closed with contributions from the coming generation of African scholars.

This volume is presented to the ever enlarging community of those concerned with African studies in the hope that it will aid constructive advances in the many areas into which such studies have spread. Never has there been more need to combine sound scholarship with creative innovation and purposeful advance than at present as the United States becomes increasingly aware of its heritage from and links with Africa.

May, 1969   Gwendolen M. Carter
                       Director, Program of African Studies
                       Northwestern University

INTRODUCTION

The basic assumption of the conference marking the twentieth anniversary of the Program of African Studies of Northwestern University was that the perspective of twenty years of study and research made it appropriate to survey our state of knowledge about Africa and to consider priorities for future lines of inquiry. In 1948, when the Program was officially founded, the majority of scholars as well as of the general American public had known little, and indeed cared little, about African culture and society. At that time the major part of the continent was still under colonial control; although national movements were becoming visible in many African areas, few could anticipate the rapidity and direction of change.

Moreover, while there had long been scattered intellectual interest and moral concern in the United States for Africa and Africans, there were few African specialists by the end of World War II who were both committed to the scientific study of this area and equipped to undertake such study. The generation of young Americans who had gained some awareness of the significance of this continent—and who were eager to understand the processes of change already visible, to gain hard data about Africa, and to acquire an appreciation of African culture in time and space—could find few places at home or abroad where the scientific study of Africa was firmly established. Slowly at first, and then with striking acceleration of pace as the United States assumed a more effective role in the international community, American universities addressed themselves in a more systematic fashion to the study of Africa. This development of African studies in the United States makes an exciting chapter in the history of higher education, for universities have increasingly responded to the challenge to explore and add to our knowledge about the rich and varied cultures of Africa.

The history of the growth of African studies in the United States has been strongly influenced by the pioneering efforts of the late Professor Melville J. Herskovits. While his intellectual contributions are well known to students of Africa the world over, the conference marking the twentieth anniversary of the Program of African Studies, of which he was the founder and for fifteen years the director, was living testimony to his sustained influence on American education about Africa.

Since one facet of the conference was directed toward registering the current state of African studies, it is worth noting some of the changes that have taken place in the last twenty years. Had such an international conference been attempted in 1948 the participants would have come from fewer fields and would have had more concern for the unusual than for correlations. African representation would have been minimal, or perhaps nonexistent. In a sense, therefore, the Twentieth Anniversary Conference not only testified to the maturity of African studies in the United States, as represented by the Program of African Studies at Northwestern University and the numerous other programs that have been established more recently, but also to the distinction of African scholarship in making profound and ever increasing contributions to the advancement of knowledge about Africa.

Beyond registering how far and how broadly African studies have developed, and demonstrating by its composition the richness of disciplinary concentration and interdisciplinary cooperation in the African field, the conference was intended to suggest guidelines for the next twenty years. These guidelines were to consider both substance and methodology. Moreover, recognizing that new methods and techniques have become essential equipment of the social sciences and humanities, attention was given to how these tools of analysis could more adequately contribute to substantive inquiry. Not all the participants accepted the usefulness of behavioral approaches and the use of statistics in identifying trends and seeking further insights. There was also a division of opinion and approach as to what should be the purpose and character of research. Some participants urged a search for knowledge directed by individual and broadly theoretical interests; others advocated studies directed toward practical problems faced by African governments. A great merit of the conference was the diversity which marked the discussions. The range of contributions represented a wide variety of approaches and elicited a frankness of comment from all sides.

As papers in this volume demonstrate, there were many substantive contributions to the conference from scholars who presented perspectives on developments in their own fields and indicated directions and priorities for work in the future. Victor Uchendu and Frank Willett provide wide-ranging surveys of the growth of anthropological and archaeological studies in Africa. Hamid Mowlana discusses the development and implications of communication technology in that continent, and Marshall Segall suggests directions for the rapidly expanding studies in social psychology in Africa. Other participants were particularly concerned with techniques and methods of analysis which have not been widely utilized in previous attempts to comprehend the nature and dynamics of change in Africa. Thus, John Paden, Donald G. Morrison, and Robert Mitchell report on their use of discriminant function analysis; Edward Soja discusses preliminary results of an analysis of communication patterns in interstate linkages in Nigeria; Remi Clignet reports on his handling of particularly rich statistical data from Yaounde and Douala in the Cameroon Republic; Jack Berry suggests insights to be secured from the uniquely detailed collection of material on the role of multilingualism and the process of linguistic integration in Madina, Ghana; James Fernandez discusses quantitative techniques which may enable the anthropologist to ask more complex questions than in the past; and Irma Adelman stresses the insights to be gained from factor analysis. In contrast, Harold Schneider challenges some prevailing approaches. Still other papers—like those of Peter Gould in geography, Klaus Wachsmann in ethnomusicology, and Robert Armstrong and Daniel Crowley in aesthetics—combine far-reaching surveys with indications of new methods of analysis.

While these substantive and methodological papers chart new directions for well-established fields, there are other papers that explicitly or implicitly suggest changing the focus of African studies. Thus Sterling Stuckey, in relation to Afro-American studies, and Peter Hammond, in a still wider outreach to the experience of Africans in several environments outside of Africa, stress the need for research that is more broadly comparative than yet attempted. Similarly, Isaria Kimambo breaks new ground in his paper on historical research goals in Tanzania by indicating lines of intersecting investigations whose concentration on material within a single country can provide new levels of knowledge and depth of insight.

No less distinctive, though differing sharply in focus and emphasis, are three papers by African scholars who to varying degrees also have political roles or influence in their countries. S. Joshua L. Zake makes the strongest assertion of the need for African research to direct itself to the practical problems of government. Kwamena Bentsi-Enchill is no less concerned to have scholarship serve the needs of African development but sees this function performed through broad proposals for constitutional engineering. Ali Mazrui's view of the scholar's role as analyst and publicist of weaknesses as well as strengths, was an issue on which he clashed with Zake, who stressed the overriding importance of handling material in a way that will contribute to national unity.

Varied as are these contributions and those of the discussants, they suggest a number of significant indicators of the future direction of African studies. First, the disciplines are being asked to address themselves to questions hitherto omitted from their purview. Along these lines, African studies, which are already making contributions to the central concerns of the disciplines through data and new findings, may enrich and extend the disciplines still further. They may also contribute more meaningfully to decisions on public policy. Second, it is expected that methodological tools and concepts developed in relation to other bodies of material, like those drawn from research on American conditions, will be utilized more broadly and with greater frequency by African specialists in all fields. Third, if African studies are to fulfill the expectations they have aroused, some revision of training and research curricula are needed. The clear implication not only of relevant papers in this volume but also of contemporary demands is that African studies must concern themselves more seriously with those aspects of African history and culture that have had an impact on the black man wherever he may be, and that the experiences of the African of the diaspora, whether in the Americas, or Europe, or Southwest Asia, must not be disregarded by African studies.

Above all, the conference demonstrated the rich returns for study and research from cross-cultural studies and interdisciplinary interactions. In the constant and fruitful exchanges no one stopped to ask from what discipline the comment or criticism or insight came. Thus the conference brought heartening evidence that the old fear of potential conflict between discipline and area study has been resolved by awareness that the relation of substance and approach is constructive and complementary. While the disciplines remain the constant, the value of area concentration lies in its stimulus to well-founded comparisons, searching analysis, and interdisciplinary interaction. The formulation of these objectives has been a contribution of African studies over the last twenty years. The challenge of the next twenty years is that African studies strengthen and contribute still more fully to the realization of these goals.

Gwendolen M. Carter
Ibrahim Abu-Lughod

EXPANDING HORIZONS
IN AFRICAN STUDIES

PRIORITY ISSUES 1.
FOR SOCIAL ANTHROPOLOGICAL RESEARCH
IN AFRICA
IN THE NEXT TWO DECADES

Victor C. Uchendu

The mandate of anthropology is the "study of man and his works."[1] This broad definition of anthropology represents a "declaration of intent" which all anthropologists seem to accept whether their specific frame of reference is "society" or "culture." But what anthropologists *do* in actual fact is another matter. The title of John Beattie's recent book summarizes the traditional concern of anthropologists: *Other Cultures*. In terms of what anthropologists do, anthropology remains in practice "the study of other cultures by other culture bearers," who are by tradition Western scholars. This distinction between the "mandate of anthropology" and the "traditional concerns" of anthropologists has many implications, including the question of the priorities which Western anthropologists have traditionally set for themselves and their subjects. In this paper, I argue that the factors which determine priority issues for research in our discipline are no longer entirely determined by scientists and scientific institutions outside the developing world. The rate of social, economic, and technological change in the societies traditionally studied by anthropologists has become so accelerated that whatever may be the disciplinary perspectives and traditional concerns of Western scholars, the research demands generated in these societies must increasingly deserve attention.

1. Melville J. Herskovits, *Man and His Works* (New York: Knopf, 1952).

Research Traditions: A Historical Note

Because of the all-embracing character of the mandate of anthropology, anthropologists, unlike other social scientists, did not normally engage in endless and fruitless debate over the nature and the boundary of their discipline. On the other hand, anthropologists have consistently worried about their limited scientific manpower problem: too many societies with unwritten cultures vying for the attention of too few trained anthropologists. The "manpower problem" is the basis (or is it the rationale?) of the "urgent anthropology" which characterized the history of our discipline at the turn of the nineteenth century, and which in its wake created the revolution in the field work and field-work methodology to which we are the heirs.

From the late nineteenth century to the third decade of this century, priority issues in anthropological research were focused on small, isolated tribal societies with unwritten history rather than on "problem areas." Field work was dominated by anthropological expeditions involving teams of workers, which were gradually but increasingly replaced by single-society studies by individual workers. In making his case for "urgent anthropology" and in setting his priority for African research—and he gave priority to the Bushmen and the Hottentots—Rivers argued that owing to the "perishability" of ethnological data, "Ethnology cannot stand delay. . . . In many parts of the world, the death of every old man brings with it the loss of knowledge never to be replaced."[2] It is six decades since Rivers wrote, yet "urgent anthropology" is still being discussed in *Current Anthropology*.[3] Lévi-Strauss summarizes the traditionalist view on the subject when he writes: "It is precisely because the so-called primitive peoples are becoming extinct that their study should now be given absolute priority."[4]

2. W. H. R. Rivers, "Report on Anthropological Research Outside America," in *Reports upon the Present Condition and Future Needs of the Science of Anthropology*, ed. by Rivers *et al.* (Washington, D. C.: The Carnegie Institution of Washington, publication 200, 1913, pp. 5–6.

3. W. C. Sturtevant, "Urgent Anthropology," *Current Anthropology*, VIII (October, 1967), 355–59.

4. C. Lévi-Strauss, "Anthropology: Its Achievements and Future," *Current Anthropology*, VII (April, 1966), 124–27.

It would be distorting historical perspective to attribute all the single-society studies since the 1920's to the demands of "urgent anthropology" and the limitations of scientific manpower. The reactions against the single-minded evolutionary theories of the late nineteenth century and the desire to generate hypotheses which could be tested cross-culturally were important factors in this enterprise. In colonial Africa especially, the problems of administration created the demand for anthropological investigations, priority usually being given to those societies which seemed to receive every administrative innovation with hostility.

Other Developments and Trends in Anthropology

Two major factors which decided research priorities in social anthropology have been outlined: the shortage of trained field workers and the demand from colonial administrations. The invaluable ethnographic contributions made by the missionary writers and colonial administrators cannot be ignored, but their work was only a by-product of their other interests.

A break in the tradition of single-society studies came slowly. Theoretical developments in anthropology as well as in other social science disciplines raised new issues from the 1930's on. The development of "problem areas" as a focus of academic research became increasingly important, especially as the impact of Herskovits' works on Africa and its connections with the Americas started to attract attention. Although data collection from single-society studies remained important, this activity was no longer viewed as an end in itself. The cross-cultural implications of field data acquired a new dimension and contributed more effectively to the testing of hypotheses as research traditions moved away from single-society studies to the "problem areas" shared by a number of societies. The major "problem areas" which attracted the attention of social anthropologists working in Africa, especially after World War II, included the patterns and problems of labor migration; the problems of urban adjustments and the associational structures emerging in urban settings; the impact of the market economy on traditional African economies, especially as they affect the ability of the African cultivator to produce for the market; the "content" of land tenure; the changing role of the chiefs in the working of modern political institutions; and the new elite groups that direct the political, economic, and social life of modern African societies.

The interest in "problem areas" as a research focus coincided with increasing financial support for social anthropological research by the colonial governments and by private foundations in the United States.[5] The number of institutions and scholars interested in African problems was growing just at the time that the sub-disciplines of anthropology were becoming not only specialized fields but were developing their own sophisticated field methodologies and theoretical foci. Although the institutionalization of area programs was late in coming, this fact did not seriously limit research efforts and output. As of the mid-forties, it was becoming difficult for anthropologists to keep up with the flow of materials from their respective sub-disciplines—a problem that is still with us. To cope with this communication problem, periodic stock-taking of the state of our science became an urgent need.

Let me call attention to a few publications, sponsored by scientific institutions in the mid-forties but published in the fifties, which were essentially stock-taking exercises. The *Yearbook of Physical Anthropology* started its publication in 1947. Sponsored by the Wenner-Gren Foundation for Anthropological Research, the *Yearbook of Anthropology,* edited by W. I. Thomas, Jr., made its first appearance in 1955. Its purpose was defined as "to represent the major accomplishments and trends" in selected aspects of the field of anthropology during 1952–54. *Anthropology Today,* edited by Kroeber *et al.,* was published in 1953. Through individual papers and extensive bibliographies contributed by some of the best minds produced by our science, it summarized the recent scholarly achievements in anthropology up to that date.

The reception given to the *Biennial Review of Anthropology* since its first publication in 1959 shows that there is a growing demand for this periodic stock-taking. Edited by J. Siegel, the *Biennial Review of Anthropology* undertakes to "describe and summarize in a systematic manner" the more noteworthy papers and monographs published in a selected number of "fields" within the review period. Besides periodic reviews sponsored by institutions, individual contributions have been quite substantial as well as outstanding. Kroeber's paper "A Half Century of Anthropology" is a general review

5. L. Mair, "The Social Sciences in Africa South of the Sahara: The British Contribution," *Human Organization,* XIX (Fall, 1960), 98–107.

of "trends" in the discipline.[6] Other contributions like those of E. M. Mendelson and Heine-Geldern are focused on national developments, especially in Germany and France.[7]

The African area, especially sub-Saharan Africa, has not been neglected in these reviews. A special issue of *Human Organization*, devoted to the theme "Social Science in Action in Sub-Saharan Africa" and edited by Miner, documents "some of the European tradition of African studies and the current activities to which this work has led." According to the editor, the purpose of the review was "to provide an introduction to, and general survey of, the role which the social sciences play in Africa."[8] In examining the British contribution to research in English-speaking Africa, Lucy Mair discusses the organization of research and the growth in research output in East, Central, West, and South Africa, especially between the two world wars and after.[9] An inventory of research efforts in French-speaking Africa by Balandier and in the Congo and Ruanda-Urundi by Nicaise also appeared in this 1960 special issue.

After World War II African studies entered a phase of sustained growth in terms of overall research commitments made and the quality of the research output achieved. An inventory of this effort is contained in *The African World*. Edited by R. A. Lystad and published in 1965, this study carried contributions from a number of disciplines ranging from prehistory to folklore.[10] Basically a "fact-gathering" and a "fact-communicating" inventory of research efforts, the study is also "forward-looking" insofar as individual contributors made some attempt to document the trends in African research, point up the gaps in our knowledge in the various disciplines, and map the probable directions of future research.

6. A. L. Kroeber, "A Half Century of Anthropology," *Scientific American*, CLXXXIII (September, 1950), 87–94.

7. E. M. Mendelson, "Some Present Trends in Social Anthropology in France," *British Journal of Sociology*, IX (September, 1958), 251–70; R. Heine-Geldern, "One Hundred Years of Ethnological Theory in the German-Speaking Countries: Some Milestones," *Current Anthropology*, V (December, 1964), 407–18.

8. H. Miner, ed., *Social Science in Action in Sub-Saharan Africa*, special issue of *Human Organization*, XIX (Fall, 1960).

9. Mair, "The Social Sciences in Africa South of the Sahara," pp. 98–107.

10. R. A. Lystad, ed., *The African World* (New York: Praeger, 1965).

This brief survey of the trends and developments in anthropology as a whole, and in the African area in particular, is designed to underscore the fact that while long-range research and theory development remain the goal of our science, interest in short-run problems has never flagged. Anthropology is a living science. The problems of society keep it alive and have helped to shape its research priorities in the past. The social priorities which non-Western societies now set for themselves throw a major challenge to our science, and in fact they question the traditional concern of anthropologists. The unresolved questions are: How much time and what resources can we afford to give to the nineteenth-century "priority issue" which Lévi-Strauss has restated firmly in the 1960's? Or, are anthropologists prepared to accept the broader implications of the mandate of our science which probably influenced Lévi-Strauss to write: "If society is in anthropology, anthropology is itself in society; it has been able to enlarge progressively the object of its study to the point of including therein the totality of human societies"?[11] This is probably a major achievement. However, the problem facing anthropology in a modern age is not so much whether anthropologists can provide a complete ethnography for each living ethnic population (desirable as this may be) as whether anthropologists are willing and able to attempt to grapple with the problems that a constantly changing world presents.

Priority Issues for Research

This brings me to the key phrase in the title of this paper—the priority issues. Issues of a priority nature arise because resources are limited. This factor of scarcity dictates not only a choice between alternatives but the ranking or time sequence in which issues can be handled. To minimize arbitrary ranking of issues, we need to establish a criterion for ranking them. There may be disagreement about the criterion selected, but very few would quarrel with the criterion of relevance. It is when we get an answer to the question "Relevant to what?" that opinions are bound to vary. Some anthropologists are bound to rank high in their scale of research activities those which can contribute to theory building and development.

11. C. Lévi-Strauss, "The Scope of Anthropology," *Current Anthropology*, VII (1966), 122.

Others may be more inclined to research activities which will bring them in contact with the changing problems of society. These polar views, which are often framed in terms of applied versus non-applied anthropological research, seem to pose false issues, and, in the final analysis, turn out to be definitional problems.[12] Research which contributes to theory formation and theories which illuminate practical problems of society and thereby contribute to their solution are not necessarily in competition but are complementary. In a rapidly changing society this kind of research activity should command priority. How can a scientist find out the limitations of his theories unless he brings them in touch with the problems of society?

Fortunately for African studies, these controversies have not prevented a forward-looking approach—a kind of "perspective plan" for future research in some of the problem areas generated by the dynamics of African social systems. Following World War II, the problems of African societies became important factors which helped to determine research priorities. In 1947 Firth made a comprehensive survey of conditions in the English-speaking sector of the West African region and concluded as follows: "It seems abundantly clear that systematic sociological research should be at least a concomitant of a development and welfare program if it cannot now be a prerequisite to it."[13] In his recommendations for future research Firth stressed the need for basic data on population distribution and its relation to resource endowment, the relation between the social structure and the emerging farming systems, and the study of family and class structure in urban areas. He put a high priority on the study of internal trade and marketing and of labor migration and its effects on traditional economy. In emphasizing the need for interdisciplinary cooperation or interpenetration, he called attention to the assistance which anthropologists can render in nutritional research. Forde's earlier recommendations on anthropological research in Gambia were more in line with the traditional practice of anthropologists than Firth's.[14] Even

12. D. Brokensha, "Applied Anthropology in English-Speaking Africa," Monograph 8 (Lexington, Ky.: Society for Applied Anthropology, 1966).

13. R. W. Firth, "Social Problems and Research in British West Africa," *Africa*, XVII (April, 1947), 77–91, and XVIII (July, 1947), 170–80.

14. D. Forde, "Notes and News: Research on Gambia," *ibid.*, XVI (April, 1946), 115.

here, however, there was a recognition of the social problems of increasing urbanization when he recommended a social survey of Bathurst as well as the collection of ethnographies.

The eastern and the central African regions were not neglected. Lists of research priorities were drawn up for various countries: Schapera for Kenya, Stanner for Uganda and Tanganyika, and Gluckman for the central African area.[15] Gluckman's recommendations deserve attention not only because of the priority issues put forward but because of the way he relates these issues to his central thesis. This thesis is that industrialization and labor migration dominate the whole trend of social development in the central African area. From these two factors he deduced his two-pronged research foci: first, the mining and non-mining urban centers and their peculiar problems, and second, the rural areas whose economies exert different influences on migration trends as well as on migrants' behavior. It is no wonder that he stressed three major problem areas for research: (1) the causes and effects of labor migration; (2) the economic, political, and religious values of the traditional societies; and (3) the formation of new groups and associations in the urban settings.

The Next Two Decades

Looking back on the achievements of the last two decades in African anthropology,[16] one cannot help claiming that anthropologists have made considerable progress in spite of their traditional concerns. There are still gaps in our knowledge. Basic ethnographic information is lacking for many social groups in Africa, and there are many societies that are inadequately studied or reported upon. Insofar as this gap remains, fact-finding and ethnographic documentation will remain an essential, but not necessarily a dominant, concern of African anthropology. In my view, the problems of Africa, especially the social goals which the states have set for themselves, will increasingly influence research priorities in the next two decades. Two developments make this view predictive of the fu-

15. I. Schapera, *Some Problems of Anthropological Research in Kenya Colony*, International African Institute, Memorandum 23, 1949; W. E. H. Stanner, *Report on Social Science Research in Uganda and Kenya* (n.p., 1949); M. Gluckman, "The Seven-Year Plan of the Rhodes-Livingstone Institute," *Rhodes-Livingstone Journal*, IV (1945), 1–32.

16. P. H. Gulliver, "Anthropology," in *The African World*.

ture trends of events. These are the fact of Africa's political independence and the emergence of African-based institutions of higher learning.

Let us consider the political development first. The greatest revolution in Africa within the last two decades is the achievement of political independence. This sovereign status has compelled African leaders to cultivate a new image for their nations and for the continent. So far as I can tell, no one has defined this "new image," but the search continues around such vague concepts as "negritude" and the "African personality." Implicit in the thinking of many Africans is a conscious rejection, not of "anthropologists" but of "anthropology," or, if you like, "bad anthropology." Although the foundation of the sociology departments in many African universities was laid by eminent anthropologists, there is no department of anthropology in the independent African-controlled area—the greatest concession so far is a combined sociology/anthropology department. There is, in fact, an ambivalent attitude toward anthropology in many African countries today. Maquet states the case clearly when he relates this ambivalence to the accidental factor of colonial experience:

> Anthropologists expected that their discipline would be
> well received in the newly independent [African] nations,
> particularly by the University trained Africans who
> usually constitute the political and administrative elite.
> The term "anthropology" and its French counterpart,
> *ethnologie*, are frowned on in many quarters; they are
> suspected of being tinged with colonialism. New research
> projects are not always encouraged and some African au-
> thorities manifest more distrust than enthusiasm when
> asked to support or facilitate anthropological field
> work.[17]

It would be reading the trends in Africa wrongly to conclude that anthropology has no future on the continent. Problems which face African societies are partly anthropological in nature and will continue to be so, but the orientation of anthropological research will have to change. This is exactly what Onwuachi and Wolfe had in mind when they declared, "If anthropology is to have a place in the future of Africa, the relevance of anthropology to problems of Africa must be

17. J. J. Maquet, "Objectivity in Anthropology," *Current Anthropology*, V (February, 1964), 47–55.

made clear."[18] On a more positive note, Maquet writes, "It is an illusion to believe that one can still study today an African society living as if modern technologies and institutions did not exist."[19] Relating African cultures to the problems created by the modern institutions and technologies which are part of their wider society will increasingly become important research problems for the future.

The emergence of national universities and research institutions in Africa in the last two decades implies a new division of labor in research as well as opportunities for inter-institutional cooperation in research in a few problem areas between African-based research institutions and Western institutions interested in African problems. There is evidence that this kind of cooperation is increasing, and we hope that it is a trend which will strengthen in the future. This kind of institutional cooperation will definitely help to eliminate the duplication of research efforts which are wasteful of scarce resources; it will also help those institutions that are based outside Africa with the problem of "clearance" of research projects in independent African countries.[20]

The growing interest in African studies in Europe and America will definitely affect research priorities for Africa. Brokensha and McCall have documented this interest among American scholars,[21] and Greenberg has called attention to the interdisciplinary implications of this development.[22] For Western Europe, the role of British institutions and scholars in the field of African anthropology is too well known to require documentation. But French contributions and the growing interest of Belgian institutions and their scholars in African studies deserves attention.[23] In the next two decades

18. P. C. Onwuachi and A. W. Wolfe, "The Place of Anthropology in the Future of Africa," *Human Organization*, XXV (1966), 93.

19. Maquet, "Objectivity in Anthropology," p. 51.

20. V. McKay, "The Research Climate in East Africa," *African Studies Bulletin*, XI (April, 1968), 1–17.

21. D. F. McCall, "American Anthropology in Africa," *African Studies Bulletin*, X (September, 1967), 20–34; D. Brokensha, "African Studies in the United States," *ibid.*, VII (April, 1964), 12–24; *ibid.*, VIII (April, 1965), 1–28; *ibid.*, IX (April, 1966), 38–80.

22. J. Greenberg, "Interdisciplinary Perspectives in African Research," *African Studies Bulletin*, IX (April, 1966), 8–23.

23. G. Balandier, "The French Tradition in African Research," *Human Organization*, XIX (Fall, 1960), 108–11; J. Nicaise, "Applied Anthropology in the Congo and Ruanda-Urundi," *ibid.*, 112–17.

Western institutions interested in Africa will no doubt continue to define their research priorities in a way that reflects their theoretical interests, their traditional concerns, and the individual interests of their graduate students who are specializing in African problems. But increasingly they must take the social realities in Africa into consideration.

The question might well now be asked: What are the problems facing independent Africa, the study of which not only can contribute to theory development but can also help decision-makers to become increasingly aware of some of the sociocultural implications of the choices they make? Anthropological opinion varies widely on this issue, and the variation in opinion reveals a generation gap. Generally, elder members of the anthropological lineage tend to think that our science would lose caste by getting involved in issues of policy and might lose its personality by studying emerging societies.[24] But the younger generation of anthropologists do not seem to care whether their research problems force them either outside the traditional paths or across the disciplinary boundary to find in other disciplines workable theories that give meaning to their data.[25] The fact is that anthropologists can no longer be unconcerned—and recent publications do indicate concern —with the pressing economic, social, and political problems in the developing world.

In the next two decades, and certainly for a longer period, the two problems which will confront independent Africa will be nation-building and economic and social development.

Anthropological Implications of Nation-Building

The "tribe" has been the traditional unit for anthropological study in Africa. Gulliver has described it as "the 'natural' unit of study—a unit of marked differentiation in sociocultural terms." [26] The fact is that where a "tribe" did not exist, anthropologists tended to invent one. The resultant loose definition of the term, which seldom makes any concession to

24. Lévi-Strauss, "Anthropology: Its Achievements and Future," p. 126.

25. R. Cohen, Comments on "Anthropological Theory, Cultural Pluralism, and the Study of Complex Societies," by Leo A. Despres, in *Current Anthropology*, IX (February, 1968), 18.

26. Gulliver, "Anthropology," *The African World*, p. 65.

demographic facts, makes this exercise quite unjustifiable. The accidental factor of colonial interests which brought many African ethnic groups into larger political units and the fact of political independence based on these units imply that the nation, or the nation-state, must be accepted as the unit of anthropological investigation. I can picture anthropology in the next two decades moving from a "tribal" to a "national" frame of reference. The anthropology of the nation holds the key which will open the door to the study of those technologically simple cultures which are now part of a wider society— the nation-state. The Kusasi of northeastern Ghana will be studied not as a "museum culture" but as part of modern Ghana. Given the present image of anthropology in Africa, it appears to me that the only practical way of extending our ethnographic knowledge of many ethnic groups for whom we have no data is to adopt a field strategy which relates the problems of the nation to the adjustment problems of the smaller social units which are experiencing rapid change.

The demand for the anthropology of the nation is not restricted to Africa. Patch has recognized this need for the Latin American area. He sees it as "an anthropology concerned not only with the small community but also with the fabric of culture and behavior which relates communities to one another and which makes more intelligible the structure and functioning of national institutions, as well as behavior and attitudes which derive from the unit of the nation." [27] The field of national problems, viewed in a national context, will be engaging the attention of anthropologists in the years ahead, whether their areal specialization is Africa, Asia, or Latin America. Anthropologists, who were the first social scientists to discover Africa, cannot afford to allot those problems which are generated by the internal dynamics of new nations to engineers, economists, political scientists, psychologists, and rural sociologists. The national frame of reference can illuminate many theoretical problems. Two decades ago it was tacitly assumed, if not believed, that African laborers were incapable of making long-term urban job commitments. Migrant labor problems consumed a lot of research resources as efforts were made to understand the reasons for what was assumed to be a high rate of labor turnover. It did not occur

27. R. W. Patch, *A Strategy of Anthropological Research in the Nation,* West Coast South America Series, XII (New York: American University Field Staff, 1965), p. 5.

to anybody that the political boundaries created by colonialism created an expanded economic system upon which some Africans could draw as their differing economic pressures dictated. The problem has changed radically in the 1960's. The vexing problem is no longer that Africans will not accept urban jobs but that they will not stay in their impoverished villages even though there are few jobs in the cities. "Back to the village" has become a current slogan strategy in many African countries, but in the absence of any worthwhile incentives this slogan seems to achieve no effective result.

Economic Development as a Goal

If there are anthropologists who still subscribe to the view that their African subjects are happy with poverty, poor health, and ignorance, they have misread the trends in that continent. The important fact about African societies in this decade is their rapid change. African leaders are making increasing commitments to social and economic development, and, of course, they are faltering in the process. There is every indication that this trend will continue.

Rapid change involves increasing conflict, a readjustment of existing social relations, and the restructuring of traditional priorities and loyalties. But the forces behind these changes are only dimly understood and should therefore receive priority in research. This is an area where we cannot allow the fruitless controversy about applied versus non-applied anthropological research to distract us from the great contribution which anthropology can make to the social and economic development of Africa. If anthropology is not a policy science and if anthropologists are not technical magicians, our science is not without valuable insights about the problems of changing societies and cultures. A planner, an administrator, or a change-agent cannot ignore these insights. McKay makes this point when he documents the widespread demand in Africa for "studies geared at least in part to help African governments in their economic, social and educational development planning." [28]

In which areas can anthropology be of help in Africa's economic development? Before answering this question, I must enter a caveat. Although the sub-discipline we call eco-

28. McKay, "The Research Climate in East Africa," p. 1.

nomic anthropology is acquiring some strength, anthropologists know that they are not economists. They do not claim that the phenomenon and the problems of economic development fall within their professional discipline. In fact some professional economists are not even sure that the field of economic development is entirely within the scope of economics because the problems of economic development are not strictly economic. The variables which economists have traditionally assumed to be unimportant in their analysis are crucially important for understanding change. This is where the strength of the science of anthropology lies: in our familiarity with the cultures, our holistic approach, and in our interest in pointing up those variables which tend to frustrate change.

To return to the question, anthropologists may approach the matter of identifying the relevant issues raised by programs of directed change and institutional transformation from a number of points. But two sources of information immediately suggest themselves. First, we can look at the elegant development plans which every African country is forced to prepare, either under internal pressure or to meet the requirements of external aid donors. Second, we can see what developments are taking place on the ground—new dams, tractor schemes, group farming, resettlement, and new industrial complexes, to name a few. These two sources of information provide important guidelines. But we must look beyond these guidelines if we are to understand the dynamics of African societies and the problems they generate for future research.

The following problem areas are unranked, and the list could be extended, but these represent the range of problems which will face many African countries in the years ahead:

1. The population problem
2. The human problems of resource and environmental development
3. The diffusion of agricultural innovations
4. The special problems of pastoral economies in the age of money economy
5. The anthropology of rural and urban communities
6. The African in commerce and in business
7. The politics of uneven development
8. Nutritional research
9. Child-development studies
10. African values, including religion, that are compatible or incompatible with rapid change

Population dynamics

Accurate information about the population of many African countries is not available. In the colonial days, many African peoples tended to underenumerate, either because of the traditional fear that one should not "boast" of children whose chances of survival were uncertain, or because they wanted to evade possible taxation. But in the charged political days following independence, some have tended to overenumerate. We know, however, that with the impact of modern medicine death rates are falling while birth rates are rising. The population problem of Africa needs to be precisely defined. This will vary from country to country. But the three central issues are (1) the relation between population and resource endowment, (2) the urban character of the population dynamics, and (3) population growth and economic development.

The trend toward urban migration and urban unemployment is politically irritating. But we need more information, not only on the urban-rural resource imbalance but on rural-rural resource imbalance. The population-resource imbalance must be lifted from mere statistics to a more concrete level. This will raise the question of land tenure and local sovereignty in land. Why are land-surplus and land-deficit economies coexisting in the same national economy? What processes lead to the emergence of a national land policy? Another question worthy of investigation is the attitude of different peoples toward family planning.

Resource development

There are a lot of human problems raised by technical change, especially when thousands of people are forced to abandon their traditional villages in order to make room for a dam or a slum clearance. The man-made lakes in Africa—the Kariba, the Volta, and the Kainji, to cite familiar examples—provide unusual opportunities for longitudinal studies and interdisciplinary cooperation. The archaeologist has the opportunity to study areas that are to be flooded or that are endangered by large-scale slum clearance and commercial activities. The social anthropologist can study the immediate consequences and the aftereffects of these schemes, as well as the adjustment problems of people resettling in a new ecological area. On a modest scale are the opportunities which the growing number of farm settlement schemes provide for the study of institutional and knowledge transfer, interethnic stereotypes among various settlers, and the new values and structures induced by a changed environment.

Diffusion research

Anthropological interest in diffusion research is not new. Since the nineteenth century anthropologists have shown an interest in the study of the spread of cultural traits among different cultural groups. But, with few exceptions, they have tended to ignore the processes by which cultural elements have become diffused within a particular culture. Although anthropologists have made a pioneering contribution to the theory of diffusion (Barnett has recently synthesized anthropological data on diffusion studies into a useful theoretical framework),[29] it is nevertheless true to say that generally anthropologists working in Africa have almost abandoned diffusion research. In the United States the requirement to assess the impact of U.S. Extension Services on the farming communities brought rural sociologists, especially in the land-grant colleges, to this field, which they now dominate. In a recent survey of the literature on diffusion research, only two of the 468 bibliographic items listed by Jones are on tropical Africa.[30] Rogers estimates that 50 per cent of all the reports on diffusion research since 1950 were contributed by rural sociologists, who also account for about 40 per cent of the total literature available on the subject.[31] But tropical Africa is grossly neglected.

Although the United States still dominates diffusion research, the progress made in Asia and Latin America in the last decade is substantial, and it is increasing. The African area remains a virgin field for diffusion studies. Innovations in African agriculture, especially the impact of the extension services on the farming communities, demand immediate

29. H. G. Barnett, *Innovation: The Basis of Cultural Change* (New York: McGraw-Hill, 1953).

30. G. E. Jones, ''The Adoption and Diffusion of Agricultural Practices,'' *World Agricultural Economics and Rural Sociology Abstracts,* IX, 1967, abstracts 2333–3427.

31. M. E. Rogers, *Bibliography of the Diffusion of Innovation* (East Lansing: M.S.U. Dept of Communication, *DIR* Report 6, 1967).

study. Bohannan has analyzed the impact of the introduction of money on Tiv economy.[32] Cohen has called attention to the human factors in the diffusion of innovations and the problems of communicating technical innovations through an effective demonstration in his suggestive paper, "The Success That Failed." [33] With the exception of three recent studies, there are few research projects directed toward this neglected field.[34] Is it not time we moved on from the analysis of the social consequences of the steel ax among the Yir Yoront to the study of the diffusion of modern farm technologies like insecticides and spraying regimes among Yoruba farmers? Diffusion studies directed at the farm level will help us to understand more clearly the interplay of forces—economic, political, social, cultural, and psychological, as well as the value systems—which influence individual decision-making among African farmers. Such studies will reveal the various channels of communication operating within and without the rural community and how individuals receive, interpret, and use the messages transmitted. These studies will also emphasize the need for interdisciplinary cooperation. But more important, the results of the empirical investigations might help not only to further the development of theory in social sciences but may contribute to the rational discussion and solution of operational problems.

Pastoral economies

The problems of the pastoral and semipastoral peoples and their economies will need more emphasis as national economies in Africa strive to bring all their different sectors into a

32. P. Bohannan, "The Impact of Money in an African Subsistence Economy," *Journal of Economic History*, XIX (December, 1959), 491–503.

33. R. Cohen, "The Success That Failed: An Experiment in Culture Change in Africa," *Anthropologica*, III (1961), 21–36.

34. The Consortium for the Study of Nigerian Rural Development (CSNRD), Michigan State University, has completed a study of farmer receptivity to agricultural innovations in certain parts of southern Nigeria. The Department of Agricultural Economics, Makerere University College, is carrying out similar studies in Kenya and Uganda. The food Research Institute, Stanford University, has just completed a field study of economic, cultural, and technical determinants of change in tropical Africa. In this project, case studies were made of the problems and processes of the diffusion of agricultural innovations in Teso, Kisii, Geita, Mazabuka, Kusasi, Akim-Abuakwa, and Katsina.

market network. The symbiotic economic relations between settled agriculturalists and the pastoral communities have been emphasized. As the pressure of population increases, thus using up marginal land, the land rotational system will no longer be a mode of adjusting to increased population. Continual cropping on the same piece of land will necessitate the use of modern technologies like new seed varieties and fertilizers. This is already happening in many parts of Africa. The social implications of this technical change for the pastoral economies have not been understood. Questions of land tenure, especially jural control of land and privileged use of pasture, will become important as the pace of economic development is accelerated; and these practices might clash with the concept of "national land policy" where this policy exists. We need more accurate information about the attitude of pastoral peoples toward innovations. "The generalization that pastoralism implies an especially strong and characteristic resistance to social change" has been questioned by Jacobs.[35] We need more information about the kinds of innovations that pastoralists tend to accept or reject, either as social groups or as individuals.

The rural and the urban areas

The anthropological study of the urban and the rural areas will continue for many decades to come. In rural areas, increasing attention will be paid to the question of rural inequality and its effects on the community structure. Rural crimes have been neglected as a field of study. There are rural crimes other than homicide, murder, and incest. Does the incidence of rural crime rise or fall with varying levels of socioeconomic attainment? How do we explain the difference in crime rates among rural communities of similar socioeconomic status? The rural areas will tend to receive more research attention because most of the needed diffusion studies will be done in these settings. The role of the rural migrant as a "settler" who helps to accelerate economic change needs further documentation. Polly Hill has documented the case of the Ghanaian migrant cocoa farmer.[36] But there are other

35. A. H. Jacobs, "African Pastoralists: Some General Remarks," *Anthropological Quarterly*, XXXVIII (July, 1965), 153.

36. P. Hill, "*Migrant Cocoa Farmers of Southern Ghana*" (Cambridge: Cambridge University Press, 1963).

cases and other problems which the study of the economic life of the rural society can reveal.

We also need information on the African in trade and in commerce. Everywhere in Africa government economic policies stress and encourage the participation of African businessmen in trade and in commerce. What problems of entry do these local entrepreneurs face, and how do they fare in a complex commercial world involving not only their national institutions and local contacts but also foreign and often mysterious institutions and contacts?

The problems of urban and rural areas can no longer be seen in isolation, because they are quite interdependent. Developments in the industrialized West suggest that urban life is hostile to the aged. Many African cities—Yoruba and Hausa cities are exceptions—are of recent development. It will be interesting to document how the aged in urban areas of Africa view their future and where they plan to retire after their active days are spent. Unemployment problems in the cities, the human problems in industry, the social ecology of the growing town, and the problems of the young will probably receive more attention in the future than will studies of the elite.

Other problem areas are likely to become increasingly important. More nutritional research will be necessary, not only as a contribution to medical anthropology but as a way of fighting malnutrition and raising the quality of rural life in Africa. This study has a contribution to make to child development, a new vista for African research. Psychological studies, especially in the area of personality formation, should receive more attention. A comparative study of African religious systems is needed. How do values—religious or otherwise—adjust to social change? The economic rationality of the African is no longer doubted. Can we test Weber's thesis with data derived from the study of African religions? In short, what features of African religious thought and practice are consistent or inconsistent with the Protestant Ethic?

The politics of development

The most sensitive area for research in the future will probably lie in those fields where honest investigations cannot avoid coming into friction with contradictions in government policies. I am thinking about the problems of the politics of unequal development and its implication for national integration and development. Economists may worry about this, but anthropologists will go on to explore the issue of "polity primacy" and its implications for social and economic development.

Conclusion

There will be no sharp break in research tradition between what anthropologists interested in Africa have done in the last two decades and what they are likely to do in the next two decades. There will, however, be a shift in emphases, for two reasons. First, the number of anthropologists working on African problems has increased and may continue to grow in the next two decades. Young and often resentful of the traditional disciplinary boundaries which inhibit communication, these scholars are not afraid to strike in new directions or to adopt any theories or theses that help to order their data. Second, developments in Africa and the trends of future events, if they are predictable, indicate that the definition of African problems, even for research purposes, should increasingly take into consideration the African point of view. I have attempted to define future research priorities from the latter perspective; this, of course, remains one man's point of view.

Whatever the priorities, certain trends in social anthropology will definitely continue. Some of these trends will strengthen research in those problem areas to which I have called attention. If my priorities are heavily biased in favor of economic development, I make no apology. This is the area to which I have directed my thinking during the last two years; it is a broad field capable of catering to many and diverse disciplinary interests.

Let me emphasize the trends which are likely to continue in future:

1. There will be increasing interdisciplinary cooperation because the problems of the future will require the assistance of the various social and natural sciences for a solution. The growing importance of area-studies programs, the rising index of cross-citation in published papers, and the increasing participation of anthropologists in research projects involving other social and natural scientists indicate the trend for the future—the breakdown of disciplinary isolationism and an increasing interdisciplinary penetration.

2. The longitudinal study of small communities, preferably by the same team, over a long time, will tend to become more important than it is at present. We know about the Nuer of the 1930's, the Tallensi of the 1940's, and the Tiv of the 1950's. We want to know what happens to them every five years, or less. Ethnographic snapshots, which capture a people and their culture over a year or two, leaving them literally fossilized in time, are not adequate for studying social change. Surely they provide a most important documented bench mark, which makes rapid surveys in a longitudinal framework not only easy but intellectually rewarding. But their limitations should be stressed. Colson and Scudder Thayer have recognized this need for the Tonga. I do not see why this trend should not become a tradition in anthropological research.

3. The study of complex institutions and societies will also continue.

4. Basic information on cultures for which data are either not available or not well documented will continue to be gathered. The collection of such data can no longer be viewed as an end in itself but might well be a by-product of other studies with a different frame of reference. The ethno-archaeological studies of many existing African populations like the Bushmen, the Hottentots, or the Ndorobo can be done as part of a wider study on the problems of their socioeconomic transition.

5. The search for an integrated theory of social action will continue.

Alvin W. Wolfe

Dr. Uchendu's review of past research trends shows that anthropologists have been influenced in the choice of priorities by contemporary events, events as Western anthropologists saw them at any particular time. As Uchendu puts it, "Anthropology is a living science. The problems of society keep it alive and have helped to shape its research priorities in the past." He goes on to suggest that "The social priorities which non-Western societies now set for themselves . . . question the traditional concern of anthropologists." And he gives us his view that "the problems of Africa, especially the social goals which the states have set for themselves, will increasingly influence research priorities in the next two decades." He cites nation-building as one such social goal, and economic and social development as another.

I want to comment on the limitations of Uchendu's clearly stated attitude that "the nation, or the nation-state, must be accepted as the unit of anthropological investigations." He remarks that he "can picture anthropology in the next two decades moving from a tribal to a national frame of reference." This is not to say that I am opposed to anthropologists working at the national level of integration or to the use of concepts valid at that level; rather, I am opposed to anthropologists, or any single anthropologist, becoming arrested in their investigations at any particular level. Dr. Uchendu may mean to encourage us to be broad-minded and expansive, to accept the nation-state *as well as* the "tribe," but in his enthusiasm he comes close to a rigidity of his own. I urge him, and all of us, to keep wide open the range of scale of the units which anthropologists may wish to describe.

At this moment in human history the nation-state may appear as the most salient unit commanding our destiny. But surely ten thousand years ago, the "tribe" must have seemed the last word in efficient management of resources. And before that a well-equipped composite band probably couldn't be beaten. I don't mean to sound flippant, for I am serious in my belief that men are developing systems of wider scale social units than the nation-state, at a level that can be called the supranational level of integration. In referring to systems at supranational levels of integration, I am talking about social systems relevant to some of the most pressing and unresolved problems of Africa today—problems of white supremacy, problems of regional economic development, problems of neocolonialism. There is nothing mystical here, just events not yet adequately studied. And I think anthropologists should be ready for new *concepts* because anthropology is, as Victor Uchendu says, a living science. Political scientists, in fact, are so wedded to the *state* concept, and economists so stuck with *national* accounts, that identification of something genuinely new with respect to social organization may well be left to the anthropologists.

Dr. Uchendu is right, of course, that in setting research priorities we must not restrict anthropology to the local community (as Brokensha almost does in his section on community studies in *Africa in the Wider World*), and we must not restrict anthropology to tribal studies (as Gulliver comes close to doing in his section in *The African World*). But for those same reasons, neither must we restrict anthropology to national studies (as Victor Uchendu appears to suggest in the paper being discussed here).

I would urge that we should take as a priority issue not only the maintenance of an open mind with respect to theory but also the continuing development of methods. The history of anthropology, into which fit those trends and developments of which Dr. Uchendu speaks, is largely the result of improvements in methods, either in data-collection or in data-analysis. The major contribution of those anthropologists we think of as great—Malinowski, Kroeber, Herskovits, Gluckman—was methodological. As one reads not only Uchendu, but Gulliver, Brokensha, Epstein, Lystad, Mair, and others who have recently looked to the road ahead, one comes to see that a successful attempt to improve one's methods has a payoff beyond one's own research domain. As methods improve in any science, discoveries, both sought for and serendipitous, are made. Possibly the time has come for anthropology to make method itself a priority issue, in the hope that novel methods will make us not only more efficient in African studies but wiser about Africa.

CONTEMPORARY AFRICAN RELIGION: 2. CONFLUENTS OF INQUIRY

James W. Fernandez

Let me ask the big question: Why study religion in Africa? It may not be easy to see—amidst the hortatory imperatives which quite naturally characterize the new Africa's first decade—what advantageous knowledge we can get from the study of religion. Africa must unite! Africa must industrialize! Africa must develop its local communities! Africa must educate its populace! What equivalent and compelling exhortation can the student of religion offer to support his collection of data? It would be dubious, if not umbrageous, to suggest: "Africa must Christianize!" or "Africa must Islamize!" It is hardly more compelling to say, "Africa must revitalize!" In a situation of modernization so full of stern imperatives, whatever the best ones may be, it seems fatuous to proclaim, "Africa, know thyself," although the study of religion in any society, one could suggest, yields a valuable lot of self-knowledge. It may seem ironic that that social institution most given to exhortation cannot easily be associated with an imperative that would justify its students in their undertaking.

Perhaps I'm leaning over too far to indulge the Philistines. Those of us who have studied religion in Africa appreciate its crucial role in the development which has, and has not, taken place on that continent. It is hard to deny the role of the mission churches in providing a base—education and medical services, primarily—for modernity. These churches may also have had a role—the question gets complicated here—in resisting modernity. They, like so much in traditional religion, may have resisted "the thinking and habits of the civilization of science and technology which is the pattern and driving force of human progress today."[1] In any case, if "a country is developed when its science and technology have ceased to be a magic potion imported from abroad and have become a living integrated part of its culture," then religion has a good deal to do with development. The student of religion in Africa, both African and European religion, is better aware than most others, it may be hazarded, of those habits of thought inimical to the development of the spirit of science in Africa's developing states—those habits of thought which persist in imposing will and imagination upon nature in place of a Baconian submission.

If to the more practical-minded interlocutor knowledge of habits of thought is not worth the candle of inquiry, then the student of religion may point to the importance of practices of a religious type in obtaining national integration in a highly disparate population.[2] It may be, in fact, that the question of the nature of leadership itself is as much a religious problem as it is a political problem. For these and other reasons religious studies in Africa should have a relevance to students of other disciplines. But we should not have to extend ourselves in justification.

If the rich varieties of traditional African religion—some of which are still quite viable, as among the Fon of Dahomey —do not sufficiently attract our interest for the knowledge they bring of the broad spectrum of human cultural creativity, then we should at least be attracted by the creativity going on in African Christianity. This creativity has been compared to Christianity's second century in respect to the development of theological and liturgical forms.[3] African religious movements, though the great majority have been

1. Ghana's uncertain accession to this "civilization" is discussed by L. H. Ofosu Appiah, editor of the *Encyclopedia Africana*, in the *Legon Observer*, I (1966), 17.

2. The classic article on this is by David Apter, "Political Religions in the New Nations" in *Old Societies and New States*, ed. by Clifford Geertz (New York: The Free Press, 1963), pp. 57–104.

3. This point is made by T. Beetham, *Christianity and the New Africa* (London: Pall Mall, 1967); and also by H. W. Turner in his two-volume study of the Church of the Lord (Aladura), *African Independent Church* (Oxford: Oxford University Press, 1967). Turner looks to a certain reinvigoration of Christianity and a primordial spiritual insight as coming from this church.

strongly influenced by Christianity, are phenomena of such dynamic variety as to provide experience on almost any problem of society and culture to those whose interest in human behavior is not sectarian but universal. Many of them are "cosmogenizing"—building a new and more satisfying religious universe in which to dwell. They are engaged, one might say, in a kind of ultimate community-development project.

If we can accept, on a variety of grounds, the relevance of the work of the student of African contemporary religion, beyond his own fully worthwhile interest in religion per se, I should like to go on and assess some problems in our present study of that religion and suggest methods which we must put into practice in the future if we are to come to better terms with the problems and insure a fruitful and orderly development of our interests. Since the range of these interests can be very great, I should like to concentrate upon certain of the difficulties that can act to hinder a high level of scholarly communication and thus obstruct a progressive study and resolution of the main propositions that would seem to apply to our universe of interest.

Number Facts

Basic to any generalization we may care to make upon cult, sect, church, or mosque activity in Africa are the statistics of religious allegiance. We have usually had to work in a penumbra zone here, being content with some wry comment or another on "pious forms of prevarication." In almost all the religious movements with which I have worked, I received greatly exaggerated figures of membership. In most cases a more careful inquiry has reduced the figure by at least half. The Church of the Lord (Aladura) was represented to me in West Africa as having a membership in the hundreds of thousands, but H. W. Turner, the authority on this church, gives us a greatly reduced figure: 10,000 total in four countries.[4] It can be well understood how, in the competition for membership and out of a sense of weakness, the size of the communion is subject to hyperbole of estimate. But, of course, the same thing has occurred in the established mission-derived churches, where estimates have swung back and forth between

---

4. Turner, *African Independent Church*, II, 14. In fact, a figure of over one hundred thousand has frequently been quoted for this church.

boosted figures calculated to put mission activity in the best light for the supporting faithful at home to narrowed estimates which reflect a desire to distinguish very carefully between a merely nominal membership and the membership actually communing. This disparity between the nominal and the communing membership is seen in more recent official government census data (in the Ghana 1960 census, for example) where claims of church allegiance made to census-takers exceed church returns and church records by 20 to 40 per cent.[5]

The problem of the disparity between nominal claims of allegiance and steady communion affects the established and mission-derived churches more than it does the independents, in which the grasp of a communing membership comes much closer to the spiritual reach. The observation is complicated by the custom of accepting dual membership in some of these groups—Bwiti in Gabon, for instance, and Amakhenleni in Natal—so that a man might claim to be a good Catholic as well as a good Bwitist. The underlying problem of the vagaries of religious statistics is in the obfuscation of the actual acculturative processes and the extent of conversion, syncretism, compartmentalization, stabilized dualism, and assimilation. In mission milieus the deep problem has always been who of the *soi-disant* are real Christians, reflecting deep doubt in many Christians themselves as to their own "imitation of Christ." But these are problems of the form and substance of religious adhesion which, although they affect categorization in any census, are not subject to resolution by any census.

In any case, it is to be hoped that the many censuses being brought forth by the new states (such as the Ghana census of 1960, which was reported in six volumes) [6] will give us more accurate figures, if only of claims of allegiance. Unfortunately the tendency in the francophone countries, as in the Gabon census of 1960–61,[7] is to exclude figures on religious allegiance. The student of religion in Africa, in short, must in every instance do careful work on attendance and allegiance

5. Beetham discusses this disparity (*Christianity and the New Africa*, p. 164), though he seems to accept claims of allegiance rather than church figures for his total figure of sixty million for the African Christian community.

6. *Ghana Census*, 1960, Special Report E., p. lxxxiv. Religion is given only for those over the age of fifteen.

7. République Gabonese, *Recensement et enquête démographique 1960–1961: Résultats définitives* (Libreville, 1965).

so as to compile those facts of "religiosity," so basic to our generalizations, from the social point of view. From the cultural point of view such number facts are of less interest.

Taxonomy and Typology

The numerous attempts to provide a taxonomy, or a dynamic typology, of mutually acceptable reference in religious studies in Africa have not yet reached any resolution. While diversity in this matter afflicts the social sciences generally and reflects both the complexity of the subject matter with which we deal as well as the seemingly ineradicable personal element in inquiry, we can probably come much closer to consensus than has heretofore been the case. But the problems are formidable, and this may be illustrated by a taxonomy which takes the Bible as its frame of reference.[8]

Distinctions between various African religious groups are drawn first on the basis of their biblical orientation: Is the group Hebraist (Old Testament) or Christian (New Testament)? If it is Hebraist, does it model itself on the classical religion of Israel (Israelitish) or has it shifted from direct revelation through prophets to an emphasis upon laws and rituals? This taxonomy, which reflects theological interest in the phenomena, may be questioned on a number of grounds. It excludes many interesting religious movements which make little or no use of the Bible. In my experience, religious movements which do make strong use of the Bible range so eclectically over the entire Bible as to render difficult any judgment as to their primary locus of interest. It is not that in the end—by various kinds of content analysis of a substantial body of testimonies, sermons, and songs—distinctions cannot be made. It is rather that such distinctions may be based on features that are of secondary importance in discriminating between movements. One suspects that these movements search the Bible out of their most basic needs and that they choose those scriptures most representative of these needs. It is natural for those who have been connected with the evangelical enterprise to assume that the Bible, the basic vehicle of that enterprise, is an independent variable upon which a great deal of any contemporary African religion depends. But it

8. As, for example, in the typology of H. W. Turner, "A Typology for African Religious Movements," *Journal of Religion in Africa*, I (1964), 1–34.

may be equally argued that the Bible is a very diversified and ambiguous document into which a great deal is projected out of a social and cultural nature that is already constituted. It is surely a rich stimulus which gives rise to a constellation of diverse motives and attitudes, but we cannot say that it is primary and causative any more than we can call any projective instrument causative of the personality features of which it gives evidence.

On the other hand, there is evidence that the Bible is an important independent variable. The availability of the Bible in the vernacular, it would seem, correlates highly with independency in African ethnic groups.[9] No doubt at some point the mythology and sacred historical experience which Bible reading offers (and some African groups read the Bible very closely indeed) have been influential in the formulation of religious movements and the development of their beliefs, liturgies, and sociopolitical structures. It may well be a fact that direct access to the Bible and the ancient Mideast culture it portrays (in so many ways similar to African culture) gave cause for resistance to the missionary attack on African culture which was part and parcel of most evangelization. But I would still argue skepticism lest the long debate in Christendom on direct access to the scriptures cause us to overinterpret their primordial character in the new African religions. If, for example, independency correlates with the availability of the Bible in the vernacular, the Bible itself may be only representative of a much fuller evangelical effort which had as its end products both the strain toward independency and a Bible in the vernacular. We must very carefully sift the relationship between the religious documents taken up by the new religions in Africa and the reconstituted natures of these documents.

The taxonomic problem, it has been frequently recognized, is that there are a great many dimensions upon which we can measure and classify religious movements, and the student is likely to choose those which most interest him and which conform to his own sense of reality. There is some bias in this, perhaps, for the sociologist or comparative theologian coming

9. David Barrett, "Reaction to Mission" (Ph.D. dissertation, Columbia University, 1965). This has been published in book form as *Schism and Renewal in Africa* (Nairobi: Oxford University Press, 1968). Among the many variables considered by Barrett for their impact on independency, the availability of the Bible in the vernacular shows next to the highest correlation.

at contemporary African religion is likely to single out the socially modernizing or Christian aspects of the phenomena and neglect their cultural depth. The anthropologist is as likely to transpose that emphasis in favor of cultural continuity that, in fact, has been much recast and even repudiated. But such biases in perspective do not really weaken the observation that there are a great many valid dimensions from which to choose, and that the student, because of the need for economy in his work (unless he is to embark on a massive multivariant analysis), will generally focus on those that seem for his purposes to exhaust the phenomenon as he has known it.

My own view is that, given the diversity of disciplines from which those of us interested in African religion come, communication among ourselves would be aided if we could accept a manageable number of dimensions reasonably abstracted from any set of particular interests (such as Christian theology or African personality) and reasonably necessary, though not sufficient, to the explanation of these movements. Acceptance of, and empirical inquiry into, these dimensions would give us a good initial grasp of the nature of these movements. By acceptance and empirical inquiry, I mean an understanding of sets of diagnostic features which may be quantified and scaled upon the dimension. This should enable us to be absolutely clear, as we are not now, by what criteria we classify, and against what features we judge, similarity or dissimilarity of movements. If we choose to arrange these dimensions so as to create a matrix, then the problem of types is solved by giving an appropriate name to each cell and letting our measures determine our classifying—by successive measures we get a longitudinal sense of dynamics.

In the acculturative situation in which so many of the African religious phenomena appear, I have long believed three dimensions to be not only most manageable but fundamental: the content dimension describing the source of the religious symbolism (acculturated or traditional); the action dimension describing the way in which this symbolism is manipulated, whether expressively or instrumentally; and the intention dimension describing, in respect to the membership, whether the movement is therapeutic or redemptive in its objectives.[10]

10. The eight cell-types of this scheme are Separatist, Faith-Healing, Zionist, Prophetic, Reformative, Ethiopian, Nativistic, Chilliastic. The three polarities, each defined in relationship to its opposite, can be re-

The symmetry of this scheme (Fig. 1) should not belie the fact that despite the bipolar arrangement of these characteristics they are not necessarily mutually exclusive in the empirical case. We are measuring dominant emphases, and these may not be in linear relationship. But the very high-level hypothesis bound up with this model is that religious movements appearing in the acculturation situation move from a traditional to an acculturated symbolism, an expressive to an instrumental technique, and a therapeutic to a redemptive intention. There are many exceptions to prove this rule, but at least we are better off than with no rule at all, or with a multitude of particular rules to cover each case in Africa.

FIGURE 1

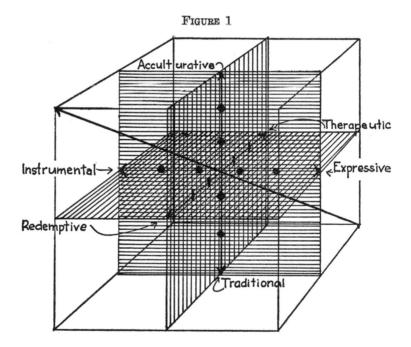

In this day of computers where multivariant analysis and multiple-regression computations can be given back to us in one-tenth of a second, the three manageable dimensions from the human point of view are virtually indistinguishable from

---

duced to a measure of qualitative state-expressiveness, therapeuticness, acculturatedness. Scaling on each dimension follows its nature. Content analysis of beliefs and symbols provides us with a measure for acculturatedness. Expressiveness is defined by three attributes: organization, ritualization, and exocentricity. Each of these, in turn, is defined by low-high measures of four attributes.

"n" dimensions for the central processing unit (CPU). Many social scientists interested in these religions are thus free to consider many variables and to make much finer analytic discriminations on individual movements than was previously possible (in quantitative form). The complicated trait profile suggested for African religious movements by Kopytoff,[11] for example, should now receive from us the most serious analytic attention insofar as we want to, and can, move in the direction of multiple discrimination. Of course, social science moves in two directions, and I can't resist being contentious here by suggesting that eventual factor analysis of the multitude of dimensions we can distinguish will bring us back to many fewer dimensions, perhaps not too dissimilar to the ones suggested in the model above.

Comparisons and the Comparative Method

If we can agree on some taxonomic principles, and even if we can't agree, our understanding is much enhanced by extended comparisons between various movements, not only those bound together in the same phylogenetic tree—such as the Zionists in South Africa, the Watchtower groups in central Africa and the eastern Congo, the Bougistes in the lower Congo and equatorial Africa, and the Aladura groups of West Africa— but also those arising out of quite different circumstances. Sundkler's work has the great virtue of offering us an extended and careful comparison of "Zionist" and "Ethiopian" South African churches.[12] The comparison is productive of an insight that the consideration of either group alone could not achieve. Sundkler's work is not, as is often the case, simply a description of the features of the various movements or the treatment of a variety of movements in discrete fashion. The discussion of the one group of churches constantly interacts with the discussion of the other group, sharpening our sense of the total organization of traits, as well as differences

11. Igor Kopytoff, "Classifications of Religious Movements: Analytical and Synthetic," *Symposium on New Approaches to the Study of Religion*, Proceedings of the 1964 Annual Spring Meeting of the American Ethnological Society, Seattle, 1964, pp. 77–90. This article is one of the most insightful we have on the problems of taxonomy in African religious movements.

12. B. Sundkler, *Bantu Prophets in South Africa* (Oxford: Oxford University Press, 1959).

and similarities in traits, and causal factors between them. Even a comprehensive study of one movement benefits by intermittent, if brief, comparative reference to other movements. Turner's two-volume study of the Church of the Lord adds this quality to the admirable scholarly patience with which it has been prepared.[13]

Our power to make these comparisons can arise in different ways—by research experience in various groups, by careful consideration of the literature,[14] or by use of the comparative method as developed in anthropology. In actual fact the comparative method in anthropology has two branches: the method of controlled comparison and the cross-cultural method associated with the Human Relations Area Files and the *Ethnographic Atlas*. The method of controlled comparison is of that kind practiced by Sundkler, although more rigorous, where two distinct cultural phenomena are carefully controlled in all particulars with an eye to singling out those variables that account for their differences.[15] The cross-cultural method rests upon a long-term effort in anthropology to rate all those societies on which we have any adequate information (well over 1,200 at the present time) on pertinent attributes in which we have interest (this now approaches 100 attributes, of which some are presented in presence or absence format and some are scaled as dimensions). With these attributes coded on this many societies, we are able to run trait by tribe or tribe by trait contingency tables, and gain, through the common statistical measures, some modest and introductory sense of strength of association and significance of relationship of various traits or tribes. I say modest and introductory because there are many problems of sampling and rating in the *Ethnographic Atlas,* and also because the measures we usually apply—phi, Q for association, or chi square for significant relationship—often tend to be arbitrary in respect to the thresholds for rejection of the null hypothesis.

13. Turner, *African Independent Church.*

14. Consideration of the literature is rendered much easier by the recent bibliography by R. Mitchell and H. W. Turner, *A Bibliography of Modern African Religious Movements* (Evanston: Northwestern University Press, 1967).

15. The student of African religion has two excellent examples of this method in S. F. Nadel: "Witchcraft in Four African Societies: An Essay in Comparison," *American Anthropologist,* LIV (1952), 18–29; and "Two Nuba Religions: An Essay in Comparison," *ibid.,* LVII (1955), 661–78.

We have recently had in just this area of method an extended study by David Barrett of African independent movements.[16] I should like to examine Barrett's work by way of noting the strengths and weaknesses of this method. The study arises from an understandable skepticism about the prevailing tendency to argue over one- or two-factor explanations for the rise of independent movements, such as status or comparative (economic) deprivation, or the search for autonomy and a new whole culture, or reaction to sterility, logicalness, and pessimism in Christianity. There always seem to be, somewhere, exceptions to any one- or two-factored rule explaining the emergence of these movements. The better approach is to draw up a much more elaborate profile of variables, and then by a statistical test of association or significant relations locate those variables which correlate with independency. Barrett begins with 100 social and religious variables abstracted from the nature of tribal culture, the nature of the colonial and missionary situation, and the nature of the contemporary situation. He then singles out 18 variables.[17] From these he constructs an index of religious strain on which every tribe on the continent can be placed. The incidence of the phenomenon of independency and the intensity of involvement can be accurately determined by the position of a tribe on the index (how many variables it manifests). Murdock's compendium, *Africa: Its Peoples and their Culture History,* and the *Ethnographic Atlas,*[18] in which African tribes are well represented (some 400), are employed for judgment as to tribal, social, and cultural variables exclusive of religious variables which are pursued into the literature. Inquiry on the present status of independency in the various areas was made by questionnaire to local missionaries. The results, however, were not satisfactory.

One can only applaud this effort by Barrett. It is just the kind of multivariant analysis that we, or some of us at least,

---

16. Barrett, "Reaction to Mission."

17. These variables are Bantu tribe, population, polygyny, earth-goddess cult, ancestor cults, date of colonial rule, white settlers, national average income, arrival of missions, publication of scripture, of New Testament, of Bible, date of publication of New Testament, ratio of missionaries to population, percentage of Muslims, percentage of Protestants, percentage of Catholics, independency in adjoining tribe.

18. G. P. Murdock, *Africa: Its Peoples and Their Culture History* (New York: McGraw-Hill, 1959); and *Ethnographic Atlas* (Pittsburgh: University of Pittsburgh Press, 1967).

should be doing. On the other hand, we should be aware of some of its weaknesses. First of all, as is well known, correlations are not causation, and statistical analysis such as this should be followed up by more focused firsthand field work in which we search for more direct empirical evidence of the actual dynamics of these movements. A technique such as that employed by Barrett does not, as indeed the author recognizes, replace hard work in the field. Rather, it is ancillary to this basic source of our understanding; only points the way and shows us new lines of research. Finally, though the technique seems to, and in fact does, make a notable advance in comprehensiveness—treating complex phenomena with the complexity they deserve—it also, as so often happens in statistical analysis, makes some quite simple-minded assumptions which are bound to be reflected in the conclusions. It assumes, for example, that we can take the tribe as the basic discrete unit of analysis and of statistical correlation. In anthropology, at least, this is no easy assumption. One man's tribe is another man's super-tribe and a third man's sub-tribe. It has always been one of the most tangled areas in our taxonomies. Time and again we find the literature treating as one tribe— "one territorially contiguous, common-language common-culture bearing unit"—entities which are regarded by Africans as distinct cultural units (or vice versa). Even if we have satisfactorily defined our tribes in the majority of our sample, we are still confronted with Galton's problem—the problem of diffusion which fuzzes the discreteness of tribal units. Different tribes may in the process of historical diffusion turn out to be simply reiterations of the same entity and not truly discrete. Since the statistical measurements of association and significant relation undertaken by Barrett assume the discreteness of each instance, and since he accepts relatively low levels of correlation (above .17) as significant, if he followed the 3° rule [19] or threw out all tribes (but one) which might by diffusion be in important ways instances of each other, his results might be radically altered.[20] Moreover, since the chi-

19. The 3° rule, discussed by Murdock in the *Ethnographic Atlas*, proscribes treating as part of one's sample any tribe closer than 3° to any other.

20. I simply cannot accept the general applicability of Barrett's view that discreteness is "proved by the extraordinary religious independence of so many adjacent tribes. On crossing tribal boundaries one not only enters a quite new language area, one frequently enters on a different religious world." Barrett, "Reaction to Mission."

square measure depends upon strictly random sampling in one's universe, and since the ethnographic data in Africa, despite our attempts at diversity, have not been randomly collected, the application of this measure demands some indulgence. His use of the term "magic" to type certain African religions also demands some indulgence (the Nilotic peoples are so typed), as does his assumption that the correlation of high per capita national income with independency belies the comparative deprivation theory of the rise of religious movements.

This is not the place to pursue statistical problems and questionable assumptions which arise in this particular use of the comparative method. I heartily endorse Barrett's contention that the variables of tribal culture help us predict the emergence of modern religious movements, although in the end only 5 such variables out of 18 are relevant in establishing his index of propensity to independency: "Bantu-ness," size of tribe, polygyny, earth-goddess cult, and ancestor cult. In his concern with independency, defined as African-initiated and -led churches which are Christian in their acknowledgment of the Lordship of Christ, Barrett ignores other, in his term, heterodox movements. Such movements have arisen, by his measure, in more than one-third of the African tribes, and they provide us with some of our most interesting data on processes of syncretism and acculturation. Indeed, since Barrett's dynamic theory of independency comes down in the end to the reaction on the part of Africans to the denigration of their culture and family life present in Christian mission, he would have found some of the best examples of cultural revitalization in the heterodox and not the independent movements.

Africanization or Christianization

Barrett's assumption that one begins with the tribal variables in explaining independency and that to some degree independency is an assertion, under evangelical threat, of African cultural integrity takes us down one slope of the watershed which is always present in the study of African contemporary religions. It happens to be the slope I find primary, but we should be cautious of the tendency to assume that the predominant thrust of any movement is either Africanization or Christianization. The tendency of missionaries and theologians, of course, is to assume the latter, while anthropologists tend to assume the former. We tend to ask either "Is African religion being Christianized?" or "Is Christianity being Africanized"? But these questions are too simple. An evenhanded acculturative approach would recognize the complexity of the situation, with Christian and African influences in many complex forms of syncretic interaction and persistent tension. The interactions of the various cultural fields, Christianity, animism, Islam, and the Western secular culture of commerce, science, and technology produce a multitude of permutations and possible qualifications, modifications, and conditions.[21] It is incumbent upon us to study this acculturative process, this tension, in the greatest detail, and in doing so we come that much closer to the real nature of evangelization and conversion. We miss it when we opt for the overwhelming weight of one culture or another. Within the Catholic church in Africa, where some might presume an inevitable Christianization, there is an acculturative interplay which is well described by Thomas.[22] He details the tension between religious cultures in what he calls the third stage of evangelization in Africa—the stage of *decolonization spirituelle*. The tension concerns the African incarnation of the church and proceeds by three stages:

1. A period of preparation in which animism is accepted as an authentic religion and in which attributes of African religious culture such as the power of oral tradition, the importance of life and fertility, the conception of collective responsibility and hospitality to strangers, the place of dance, song, and poem are all recognized as worthy of incorporation. The central theme in this phase is a conversion of the African spirit of community into a community spirit of the church. The attempt is made to relate the sacraments to animist rituals.

2. A dialogue is begun with animism. In order to achieve as rich an articulation of Christianity in African culture as possible, African modes in architecture and sculpture, catechism and liturgy, are incorporated (ideally by African clergy).

21. This complex interaction of cultural fields is discussed by J. S. Trimingham, *The Christian Church and Islam in West Africa* (London: S.C.M. Press, 1955).

22. V. Thomas, "L'Eglise chrétienne d'Afrique noire," *Tam Tam revue des étudiants catholiques africains*, No. 7–8 (December, 1963), pp. 7–21.

3. The African pole of the dialogue begins to assert itself as the two cultural versions of the sacred become confounded. Celibacy is confronted with the ideal of procreation. Sacramental efficacy is challenged by more practical, "magical" methods, and the supernatural is put to more frequent use in attaining utilitarian ends.

The result of this spiritual dialectic is by no means clearly seen. Hopefully, Thomas asserts, it will be a new African Christian culture, though others have asserted that Christianity will eventually prove incompatible with the African milieu.[23] But the point is that we miss the process and the dialogue if we lean too heavily in our work upon one religious culture or another in an arena where many culture fields are making their claim and asserting themselves through various mechanisms which are not usually simple assimilations of one to the other.

Confluents of Inquiry

The note I should like to conclude on is implied, I believe, in the way I have treated the several problems and approaches I have discussed (although by no means comprehensively.) It seems to me that for various reasons—the cybernetic revolution, attachments to the perquisites of a high standard of living, the increasing impatience of many Africans with some phases of social science research—we have been moving toward a new epistemology in the African social sciences, one which is exclusivistic and proclaims that knowledge which cannot be attached to some manifestation of number and estimation of quantity is not knowledge at all but illusion.

This doctrine, which should enjoy a portion of our support in all social sciences, and perhaps all of our support in some social sciences, cannot now, if ever, entirely commit us in the study of contemporary African religion. For one thing, there are too many phenomenologists of various academic persuasions participating in that study who would be unwilling to reduce all knowledge and experience to number and formal statement. For another thing, the information we now have to manipulate quantitatively is too meager to give us any confi-

23. P. Welbourne and B. Ogot see a failure of the established church in Africa and a consequent Africanization of Christianity in *A Place to Feel at Home: A Study of Two Independent Churches in Western Kenya* (Oxford: Oxford University Press, 1966).

dence in analyzing it in this way entirely. We have some, but we need many more, field studies of contemporary African religious groups, and by that I mean case studies in which participant observation, and not simply a short-term saturation with questionnaire schedules, is the guiding principle of inquiry. Only on such a basis—my own experience is that hospitality is extended almost without exception to the one who seeks to participate in the spirit of honest inquiry—can we get penetration into these deeper and complex questions of religious allegiance, of therapeutic or redemptive intent, of cultural reaffirmation, and of the syncretic dialogue between religious cultures.

In respect to my own primary interests in these movements, interests which focus on symbolic cosmogenization and organizing imagery in discourse and liturgy, I do not see any social science technique which can be employed in lieu of participant observation in gathering and interpreting texts and rites,[24] nor do I yet see any easy way to quantify the patterns which the African prophets produce. There is yet many a slip 'twixt computer and lip.

Let me suggest a problem, very important to my own work, for which only long-term field involvement at many levels of research awareness can supply adequate information. I have been interested in the old problem of how we use the body to represent the articulation of our social parts and our relation to supernatural forces. We are all aware of the "real metaphor" of the mystical body of Christ—the way in which Christians extend the body of Christ to incorporate all the communing faithful. It is that body which Christians incorporate by communion and imitation. In turn, through their exemplary activity, it is projected out into the world. We know, at any rate, in reviewing the microcosm-macrocosm problem that "the whole body can be taken as a map whose interior and exterior terrain can be categorized and extended in our grasp of the world."[25] What I have been interested in is how the membership really understands and experiences

24. As I have argued in "Revitalized Words from the Parrot's Egg and the Bull that Crashes in the Kraal: African Cult Sermons," *Essays on the Verbal and Visual Arts*, Proceedings of the 1966 Annual Spring Meeting of the American Ethnological Society, Washington, D. C., 1967, pp. 45–63.

25. James B. Watson and Harold E. Nelson, "Body-Environment Transactions: A Standard Model for Cross Cultural Analyses," *Southwestern Journal of Anthropology*, XXIII (Autumn, 1967), 294.

its spiritual and social communion. This is not an interest in what the religious experience is in itself—that will have to remain a *mysterium tremendum* for social science—but in how it is represented. We can hazard that the way it is represented has something to do with what it is.

Furthermore, these representations have something to do with the actual organization of behavior in the cult groups. This is implied in the name—organizing metaphors. If you represent yourself or your metaphoric objective to be "one-heartedness" (Bwiti in Gabon), or pneumatic incorporation of the circumambient Holy Spirit (South African Zionism), or purgation of bilious impurities and superfluidities (Amak-hehleni curing cult of Natal), this will have an inevitable impact upon the dynamics of the cult. Cult life is organized, we may say, to achieve the metaphoric transfer of focus from suffering self to religious body. A metaphor, it is to be argued, is to some degree a plan of behavior, and, in the case of religion, a plan of salvation.

It is not an easy matter to assess these metaphors without considerable participant observation. But our problems are not limited to making out such figures of speech and behavior —the principal ways in which the microcosm is projected into the world and the world condensed into the microcosm; we must inquire how religious cult life operates in the transformation of the member's experience by the manipulation of metaphor and metonymy.

We do not have to complicate this discussion, for our only purpose here is to indicate one confluent of inquiry which is at present imperfectly susceptible to parsimonious research of a quantitative sort. It is sufficient to say that cult members appear to represent their experiences in various modes keyed by organizing metaphors such as the ones put forth above. Each of these modes, or universes of metaphoric discourse, contains a set of related images which form in conjunction a metonymous whole. If we take the Bwiti cult of northern Gabon we find that the night-long ritual celebrates three progressive states in the coalescence of the membership: common clanship (*ayoñ da*), common membership in a hunting team (*esamba*), and one-heartedness (*nlem mvore*). Each of these three organizing metaphors carries in association with it, by metonymy, a set of related images, the vocabulary so to speak of that particular metaphoric universe. This "vocabulary" emerges in the ritual events and objects, in the songs and myths attached to the rituals, and in other ways. In general the "vocabulary" shifts as the organizing metaphor shifts. But the matter is more complicated yet, because links between the vocabularies of the various metaphoric universes create a constant cross-referencing and interplay. It is this which contributes to the thickness or the multileveled richness of the ritual experience. We may speak of a kind of looping process in the ritual by which the association between colors during the *ayoñ da* phase of the ritual, for example, brings to representation elements of the *esamba* or *nlem mvore* phase (see the paradigms in Fig. 2).

FIGURE 2

Ayoñ da ———→	*Esamba* ———→	*Nlem Mvore*
oneness of brain, bone, and umbilicus	oneness of existing body	one-heartedness
white	black	red
sinews and tendons	trails of the forest	veins and arteries
semen	sweat and exuviae	blood
maleness	neuter state	femaleness
distillation of bodily processes into essence	expulsion of bodily processes	commingling of bodily processes
lineal structure	corporate grouping	absolute identity
structuring	massing	liquefying

What happens in ritual, then, is that we get a constant recasting of experience from one "vocabulary" to another—whether by congruence of association or by the provocation of opposites. The process is one of constant transformations. We start, for example, by representing ourselves as one clan and lineage (*ayoñ da*), scanning all or some of the "vocabulary" in that metaphoric domain while eliciting the associated feelings. We may then recast or transform to "one-heartedness" (*nlem mvore*) or the state of *esamba*. This looping through various "vocabularies" produces that "thick complex condition," the experience of which is potent and meaningful.

I hope that such a brief *aperçu* as this can give us an indication of the kind of study which we should be undertaking of the enormously creative arena of African religion. Recognizing the complexity of such study and the complexity of religion as symbol and experience, it is not possible, for obvious reasons, to commit oneself entirely to the new epistemology we discussed earlier in this paper.

But on the other hand, there is no reason why the two perspectives on our materials should not exist complementarily. Along with this participant inquiry should go, therefore, a knowledge of the multiple variables that have been advanced to structure and account for our phenomenon. We should be making constant efforts to improve the ratings in respect to the cultures in which religious movements arise as well as to improve scalings of the movements themselves. In this way our method should be two-phased, quantitative and qualitative, aimed at as fine a knowledge of the patterning, the Gestalt, of particular movements as is probable, while striving for as great an accuracy in our variables, our scales, and our indexes as is possible. Some complementary specialization is inevitably needed, and seems in fact to be emerging, in respect to African religious studies.

For myself, I will admit, long-term participant observations bring me much closer to an understanding of the reality of religious culture than multivariant analysis—though I would rather rest my predictions on the latter. This has often been the way of anthropologists. Our great students of religion have been those who have lived as close as possible to the phenomena—Sahagun, Malinowski, Evans-Pritchard, and Herskovits himself, the founder of the Program of African Studies whose twentieth anniversary we bear witness to in these sessions. He was one of the great students of African religion and its syncretisms in the new world. It would not be out of place to recall as one kind of model for our inquiry those penetrating descriptions of the religious life in the bush of Surinam, in the ancient kingdom of Dahomey, in Trinidad and Haiti and Bahia. That kind of comparative knowledge gained firsthand by one man has not been seen since. But cooperatively, by an interplay of case study and multivariant analysis, we can build on that tradition and bring it to fruition.

THE GROWTH OF PSYCHOLOGY
IN AFRICAN STUDIES

3

Marshall H. Segall

Melville Herskovits, America's first Africanist, was among the first to conceive an important role for psychology in African studies. I have always believed that he would have been a psychologist himself had he not committed himself to anthropology. In many respects, of course, he was a psychologist. His classic 1927 book, *The Negro and Intelligence Tests,* and his work just before his death in 1963 on *The Influence of Culture on Visual Perception* were early and late contributions to psychology,[1] illustrating his continuing interest in the field. There were many other important works issued over a forty-year period. In his teaching too he was never very far from psychology. From the earliest days of Northwestern's Program of African Studies, he made a place in it for psychology. His conviction that psychology would become a key discipline in African studies came to be shared by many others. However, that conviction was, until quite recently, little more than a hope.

There were some pioneering efforts in psychological research in Africa during the 1950's, such as those of Doob, LeVine, Campbell, and a few others. A few centers of psychological research were located in Africa, such as the Institut

1. M. J. Herskovits, *The Negro and Intelligence Tests* (Hanover, N. H.: Sociological Press, 1927); M. H. Segall, D. T. Campbell, and M. J. Herskovits, *The Influence of Culture on Visual Perception* (Indianapolis: Bobbs-Merrill, 1966).

des Sciences Psychologiques et Sociales in Dakar and the Institute for Personnel Research in Johannesburg. African studies symposia usually contained a section on psychology, and a few books on African studies included chapters, often written by one or another of the few well-known pioneers. It was, in fact, a rather embarrassing period for psychologists interested in African studies, with four or five of them regularly reviewing one another's writings, which usually were composed largely of references to the others' earlier works.

From time to time, one or another of these pioneer psychologists was called upon by fellow Africanists to prepare a statement on the current status of psychology in Africa. In most of these statements the point would defensively be made that psychology had not yet come of age in Africa, that little *genuine* psychological research had yet been accomplished, but that research opportunities for the psychologist were many and enticing and that there might be a burgeoning of psychological activity in the near future. Doob said so in his chapter in Lystad's *African World*, LeVine said so in his chapter in Hsu's *Psychological Anthropology,* and I said so more times than I care to recall. One either sang or heard the same song at successive annual meetings of the ASA. But I believe that it is possible today to claim that Melville Herskovits' expectations about psychology in Africa are at last being realized. At least, we have reached the point where one can meet a bona fide stranger at a psychology session of an ASA meeting. More significantly, perhaps, one can now compile a bibliography composed of studies by relative strangers, cited for their intrinsic merit.

In 1961, at an ASA meeting, I said that "psychological participation in African studies has thus far been minimal" and that "even though it is destined to grow, it may not grow at as fast a rate as some of us might wish." Today I will argue that the rate of growth of psychology in Africa is greater than any of us expected—any of us, that is, with the possible exception of Melville Herskovits.

What I propose to do here is review some recent and current developments in psychology in Africa. I will refer to some new research centers and to some research that has been produced at these centers. The review will not aspire to be comprehensive. The developments, happily, have been too numerous for that to be a realistic goal for a paper of this length. Instead, I will concentrate on those developments which appear to me to illustrate the likely trends in the future growth of psychology in Africa. To get a truer picture of what is going on, bibliographies prepared during the last few years should be consulted. The fullest of these are by Doob, Klingelhofer, Evans, and Irvine.[2]

I believe that two features stand out in the recent developments in psychology in Africa. The first is a set of new content-emphases in the research done in Africa. The second is the creation of psychological research and training institutions in Africa. These two features are not unrelated. As psychological research has increasingly come to be indigenously based, influenced, and directed, its goals have come closer to reflecting what Africans feel that *they* need to know. The research goal is no longer merely to satisfy the curiosity of non-Africans who wonder what makes Africans tick, although in some forms that remains a perfectly respectable end.

One of the new centers for psychological research is that in Lusaka, at the University of Zambia. There, Alastair Heron and several of his colleagues have recently opened a well-equipped psychological laboratory. It is, I believe, the first such installation in Africa. What is most noteworthy in this development is the fact that it is a laboratory. The research which is beginning to emerge from Zambia is, therefore, research into psychology *in* Africa, as opposed to psychology *of* Africa. I believe that this reflects a significant new emphasis in psychological research in Africa. That same emphasis is reflected in work now being done at Makerere University College in Uganda, where a teaching and research program was inaugurated in 1967. A similar view prevails in the University of Ghana, where Cyril Fiscian has just begun a psychology program. In all of these new centers, much of the research being done could be done anywhere. It is basic research concerned with psychological processes and should interest psychologists whether or not they are interested in Africa. It yields information that is relevant to understanding of human behavior, and the fact that the subjects in the research happen to be Africans is, for the most part, irrelevant. At the same time, however, the fact that the research is done with African

2. L. Doob, ''Psychology,'' in *African World*, ed. by R. Lystad (New York: Praeger, 1965); E. L. Klingelhofer, *A Bibliography of Psychological Research and Writings on Africa* (Uppsala: Scandinavian Institute of African Studies, 1967); J. Evans, *Children in Africa: A Review of Psychological Research* (New York: Teachers College Press, forthcoming); S. H. Irvine, ''Human Behavior in Africa: A Bibliographic Overview,'' unpublished manuscript.

subjects means that the behavioral impacts of certain social, cultural, and linguistic factors that do not exist elsewhere are being revealed by this research. Thus, the African research setting provides a necessary extension to the empirical domain which is the basis for all advances in psychological theory-building. But the research also has potential applicability to contemporary problems in Africa.

One substantive problem area in which research done in Africa is contributing correctives to psychological theory is human cognitive development. This is a field in which most contemporary theory derives from work done largely in a very few research centers in Europe and the United States. Most theories of cognitive development are based on Piaget's research in Geneva and the work of several American psychologists in a few centers in the United States. Contributors to these theories have not been unaware of the narrowness of their data base, and many have themselves called for research to be done in non-Western settings. Some have done research in Africa. Gay's and Cole's work in Liberia and Greenfield's work in Senegal are recent examples of such research.[3] One of the leading American cognitive theorists, Jerome Bruner, has developed a keen interest in research done in Africa. He has employed African data in several of his recent publications concerned with cognitive development. Milly Almy, who recently completed several Piagetian studies among school children in New York City, has undertaken some pilot studies in an effort to replicate her American research in Ugandan schools.[4] One of Heron's colleagues in Zambia, Robert Serpell, has published several papers which report the results of experiments on basic cognitive processes, notably sorting and classifying, among Zambian children.[5]

One of the theoretically relevant reasons for doing such research in Africa is the relative ease with which one can in Africa separate effects of maturation from effects of schooling and other experiences. There it is quite possible to compare

3. J. Gay and M. Cole, *The New Mathematics and an Old Culture* (New York: Holt, Rinehart & Winston, 1967); P. M. Greenfield, "On Culture and Conservation," in *Studies in Cognitive Growth*, ed. by Jerome Bruner (New York: Wiley, 1966).

4. M. Almy, *The Usefulness of Piagetian Methods for Early Primary Education in Uganda: An Exploratory Work* (Kampala: National Institute of Education, 1967). Mimeographed.

5. R. Serpell, "Selective Attention in Children," *Bulletin of the University of Zambia, Institute of Social Research*, No. 1, n.d., pp. 37–41.

groups of subjects of similar age who have had strikingly different kinds of experience. Even within a single ethnic group, school-going children can be compared with nonschool-going children, and urban children can be compared with rural children. These and other feasible comparisons make it possible to discover the role of experience in shaping cognitive development. Until very recently maturation was many theorists' favorite explanation for cognitive growth. Because growth is correlated with age, and because age is correlated with year in school and other experiential variables, both age and experience are equally good candidates to explain cognitive growth, with age providing the simplest and most parsimonious, but psychologically less interesting, explanation. In the United States and Europe the variables which were available as alternative explanations tend much more to be confounded with age than they are in Africa. The result has been that research done in the U.S. and Europe could provide little in the way of choice between the two kinds of explanations, one based on age, the other on experience. Recent research done in Africa has helped to make a choice possible. The African research has tended to show that it is the nature of the experiences had by the child as he grows older, and not his growing older per se, which determines the way in which he comes to do his thinking about the world in which he lives.

A few studies just completed in Uganda may serve to illustrate this. The first of these was an experiment conducted by Mrs. Judith Evans, a research associate in the Makerere psychology program, in which Ugandan subjects, mostly children, were given an opportunity to learn to use two different rules of equivalence grouping, one based on color and the other based on function, in the sorting of pictures of familiar objects. Several previous studies, done in Africa and elsewhere, had found that color was a highly preferred basis for sorting objects, and that sorting by function was a tendency displayed by only a few subjects. In the previous African studies, functional sorting was extremely rare, even among adult subjects. However, in the previous studies, subjects were merely asked to sort objects; in the Ugandan study, they were forced to learn to sort them both ways; that is, in accord with their color and on the basis of their function. Differential ease of learning was the index of the subjects' skill in sorting according to color and function. The basic findings in this study were that (1) sorting by color was learned more rapidly than sorting by function by most subjects. This relative ease showed up both in rate of learning and in numbers of subjects failing to reach an arbitrary criterion of learning. However, (2) performance in sorting by function improved significantly as a function of years in school. Moreover, (3) age could not account for improvements in sorting-by-function performance, since older unschooled children and adults who had completed minimal amounts of formal schooling had as much difficulty learning to sort by function as did younger school children. Finally, (4) children in the fifth form of primary school actually learned to sort by function as readily as they learned to sort by color.[6]

In considering these findings, Judith Evans and I were forced to conclude that all previous findings, which had shown functional sorting to be a later development than color sorting, could no longer be interpreted as revealing a maturational unfolding of conceptual ability. Our findings suggested to us the following alternative. Unless subjects are induced by the experimenter to seek some less obvious characteristic than surface color, and unless they have some tendency to look for the less obvious, a tendency which we believe is reinforced by some experiences but not by others, they will employ color or some other superficial characteristic for the classification of objects. Our school-going subjects, at least those who had reached primary-grade five, had such a tendency. We also found some evidence that an urban, as opposed to a rural, environment enhanced this tendency. Sorting by function is not, then, merely a manifestation of intellectual maturity, but an end product of experience.

It is unlikely that the findings of this study will startle psychologists interested in cognitive development. Few psychologists today consider maturation to be a potent explanatory variable. However, they would be stuck with maturation as a tenable explanation were it not for the possibilities of eliminating it as such that are present in settings like Uganda. That Evans and I could compare school-going and nonschool-going, and rural and urban, children and adults was the principal reason for the fact that this study illuminates the role of experience, separate from maturation, in the development of cognitive processes.

Another member of the Makerere research team, Miss Myra

6. M. H. Segall and J. L. Evans, ''Learning to Classify by Color and Function: A Study of Concept Discovery by Ganda Children,'' *Journal of Social Psychology*, LXXVII (1969), 35–53.

Schiff, a graduate student in psychology at Syracuse University, has completed a study in and around Kampala that deals with the role of early childhood experience in the shaping of cognitive habits.[7] Her major concern in this study was the relationship of the mother's behavior and attitudes toward her preschool child and the child's manifest curiosity. The crucial comparisons in her study involve an acculturation dimension, for pilot research had indicated that traditional Ganda child-rearing practices emphasize obedience, whereas modern, European-influenced Ganda tend to be permissive and approving of active exploration in their children.

Miss Schiff worked with a large sample of mothers and their children. Her data-collection efforts were of two kinds. She administered a standard interview to each mother, and she completed a set of observations of interaction between mother and child in relation to a set of play materials which she introduced into the observation setting, which in all cases was the subject's own home. The materials were designed to provide measures of the manner in which the child dealt with attractive, novel, and problematic situations and the manner in which the mother responded to the child as he was in the course of responding to the materials. Some of these materials were taken from a test battery designed by Professor Thomas Banta of the University of Cincinnati, who was himself at Makerere for the academic year 1968–69. Banta's test battery had previously been employed with various subcultural groups of American children as a measure of what Banta calls "autonomy," a concept which includes creativity, innovativeness, persistence, curiosity, and other stylistic aspects of cognitive behavior. "Autonomy" correlates positively with intelligence, but not so highly as to be confused with it.

In addition to the Banta battery, Miss Schiff's measures included indexes of other kinds of behaviors which theoretically ought to be relevant to success in intellectual endeavors. One of these might be called active, or aggressive, curiosity. It is the sort of behavior that is displayed when a child takes advantage of an opportunity to deal with and learn something about a new stimulus which appears before him. It may be thought of as the opposite of shyly holding back, for whatever reason, from interaction with such a stimulus. In Miss Schiff's

7. M. Schiff, "Some Consequences of Child-Rearing Practices Among the Ganda" (paper delivered to the African Studies Association, Los Angeles, October, 1968).

study, one measure of the child's active curiosity is obtained near the outset of the session, when Miss Schiff, upon entering the room in which the interview is to be conducted, knocks over a basket of toys, seemingly by accident. This provides the occasion for an observation of the child's reaction to the toys and the mother's reaction in turn to the child. Over many observations in the course of a year, a wide range of reactions was elicited and recorded. Some children attacked the toys with apparent relish, others politely picked them up and put them back in the basket, and still others remained aloof. These individual differences in the children's behavior, and comparable differences on other measures, correlate in interesting ways with the mothers' behavior toward the children, as revealed both by observations and responses during the interview. Moreover, both sets of differences, in the children's and in the mothers' behavior, relate to acculturation. In general, traditional mothers actively discourage their children from asking questions, from exploring, and from otherwise learning how to be autonomous. The children of such mothers tended to earn the lowest autonomy scores and the highest passivity ratings yet observed with the Banta-type materials.

The findings of this study have both theoretical and practical implications. The former concern the role of experience in establishing habits of dealing with novelty, of seeking information, and of learning. Viewed from this perspective, Miss Schiff's study falls under the culture and personality rubric, for it illuminates a possible impact of Ganda cultural values on typical Ganda behavior. What Miss Schiff observed in four-year-olds is not unrelated to the passivity, fatalism, and respectful acceptance of things as they are that one sees in rural Ganda and other East African adults. The practical implications of her findings are obvious when one shifts attention for a moment to what goes on in East African schools: reliance on rote learning, rigid adherence to a syllabus, reluctance of teachers to elicit questions, and the concomitant reluctance of pupils to ask them. These phenomena obviously do not exist in a cultural vacuum, nor are they solely the product of colonial styles of formal education. They seem to have deep roots in child-rearing techniques and in the early behavior patterns which those techniques produce. Assuming that East African educators wish to modify the present situation, Schiff's findings suggest that corrective action will have to take into account such cultural influences.

Richard Kingsley, another Syracuse graduate student working at Makerere, focused on cognitive style in school-age children.[8] His research was concerned with the manner in which Ganda children attacked a simple concept-formation problem. He employed several different tasks, designed so that performance could be either enhanced or depressed by attending to the experimenter on the one hand, and focusing on the problem on the other. A hypothesis which Kingsley was testing in his research was that Ganda children who were in school would perform better on those tasks which favored attending to the experimenter rather than to the problem itself. His hypothesis was based on a hunch that Ganda tradition, reinforced by teachers' behavior, favors the development of a cognitive style in which one does what works so long as it works, and then one shifts to whatever else is found to work. Such a style leads to social reinforcement and is highly efficient when authority is the criterion for being correct. Probing the nature of the problem and worrying about why the correct response is correct detracts from success in such a setting.

Kingsley's study is cross-cultural. He plans to collect data with comparable children exposed to the same problems in other cultural groups, where there is reason to expect the children to perform better on tasks where they must attend to the problem rather than to the experimenter for feedback on their performance. If the expected differences are found across cultures, Kingsley will have demonstrated an important culturally determined source of cognitive style, and his study will help to explain why Ganda students behave so passively in the classroom.

The Schiff and Kingsley studies illustrate how research on cognitive development in Africa can reveal something about African behavior that is of practical significance, at least to African educators, and at the same time reveal relationships between culture and behavior that must affect theories of cognitive development of human beings in general.

Because such research done in Africa has these two kinds of payoff, practical and theoretical, I expect we shall be seeing much more of it in the near future. What its results are likely to show us is that culture helps determine not only what is learned but also how people go about learning it. We shall not discover an African mind, but we shall learn from research

8. R. Kingsley, ''Culture and Cognitive Style'' (paper delivered to the African Studies Association, Los Angeles, October, 1968).

done in Africa how culture affects the thinking process of all human beings.

Linguists have argued for many years that language is one of the most important aspects of culture affecting cognitive processes. As psychological research in Africa develops, psycholinguistic studies must be a part of that development. The importance of linguistic factors in basic cognitive processes cannot be overstated, partly for methodological reasons. Much published research on cognitive development has suffered from a failure to take linguistic factors into account, paradoxically because the researchers typically worked in their own language with subjects who spoke that language. In Africa it is much easier to be aware of how language affects cognitive processes for the simple reason that the subjects' language is usually different from the experimenter's. What at first glance is a methodological hurdle is, in fact, a theoretical advantage.

At Makerere in 1967, we were concerned about what our instructions to subjects in our several experiments would really mean to them. In the course of considering this, we decided to do an experiment expressly designed to reveal possible subtle effects of linguistic variables on simple cognitive behaviors.

The task employed in this experiment was again a sorting task, in which the subjects had to learn to classify stimuli according to a criterion determined by the experimenter. Thus, the task was a concept-discovery problem. The concepts to be discovered were form and number and every set of stimuli could be sorted either way. For any particular subject, one or the other classification rule was in effect, its choice determined randomly by the experimenter.

A subject would be confronted with a set of four stimuli on each of several trials. An example of such a set would be one composed of a star, a circle, four stars, and four circles. Obviously, if the subject were to sort these stimuli in terms of number, he would place the single star and the single circle in one class and the four stars and four circles in another; whereas, if he were to sort by form, he would place the single and multiple stars in one class and the single and multiple circles in another. On successive trials, one of the forms would always be present (say, the star) in combination with any of seven other forms. Similarly, on each successive trial, there would always be singleton versions of two forms and multiple versions of those two forms, with the multiples numbering either two, three, or four. Thus, for a given subject, all trials would be composed of two singulars and two plurals, and simultaneously of two stimuli of a standard form and two of some variable form. Each subject had to discover, via trial and error, the correct way to classify the four stimuli presented on each trial, with the rule held constant over all of his trials. He either had to attend to number and ignore form, or attend to form and ignore number.

The crucial psycholinguistic aspect of this experiment was imbedded in the instructions read to each subject. All subjects were instructed in the same manner except for one critical pair of terms. Here, in a somewhat abbreviated form, are the instructions that a randomly selected one-half of our sample received:

> We are going to play a game together. I am going to show you some pictures of things, and you are going to guess what they are called. The names of the things are *Makalo* and *Mikalo*. You will have to guess which ones are called *Makalo* and which ones are called *Mikalo*. I will always show you four things at a time. You must guess which of the four are called *Makalo* and which of the four are called *Mikalo*. The ones you think are called *Makalo* you should put here and the ones you think are called *Mikalo* you should put here.
>
> Every time you do this, I will tell you which ones you have correctly guessed. I want you to try to get as many correct as you can. Each time you get all four correct I will give you ten cents.
>
> After I have told you how many you guessed correctly, we will try again with another set of four things. Remember, each time you get all four correct, you will win ten cents. Try to get as many ten-cent pieces as you can.

The other half of the subjects heard the same instructions, except that the words *Kaloma* and *Kalomi* replaced *Makalo* and *Mikalo*. It will be noted that both sets of words are composed of the same syllables, *ka, lo,* and *ma,* or *ka, lo,* and *mi,* but that in one case the *ma-mi* variation occurs first, as if in prefix position, and in the other case the *ma-mi* variation occurs last. As far as we know, the words composed of these syllables are not real words in Bantu languages spoken in Uganda, but they are possible words in the sense that they follow structural rules in force in Bantu languages. Indeed, it is these structural rules that inspired the experiment.

In Bantu languages the stem of all nouns appears at the end of a word. Prefixes are employed to designate noun classes and number. Thus, if something were called -*kalo*, it is conceivable that one -*kalo* would be called *Makalo* and several would be called *Mikalo*. Similarly, if something were called -*loma*, something else could not also be called -*loma*, but might be called -*lomi*. A word difference occurring only at the front of the word could thus imply the same thing in different quantity, whereas a word difference occurring at the end of the word would imply different things.

If these structural rules of Bantu languages had any influence at all on the cognitive processes of subjects in the experiment, then those whose instructions included the class designations *Makalo* and *Mikalo* should have found it easier to learn to sort the stimuli in terms of number, while for those whose instructions included the class designations *Kaloma* and *Kalomi* should have found it easier to learn to sort the stimuli in terms of form.

We conducted the experiment with several hundred children, most of whom were between the ages of seven and eleven years, in two Bantu-speaking groups, Ankole and Ganda. Most of them were in school, in primary-grades three, four, and five. Preliminary examination of the data indicates that the predicted interaction between task and class designations is present. There are some very interesting qualifications, since some differences exist between the two ethnic groups and across age and year in school, but I am not yet prepared to comment on these. For the present, I wish to stress that the experiment revealed that the nature of the meaningless class labels employed in the instructions was related to the ease with which the two sorting rules were discovered by the subjects. As predicted, among those who had to discover that they were to sort by number, an advantage existed for those whose instructions employed the terms that satisfied the Bantu grammatical rule for designating number. Similarly, an advantage accrued to those in the sort-by-form group whose instructions included terms that satisfied the rule for designating different things. This subtle force was sufficient to show up in spite of other behavior determinants which must have existed in this situation, including age-related preferences for number or for form.

Whatever else may have acted to assist or detract from the subjects' efforts to discover what they were supposed to do, the position of two syllables in the instructions had an effect on their thought processes. To put it rather dramatically, the experiment demonstrated that what a thing was to be called influenced how it was processed conceptually. I believe this is what psycholinguistic theory is all about, at least that part dealing with relationships between language and thought. It is my view that one must study both to understand either, since neither occurs without the other. Thinking always occurs in a linguistic framework, so that what is thought and how it is thought are influenced by the thinker's language. If we are to do cognitive research, we must attend to linguistic variables. If we are to investigate linguistic factors in cognition, I cannot think of a better place to do it than in Africa, where the linguistic complexities present even in a single country like Uganda make such research an eminently practical possibility. Moreover, the fact that so many available subjects are multilingual opens up some particularly intriguing possibilities for research of theoretical and practical significance.

In East Africa, psycholinguistic research will be, I suspect, a major activity during the years to come. A large-scale program in basic linguistic research has been launched there, in the form of a language survey, and psychologists can and will work in conjunction with that program, leaning heavily on the work of the linguists and contributing to it by focusing on related psychological issues. The effects of such collaboration will undoubtedly be of mutual benefit to the two disciplines. Again, this should be accompanied by considerable practical payoff for educators in Africa.

The studies I have referred to thus far concern cognitive processes, their development, and the role of language in their determination. This area is the one in which I think we will see the greatest emphasis during the coming years. I would like to consider, however briefly, some other problem areas which are engaging psychologists in Africa.

The first, severe malnutrition, involves a joint sociopsychological and medical problem in many parts of Africa. Its root causes are largely social and psychological since they involve tradition-influenced dietary habits, and there is reason to believe that some of its end products are also social and psychological, since both short-term and long-term effects on personality, ability, and energy seem likely. Medical personnel in many parts of Africa have long called for psychological research as part of their own programs of investigation into the causes and methods of eradication of this widespread phenomenon. Psychologists have begun to answer these calls. At

Makerere, several psychological studies have been started. Leonard Doob in 1967 began to survey attitudes in Uganda toward health issues, including diet, and these surveys are to continue over a period of years so that shifts can be detected. This very basic study is being done elsewhere in Africa too. Doob also designed a study on the transmission of recommended dietary practices among housewives in Ganda villages. This study is now in progress, being conducted by a fellow of the Makerere Program in Social Psychology on behalf of the Medical Research Council Infant Malnutrition Unit at Mulago Hospital. Another study under way in this collaboration with the Medical School is a study of the long-term physical and psychological effects of kwashiorkor, a form of acute malnutrition which is well known in many parts of the world. These three studies are, I believe, just the start of a program of sociomedical research in which psychologists will play a major role. Similar programs are likely to develop in several centers in Africa.

Another research area that is thriving brings psychologists into a working relationship with political scientists concerned with problems of emerging nations. The psychological implication of political development is an example of psychopolitical research now under way in several African locales. Martin Doornbos of the Institute of Social Studies, The Hague, and I, with assistance from my colleague at Syracuse, Clive Davis, have just completed one such study in Ankole, in southwestern Uganda. We collected data there, in the form of questionnaire responses, during several months in 1966 and again in 1968, from several hundred male adults, all of whom were members of Ankole society. The reason for collecting the interviews in two waves was that in 1967 a new constitution was established in Uganda which, among other steps toward centralization of power, transformed the kingdom of Ankole into a "district," abolishing the traditional Hima monarchy and substituting a predominantly Iru popular regional administration. This effort by the central government to combat tribalism is, if nothing else, a splendid independent variable. Hence, we conducted two waves of data-collection, before and after the abolition of the monarchy and the several political and social reorganizations that accompanied it.

The questions this study was designed to answer concern the self-concepts, or the ways in which persons define themselves, that are characteristic of various sub-groups among the people of Ankole. The study was inspired by recent political science writings on identity crises and primordial attachments as psychological concomitants of political development. A man living in Ankole in post-independence Uganda might be expected to be confronted by an identity crisis, for he probably has more potentially conflicting reference groups that could be psychologically relevant than does any man anywhere else. Primordial ties available to him include linguistic, ethnic, tribal, religious, and kinship links. In some very interesting ways, these are intertwined in Ankole. In addition, a man in Ankole could identify himself in terms of his occupation, his academic achievements, his age, his marital status, and, of course, in terms of his nationality. The purpose of our study was to find out how, in fact, these people do identify themselves and to seek explanations for individual differences in the patterning of self-descriptions by examining some details of individual life histories, particularly educational background.

It can now be confessed that Doornbos and I did not plan the before-and-after aspect of this study from its inception. Not even as astute a political scientist as Doornbos predicted the abolition of the monarchy. After the fact, however, it became obvious to us that it provided an opportunity for a kind of natural experiment that seldom occurs, and we repeated a wave of interviewing that we had done before the abolition of the traditional monarchy. We are now in a position to make empirically based statements not only about how various Banyankole think of themselves a few years after national independence but also about how, if at all, the dramatic reformation of their homeland affects those thoughts.

A few such statements follow. A more complete report is forthcoming in a monograph. First, some findings from the pre-constitution data: The single most salient term of self-reference in the sample as a whole was "tribe." The most popular response to a totally open-ended question, "What are you?", asked at the outset of the interview, was "I am a Munyankole." Nearly half the sample made that response. In contrast, only 3 per cent of the sample replied, "I am a Ugandan." The salience of the tribe, as shown by replies to this question, varied significantly with education. It was more popular among less-educated persons. When asked how people *should* think of themselves, the proportion responding in terms of "tribe" decreased slightly, but the proportion saying "Ugandan" went up to 51 per cent. It thus appears that tribal awareness is much greater than national consciousness, but people are at the same time aware that they *ought* to be thinking of themselves as Ugandan. It also appears that education enhances national consciousness.

As for the effects of the new constitution of 1967, I wish merely to note here that there are some striking ones. While there are enough similarities to establish the reliability of our techniques, some large differences in self-referential behavior have occurred, including an apparent enhancement of the salience of the tribal designation as a term of self-reference following the establishment of the constitution. This finding, and others like it, should illuminate the psychological implications of nation-building. The blessing, not unmixed, of a psychological approach to such issues as the emergence of national identity is that reams of data are collected to serve as the basis of generalizations. Doornbos tells me that the early results of our data-analysis confirm what he had already learned via his political science methods. I, in turn, am pleased to note that his observations fit our data and offer possible explanations for them.

In this, and the other psychological studies I have referred to, there is a relevance to the concerns of some other disciplines, such as education, linguistics, medicine, and political science. Sociologists and anthropologists are also likely to find that ongoing research in psychology in Africa relates to their concerns. I believe that this is an extremely important feature of research in Africa. It seems to me that, on the one hand, social scientists who preceded psychologists into African studies recognized psychology's relevance and invited its participation, and, on the other hand, psychologists who have entered African studies have responded to the invitations by turning their attention to problems unearthed and highlighted by previous social science research. The interdisciplinary dovetailing of research efforts has been, and should continue to be, beneficial for all concerned.

If it is to continue, opportunities for interdisciplinary training with a cross-cultural focus must be expanded, and more graduate students in psychology should be encouraged to participate in such training programs. As I remarked earlier, the Northwestern Program of African Studies from its beginnings twenty years ago made a place for psychology. Donald Campbell has helped to guide the Northwestern program, and he has devoted a good portion of his professional time to research in Africa. Leonard Doob, who must be acknowledged as the *doyen* of psychological research in Africa, has long been a guiding light in African Studies at Yale. Since 1966, the Syracuse Program of Eastern African Studies has included psychology. As these centers produce African-oriented psychologists, it is to be hoped that other African studies programs will find room for them.

In Africa, too, there must be institutional development of psychology if this field is to continue to grow. Meaningful psychological research cannot be consistently done in Africa if we must rely solely on short-term projects completed by visiting psychologists with no real stake in African intellectual life. Not until there are more psychological research institutes in Africa and more departments of psychology in African universities will psychology realize its potential.

Most of the research I have described here was done under the aegis of the Makerere University Program in Social Psychology. I must apologize for dwelling on research in which I had a personal involvement. Now I must apologize again for turning to a description of the Makerere program itself. I do so because I believe that it can serve as a model for the kind of institutional development which I feel is necessary for the continuing growth of psychology in Africa. I do not mean to argue that the Makerere program should be emulated in all respects, but I think it can serve as a good model to which others might react as they plan similar activities.

The program was created in July, 1967, with generous financial assistance from the Carnegie Corporation. It is built around an undergraduate teaching program in social psychology at Makerere, and it leads to a B.S. degree. This teaching program is located in the Faculty of Social Sciences and is one of the very few such programs in Africa. Until recently, the only teaching in psychology available in African universities was to be found in faculties of education, where the subject was treated primarily as a service, or tool, discipline. Education courses did not train psychologists. Indeed, few African students were ever exposed to psychology during their undergraduate days. It is little wonder that so few Africans sought postgraduate training abroad as psychologists. The core of the effort at Makerere, then, is an undergraduate teaching program out of which will come candidates for further study in psychology.

The second feature of the program is the provision of fellowships for graduate study in psychology. At the present time, the program has only a few of these fellowships, reserved for Makerere graduates and tenable at Syracuse.

To staff the program at Makerere, Syracuse University recruits American and European psychologists who spend a year or more at Makerere teaching undergraduates, advising graduate students, and doing research. To date, psychologists from the University of Iowa, the University of Cincinnati, the University of Sussex, and Syracuse University have participated. Psychologists from the University of Bristol may soon join the program, and participation is expected from Norway in 1969. Makerere will also add permanent staff members in social psychology as candidates for these posts become available. It is anticipated that the holders of the psychology fellowships who will be completing their training during the next few years will apply for those posts, gradually eliminating the need for expatriate, temporary staff members.

On the other hand, it is a positive feature of the program that expatriate participation, although not necessarily at the teaching level, is expected to continue indefinitely, albeit at a reduced pace. Expatriate psychologists are drawn to Africa by the research possibilities which exist there. The program in social psychology at Makerere offers places to visiting psychologists who will participate in the research activities of the program and who will assist in the teaching of psychology. Similarly, graduate students in psychology are encouraged to come to Makerere, as associates of the Makerere Institute of Social Research and of the Makerere Program in Social Psychology. Syracuse University has provided some fellowships in its Department of Psychology especially to provide a year's externship in cross-cultural psychology at Makerere. Students from any psychology graduate program are, of course, welcome.

The research done by the expatriates is an integral part of the undergraduate training program at Makerere, for students in psychology are given opportunities to participate as researchers, and, at the very least, receive information about this research in their regular lectures or in research seminars.

Thus, the program is expected to contribute to ongoing psychological research in Africa, to encourage more psychologists to do research in Africa, to participate in the further development of psychology as an undergraduate subject in Africa, to assist African students who wish to become psychologists, and, in the long run, to make psychology a full-fledged, indigenously manned, productive discipline in Africa.

This last goal is a specific example of what is, today, a general trend in psychology—its spread to countries, both developed and developing, in which earlier it hardly existed. The internationalization of psychology is, perhaps, the most striking characteristic of its history during this decade. As a social psychologist, I am most impressed by the international growth of this branch of the discipline, as evidenced by new programs in social psychology at many European universities, the occurrence of international conferences and workshops, and the publication of international journals. In this country, several social psychology programs, such as those at Michigan, Rice, and Syracuse, have come to emphasize cross-cultural research training, and two prominent social psychology journals have explicitly encouraged cross-cultural research, in one case by offering immediate publication of reports of such research.

A part of this trend is a concern with the potential contributions of social psychology to the problems of developing nations. A conference on that topic was held in 1966 at the University of Ibadan.[9] That the conference organizers, who included Brewster Smith, Herbert Kelman, and Henri Tajfel, chose to convene it in Nigeria is further evidence that psychologists have at last discovered Africa. Africa has also discovered psychology. The Makerere Institute of Social Research set up a workshop at Syracuse University in December, 1968, to which psychologists from various countries were invited to share thoughts on psychological research opportunities, difficulties, and priorities. It is a happy thought that the field of psychology in Africa has become sufficiently popular to justify discussion of priorities.

Thus, it seems that psychology in Africa has come of age. I trust that the cursory review I have provided of some of the current activities of the Makerere Program in Social Psychology, the few recent studies which I have described, and other developments which have occurred elsewhere justify this assessment.

9. J. DeLamater, R. Hefner, R. Clignet, and an international editorial committee, "Social Psychological Research in Developing Countries," *Journal of Social Issues*, XXIV, No. 2 (1968).

DISCUSSANT'S COMMENTS   3.

Lance R. Sobel

In the discussion following Professor Segall's presentation of his paper on the growth of psychology in African studies, a number of questions were raised concerning the manner in which much psychological research is conducted in Africa, the nature of the questions asked by the people conducting this research, the direction in which currently existing training programs in Africa are moving, and the relevance of training programs and current research to some of the practical concerns of African nations. While it is true that most participants at this session shared Segall's enthusiasm over the development of the study of psychology in African universities and the growing role of Africa in psychological research, I believe that I am conveying the spirit of the discussion at this session by questioning his conclusion that "psychology in Africa has come of age." Reflecting a recurrent theme in the discussion, I would like to devote the major part of my comments to a consideration of the ethnocentric nature of psychological inquiry in Africa. This is an issue which is important to any further consideration of the independent development of the discipline in Africa.

An examination of recent bibliographies of psychological research done in Africa, of international journals, and of international conference reports [1] shows that the overwhelming majority of this research is carried out by North American and European scholars. Judging from the size of programs such as that at Makerere it is reasonable to assume that this situation will not change appreciably in the near future, especially in view of the fact that the immediate impact of such programs is usually the initiation of research projects by the expatriate staff at these institutions. Certainly there is

1. See, for example, Remi Clignet, "Psychological Research in Africa: Significance and Method," unpublished manuscript, 1968, which includes a bibliography of ninety-five sources in English and French; see also the *International Journal of Psychology*, and the recently established *Cross-Cultural Social Psychology Newsletter*. The *Journal of Social Issues*, XXIV (April, 1968) includes papers presented at the 1966 Ibadan Conference on Social Psychological Research in Developing Countries and includes biographical sketches of conference participants.

value in research conducted by non-African scholars—Segall makes the point that "the African research setting provides a necessary extension to the empirical domain which is the basis for all advances in psychological theory-building." But it is necessary to ask to what extent the outcome of such research is determined by the facts that the hypotheses being tested and the methodologies used were developed in a Western cultural milieu and that data are analyzed and interpretations made within an essentially Western frame of reference.

Clignet, in a recent paper on psychological research in Africa[2] notes that psychologists as well as other social scientists "have often been characterized by a high degree of ethnocentrism." He identifies three facets of this ethnocentrism, including the one-sided relationship between the African subject and the non-African investigator ("all observers expect that African individuals give the *White Man* the answers they think he wants to hear"), the choice of instruments devised for the investigator's own culture or discipline which have not been tested in the (African) research setting, and the definition of variables whose choice and treatment are often influenced by the ideological as well as the cultural background of the investigator. It is not difficult to find articles which provide concrete examples of the problems raised here. However, examples of how these problems may be solved are also available.

LeVine has reported on efforts in South Africa and the Congo to discover modal culture-determined responses to projective tests that may be used as the background from which to evaluate individual responses on these tests.[3] The lack of such background knowledge has led to gross misinterpretations in the use of these tests, and some investigators have questioned the validity of projective testing in cultures other than those in which they have been developed. An important implication of LeVine's study is that psychologists working in Africa can overcome some of the difficulties inherent in doing research in cultures foreign to them by spending the time to gather background on these cultures through cooperation with

2. Clignet, "Psychological Research in Africa."

3. Robert LeVine, "Africa," in *Psychological Anthropology*, ed. by Francis Hsu (Homewood, Ill.: Dorsey Press, 1961). Clignet, in the paper cited, also gives examples of problems of misinterpretations in the use of projective tests in Africa.

anthropologists and by developing their own observational skills. This does not, however, obviate the need for cross-validation of outsiders' interpretations of cultural patterns by members of the "in-group."

In a paper specifically devoted to the mutual relevance of the methods of anthropology and psychology, Campbell gives a number of examples of how ethnographic data have been used to test conflicting hypotheses derived from existing psychological theories.[4] A number of these examples are used to show how data from anthropological investigations in African and other non-Western cultures support a learning-theory rather than a psychoanalytic explanation of the relationship between early childhood experiences and later behavior. Campbell's concern was with tests of the universal applicability of existing psychological theories and not with the extent to which the anthropologists whose data he used were able to explain or account for behavior in the societies they studied.

My own feeling is that it is not surprising that psychoanalytic theory, especially that of the Oedipus complex, did not hold up when examined in cultural settings where family patterns and sexual mores bore little or no resemblance to those existing in Freud's Vienna or those existing in contemporary Western settings. What is surprising is that so many investigators have gone to such great lengths to apply this theory in a variety of cultural settings. It may be argued, however, that these attempts reflect a significant heuristic value of Oedipal theory in spite of its apparent lack of universal applicability. It is on this basis that I find Fernandez' proposal that the myth of the legendary Zulu hero, Shaka, is a "more relevant symbolic statement of the agonies of African family life" than that of Oedipus[5] more important than Campbell's finding that learning theory may be more universally relevant than Freudian theory. Fernandez derives a syndrome he calls the "Shaka complex" from this Bantu myth and shows how it may relate to political behavior in Africa and to "certain family characteristics of many African societies in transition." The Shaka complex is likely to prove as culture-bound as is the Oedipus complex, but I feel that psychology is likely to develop theories of universal ap-

4. Donald T. Campbell "The Mutual Methodological Relevance of Psychology and Anthropology," in *Psychological Anthropology.*

5. James Fernandez, "The Shaka Complex," *Transition,* XXIX (February–March, 1967), 11–14.

plicability only when more such partially relevant theories from a wider range of cultural perspectives exist.

Another example of misinterpretation due to insufficient knowledge of the cultural setting is given by Clignet in a discussion of one of his own investigations. He explains his failure to replicate the findings of Small and Campbell in his conformity experiment done in the Ivory Coast on the basis of his failure to use "experts" in the experimental manipulation whose behavior conformed with local conceptions of expertise. Being wise enough to have asked his subjects to explain their behavior at the conclusion of the experiment, he learned that "the lack of unanimity of the so-called 'experts' indicated very clearly that after all they were not [from the point of view of his subjects] experts." [6] Since it appears that expertise is confounded with consensus in this culture, it does not seem possible to carry out the replication that Clignet intended. Here we are again faced with a situation where a new culturally specific theory of conformity might prove more productive for the long-range goal of universal theory than tests which assume the cross-cultural relevance of existing theories. Note also that in Clignet's experiment the subjects were able to utilize knowledge of their own culture to explain the outcome.

Thus far I have mainly considered the ways in which expatriate researchers can utilize existing knowledge of their own sensitivities to overcome some of the cultural barriers to meaningful psychological research in Africa. At this point I would like to move on to a consideration of some proposals for reducing the degree of expatriate domination of psychological research in Africa. Although my primary concern here is to deal with the problem of expanding the perspectives of the discipline, thus increasing its relevance both theoretically and practically to Africa, it should be mentioned that the imbalance in the source of influence and direction of research in Africa may be considered an ethical and political problem as well. The term "intellectual neocolonialism" was used at the conference with regard to the attitude evidenced by some investigators who appear to have taken access to Africa for granted without regard for the needs, interests, or privacy of individuals in the host country. In an article on project Camelot in the East African journal *Transition*, Galtung has used the term "scientific colonialism" to describe the "proc-

6. Clignet, "Psychological Research in Africa."

ess whereby the centre of gravity for the acquisition of knowledge about [a] nation is located outside the nation itself.''[7] In view of the number of African studies programs existing in the United States and Europe, this is an all too accurate picture of the state of social science information concerning Africa. Galtung proposes as one corrective for this situation ''devising social science methods that are so good and so cheap that they can be used by anybody with a sufficient level of training,'' and he goes on to discuss the various ways in which correcting the current state of imbalance is of scientific and practical value both to the developed and the developing nations.

Kelman, Tajfel, and Campbell have each presented programs designed to increase the cooperation between scholars from the developed and the developing nations in psychological research.[8] All agree that the major goal of such programs should be to facilitate the development of professional skills in the developing nations, and all make the point that this goal is not predominantly an altruistic one. The ''growth of the discipline,'' development of an ''optimal social science,'' and the achievement of a ''properly international and cross-cultural'' social psychology all depend on a reduction of the influence of the United States and an increase in contributions from ''all provinces'' or ''many positions of approximately compatible professional strength.'' The message is clear, but a number of important questions are raised concerning the means of achieving this mutually desired end.

Kelman, like Segall, argues that basic research concerned with long-range issues should be the focal point of his proposed cooperative research program. By concentrating on the general area of social change and using ''problems of developing societies'' as the starting point for this research, he feels that his program can gain support from scholars in these nations and attract some of the most promising students.

Tajfel takes issue with Kelman on a number of points. He

7. Johan Galtung, ''Scientific Colonialism,'' *Transition*, XXX (April–May, 1967), 11–19.

8. Herbert C. Kelman, ''Psychological Research on Social Change: Some Scientific and Ethical Problems,'' *International Journal of Psychology*, II (1967), 301–14; Henri Tajfel, ''Second Thoughts about Cross-Cultural Research and International Relations,'' *International Journal of Psychology*, III (1968), 213–19; D. T. Campbell, ''A Cooperative Multinational Opinion Sample Exchange,'' *Journal of Social Issues*, XXIV (1968), 245–56.

argues against placing the emphasis on cooperative research projects, on the basis that these projects tend to reflect the interests of the scholar who has the funds to support them and further that such projects are limited to nations within "the various economic and political spheres of influence" and thus are not likely to avoid a "global political ethnocentrism." He also questions the appropriateness of basic research for solutions to practical rather than to theoretical problems, claiming that the "fundamental answers to long-range problems" sought by Kelman have "a way of manufacturing their Pandora's boxes, the contents of which are highly unpredictable to the scientists themselves."

Tajfel proposes the use of international training seminars, small international conferences, and short-term exchanges of scholars as means of fostering the indigenous and preferably autonomous development of the discipline in different countries and at the same time maintaining open channels for international communication and cooperation. He suggests that the short-range goal of practical relevance in research is distinct from the longer range goals of advancing knowledge and promoting the indigenous growth of the discipline, and that scholars from the developed nations can be useful to the developing nations by helping to do research which, primarily, has immediate objectives and which only secondarily may have theoretical implications.

The proposal put forth by Campbell takes a slightly different tack. By placing a great deal of emphasis on methodology, that is, the use of instruments and techniques that would allow his multinational opinion-sample exchange to be classified in the category of "no-budget research," he avoids the problem of asking scholars in the developing nations to depend on outside funds, and therefore on the initiative of scholars from the developed nations. Campbell has also chosen an area—attitude or opinion surveys—that may provide a meeting ground for social scientists of all disciplines. This is important for two reasons. First, the number of cooperative ventures in basic psychological research in Africa is limited by the small number of African psychologists and the even smaller number of African *social* psychologists, and such programs may prove attractive to sociologists and political scientists and possibly anthropologists, as well as psychologists. Second, its multidisciplinary nature avoids imposing existing disciplinary boundaries on scholars in Africa who are likely to be in the process of making decisions concerning the future course for social sciences in their own nations or regions. Campbell also offers suggestions for the training of undergraduates and enlisting the aid of high-school students, as well as a discussion of the implications of reducing dependence on existing methodological techniques and instruments. The implementation of this proposal on even a modest scale could result in a major step in the direction of the universally utilizable social science methodology called for by Galtung.

One of the aims set forth in a statement of purpose by the *International Journal of Psychology* is to "enlarge the scope of psychology beyond local limits" through an *"international confrontation of theories and methods,* on which psychologists from various countries differ, because of their native culture and training." Note that the emphasis here is on *psychologists* from various countries and not on research subjects from various countries. Most of my remarks up to this point have been devoted to considering how and why attempts should be made to increase participation in this international confrontation by psychologists whose cultural background is African.[9] At this point I would like to consider in more detail the training of psychologists in an African setting. This is an especially important point since the existing programs for training psychologists in Africa are still in the formative stages.

Segall's discussion of the Makerere University College program in social psychology provided the starting point for a good deal of the discussion at this conference session. While Segall chose to emphasize the fact that the Makerere program, by teaching psychology as a separate or distinct discipline, was producing candidates for graduate study abroad, most of the questions that were raised concerned the nature of the teaching of this discipline. One discussant made reference to what he considered the disappointing state of affairs in Indian universities where the curricula in psychology are simply images of those existing in British or American universities with no attempt made to incorporate local philosophical or cultural ideas. He suggested that Western scholars are in need of the "breath of fresh air" that comes with exposure to the ideas of those raised in non-Western cultures, but wondered if this exposure would be possible if African psychology pro-

9. I do not mean to attribute homogeneity to the many and diverse cultural groups in Africa but to use this as a category equivalent to "Eastern" and "Western."

grams followed the Indian example and provided no outlet for the expression of non-Western ideas.

Segall's comments concerning the continuing participation of expatriate faculty in the Makerere program was another point for discussion. It was mentioned that his view of the contributions that expatriates can make to the growth of the discipline in Africa was one-sided in that he failed to consider the fact that not only do interesting research possibilities exist for expatriates in Africa but interesting research possibilities exist for African psychologists in Europe and the United States as well. Further, it was stated that he ignored the contributions that African psychologists can make to Western universities.

Although I am not sure that he meant it that way, Segall seemed to imply that Africa should send its students abroad to gather ideas and knowledge, while other nations will send faculty and some students to Africa to gather data. The teaching of psychology in African universities does not by itself contribute to broadening the perspectives of the discipline, that is, to reducing its ethnocentric nature. It should be evident that many of the problems raised earlier concerning the dominance of expatriate influence in research in general apply to the Makerere program, its funding, its faculty, and the research that is done there. If there are not yet African faculty available for the Makerere program then it is not enough that students are "given opportunities to participate as researchers, and, at the very least, receive information about this research in their regular lectures or in research seminars." If they are the ones who can bring local cultural perspectives to bear, then it seems that they should be given that opportunity. Campbell has suggested that social psychologists draw on the "local problems, values and images of man for the content and setting of comparative research." [10] This suggestion seems equally appropriate for the design of a university curriculum, for only when these values and images are reflected in the development of the discipline in Africa and in the African contribution to the international confrontation mentioned above will it be possible to say that "psychology in Africa has come of age."

10. Campbell, "A Cooperative Multinational Opinion Sample Exchange."

HISTORICAL RESEARCH
IN MAINLAND TANZANIA

4

Isaria N. Kimambo

Although a good deal of research into the history of Tanzania has been conducted throughout the past ten years, several factors have placed limitations on historians' efforts to develop the framework necessary to a comprehensive study. Tanzania contains a large number of distinct ethnic and geographical units, each of which requires separate study before an adequate territorial coverage is possible. Sources, also, are widely dispersed and require a variety of linguistic skills. Much recent work in Tanzania has been colored by the preoccupations of independence, although these concerns are rapidly being superseded by other problems.

Early History

Research into the early history of Tanzania (like that of many countries in Africa) has suffered also from the attitudes of historians toward the value of oral traditions as a source of information. Fortunately, these attitudes have changed considerably in the past few years. While formerly oral traditions were regarded as legends useful only to ethnographers, today many scholars are collecting oral traditions with the conviction that through these sources they can recover the history of nonliterate societies. This change in attitude can in large measure be attributed to the work of certain pioneers who have illustrated that a methodology can be formulated to handle oral evidence as scientifically as other evidence. Jan Vansina's *De la tradition orale*,[1] published in 1961, is perhaps the best example of such efforts.

In mainland Tanzania serious collection of oral traditions started in 1956 when Kathleen Stahl began her work among the Chagga. This work continued until 1961, and the result was published three years later.[2] The preliminary results of the work of seven other scholars who have collected oral traditions in Tanzania have been published as chapters in a book edited by Andrew Roberts,[3] and oral traditions which I collected among the Pare in 1965–66 are included in a forthcoming book.[4]

During the past ten years archaeologists have done much in the interior to provide a background for the study of oral traditions by illuminating the many centuries of the iron age which lie beyond the reach of historical memory. In 1964 Hamo Sassoon made his first systematic excavations at the stone ruins of Engaruka in northern Tanzania. He continued these excavations in 1966, and in the same year Brian Fagan excavated salt-working dumps at Ivuna, near Lake Rukwa. Meanwhile J. E. G. Sutton surveyed other sites for possible excavation, and in 1967 he revealed a long iron-age sequence at the brine springs of Uvinza, near Kigoma. In the same year Robert Soper discovered early iron-age sites in the Pare Mountains and elsewhere in northeastern Tanzania. Comparison with linguistic evidence indicates that these sites may mark the earliest stages of Bantu settlement in East Africa.[5]

1. An English edition translated by H. M. Wright appeared as *Oral Tradition* (London: Routledge & Kegan Paul, 1965; Chicago: Aldine, 1965).

2. Kathleen M. Stahl, *History of the Chagga People of Kilimanjaro* (The Hague: Mouton, 1964); see also her "Outline of Chagga History," *Tanzania Notes and Records*, LXIV (1965), 35–49.

3. Andrew Roberts, ed., *Tanzania Before 1900: Seven Area Histories* (Nairobi: East African Publishing House, 1968). Contributors of oral histories included in this volume are B. Brock among the Nyiha of Mbozi (1961); Alison Redmayne among the Hehe (1961–63); R. G. Willis among the Fipa (1962–64); A. Shorter among the Kimbu (1964–67); I. N. Kimambo among the Pare (1965–66); S. Feierman among the Shambaa (1966–68); and Andrew Roberts among the Nyamwezi (1967).

4. I. N. Kimambo, *A Political History of the Pare of Northeastern Tanzania, c. 1500–1900* (Nairobi: East African Publishing House, forthcoming).

5. Preliminary reports on these excavations have appeared in *Azania*, I (1966) and II (1967); in the *Journal of African History*, VIII (1967);

As a result of this work, our understanding of Tanzania's precolonial past has been considerably advanced. This recent research however is confined to two areas: the northeastern region and the western region, which extends into the southern highlands. A large part of the country therefore remains untouched. With the exception of three staff members from the University College, Dar es Salaam (J. E. G. Sutton, A. D. Roberts, and myself), most of the workers who have collected oral traditions are research associates from overseas. Dr. Roberts, who has held the position of Research Fellow in Oral History (supported by the Ford Foundation), has been responsible for coordinating and encouraging the visiting researchers, even those whose primary interest is not in the collection of oral traditions for historical reconstruction, and it is due largely to his efforts that the results of this recent research have been made available.

Although the completed research is limited to a few areas, it has already provided information on four major points: (1) the character of oral evidence in Tanzania, (2) the question of origins and spread of chieftainship, (3) the growth of contact between the coast and the interior, and (4) the kind of political changes which were taking place in the nineteenth century.

Character of oral evidence

It has been clearly demonstrated that oral traditions reflect the social and political structures of the areas concerned. In most of the areas studied, traditions of chieftainship are richer both in quality and quantity than other types of traditions, and in the numerous small chiefdoms of western Tanzania, traditions of chieftainship are in fact the only ones available. In the larger political units like Usambara and Ugweno in North Pare, more detailed traditions can be found, but nowhere are there "professional historians" of the type known in the large kingdoms of West Africa. In most of these examples, therefore, genealogies are short and obviously telescoped, except in the case of Ugweno where accuracy of genealogies and historical memory were greatly increased by initiation periods requiring the continuous participation of all

and in *Tanzania Zamani* (research bulletin of the Department of History, University College, Dar es Salaam), No. 2 (1968).

adults. Also, fortunately, in the other chiefdoms traditions overlap, and so through careful comparison one can trace certain events back to the seventeenth century. The second point to be noted is that when political changes took place, changes in the traditions could also be expected. Thus, when the Kilindi took over political power in Usambara in the eighteenth century, they endeavored to suppress the older traditions. Similarly the unification of the Hehe by Munyigumba and Mkwawa in the nineteenth century resulted in such a complete transformation of society that Alison Redmayne's researches have thrown little light on pre-nineteenth-century Hehe history. Yet this is by no means a general hypothesis, since among the Kimbu, for example, Father Shorter found that the unification brought about by Nyungu ya Mawe in the nineteenth century sharpened interest in chiefdom traditions.[6]

Origins and spread of chieftainship

It was formerly thought that the whole development of chieftainship in Tanzania could be traced to a single *ntemi* tradition originating in one area, possibly the interlacustrine region, from which it spread to the Nyamwezi-Sukuma area, from which it reached southwestern Tanzania by the sixteenth century. From there it was thought that a secondary movement went north and northeastward to Uhehe, Morogoro, Usambara, and Kilimanjaro. The new evidence brings out two points: First, in the case of the Pare Mountains, there is a clear picture of evolution of political organization within the society. Secondly, even in the Nyamwezi-Sukuma area there is a complex picture of movements of groups from many directions, each forming its own chiefdoms, although in no case before the seventeenth century. Certainly a diffusionist hypothesis is proving to be too simple to explain why innovations in these societies were acceptable, possible, and even necessary. In Ugweno, for example, as early as the sixteenth century far-reaching reforms were initiated from within, while in Usambara the same kind of centralization was achieved when the Kilindi took over political power in the eighteenth century. In both cases it is becoming clear that nothing can be explained without understanding the forces which were stimulating changes within these societies.

6. Redmayne, in *Tanzania Before 1900;* and Shorter, *ibid.*

Growth of contact between the coast and the interior

Although the coast of Africa had developed a network of contacts with the Indian Ocean world, its contact with the interior developed rather late, and when it did develop the initiative came from the interior rather than from the coast. Recent studies help to explain both politically and commercially why contacts did not occur earlier. Because of the marginal nature of the land in the *ntemi* area, territorial chieftainship did not develop until the period between the sixteenth and eighteenth centuries, and, from the evidence available, the institution of territorial chieftainship encouraged the trade contacts which followed. For example, the prestige attached to the shell of the giant clam, which had been used since the end of the eighteenth century as regalia of chieftainship in Ukimbu and Unyamwezi, encouraged expeditions to the coast. Economic motives may have been even more crucial. The attempts by rulers to control iron trade and salt trade are well illustrated, and contacts grew from the organization of regional trade networks. As the commercial scale expanded, the trade value of ivory came to be realized. It is significant that by the end of the eighteenth century the Igulwibi group were moving from Iramba to Ukimbu in search of ivory. It is also significant that the first Nyamwezi traders arrived on the coast around 1800.

Changes in political and military organization in the nineteenth century

With the possible exception of the rulers of Ugweno, Usambara, Ufipa, the Hinda states, and Buha, most chiefs relied primarily on kinship and ritual for their authority. But long-distance trade helped to spread new crops such as maize, rice, and cassava, as well as iron hoes for cultivation, and in the nineteenth century many chiefs accumulated goods through trade and plunder. This increased agricultural and material wealth enabled certain rulers to support followers who were entirely dependent on them. Thus such rulers as Ghendewa of Ugweno, Kimweri of Usambara, Rindi and Sina of Kilimanjaro, Kapuufi and Kimaraunga of Ufipa, Mirambo of the Nyamwezi, Nyungu of the Kimbu, and Mkwawa of the Hehe were all operating in this new atmosphere. Their new source of political power had radically affected the size of their political units. In the cases of Mirambo, Nyungu, and Mkwawa there was a remarkable enlargement of political scale. But in the cases of Upare and Usambara there was a reduction in political organization as the scale of contact expanded, mainly because those in traditional centers of power found themselves isolated from the caravan routes, and thus their subordinates who were in touch with the new source of power were encouraged to rebel against them.

Continuing research

This short summary of the results of recent research in the early history of Tanzania indicates how much such researches can contribute to the overall understanding of the history of this country. At present more work is going on in collecting oral traditions,[7] and these researches are likely to add dimension to the studies already done in the two regions mentioned earlier.

This discussion of the early history of Tanzania has omitted the coastal area, about which more is known. Yet recent research has indicated that much remains to be done in this area also. H. N. Chittick's work on Kilwa has revealed how archaeology can increase our knowledge of the development of coastal societies and how it can give us a more accurate perspective through which to interpret the existing coastal manuscripts.[8] Edward Alpers has indicated that valuable information still lies buried in Portuguese archives. His work on Yao trade has already shed light on what was happening between Kilwa and the interior during the Portuguese period, and his work in the Goa archives has helped to revise the chronology of the sultans of Kilwa in the eighteenth and nineteenth centuries.[9] There is no doubt that work of this kind is still needed for the settlements of the coast.

7. C. F. Holmes is working on the Kwimba chiefdom of the Sukuma; P. Pender-Cudlip is collecting traditions in Iramba; D. C. Sperling is working among the Digo; A. Unomah from Ibadan is working on the history of Tabora; W. Brown on that of Bagamoyo; and Alan Jacobs is following up his earlier work in Masailand.

8. H. N. Chittick, ''The 'Shirazi' Colonization of East Africa,'' *Journal of African History*, VI (1965), 275–94; see also his articles in *Azania*, I (1966) and II (1967).

9. Edward Alpers, ''The Role of the Yao in the Development of Trade in East-Central Africa: 1698–c. 1850'' (Ph.D. dissertation, University of London, 1965); also Alpers, ''Malawi and Yao Responses to Chang-

So far as the Department of History at the University College, Dar es Salaam, is concerned, two projects which are now in progress are of great importance. One is the collection of oral traditions in Karagwe by I. Katoke, a member of the department. It is hoped that his work will shed light on the nature of the Hinda kingdoms about which so little is known. It is also hoped that the work of C. Hartwig, a research associate, in Ukerewe will tie up with Mr. Katoke's research. The second study, which will be discussed below, is a comprehensive departmental project on the Maji Maji Rising.

For the early history of Tanzania, however, a high priority is to institute a massive program of collecting oral traditions in the vast untapped areas of the country. Ideally such a program should go hand in hand with archaeological and linguistic studies, but it is unlikely that the Department of History at the University College, Dar es Salaam, will in the next few years be sufficiently equipped with the manpower and other resources required to meet this need. We shall continue to rely on research associates from other countries for some time, but our experience indicates that the best results can be obtained from a coordinated program, and we expect that coordination will be our main role for some years to come.

Modern History

Political studies

The most valuable research of recent years has undoubtedly been on the history of regional politics. The work of Andrew Maguire in Sukumaland, R. P. Abrahams in Unyamwezi, Basil Mramba in Kilimanjaro, and Ralph Austen and Goran Hyden in Buhaya is already available,[10] while Susan Geiger Rogers

---

ing External Economic Forces, 1505–1798,'' in *East Africa and the Orient: Problems of Cultural Synthesis in Pre-Colonial Times,* ed. by H. N. Chittick and R. I. Rotberg (Cambridge, Mass.: Harvard University Press, forthcoming) ; and Alpers, ''A Revised Chronology of the Sultanas of Kilwa in the Eighteenth and Nineteenth Centuries,'' *Azania,* II (1967).

10. G. A. Maguire, ''Towards 'Uhuru' in Sukumuland'' (Ph.D. dissertation, Harvard University, 1966) ; R. G. Abrahams, *The Political Organization of Unyamwezi* (Cambridge: Cambridge University Press, 1967) ; Basil P. Mramba, ''Some Notes on the Political Development of

(Kilimanjaro), Paul Puritt (Meru), J. Gus Liebenow (Makonde and Makua), Richard Juma (Usambara), and the author (Upare) are all engaged on roughly similar subjects. Such studies are valuable, and more are needed, for example in the Lake Tanganyika region and the Songea, Iringa, Rungwe, Mbeya, Morogoro, Kisarawe, Kondoa, Bagamoyo, Handeni, Korogwe, and Musoma districts. The list is formidable, especially when it is remembered that all the completed studies concentrate either on the earlier or the later colonial period but not one covers the whole colonial period in its chosen area. A study of this kind, which would combine the basic administrative and mission records with a limited range of private sources in African hands and with interviewing, is one of the most valuable things a graduate student with history training can do. The Department of History of the University College, Dar es Salaam, is planning a one-year research-training course for graduates which will concentrate on work of this kind, while Dr. Iliffe is attempting a synthesis of material presently available in his study of politics and society in Tanzania from 1907 to 1954.

Economic history

All the existing area studies share a preoccupation with politics. This was to be expected in 1961, but such studies are increasingly anachronistic. From the viewpoint of the administrator, social scientist, or teacher, what is most needed from the historian of modern Tanzania is painstaking and detailed economic history at the regional or district level, that is, a transfer of energy from area politics to area economics, similar to the transfer from national to area politics that took place soon after independence. In Tanzania, at least, area political studies have lacked detail in their economic treatment (although James Graham has recently attempted a

---

the Chagga of Kilimanjaro'' (B.A. research paper, Makerere University College, 1967); R. A. Austen, ''Native Policy and African Politics: Indirect Rule in Northwest Tanzania, 1889–1939'' (Ph.D. dissertation, Harvard University, 1965); Goran Hyden, *TANU Yajenga Nchi: Political Development in Rural Tanzania* (Lund, 1968). See also the section on Ukaguru in *Contemporary Change in Traditional Societies: Volume I,* ed. by J. H. Steward (Urbana: University of Illinois Press, 1967).

purely socioeconomic study.)[11] Apart from the work of Michael von Clemm,[12] such research as has been done in economic history has generally been background work by lawyers, economists, or political scientists concerned chiefly with contemporary issues (for example, R. N. James's work on Haya land tenure and John Saul's on the cooperative movement). Local agrarian research concerned with economic history is now giving a new dimension to historical studies in India, yet in Africa, outside Egypt, very little work of this type has been done save the pioneering work of Polly Hill and the sociologically oriented studies of the Rhodes-Livingstone Institute and the East African Institute of Social Research in the 1950's (for example, P. H. Gulliver's work in Unyakyusa, which is still the best available in Tanzania).[13] Such agrarian studies are difficult to undertake, for rich source materials such as exist in India are unlikely to be available in Tanzania. Possibly a number of new techniques will be needed. But the present Tanzanian emphasis on reconciling rural development with egalitarianism puts a high priority on provision of the background data on what has in fact happened when agrarian systems have been opened to the world economy. A number of social scientists in other disciplines share this concern. Graduate schools might show a special tolerance toward the experimental techniques and tentative conclusions which must accompany early research in this field.[14]

Economic history at the industrial or territorial level remains fragmentary.[15] As yet there is no coherent study of the

11. J. D. Graham, ''Changing Patterns of Wage Labor in Tanzania: A History of the Relations between African Labor and European Capitalism in Njombe District, 1931–1961'' (Ph.D. dissertation, Northwestern University, 1968).

12. Michael von Clemm, ''Agricultural Productivity and Sentiment on Kilimanjaro,'' *Economic Botany*, XVIII (1964), 99–121.

13. P. H. Gulliver, *Land Tenure and Social Change Among the Nyakyusa* (Kampala: EAISR, 1958).

14. For further thoughts on this subject, see T. O. Ranger, ''Historical Studies of Rural Development in Tanzania'' (East African Academy Symposium paper, Dar es Salaam, September, 1968).

15. A. C. Mascarenhas is working on histories of Dar es Salaam port and of the labor force in the sisal industry; J. F. Rweyemamu is contemplating a history of Tanzanian political economy; and there is material on the settler economy in German times in John Iliffe's book on the 1905–12 period, *Tanganyika Under German Rule 1905–1912* (Cambridge: Cambridge University Press, forthcoming).

impact of the capitalist economy, such as has been attempted by G. Arrighi in Rhodesia and by M. P. K. Sorrenson in Kenya. John Masare is investigating the political history of the Asian community, and this research will soon be supplemented by M. Hatim Amiji's more wide-ranging work on the Ismailis, but no serious account of Asian business enterprise exists; it might be impossible for anyone but an Asian to write one. A comprehensive history of the labor movement is also needed; at present there is only A. C. A. Tandau's work.[16]

Urban history is receiving more attention, although this is again a difficult field for the foreign researcher. Kibodya is studying the history of Tanga, and the work of Unomah on Tabora and Brown on Bagamoyo, although primarily concerned with the nineteenth century, will doubtless also illuminate the later history of those towns. Amateur historians are working on urban history in Moshi, Same, and Bukoba. It is possible to list important research areas that are untouched— the impact of the 1929 depression, for example, and the whole field of British economic policy, on which there is only Leubuscher's work and articles by Ehrlich.[17] But, in general, these broad questions will be answerable only when the detailed local studies are available.

African resistance movements

Besides leading historians to ignore economic history, the preoccupations which characterized the nationalist period have colored other research fields. One point where research might have been concentrated is the tradition of African resistance, but even here only a very few topics have been covered. The major work is undoubtedly F. F. Muller's purely documentary study of the coastal resistance of 1888–89,[18] a subject which could now be elaborated from oral materials, hopefully collected and analyzed by a Tanzanian from the

16. A. C. A. Tandau, *Historia ya Kuundwa Kwa TFL na Kuanzishwa kwa NUTA* (Dar es Salaam, 1966).

17. Charlotte Leubuscher, *Tanganyika Territory: A Study of Economic Policy under Mandate* (Oxford: Oxford University Press, 1944); Cyril Ehrlich, ''Some Aspects of Economic Policy in Tanganyika, 1945–60,'' *Journal of Modern African Studies*, II (1964), 265–77.

18. Fritz Ferdinand Muller, *Deutschland-Zanzibar-Ostafrika: Geschichte einer deutschen Kolonialeroberung 1884–1890* (Berlin, 1959); see also J. A. Kieran, ''Abushiri's Resistance,'' in *Hadith*, II, ed. by B. A. Ogot (Nairobi, forthcoming).

coast. Tribal resistance and revolt is considered by Kathleen Stahl (Chagga), Alison Redmayne (Hehe), and M. Jellicoe (Nyaturu),[19] but none of these studies is fully satisfactory. There must be at least twenty tribal resistances in Tanzania which require a monograph and which, had they taken place in West Africa, would by now have received one. Study of a resistance requires a knowledge of German, fluency in Swahili, and a very considerable knowledge of the society in which it took place; ideally, such a study should be combined with oral work on the nineteenth century and earlier, as Stephen Feierman has recently done in Usambara.

The most dramatic incident in Tanzanian resistance, the Maji Maji Rising of 1905–7, has naturally been a first priority for the University College, Dar es Salaam. John Iliffe has written on the documentary sources, and G. C. K. Gwassa is preparing a thesis on the oral and written materials on the outbreak of the rising.[20] The college is also engaged in related research conducted at the village level by its undergraduate students, financed by the Rockefeller Foundation. Twenty-five students were employed on this project in 1968. There is still much room for further research, for Maji Maji may come to absorb as many generations of students as the Indian Mutiny. The principal need is for oral historians with anthropological training to work in the Southern Highlands, the Kilombero Valley, and Ungoni.

Political activity at a supratribal level cannot be studied adequately until further regional work is completed. Ralph Austen, J. M. Lonsdale, and John Iliffe have contributed preliminary papers,[21] but the main source for the next few years is likely to be Daud Mwakawago's forthcoming Swahili

19. Stahl, *History of the Chagga People;* A. H. Redmayne, ''The Wahehe People of Tanganyika'' (D.Phil. thesis, Oxford University, 1964), and ''Mkwawa and the Hehe Wars,'' *Journal of African History,* IX (1968), 409–36; M. Jellicoe, ''The Turu Revolt, 1908'' (University of East Africa Social Science Research Conference paper, Dar es Salaam, January, 1968).

20. John Iliffe, ''The Organisation of the Maji Maji Rebellion,'' *Journal of African History,* VIII (1967), 495–512; G. C. K. Gwassa and John Iliffe, eds., *Records of the Maji Maji Rising: Part One* (Nairobi, 1968).

21. R. A. Austen, ''Notes on the Pre-History of TANU,'' *Makerere Journal,* No. 9 (1964), pp. 1–6; J. M. Lonsdale, ''Some Origins of Nationalism in East Africa,'' *Journal of African History,* IX (1968), 119–46; John Iliffe, ''The Role of the African Association in the Formation and Realisation of Territorial Consciousness in Tanzania'' (U.E.A.S.S.R.C. paper, Dar es Salaam, January, 1968).

history of TANU and its predecessors. The party itself has apparently earmarked funds for the writing of an official history, but no one has yet undertaken it; probably this field must be reserved to Tanzanians for some time, save at the regional level as in Goran Hyden's work. For the post-1945 period, there is some published material on the Meru Land case, most of it rather unsatisfactory.[22] The rural unrest of the 1950's has also been studied,[23] but definitive research on this question will probably need to be integrated into regional agrarian history covering a longer period.

Intellectual and religious history

The most barren field of all, in terms of published work, is intellectual and religious history. All work to date has been written from the mission viewpoint. This would include Marcia Wright's study of Evangelical missions in the Southern Highlands, J. A. Kieran's work on the Holy Ghost Fathers, and Pastor C. J. Hellberg's work on Buhaya.[24] There is also work in progress on the Benedictine mission in the Mahenge and Peramiho areas, the Christian Mission Society, the Universities' Mission to Central Africa in Masasi and Magila, and the White Fathers in Ukerewe. This still leaves the field very wide open, and even areas of early and successful mission work, like Kilimanjaro and Ufipa, remain virtually untouched. As with area political studies, further accounts of individual missions, concentrating perhaps on African response, are still needed. The more purely educational field has

22. I. M. Wright, ''The Meru Land Case,'' *Tanzania Notes and Records,* LXVI (December, 1966), 136–46; Nkura Kirilo Japhet and Earle Seaton, *The Meru Land Case* (Nairobi: East African Publishing House, 1967); Anton Nelson, *The Freemen of Meru* (London: Oxford University Press, 1967).

23. L. Cliffe, ''Nationalism and the Reaction to Enforced Agricultural Improvement in Tanganyika during the Colonial Period'' (E.A.I.S.R. conference paper, January, 1965); N. R. Fuggles-Couchman, *Agricultural Change in Tanganyika: 1945–60* (Stanford: Stanford University Food Research Institute, 1964); J. D. Jesby, ''Warangi Reaction to Agricultural Change'' (E.A.I.S.R. conference paper, January, 1965); Maguire, ''Towards 'Uhuru.' ''

24. C. J. Hellberg, *Missions on a Colonial Frontier West of Lake Victoria: Evangelical Missions in North-west Tanganyika to 1932* (Lund, 1965); Marcia Wright, ''German Evangelical Missions in Tanganyika, 1891 to 1939'' (Ph.D. thesis, London University, 1966); the title of the unpublished thesis by Dr. Kieran is not at hand.

been researched by A. R. Thompson (a study of British policy, especially in relation to missions), Patricia Saul (a study of agricultural education in Buhaya), and J. E. F. Mhina, whose forthcoming history of St. Andrew's College, Minaki, may hopefully stimulate rival school histories. James Coleman and Carl Rosberg are engaged on a study of Tanzanian elites.

The Christian impact, however, is only one aspect of intellectual and religious history. There remains the study of Islam, of African religions, and of more secular intellectual activity. No one has ever worked seriously for any length of time on Tanzanian Islam, yet it has certainly influenced contemporary patterns of thought as powerfully as have the Christian missions. B. G. Martin has recently made preliminary investigations into the history of the Qadiriyya movement, and has proved that material is available to justify the interest of trained Islamicists.[25] This field is now vacant, while the field of "traditional" religious history has been virtually vacant, with the exception of Monica Wilson's *Communal Rituals of the Nyakyusa.* Peter Lienhardt, Terence Ranger, and A. V. Akeroyd have focused interest particularly on popular movements to eradicate witchcraft,[26] while Professor Ranger has shown that a wide range of important subjects exists in the field of popular religious thought and artistic expression. His papers on this subject might be useful to anyone establishing research priorities, for they are correctives to the political-economic bias that colors so much that is written and learned about Africa.[27] Finally, in the intellectual field, there is the quite unexplored area of secular intellectual history: the material which might be recovered from legal records, for example, or from popular Swahili poetry, or

25. See the notes to his translation of C. H. Becker, "Materials for the Understanding of Islam in German East Africa," *Tanzania Notes and Records,* LXVIII (February, 1968), 31–61; see also J. S. Trimingham, *Islam in East Africa* (Oxford: Oxford University Press, 1964).

26. Peter Lienhardt, *The Medicine-Man: L Swifa Ya Nguvumali* (Oxford: Oxford University Press, 1968); T. O. Ranger, "Witchcraft Eradication Movements in Central and Southern Tanzania and Their Connection with the Maji Maji Rising" (research seminar paper, University College, Dar es Salaam, 1966).

27. T. O. Ranger, *The African Churches of Tanzania* (Nairobi: East African Publishing House, 1968), and "Tanzania: The Movement of Ideas, 1850–1939," in *A History of Tanzania,* ed. by I. N. Kimambo and A. J. Temu (Nairobi, forthcoming). This latter book will also contain general chapters by Gwassa on the 1885–1907 period, Iliffe on 1907–45, and Temu on 1945–61.

indeed from the Swahili press in general, which has a fairly continuous history back to 1891.

Further research on the colonial period

Three other topics should perhaps be mentioned. First, East German historians and John Iliffe have used German colonial sources for the administrative history of the German period, but a great deal still remains unused in the Potsdam archives. The British administration has been studied by Margaret Bates, Ralph Austen, and J. C. Taylor,[28] and Robert Heussler is now engaged on a major analysis of British administrative attitudes, but here again the documentation available in Dar es Salaam alone remains formidable. A more urgent need, perhaps, is systematic interviewing of former British personnel; one can estimate how important this may be by noting the lack of such interviews from the German period, where it is now too late. Second, only one biography of a twentieth-century Tanzanian of importance has been written; [29] sufficient material exists for many more. Third, A. J. Temu is presently beginning a study of the impact of the First World War on African societies, and this is a subject which might repay detailed regional study.

Making sources accessible

The list of gaps is formidable, but one further point should be made before an attempt is made to select priorities. This outline, like most research schemes, proceeds from the assumption that the natural focus of research will be a clearly defined historical topic and that the natural outcome of it will be a thesis or book setting forth the author's evidence and conclusions. It would be naïve to think that this pattern is likely to change soon. From the viewpoint of a historian resident in

28. M. L. Bates, ''Tanganyika under British Administration, 1920–1955'' (D.Phil. thesis, Oxford University, 1957) ; Ralph A. Austen, ''The Official Mind of Indirect Rule,'' in *Britain and Germany in Africa*, ed. by P. Gifford and W. R. Louis (New Haven: Yale University Press, 1967), pp. 577–606; J. C. Taylor, *The Political Development of Tanganyika* (Stanford: Stanford University Press, 1962).

29. G. R. Mutahaba, *Portrait of a Tanzanian Nationalist: The Life of Ali Migeyo* (Nairobi, forthcoming).

Tanzania, however, it is by no means obvious that this is the most useful contribution that the visiting researcher can make to the historiography of the country. It is difficult to estimate the Tanzanian public, but two other sorts of publication might be more valuable to it. One is the thirty-page pamphlet, summarizing the historian's evidence and conclusions in a low-cost publication which can be purchased widely in a society still not geared to book-buying. Anything that can be done to persuade researchers to summarize their work in this form should be very strongly encouraged.

The second urgent need is for the publication of collections of sources—not readings, but original documents. A major problem of writing Tanzanian history is the inaccessibility of the sources. To give one concrete example, southern Tanzania has several vast Benedictine abbeys, founded and staffed largely by Germans. These houses keep their chronicles in the traditional form. There is a deep amateur interest in the history of the area, and it is frustrating to the local historian to know that one of the main sources for the modern history of his region is a chronicle he cannot see in a language he cannot read. (One schoolteacher recently vowed to learn German specifically for this purpose.) This is not particularly the fault of the mission, but it is a symptom of the general difficulty of encouraging historical interest in a country where "history" normally means a foreigner's conclusions about one's past, based on material one cannot obtain. A project, adequately financed and staffed, to edit and publish the more important collections of documents—both oral and written—would in the long run be more useful to the history of Tanzania than any multiplication of unpublished doctoral dissertations.

Conclusion

The survey given in this paper has indicated how interest in historical research in mainland Tanzania has been growing in the past ten years. It has also indicated that much remains to be done before a detailed history of Tanzania can be attempted. As a rough guide to future research, therefore, seven priorities can be summarized in a rather arbitrary order from this survey: (1) an urgent, massive program of collecting oral traditions; (2) serious experimentation with agrarian history; (3) a continuing direction of research toward basically political studies at the area level; (4) an attempt to make research material available by publication of conclusions in pamphlet form and by publication of documentary collections of a fairly high standard; (5) an extension of oral research into the earlier colonial period in order to cover response to invasion and early colonial rule; (6) a greater concern for intellectual history in addition to political-economic history; and (7) continuation of research on coastal settlements and societies. It is hoped that the research strategy outlined here will act as a guide in our efforts to reconstruct a detailed history of Tanzania as soon as possible.

Frank Willett

The Past and the Present

It could be argued that the fascination of archaeology is largely due to the fact that it is so much involved with other kinds of study. More than most other subjects it cuts across the whole range of academic disciplines and participates in the natural sciences, in the social sciences, and in the humanities. Archaeology is not itself an academic discipline, but rather a technique for the study of the past, and in investigating different periods of the past it takes upon itself, chameleonlike, the coloring of the disciplines whose aid it enlists as most helpful to the problems at hand.

There are very good historical reasons for this, for archaeology grew out of two separate disciplines, geology and the classics.[1] Geologists of the Pleistocene period began to find stone tools made by early men, evidence of the animals they killed, and sometimes even human bones. Gradually the traditional stratigraphic and paleontological studies were refined to provide the basis of archaeological field technique. Because of the relevance of these investigations to the study of human evolution, cultural as well as physical, they became absorbed

1. This of course is an oversimplification, nor do I consider it relevant to discuss such pioneer archaeologists as St. Helen, who conducted excavations to find the Holy Cross and, finding three, conducted a scientific experiment to establish which one was the True Cross.

into anthropology. Classical archaeology, in contrast, set out to illustrate the literature of antiquity, or to prove the validity of historical documents. Schliemann's famous exclamation during his excavations at Troy, "Today I have gazed upon the face of Agamemnon," demonstrates the attitude. From the classics, the technique spread to biblical studies, and even as late as 1929 Sir Leonard Woolley was gratified to have found at Ur conclusive evidence of a flood which must have fathered the story of Noah. This tradition of archaeology has stayed close to the study of classical and Oriental languages and has become associated also with art history. Egyptologists have usually grown up in this tradition, but most archaeologists working in Africa south of the Sahara have been trained as anthropologists, that is, as prehistoric archaeologists.

African archaeology is a very rich and rewarding field, so vast in its time span and techniques that an incipient polarity is developing between archaeologists working at the two ends of the time scale, a polarity which is emphasized by the different company kept by archaeologists working with different kinds of data. Archaeologists who work on the earliest phases of human history in Africa are involved with problems of man's bodily evolution and his dependence on, and gradual conquest of, his environment. Consequently they associate with physical anthropologists, zoologists, ethologists, botanists, palynologists, paleontologists, geomorphologists, stratigraphers, and pedologists. Archaeologists working in the later periods—the late stone age and the iron age—are more historically oriented. To a large extent man had by then gained the upper hand over his environment and was producing his own supplies of food. The archaeologist working at this end of the time scale, therefore, is involved with historians (using documents as well as oral traditions), ethnologists, social anthropologists, agronomists, ethnobotanists, economic historians, and art historians, but also with zoologists, palynologists, and pedologists. Thus in the earlier period, archaeologists are more heavily involved with the natural sciences, and in some respects the archaeology of early man may be regarded as a branch of the natural sciences. In the later periods, although the archaeologist is still concerned with environmental problems—especially those which affect human culture, such as characteristics of the soil and raw materials available to the community—the emphasis is increasingly akin to that of the social, and particularly the behavioral, sciences. This tendency to polarization seems likely to increase in the future because the range of ancillary disciplines involved is likely to grow. From their student days archaeologists are likely to need specialized training to prepare them for work in either the early stone age or the late stone age and iron age.

Inevitably, the links with so many disciplines—which sometimes make one feel that archaeology is perhaps not so much a science in its own right as the art of getting scientists to work for one—will lead to teamwork in the field as well as in the laboratory. It is increasingly clear that the scientists whose help we solicit need more information than the archaeologist is trained to record; the specialist needs to do his own sampling so that he can observe for himself the conditions of occurrence. Palynologists have long since insisted that they must collect their own pollen for analysis in order to be sure that the samples are free from contamination and to ascertain whether they represent a continuous or a discontinuous deposition. The teams that undertake field work, however, will be differently composed, depending on the period being investigated. A zoologist and a botanist (especially a palynologist) will be required on most sites, but in general an early stone age team will consist almost exclusively of natural scientists, whereas a team working in the later period is more likely to consist predominantly of social scientists and humanists.

A major problem which is likely to require the attention of interdisciplinary teams is that of the origins of the Bantu-speaking peoples. A recent conference envisaged that such a team "should include a botanist, an ecologist, an oral historian, a zoologist, a Bantu linguist, an ethnographer with archaeological training, and a physical anthropologist."[2] Without this kind of cooperation, the problem of Bantu origins may well never be resolved.

Present Ignorance and Its Future Cure

A number of articles in the *African Studies Bulletin*[3] have drawn attention to the many areas of Africa which are effec-

2. *African Studies Bulletin,* XI (September, 1968), 229.

3. In preparing this paper I have utilized the following articles: Frank Willett and Brian M. Fagan, "Report on the African Research Committee Conference on the African Iron Age," *African Studies Bulletin,* X, No. 1 (April, 1967), 43–50; J. Desmond Clark, "The Position of Research in African Archaeology: Future Developments and Needs," *ibid.,* X, No. 2 (September, 1967), 10–18; J. Desmond Clark, "Report

tively blank archaeologically. Some areas are totally blank because they have never been explored at all, while in other areas little archaeological work has been done or none is being pursued at present and thus very few sites are recorded. Most of the blank areas are to be found within the areas of Africa which are, in general, Spanish-, Portuguese-, or French-speaking. Some attempt is being made to fill in these gaps, as is witnessed by the article by R. de Bayle des Hermens in the *West African Archaeological Newsletter* [4] reporting on a preliminary archaeological survey of the Central African Republic. Clearly the way in which these gaps must be filled is by initial surveys to locate sites and make some estimate of their archaeological content, either by surface collecting or by small-scale excavation. A very careful selection of appropriate sites for larger scale excavation will then be made. A classic example of this approach is the work of Graham Connah in northeastern Nigeria. A careful survey led him to select the site of Daima for a large-scale excavation. The Daima excavations have produced a sequence from the late stone age right through into modern times. [5] In cases where blank areas lie adjacent to areas in a neighboring state which have been explored, it may be more profitable to work from the known area across the intervening political frontier into the unknown. Although the archaeology of the Yoruba of Nigeria is still in its infancy, nothing at all has been done in Dahomey and Togo. A major investigation of the archaeology of Yorubaland ought to cross these political frontiers when the work which has been done in Nigeria would simplify the understanding of the evidence in these other two territories. The

of the Archaeology Committee of the African Studies Association for the Year 1966–1967,'' *ibid.*, XI, No. 1 (April, 1968), 33–38; and Brian M. Fagan, Roland Oliver, and Tulli Grundeman, ''Wenner-Gren Research Conference on Bantu Origins in Sub-Saharan Africa, Chicago, March 24–29, 1968: Summary Report and Recommendations,'' *ibid.*, XI, No. 2 (September, 1968), 225–31.

4. R. de Bayle des Hermens, ''Recherches préhistoriques en République Centrafricaine, 1966–1967,'' *West African Archaeological Newsletter*, No. 9 (1968), pp. 6–13.

5. See Graham Connah, *First Interim Report*, Northern History Research Scheme (Zaria, 1966), pp. 11–21; and ''Summary of Research in Benin City and Bornu,'' *West African Archaeological Newsletter*, No. 5 (1966), pp. 22–25; ''Radio-carbon Dates for Daima, ''*Journal of the Historical Society of Nigeria*, III, Pt. 4 (1967), 741–42; *Second Interim Report*, Northern History Research Scheme (Zaria, 1967), pp. 17–31; '' 'Classic' Excavation in North East Nigeria,'' *Illustrated London News*, Archaeological Section 2276, Vol. CCLI, No. 6689, October 14, 1967.

cultures of the Tanzanian coast, which are well known and are believed to continue down the coast into Mozambique and along the lower Zambezi, could be studied in a similar way. The vast area of the Congo Basin has had a certain amount of archaeological attention, but this has been restricted to widely separated districts. This is an area of particular interest to those of us who are concerned about the origins of the Bantu-speaking peoples. The fringes of the Congo, north and south, both within the Congo Basin proper and just outside it, are obviously crucial for the investigation of this problem.

Even in areas which are relatively well served by archaeology there are still some important gaps to be filled. Nigeria, for example, has attracted a large number of archaeologists, yet almost nothing is known of the archaeology of the Benue Valley in the first millennium A.D., which appears to be a period of great importance not only in the history of that area itself but also as a link between the cultures of the Lower Niger and the Sudan. Remarkable progress has been made in Nigeria, however, in filling in the gaps. Under the leadership of Thurstan Shaw a very vigorous and coordinated policy aimed at giving some archaeological coverage to the whole country has been pursued, and there are very good hopes that Professor Shaw will soon be able to arrange for a team investigation of the Benue Valley area.[6]

Survey and excavation, however, are really only the beginnings of archaeology. If the findings of surveys and excavations are not published, fully and rapidly, then the work might almost as well have been left undone. A great deal of excavation has been carried out in West Africa as a whole, but very few definitive reports have been published. It is often difficult to persuade departments of antiquities and even universities that archaeologists do need a great deal of time free from involvement in excavations so that they can write their reports. It is not an exaggeration to point out that it takes about four times as long to write an excavation report as it does to conduct the excavation on which it is based. A period

6. Thurstan Shaw's inaugural lecture as Research Professor of Archaeology at Ibadan surveyed these very problems (*Archaeology and Nigeria* [Ibadan: University Press, 1963]). His recent survey of "Radio-carbon Dates from Nigeria" provides a ready index of the progress made since that time (*Journal of the Historical Society of Nigeria*, III, No. 4 [1967], 743–51). This listed thirty-one dates, but has already been superseded by *Radio-carbon Dating in Nigeria* (Ibadan: Prepublished by the Historical Society of Nigeria, 1968), which lists seventy-two dates, and more are now available.

of consolidation probably lasting five years or more is needed, after which the archaeologist who has turned from excavation to writing will be free once again to open up new sites and new problems. Until excavation reports are published archaeologists will lack the standards of reference for describing their own material, and the writing of pioneering reports is thus more difficult and more time consuming.

The publication of archaeological reports is of course an expensive matter, but to judge by the example of the journal *Kush*, which is now self-supporting, there is sufficient interest in archaeology for new journals to be viable. *Azania* has recently been established primarily to cover eastern Africa, while the *South African Archaeological Bulletin* has been providing us with short reports of archaeology from all over Africa for many years. There will soon be an archaeological journal dealing primarily, but not exclusively, with West Africa. There will certainly be a great deal of material in hand for this journal as is indicated by the rich flow of shorter, interim reports which have been appearing regularly in the *West African Archaeological Newsletter*, another of the benefits that we owe to the energy of Professor Thurstan Shaw. In addition, we may hope that publishers (particularly university presses) and governments may combine to establish regular series of excavation reports of volume length so that those of us who write them may have some reasonable expectation of their publication. This in turn will make it easier for us to teach archaeology in universities, for at present it is extremely difficult to provide an adequate bibliography for our students, and much of our teaching has to be based on hearsay evidence, or at least on private communications from our colleagues.

The communication of information is already becoming a problem. As the subject grows and more people are involved in it, it becomes more and more difficult to keep in touch with all the colleagues who are interested in the problems which engage one's own attention. In 1966 a Conference of West African Archaeologists was established which is expected to meet annually. Such a conference gives archaeologists an opportunity to report on their latest work and to discuss topics of common interest. Indeed it is out of this conference that the proposed archaeological journal is likely to grow. In the future I expect to see more periodic conferences of this kind. Similarly, there are likely to be regular conferences based on specialized interests. The first of this kind is the Association

Sénégalaise pour l'Etude du Quaternaire de l'Ouest Africain (ASEQOA), which is already keeping us informed of what is going on in the several disciplines which are intimately concerned with the study of the Pleistocene and Holocene periods.

Communication at the intercontinental level is facilitated through the Pan-African Congress on Prehistory and its various committees. The *West African Archaeological Newsletter* and the journals mentioned above also provide communication on an international scale. Within America, we have organized through the Archaeology Committee of the African Studies Association the regular exchange of news between those of us who are based on this continent but working in Africa by inviting letters which are then edited into an article for the *African Studies Bulletin*. This was an idea which grew out of the African Research Committee Conference held at Urbana in 1967.[7] As a result of that Conference, Brian Fagan wrote to everyone we knew who was interested in the iron age in Africa, wherever they were based. The response was overwhelming, and the circular that he prepared and distributed ran to thirty-one pages. While this is extremely heartening in reflecting the rate of growth of interest in the African iron age, the increasing numbers of scholars compound the difficulties of communication. Even the preparation of an annual newsletter of this kind is a great burden. We have therefore been compelled to cut back on the original project and restrict the circulars to those based here in America, though we hope to repeat the large-scale circular at intervals of four or five years.

Conferences of course are a major method of communication, but the larger ones are becoming less effective in this function. So long as academics are expected to read a paper if they wish to have their expenses paid, the major international conferences will continue to be bogged down with papers which are often of little or no importance. This is a general problem of international conferences in any field of interest, but the solution to it has been found in an African historical and archaeological conference, namely the one which is organized every four years by Professor Roland Oliver on behalf of the School of Oriental and African Studies of London Univer-

7. Reported in *African Studies Bulletin*, X, No. 1 (April, 1967), 43–50. The first news article to appear was by Brian M. Fagan, ''African Archaeology in the United States, 1967,'' *ibid.*, XI, No. 1 (April, 1968), 63–66.

sity. From its initiation this conference has accepted and circulated papers in advance, with no papers being read at the conference, which is devoted to the discussion of topics of general interest. Even this conference has grown unmanageable in size, however. The last one was restricted to specifically chronological problems, and the numbers of those attending had to be limited by invitation. Circulation of papers in advance is, I am convinced, the only way that these general conferences can continue to be of any value. Small working conferences devoted to a single limited area or problem have proved to be very useful. Those sponsored by the African Research Committee have been exemplary in this way, and when papers are circulated in advance for a small conference the resulting discussion is far more profitable to everyone concerned. I expect to see more of these small-scale meetings in the future.

One of the problems of communication in general is that of an agreed terminology. This was discussed at the Wenner-Gren Symposium in 1965,[8] and the proposals of this symposium were discussed briefly at the Pan-African Congress on Prehistory, in Dakar in 1967. While it is not possible to legislate about archaeological nomenclature in the same way that the International Commissions on Zoological and Botanical Nomenclature can lay down rules, it is nevertheless essential that we should be able to understand one another and that we should use technical terms in the same way in different languages. The Pan-African Congress therefore set up a commission which has already circulated for discussion its first informal set of papers relating to nomenclature. Now that we have more channels of communication, there is less excuse for people working in isolation to develop their own terminology on principles quite different from those of their colleagues. We are gradually getting rid of idiosyncratic and ambiguous terminologies in African archaeology, but we have a long way to go before we are all speaking the same language.

Methodology and the Future

Archaeology is an expensive technique, and it is slow in producing results. In consequence, its methodology needs to be

8. See W. W. Bishop and J. D. Clark, eds., *Background to Evolution in Africa* (Chicago: University of Chicago Press, 1967), especially pp. 861–902.

very carefully considered if the cost is to be justified in results. When investigating an unknown area it is usual to attempt to discover what the sequence of occupation has been. This is usually done by seeking deep occupation deposits which will give a long sequence of time, probably the most profitable way of investing a relatively small sum of money in terms of the amount of information obtained. It is often difficult, however, to isolate with any precision the individual phases of occupation on such a site because the occupation surface is disturbed continually, for example in digging mud to make new buildings. After the general sequence has been established, therefore, single phase occupation sites where all the material can be demonstrated to be contemporary must be located. A large number of these can then be investigated and related to the general sequence. In many parts of Africa work is progressing to refine the techniques involved in this type of "horizontal stratigraphy," as it has been called, that is, the isolation and definition of what would be successive layers if the occupations were all on the same site.

Another line of investigation which is likely to be rewarding is the excavation of sites with known historical associations. In my own work, knowledge of the fact that Old Oyo was abandoned about 1837 has proved invaluable, as I have discovered pottery of types derivative from one of the major Old Oyo traditions on several sites where they have provided a convenient dating zone. But a line which has not yet been employed is that of tackling sites where the oral traditions record the name of the founder and the circumstances of foundation but not the date. The archaeologist should be able to recover material from such sites which could be correlated with the general sequence where that is known, or perhaps even dated fairly closely by radio-carbon or other techniques. This is a type of archaeological cooperation of which we may expect to see more in the future, and indeed a new breed of graduate likely to be trained equally in history and archaeology may be very active in this kind of problem.

In 1965 the Wenner-Gren Foundation sponsored a most important archaeological conference, the papers for which have recently been edited by W. W. Bishop and J. Desmond Clark as *Background to Evolution in Africa*. These papers survey the status of archaeology in most parts of Africa, covering both stone age and iron age, and deal also with topics which are clearly relevant to archaeology though not strictly archaeological problems in themselves. What is most impressive about this very large collection of papers is the increasing precision in analytical, dating, and interpretational techniques which are now being employed. We may expect to see increasing precision in these methods in the future.

We are indeed in a phase of transition in which not only are traditional techniques being refined and new ones introduced but the whole emphasis of interpretation is shifting from the purely technological to the essentially social. The archaeologist was once satisfied if he could classify and label the tools he found and deduce from them, and from the associated organic remains, the basic economy of the community. Nowadays a far more sophisticated approach is expected. The artifacts are no longer an end in themselves: they are a part of a complex of evidence. Increasingly we are asking how large the communities were, whether their settlements were seasonal or permanent, how long they were occupied in either case, how the buildings on the site were distributed, and whether there were areas set aside for the practice of specialist crafts and how the different occupation sites related to one another. We are interested to know whether the huts all had fireplaces, indicating that cooking took place and therefore that women lived there; from this information we may be able to deduce something about marriage patterns. In short, we are moving away from an attitude which is essentially that of the museum curator classifying and storing the artifacts from archaeological sites to an approach which is far more like that of the cultural anthropologist; we are in fact becoming paleocultural anthropologists, not only asking questions about material culture but also trying to infer as much as we possibly can about the non-material culture.

This changing emphasis on the part of archaeologists is stimulating a renewed interest in ethnography, which has of late been considered rather old-fashioned, although a broader range of application is now called for than has been employed in the past. The study of material culture is obviously of basic importance, but now an estimate of its relationship to non-material culture is also required in archaeological interpretation and understanding. Increasingly, archaeologists are undertaking ethnographic surveys for themselves, but there also seems to be a growing interest in specialization in this particular field of study among students in anthropology departments. Such ethnographic studies can throw light on archaeological problems of all time periods, but one of the particular joys of studying iron age settlements is that we can commonly draw also on historical traditions, and indeed on direct correlations with present-day ethnography.[9] Modern settlement patterns should prove a most fruitful area for studies of this sort. This is obviously one of the types of information that archaeologists can fairly easily recover from the past, and yet there is an astonishing lack of modern data with which to compare archaeological findings.

This shift of interest away from the artifact into the society which produced it does not mean, however, that we are neglecting the artifacts themselves. Indeed, artifact analysis is still a basic aspect of archaeological interpretation, and the techniques are becoming increasingly sophisticated. This is part of a more general tendency toward increasing application of quantitative techniques in archaeology.[10] Probably the most time-hallowed technique used in archaeology is the simple percentage analysis of artifact types in the definition and comparison of industries. For some decades stone age industries have been characterized by the relative proportions of tools present rather than by the presence or absence of certain critical types of tools for this method has been shown to be utterly unreliable. For this reason many of the older collections of stone implements housed in museums are useful only insofar as they indicate the geographical locations from which stone implements have come. To define the characteristics of the industry, unselective, non-biased samples of all the available material, including the waste, must be taken and analyzed. On later sites, where pottery is the artifact most commonly found, a long-established technique is seriation analysis, that is, a mathematically based study of stylistic change which is usually directed to showing how one type of decoration gives way to another with time or, alternatively, how one form replaces another. Oliver Myers was, I believe, the first to employ more advanced statistical techniques in the study of archaeological sites in Africa, particularly in the analysis of surface collections.[11] Matrix analysis has been

9. Some examples of ethnographic studies from this point of view are given in the *African Studies Bulletin*, X, No. 2 (September, 1967), 15.

10. See R. F. Heizer and S. F. Cook, eds., *The Application of Quantitative Methods in Archaeology*, Viking Fund Publications in Anthropology, No. 28 (New York: Viking Fund, 1960). The chapter by A. C. Spaulding on ''Statistical Description and Comparison of Artifact Assemblages'' (pp. 60–83) is particularly relevant.

11. Oliver H. Myers, *Some Applications of Statistics to Archaeology* (Cairo: Antiquities Service, 1950).

used by David Clarke in a study of Beaker pottery from the British bronze age, and this too is a technique which will find increasing employment in African archaeology.[12]

Some of the most interesting work in this field is being conducted by Steve Daniels at the University of Ibadan.[13] Daniels has made a most useful contribution to the concept of a type. This is a topic which has been much argued in American archaeology. Some of our colleagues seem to have a very rigid idea of what a type is, yet most classes of artifacts are extremely variable. There are borderlines of uncertainty in any system of typological classification, and this can be a great headache in any kind of statistical analysis. What we need is a system of classification which arises from the population of artifacts before us. It may be possible to avoid altogether the judgment of the limits of any class (or "type") by suitable statistical techniques. It is precisely to this end that Daniels has been working. His method is to choose as many parameters as seem appropriate on any group of material and then handle these as separate dimensions in a multidimensional space. Thus, in Daniels' method the precise location of any individual artifact in the multidimensional space is a function only of the parameters chosen; the greater the number of parameters chosen, the less the element of subjective judgment on the part of the analyst. This technique ensures that the groupings of objects correspond to the real features they possess, a sort of democratic alternative to the traditional method of dictatorially assigning artifacts to preconceived type-categories which may not always be appropriate. The method, of course, is slow, and we may well find that a strain of archaeologists will arise who will devote themselves purely to the statistical analysis of collections.

The advances currently being made in the laboratory sciences are among the most outstanding expansions of academic

12. David L. Clarke, "Matrix Analysis and Archaeology with Particular Reference to British Beaker Pottery," *Proceedings of the Prehistoric Society for 1962* n.s. XXVIII (1962), 371–82. His book *Analytical Archaeology* (London: Methuen, 1968) has reached me as this goes to press. It is mainly a presentation of a conceptual framework of archaeology, but discusses statistical and computer methods in archaeological analysis.

13. Daniels has published outlines of his methodology in the *West African Archaeological Newsletter*, No. 5 (1966), pp. 17–19; No. 6 (1967), pp. 4–6, 36–45, 48; in *Archaeometry*, IX (1966), 151–54; and as appendixes to various reports such as in B. M. Fagan's *Iron Age Cultures of Zambia*, I (London: Chatto and Windus for the National Museum of Zambia, 1967), 192–94; and II (forthcoming).

knowledge today, and we may expect that archaeology will appropriate new techniques from the laboratory sciences as they become available. We now have a journal, *Archaeometry*, published in Oxford, devoted purely to laboratory techniques in the analysis of archaeological artifacts. In many cases, the articles in this journal describe newly invented techniques which could be of great value to the practicing archaeologist if they were available to him as a regular service. We already have commercial laboratories prepared to offer services in radio-carbon and other dating techniques, and it is to be hoped that other analytical techniques will soon be available to the archaeologist on a commercial basis instead of having to find a sympathetic scientist prepared to spend time to do them for him.

In the field of analysis of the composition of artifacts, the Lawrence Radiation Laboratory at Berkeley has already undertaken a number of analyses of trace elements in pottery [14] and other archaeological materials. These techniques are proving far more valuable than the old spectrographic analyses which revealed only the gross make-up of archaeological materials. Trace-element analysis is concerned with more than thirty elements which may or may not be present in an artifact or may be present in varying quantities. Extremely small amounts are measured so that very accurate comparisons can be made between samples. This technique will be particularly valuable in questions of the composition of trade goods such as beads and pottery which hitherto have had to be assessed chiefly by visual examination.

Radio-carbon dating has proved to be the most revolutionary single laboratory technique to be used in the last ten years in Africa. It was only about three years ago that we began to have enough radio-carbon dates from African excavations to make any very useful comparisons, and now every few months we have to revise our earlier views of chronology as radio-carbon dates produce new evidence. It is becoming commonplace to obtain a block of radio-carbon dates whenever possible. Since a radio-carbon date is merely a statistical expression of probability, several dates from any given horizon are desirable in order to reduce the possible margin of error. As the number of laboratories working in this field increases and the tech-

14. I. Perlman and Frank Asaro, *Deduction of Provenience of Pottery from Trace Element Analysis*, reprint UCRL-17937, University of California, Berkeley, Ernest O. Lawrence Radiation Laboratory, October, 1967.

nique is increasingly refined, we are finding explanations for the anomalous dates that do turn up from time to time. Unfortunately we still find archaeologists, let alone laymen, who quote radio-carbon dates without reference to the standard deviation. We have a long way to go before archaeologists' training in statistical methods catches up to the sophisticated quantitative techniques which are proving increasingly valuable in archaeological study. This training is surely one of the most urgent needs in African archaeology at the moment.

We can look forward too to the further development of techniques of dating. Research is currently being conducted into thermoluminescence.[15] This technique, which was first announced about ten years ago, has produced few dates so far, and a great deal of laboratory work is needed to perfect it. Laboratories in Oxford and Philadelphia are approaching this technique from quite different points of view, and we may hope within the next twenty years that the technique will have become sufficiently perfected to be regularly employed.

Policy and Research in the Future

One of the topics which has been much discussed in meetings of Africanists has been the question of access to areas of Africa for purposes of research. On the whole, archaeology is welcomed by politicians in most African countries because it is capable of revealing the history of Africa in an unbiased way and is for the most part concerned with a relatively remote past. Since only rarely can one discover the name of the ethnic group who produced the artifacts being investigated, the subject gives little encouragement to ethnic pride and does not therefore foster interethnic tensions. Postage stamps reflect this interest: a recent Tanzanian stamp por-

15. A useful survey of scientific techniques applicable to archaeology is in *Science in Archaeology*, ed. by Don Brothwell and Eric Higgs (London: Thames and Hudson, 1963). Thermoluminescence is described on pp. 90–92. See also M. S. Tite and J. Waine, "Thermoluminescent Dating: A Re-appraisal," *Archaeometry*, V (1962), 53–79; M. J. Aitken, M. S. Tite, and J. Reid, "Thermoluminescent Dating: Progress Report," *ibid.*, VI (1963), 65–75; M. S. Tite, "Thermoluminescent Dating of Ancient Ceramics: A Reassessment," *ibid.*, IX (1966), 155–69; and S. J. Fleming, "Study of Thermoluminescent Extracts from Pottery," *ibid.*, pp. 170–73. Short notes have also appeared in the *Masca Newsletter* (Philadelphia), I, No. 1, 3; I, No. 2, 2–3; and III, No. 1, 1.

trays "Zinjanthropus," and many Nigerian stamps have shown ancient sculptures.

Difficulty of access is likely to arise, not so much from the nature of archaeological investigation as from tensions between the country in which one proposes to do the research and the country in which one is based. These tensions may not be at a political level alone. Brian Fagan and I issued an offer of help in a spirit of altruism which arose from a lively recollection of our own difficulties in the field—an offer to attempt to put archaeologists based in Africa into touch with American graduate students who would like to go out to help them—and this was construed as an effort to gain control over other people's work. Misunderstandings arise only too easily. The only counter for this kind of misunderstanding is to operate through institutions or individuals already active in the field. Individual research projects will have to be submitted for approval to the appropriate department of antiquities, museum service, university department, or institute of African studies in the area in which the research is to be conducted. I think that increasingly our graduate students will be asking the advice of institutions and individuals in Africa about what work they can best undertake, since the work in any territory is likely in the future to be coordinated through one or another institution which will function as a main clearinghouse. This is all to the good, for it means that a graduate student working in the field will have the backing of a local organization and in turn he will have obligations to his sponsors to leave behind at least a preliminary report on the work he has done before leaving the country. The very slowness of archaeological study, however, creates complications. Many African countries are becoming unwilling to permit the removal of archaeological material for study, and we may find it increasingly necessary to make arrangements for the material to be studied in the field, with the final report written elsewhere without access to the material. In this case, a return trip to the country to examine the material may well be necessary before the report is published.

In some parts of Africa political considerations do make it difficult for white archaeologists to gain access, and it may be that many of these areas contain information crucial to the understanding and solution of problems in neighboring countries. In such cases we should encourage nationals of the country concerned to undertake archaeological research themselves. To do this it may be necessary to offer fellowships for their training in our own universities.

What pattern will this training follow? Up to the present, relatively few specialists in African archaeology have been trained in America. Most have come out of anthropology departments where they specialized in archaeology and have turned to Africa for their dissertation research after taking course work about the continent. More so perhaps than in other fields of African studies, we are finding that it is desirable for students to go to Africa before they write their dissertations to get some understanding of the specifically African problems. They can be trained adequately in the techniques of archaeology anywhere in the world, but there are problems of organization and administration (legal formalities, working with local labor and local rates of pay, choice of a base, etc.), as well as more specifically archaeological problems such as the distinction of stratigraphy in lateritic conditions and problems of preservation, which are characteristically African. An introduction to these conditions under experienced guidance, together with an acquaintance with the material already known and preserved in museums, is obviously desirable before the student sets out on his own dissertation research. Students are already making these preliminary trips, and I expect such preliminary experience in Africa eventually to become part of the training of all African archaeologists.

So far as course work itself is concerned, the expansion of related disciplines which are contributing to archaeology will call forth a corresponding expansion of course content. In the study of the African iron age we can expect to see increasing numbers of people trained in both history and archaeology. A number of African universities have placed their archaeologists inside the history department. The purpose in doing this is twofold: first, all historians will receive instruction in archaeology, and second, students wishing to specialize in archaeology will have a good and adequate historical background. However, it will be necessary to provide more than mere service courses—aseptic archaeology. Courses will have to be constructed which will produce students who are professionally qualified in both fields—who will be both dirt archaeologists and historians—for we can no longer consider archaeology to begin where history leaves off.

Africa as a whole suffers from a lack of the general knowledge of archaeology which in most parts of Europe can be relied on to lend support to efforts to rescue important archaeological discoveries made in the course of commercial development. In the area around Ife and in the Plateau tin-fields of northern Nigeria the intensive archaeological work that has been carried on has stimulated this kind of interest among the local people, but a far more widespread awareness is required. If all history students graduating from African universities have had even a minimal training in archaeology they will eventually, when they go to their jobs as schoolteachers and administrators throughout the country, provide an elite with an interest in, and a knowledge of, archaeology. If they have had more than nominal training they may even be capable of acting in the way that amateur archaeological societies do in Europe—by actually undertaking archaeological work, whether independently or in cooperation with professionals. They should at least be able to undertake surveys of unknown areas in their own locality. Such local surveys would eventually contribute to a better coverage in maps showing the distribution of archaeological sites in African countries.[16]

We are entering a new phase in cooperation with African universities and other institutions such as museums and departments of antiquities. Both the preliminary visits of students and the main research for the dissertation need to be sponsored by a body in Africa not only to coordinate work but also to allay any suspicion of exploitation of African knowledge, for the potential suspicion is great. The importance of maintaining local contacts and good relations with African institutions and individual workers cannot, in the interests of the subject itself, be overemphasized. I believe that there will be a great increase in joint research projects, including exchanges of faculty between African and American universities. The African university will be able to provide the headquarters facilities which are needed, storage for materials, equipment, laboratory facilities, study space, perhaps even professional draftsmen and a photographic studio, thus keeping down the overhead costs of expeditions from outside Africa. They would also be able to provide transport, which is always a disproportionately high expenditure in any major field project. In return for these facilities a substantial proportion of the expense would have to be met from American

16. J. D. Clark's *Atlas of African Prehistory* (Chicago: University of Chicago Press, 1967) shows very effectively the distribution of both our knowledge and our ignorance of archaeological sites in Africa at the present time.

research sources. The training excavations might be conducted alternately by members of the African institution and the American one, with students from both taking part each time. Exchanges of faculty between the two universities would help to foster the feeling of common interest and to allay suspicion.

Major commercial undertakings in Africa, especially the building of large dams, have highlighted both the need for, and the difficulties of, international cooperation. The rescue work which was sponsored by UNESCO in conjunction with the Aswan High Dam shows, in the first place, how much international interest there can be in such schemes, but also how money can easily be wasted for lack of a coherent scheme to coordinate the work. The Volta Basin, on the other hand, was investigated by a small research team over a period of five years—an investigation which has produced extremely valuable results.[17] Less happy is the case of the Kainji Dam in Nigeria, where due to a series of administrative problems international cooperation was not obtained until the final season before flooding. Important evidence, however, has been rescued from the area. Even less encouraging is the case of the Cahora Bassa Dam in Mozambique, where the Archaeology Committee of the African Studies Association, backed by the National Science Foundation, pressed very hard to obtain permission to organize excavations in conjunction with Portuguese or any other scholars from southern Africa who were prepared to cooperate, but it was found impossible to organize anything. We can expect that commercial projects of a comparable scale will continue to be undertaken, and it is essential that archaeological rescue work be written into the initial proposals in order to give time for the organization of an adequate archaeological program, on the example of the federal highway programs in America, which have a fixed proportion of their budget provided for rescue work in advance of the bulldozers. The African countries themselves, however, are not going to be able to afford to set aside large sums of money for this kind of work, and it is desirable that funds should be made available through international bodies on which African countries can draw for this purpose; otherwise important archaeological data will be irretrievably lost.

17. Interim reports have appeared in the *West African Archaeological Newsletter,* and comprehensive publications of the findings of Volta Basin research teams are forthcoming.

Writing in April, 1966,[18] Desmond Clark listed a number of sites which needed to be investigated in connection with the study of early man in Africa. Already some of these sites are being investigated, notably the Omo Valley, which is producing important information. For the study of early man we need sites which show long stratigraphic sequences associated with evidence of human activity and of the animals and plants among which he lived. We also need to locate living sites and to excavate them extensively, laying bare the whole area of occupation so that we may recover all the available data by the various techniques referred to earlier. Most of the work on early man has been concentrated in eastern Africa, yet in the area around Lake Chad there are deposits which appear to correspond to many of the Plio-Pleistocene sequences in East Africa. It is to be hoped that within the next twenty years extensive investigation will be conducted there, but unfortunately there is no Olduvai Gorge cutting through them to reveal the most profitable sites for excavation.

So far as the later period of African archaeology is concerned, there is a whole battery of problems on which we are still extremely ill-informed: the diffusion of pastoralism and of agriculture; the origins and spread of the individual domesticates, whether animal or plant; the dates of introduction of exotic domesticates, both American and Asiatic; the origin and diffusion of ironworking. Very little work has been done so far on the medieval empires of West Africa and the Sudan. Archaeological investigation in Madagascar has only just begun and this may well be a crucial area for iron age studies which need to be closely tied in with the archaeology of adjacent mainland Africa. In my own special field, the history of art in Africa, the gaps are far greater than the knowledge. We know of many sites with rock art, both painted and engraved, covering a time span of six millennia or more, but our knowledge of sculpture only goes back over a period of two and a half millennia, and its history can be traced in any consecutive way only in parts of Nigeria. For the rest of the continent we have individually datable art styles, with no real knowledge of their historical relationships.

African archaeology is really still in its infancy. Stone age studies have been pursued for some decades, but real concentration on the iron age is hardly more than twenty years old.

18. *African Studies Bulletin*, X, No. 2 (September, 1967), 14.

That there are so many gaps, both in terms of geographical coverage and in terms of our historical knowledge, is not surprising, nor should it be considered discouraging. Rather, these gaps should stimulate us to spend the next twenty years in intensive and certainly profitable research. What we can predict with certainty is that twenty years from now our present knowledge of African archaeology will appear to be crude and oversimplified in the extreme.

TRADITIONAL AND CONTEMPORARY ART IN AFRICA

Daniel J. Crowley

Art historians and anthropologists, the first concerned primarily with objects and the second with functions, are well along in describing and analyzing the basic types, styles, and uses of art in traditional African cultures. Since the classic full-length studies of art in particular ethnic groups or areas by Rattray, Griaule, Olbrechts,[1] and others, there have been many detailed analyses of particular types of sculpture, such as Horton's study in *Kalabari Sculpture* of Ijo *ekine* masks, Hottot's "Teke Fetishes," and Holas's *Les Masques Kono (Haute-Guinée française)*, or of the institutions which structure or support the art, such as Lloyd's "Craft Organization in Yoruba Towns," Plancquaert's *Les Sociétés secrètes chez les Bayaka*, or Elkan's "The East African Trade in Woodcarvings" on the sources and economic foundations of Kamba tourist art.[2] By far the most popular form of presentation of

---

1. R. S. Rattray, *Religion and Art in Ashanti* (Oxford: Oxford University Press, 1927); Marcel Griaule, *Masques Dogons*, Travaux et mémoirs d'Institute d'Ethnologie, No. 33, 1958; Frans M. Olbrechts, *Plastiek van Kongo* (Antwerp: Standard-Boekhaudel, 1946).

2. Robin Horton, *Kalabari Sculpture* (Lagos: Department of Antiquities, 1965; Robert Hottot, "Teke Fetishes," *Journal of Royal Anthropological Institute*, LXXXIII (1956); B. T. Holas, *Les Masques Kono (Haute-Guinée française)* (Paris: P. Geuthner, 1952); Peter Lloyd, "Craft Organization in Yoruba Towns," *Africa*, XXIII (January, 1953), 30–44; M. Le R. P. Plancquaert, *Les Sociétés secrètes chez les Bayaka* (Brussels: Falk, 1930); Walter Elkan, "The East African

stylistic variation is the photographic anthology, but these vary widely in the quality of the specimens and plates, and in the interests and competence of the compilers. Some are scholarly catalogues of a single exhibit, private collection, or museum collection; others, such as Fagg's *Tribes and Forms in African Art*,³ while otherwise magnificently presented, overstress the relationship between art style and ethnic group. Still others eschew the available ethnographic data in favor of speculative captions supporting one or another aesthetic theory. A full-length bibliography of African art citing nearly five thousand items has recently been published,⁴ but that is not to imply that African traditional art is now fully or even adequately documented or understood. Indeed, it is no exaggeration to say that scores of mask- and figure-types have still to be delineated and their meanings or functions described in words or on film, and the majority of great living carvers and other craftsmen have yet to be studied by scholars.

Recent publications of epic poetry, declamations, praisesongs, dance-dramas, love lyrics,⁵ and other forms by a number of African peoples have forced folklorists to recognize that these and undoubtedly many other kinds of folklore and oral literature amenable to study by their discipline have remained unnoticed and undocumented until now, in spite of the truly astonishing total of over twelve thousand African folktales which have been published since 1826.⁶ Obviously our preoccupation with the forms of our own society has operated to keep us from seeing the true range of African oral literature beyond and between our categories of folktale, proverb,

Trade in Woodcarvings," *Africa*, XXVIII (October, 1958), 314–23.

3. William B. Fagg, *Tribes and Forms in African Art* (New York: Tudor, 1965).

4. L. J. P. Gaskin with Guy Atkins, *A Bibliography of African Art* (London: International African Institute, 1965).

5. See, for example, Henry F. Morris, ed., *The Heroic Recitations of the Bahima of Ankole* (Oxford: Oxford University Press, 1964); S. A. Babalola, *The Content and Form of Yoruba Ijala* (Oxford: Oxford University Press, 1966); Trevor Cope, ed., *Izibongo: Zulu Praise-Poems* (Oxford: Oxford University Press, 1968); Ahmad Nassir bin Juma Bhalo, *Poems from Kenya, Gnomic Verses in Swahili*, trans. and ed. by Lyndon Harries (Madison: University of Wisconsin Press, 1966); Eric Dampierre, *Poètes nzakara* (Paris: Julliard, 1963); Pierre-Francis Lacroix, *Poèsie peule de l'Adamawa* (Paris: Julliard, 1965).

6. William R. Bascom, "Folklore Research in Africa," *Journal of African Folklore*, LXXVII (January–March, 1964), 12–31.

riddle, poetry, drama, and the like. One can only wonder if a similar situation does not exist in graphic and plastic art.

Perceptive collectors, led by Roy Sieber, are investing in brass and other metal jewelry and ornaments because these previously little-valued items are rapidly disappearing, often being melted down by African women and replaced with gold or plastic. Scholars involved in the study of basketry are exceedingly rare, and to my knowledge not one has yet directed much attention to the thousands of baskets now gracing collections of Africana, to say nothing of the millions in everyday use in Africa. Cicatrization and tattooing, even more evanescent than basketry, have occasionally been documented photographically,[7] but close analyses and comparative studies of styles, methods, and content remain to be done. The recent growth of interest in traditional African architecture bodes well for the future of this rather distinct subdiscipline,[8] especially when those turning to this subject have the requisite architectural training as well as African field experience. There are undoubtedly many equally significant arts or crafts subjects about which existing, although scattered, information has yet to be meaningfully assembled. One hopes that these problems are sufficiently apparent and important to attract the research they deserve, especially by African scholars, before all truly traditional African artists and the socioreligious institutions that support African art are dead.

A rational approach to this problem of salvage-art-ethnography calls for team research on a much larger scale than has yet been attempted, but somewhat in the manner of Griaule and his students. Specialists in art, folklore, religion, linguistics, music, dance, theater, recording methods, and filming, plus area specialists and logistics experts, might be assembled and trained together, then moved from ethnic group to ethnic group to document each aesthetic event in season, working on the basic crafts and technology when no festivals or dances were imminent. Ethnohistorians and ethnographers could comb the published data and provide the necessary back-

7. See, for example, Jose Redinha, *Campanha Ethnográfica ao Tchiboco (Alto-Tshicapa)*, Subsidios para a Historia, Arqueologia e Ethnográfica dos Povos da Lunda, Museu do Dundo, Companhia de Diamantes de Angola (Lisboa, 1955), pp. 197–211.

8. See, for example, L. Prussin, ''The Architecture of Islam in West Africa,'' *African Arts/Arts d'Afrique*, I, No. 2 (Winter, 1968), 32–35, 70–74.

ground information, while scouts could precede the study party to establish rapport, discover the present local calendar of aesthetic events, and single out distinguished local artists in all media for intensive study later. We know that those curiously African institutions, secret and not-so-secret socioreligious societies, inspire, create, and use most of the art objects produced in Africa, and we also know that these institutions are under great pressure. It is still not too late to find out what words are sung, what dances are danced, and which masks represent which mythical beings before these mask performances die of desuetude, are radically changed to support new institutions such as political parties, or are replaced by alien forms of social control and entertainment. With the right kind of filming and editing, such performances might even have a certain popular appeal that would help repay the immense cost of such team research.

A much more thorny problem for anthropologists and art historians will be the objective documentation of the development of contemporary art in Africa. The seriousness of the problem is indicated by comparing the dearth of studies of contemporary African art with the large numbers of books, journals, and scholarly papers on contemporary African literature. Except for the Harmon Foundation compendium, *Africa's Contemporary Art and Artists,* which lists over three hundred African artists working in twenty-five countries, and Ulli Beier's useful survey of major schools and movements, *Contemporary Art in Africa,*[9] there has been little to compare with the flood of effusive, perhaps overappreciative, even patronizing, surveys that have been lavished on Africa's fledgling literature. And if the art critics, historians, and journalists with their professional training and ready formulations are as yet unwilling to approach modern African painting and sculpture, it is easy to see why anthropologists have not rushed to the task. Not only are our methods and preferences more suited to the study of moribund or attenuating cultures but also we are ill-equipped for the close analysis of techniques and minute variations in style that studies of contemporary work require.

The first and possibly the most serious problem is essentially philosophical: whether there are truly supracultural or "in-

9. Evelyn S. Brown, *Africa's Contemporary Art and Artists* (New York: Harmon Foundation, 1966); Ulli Beier, *Contemporary Art in Africa* (New York: Praeger, 1968).

ternational'' styles or forms in art, or whether a culture must invent its own forms of art expression. The issue of diffusion versus independent invention suggests a complex of related problems in the critical evaluation of art forms which are influenced by one culture or tradition and executed by an artist of another cultural origin. Art historians and anthropologists are in accord to the extent that they believe that the art of a culture must be produced by fully enculturated members of that culture, and that art as practiced by a member of a different culture or by a member of the same culture but a different epoch are equally anathema.

In this respect one would be interested to know more about the evaluation by rural Mexican audiences of the Mariachis de Uclatlan from the Institute of Ethnomusicology at UCLA, or the response of the Asian and African audiences to the UCLA Indonesian gamelan orchestra; Indian sitar, sarode, and tabla players; Japanese kota and samisen soloists; or African drum choir, all manned by earnest Californians. Institute scholars postulate the existence of true ''bi-musicality'' paralleling bilingualism, and report large audiences and a steady sale of recordings in the source countries. But an American hearing jazz played by Germans, Frenchmen, and Japanese readily recognizes the validity of the concept of culture and the difficulty of bridging the chasms between cultures.

The iron rule that the art of a culture must be produced by members of that culture exists either to exclude or to devaluate a great many superbly crafted objects—embroideries in the styles of Madeira or Appenzell made less expensively in the Philippines, Coyotepec blackware or Patamban greenware made nearer the market in Tzintzuntzan, fine ceramics in the ancient styles of Han, Sung, and T'ang created under the aegis of Ch'ien Lung, Bernard Leach, or the Imari potters, to say nothing of hundreds more degenerated styles or techniques. French impressionist paintings have been done by the Englishman Alfred Sisley and the American Mary Cassatt, and surely Wilfredo Lam's painting is Western expressionism, even though he is a Cuban of African and Chinese ancestry. One of the greatest of Spanish painters was a Cretan named Theotocopuli but called El Greco, Aesop is thought to have been an African slave rather than a citizen of Athens, and the ''exotic'' ancestries of Grieg, Kant, Thomas Mann, Heredia, Santayana, Picasso, Modigliani, and many other great men are credited as precisely the source of their greatness.

It is unlikely that the writings of Kamala Markandaya, Santha Rama Rau, Vidia Naipaul, and other talented Indians writing in English will ever be considered Indian literature either by Indians or by foreigners, but in this regard it appears that Amos Tutuola is to be credited with establishing, although unintentionally, a basis for critical acceptance of Africans writing in English. His content, style, and use of language, although deeply idiosyncratic in African terms, evidently approximated some of the Western preconceptions of how Africans might write. Although his works were seen as beautiful and compelling, they were not recognizable as "English literature" in any usual sense of the term, and hence were regarded by the critics as "African literature in English."

The respectable existence of African art in Western media was not to be established so easily, either by an artist so great as to be above national classification or by a "transitional" figure whose works approximated alien expectations. But any fair-minded judge will find only a derivative and provincial Western post-impressionism in the technically skillful but empty productions of most Africans formally trained in art schools. Occasional naive paintings are seen, such as occur in many other cultures, exemplified by the Douanier Rousseau, Grandma Moses, and the Haitian "primitives." Yet literally hundreds of African artists have been working in all media in nearly every country for at least the last forty years.

Perceptive collectors who rely on their own taste rather than on that of critics and dealers have long collected "contact art," chosen without regard to classification or continuity, but because of felicitous proportions, skillful use of materials, or significant content. With the growth of travel in Africa, the tastes of travelers are changing, and old, slightly used, frankly new, and carelessly forged sculpture in traditional styles is now available near every international airport, the authentically old pieces usually having been transported across one or more national boundaries to minimize difficulties over export permits. Some of this "airport art" is worth more consideration than is usually accorded it, for instance, the Senufo tourist figure and the wooden leopard from the carvers' cooperative at Ikot-Ekpene, Nigeria,[10] as well as many rarely displayed objects in museums, private collections, and occasional churches and public buildings, par-

10. Beier, *Contemporary Art*, pp. 11, 13, illustrations 1 and 2.

ticularly in Nigeria. The existence of these pieces strongly suggests that African artists will one day create a new tradition with some of the authority and elegance of the past.

Art historians and anthropologists have in effect demanded the impossible of African artists. If they repeat the limited forms of the past, but without the socioreligious context, the art is called debased and stereotypic; if they copy Western styles, they are called derivative, mere copyists; and if they combine the two, the result is all too often judged bizarre, ill-digested, or monstrous. Beier appropriately entitles his first chapter "Between Two Worlds." For that matter, most of Africa either never had a sculpture or painting tradition or had one, such as Sao in Chad, or Zimbabwe in Rhodesia, that has been extinct for centuries and can hardly be revived as the basis for a new style in the manner of Nampeyo with Hopi pottery.

The various European teachers who have founded the most successful art schools in Africa—Defosses in Elisabethville, Lods in Potopoto, Guedes in Lourenço Marques, and particularly Frank McEwen in Salisbury—shared their own European teachers' post-Beaux-Arts faith in uncontrolled experimentation and expressiveness in the studio and gave only minimal formal academic drawing training to their African students. The results, admittedly far from perfect, suggest that they had found the appropriate teaching method, and that African artists need materials, a place in which to work, some minimal support in attention and cash, and, most of all, solitude. This method has proved quite successful in the Mbari studios in Ibadan and Oshogbo, and evidently in Nairobi, and only the lack of finances and personnel limit its application in many permutations in other African cities. Worldly African political leaders have long since discovered the usefulness of peripatetic music and ballet troupes, international festivals and congresses, imposing museums, and government galleries or *villages artisanats* offering the best in "authentic" local crafts. Art is indeed appropriately used in the service of African nationalism and the philosophy of negritude, and artists can presumably expect continued governmental support.

The specific studies appropriate to art historians might be the detailed analysis of the development of a contemporary art style, its theoretical and methodological precepts, the relationship of the output of each member to the development of the school, their mutual borrowings and interactions, and careful documentation of materials, sources, symbolization, outside influences, and integration of each individual piece produced. The placing of a series of objects in stylistic, historic, and evaluative perspectives is also a traditional labor of art historians. Anthropologists may choose the life-history method, carefully documenting the significant events in the life of each artist as he is recognized, a method that would be equally productive if applied to our own society. They will concentrate on the uses of the object and its meaning and value to its creator and his audience or clients, and the special problems of the artist in one culture creating for a little-known and poorly understood client in another. Comparative studies of solutions to these and other problems by Scandinavian, Japanese, Mexican, and other artists and craftsmen will prove instructive, especially in showing how strong traditional crafts or styles have been modified with resounding success both aesthetically and financially. And it is through cross-cultural and cross-disciplinary studies such as these that we may some day be able to formulate the long-sought laws of aesthetic behavior.

THE ARTS IN HUMAN CULTURE: 7.
THEIR SIGNIFICANCE AND THEIR STUDY

Robert Plant Armstrong

There is no prognostication concerning the study of the arts in Africa during the next twenty years that is not also true of their study in any other area of the world. Thus I shall with the justification of necessity speak in very general terms, alluding when I can specifically to Africa.

It must be clear from the onset that what I mean by "arts" is a generalization comprising all available works of art. "Arts" is thus a large category, and a complex one as well, for I mean to include not only painting and sculpture but also music, dance, architecture, poetry, and narrative. Thus my use of the term is identical with the informed use of the term rather than with that careless use which sees works under the first two terms as "art" and the others by the particular names of their forms. The arts are amenable to serious study, and—as is true of other areas of human or natural phenomena —inquiry concerning them must be done, if it is to be done well and importantly, in terms of a method which has been rigorously devised. This particular kind of rigor is an activity superordinate to method; that is, it is *methodology.*

What does one expect of methodology? And subsequent to that, what does one expect of method? There is a difference between them despite the fact that one frequently hears the former when he knows that only the latter is meant. It is simpler to answer the second question first. One expects of method procedures that are well-articulated, reliably applied, and intelligently interpreted. One expects of methodology not only the formulation of a program or a system of investigation, but that the system be geared to the nature of the phenomena rather than determined by the erratic growth of a set of random queries which are heterogeneous rather than genetically related (a common situation reflecting more nearly the state of the investigator's mind, or his thought on the subject, than the nature of the phenomena). One expects prior to this, therefore, the formulation of a logic of procedure and the detailed determination of method within a frame of reference derived from a thoughtful consideration of the characteristics and the functions of art not only as facts of social interaction, an approach which yields one kind of information, but as works of art, a different approach which yields a wholly different kind of knowledge. This would imply not only that the persons electing to do research in the field of art should know which category of knowledge about art they are pursuing but also that they should know as much about art and philosophy as they do about the social sciences.

I am not concerned here with those social scientific studies which may use the arts as part of their data. The interesting work done by the participants of the 1965 Lake Tahoe conference on "The Traditional Artist in African Society" reflects an important concern, and while I am not competent to speak of its sociological merits, I am competent to recognize that the essays at that conference were not concerned with art, nor were they intended to be. Studies of the social dimensions of art are important and, in relative terms, plentiful. Such studies will continue to be done over the next two decades and they will enrich our understanding of society. On the other hand, there are studies purporting to be concerned with art as such which lack much in illumination because they proceed from no coherent theory of art and thus are not executed in terms of a logically and systematically planned method.

The ultimate objective of method, of course, is knowledge. The next twenty years, it is to be hoped, will see the formulation of theories and thus of methods which will mark the beginning of the rise of those studies dedicated to the accrual of information purposefully, programmatically, and discriminatingly acquired. Such pertinent information, one hopes, will be directed not so much to man and society as to man and art, as a result of which our knowledge of culture would greatly and more richly increase. What I write about here of the next twenty years is devout rather than prophetic. I write of significant lacunae rather than of certain trends. I have introduced a few rather ponderable topics, and there is no wise, nor indeed acceptable, alternative save to pursue them severally, each in some greater degree of detail.

I choose to follow the injunction given to the White Rabbit, " 'Begin at the beginning,' the King said very gravely, 'til you come to the end: then stop.' " The beginning in this case is clearly the fact that those who write about art are by and large either artists who know little about the social sciences or social scientists who know little about aesthetics. The fact of the matter is that the work of art is a special kind of thing, requiring its own science; it is also fact that the work of art is a social thing, thus standing in need of explanation in social terms. The work of art, then, is a special kind of social thing, special in that it is different from material culture, although it often has that kind of physical form, and different as well from the usual categories of mental culture—social structure, economic activities, religion, language, and so forth—even though at the periphery of its being it is non-distinctively (that is, in ways that are not essential to its special existence) involved with, or similar to, these traditional categories. Whatever its special nature as settled upon—doubtless temporarily—in the next several years, it must be recognized that the work of art exists for the sole purpose of uniquely constituting or importing something relevant to man. Thus the view of the social scientist—concerned as he is with the work of art as an item in economic transactions, as an indicator or ascriptor of social status, or as an item in religious activity—is irrelevant to that special and definitive nature of the work of art.

The special nature of that human event we call the work of art will be differently viewed by various people. But it seems to me that certain characteristics are essential to such a view if it is to suit the ends of serious comparative study, acceptable alike to humanist and social scientist: (1) It must present a useful view of the ontological nature of the work of art; (2) it must advance a relevant theory concerning the function of the work of art in human existence; (3) it must present a logic of procedure for study which will be firmly rooted in adequate, indeed rigorous, consideration of the ontological nature of the work, but which at the same time must be amenable to explicit implementation in one's study, in the archives and galleries, or in the field. It is to be hoped that such a view, with the aid of a sensitive and intelligent head behind it, will eventuate in studies that are characterized by clarity, analysis, relevance, and generalization.

We must recognize that the work of art is a serious human product—a product essential to culture, not an embellishment. The work of art is more than an artifact, although an artifact it frequently and clearly is; it is not simply, as I have already suggested, an item in other realities—rite, economy, or what have you—although, to be sure, it has these dimensions to its existence.

I think we must accept that we may no longer regard the work of art as a symbol, nor may we regard it as a product of the reason somehow gone awry, which is sometimes the case to that precise extent to which the work of art does not quite conveniently "fit" into the nature of the symbol as we have come to understand it. We have come to the understanding that the work of art is ontologically independent, a thing in itself, and that it thus contrasts with the symbol which, since it must refer to something external to itself, is not ontologically independent but dependent. Indeed, it is important to realize that the work of art is not primarily, and certainly not importantly, a work of the reason at all, but a work of the feelings. What is entailed by such a view for the study not of art alone but of human existence—of which "behavior" is only one kind of grid superimposed upon existence for the purposes of classification and analysis—is profound indeed. We come by such a road to the realization that culture is tripartite, comprised of material, mental, and affective components, not bipartite, and that that universe which has its own and unique system of expression is in fact as independent of the reason as the reason is independent of it, though there are interrelationships, to be sure, since man's consciousness is unitive and language-dominated. Once again we reach a familiar conclusion, but with new evidence added: any approach to the study of art which does not take its point of departure in the ontological independence of the work of art is simply not a relevant study of art, irrespective of what social or archaeological or historical values such a study may have.

Since at the present time the social sciences fairly well monopolize the study of Africa, it is fair to inquire whether the study of human experience and feeling is important to the social sciences. Indeed, there are here and there humanists so unresponsive to what we might refer to as the human spirit that we might also ask whether such a study is pertinent to the humanities. It is beyond the scope of this paper to demonstrate such import, and so I shall simply assert that human experience and feeling (without which experience is not likely to happen, and which is itself dependent upon experiential bases) doubtless exert profound influences upon social activities, since they affect the individual and since individuals acting in concert constitute society. Further, of course, the study of experience *qua* experience and of feeling—their textures, significance, lived-quality—is important in and of itself if we are to understand man.

The functions of the work of art thus are concerned with the objectification of human experience, such that the work of art is self-existent and ever amenable to perception and transaction, and charged with the inevitable invasion of feeling that accompanies that action and transaction. The implications of these views for a logic of procedure are clear. One proceeds in recognition of the following facts: that the work of art is a thing in itself and has no external referent; that it exists in and of its own universe of feeling; that methods of study which are relevant proceed from these facts; that if quantification is to be useful it must be relevant quantification, that is, pertinent to the work of art itself and not to irrelevant or tangential factors; and that qualification is likely to be even more useful, trenchant, and revealing. But we must be prepared, after we have explored the terrain more thoroughly, to accept the necessity for devising some completely new method of trenchant and relevant description and analysis which will derive relentlessly and inevitably from the essential nature of the work of art.

Such requirements necessitate a high degree of methodical imagination and invention. As the questions traditionally asked of art are irrelevant, so are the traditional methods inapposite; indeed, by definition, they tend to be, in both the social sciences and the humanities, reductivistic, for they treat feeling as symptom, seeking out its causes rather than treating it as an existent state in and of itself; and experience is regarded as *about* something rather than as that which is essentially self-contained. Thus, as I have observed before, that study which attempts to reduce the work of art to what it is not—to the search for causes, to the documentation of history and of influences, to examination of its functions in rite, family, or marketplace—is an irrelevant study of art.

The logic of procedure therefore dictates that basic research be directed to the task of determining what physical aspects of the work of art are distinctive in the sense that they bear, or are significantly informed with, experience and feeling, and to the means by which this reality can, apparently so inappropriately, be achieved by physical forms.

We are, with respect to the conceptualization of the field— to say nothing of the articulation of methods—farther away from a relevant system of description, analysis, and theory than linguists were to appropriate approaches to the study of language before the days of the founders of the structural approach, when the essential nature of language was basically recognized, which led logically to the development of a system of study relevant to the phenomena. Granting the recognition of the separate universe of feeling; granting the acknowledgment of the fact that the realm constituted by works of art is patterned as all other human activities are patterned; and granting the identification of the proper criteria among which to search out such regularities, the study of the work of art should proceed as dramatically and as pertinently as, in its early days, did the study of language.

Under such circumstances, workers will know how to distinguish among such terms as aesthetics, form, and style, to name only a few; and terms having clear meanings will no longer mask loose thinking but will rigorously perform honest jobs. In so doing they will lead to the accumulation of data which are revealing, which are comparable, and which will lend themselves to cross-cultural examination and, in the long run, facilitate generalization about art.

What does it mean to say that clear and precise terms and a well-articulated method will lead to such an accumulation of data? This sort of statement provokes numerous questions. For example, if the work of art is an entity among entities, and if it is self-existent and whole, self-sufficient, what relevance to it have data derived from it? The answer can only be "very little," provided that one's interest is in the work of art. If we are to consider the next reasonable question, "What kind of data, no matter how little?" we will find that we are in a sense concerned with reductions, though of a special and more relevant sort than those deriving from inquiry based upon art as symptom and symbol. This is to say that we are not reducing art to something it is not—like neuroses or ritual implements or ideas—but are factoring out from its being *qua* art certain remarkable and artistically relevant factors. Further, it is clear that such extrapolations committed upon a sufficiently representative sample have cultural significance, and by committing such activities we place ourselves in a position from which we can make certain relevant cultural statements about art *qua* art, as well therefore as certain statements about culture.

Such conclusions can be reached only by methods which are —as are those implied above—inductive. Such methods are inductive with respect to the identification of relevant characteristics of the forms of art in given cultures. They are not concerned with prior attitudes concerning the nature of the work of art to which answers have already been proposed based upon the characteristics of art in another, and perhaps very different, culture.

It is difficult to study art as art—as a special mode of affective and experiential being, one that is ontologically self-sufficient—but the fact that the study is difficult will, I think, challenge rather than dissuade. This will even more likely be the case as the problem itself is analyzed, as the proper questions are asked, and as the nature of the phenomena becomes sufficiently clear for us to define some proximal, if neither medial nor distal, objectives.

Some objectives are clear, and I should like to devote a few paragraphs to one important area of problem and objective.

I have mentioned that when I write of the arts, or of "art," I am thinking of each of the arts. It will perhaps be useful therefore if I indicate in very general terms the influences such views as I have presented here will have upon the studies of the various forms—sculpture, painting, music, dance, architecture, drama, costume, poetry, and narrative.

One must accordingly find those areas of the existence of the forms which are of affecting significance, and for each of the arts, as I see them, these are as follows:

sculpture:	surface, color, volume, movement (in the case of a mobile)
dance:	volume (of the body), movement, situation
graphic:	surface, color
music:	tone, movement
architecture:	surface, color, volume
drama:	color, movement, situation

narrative:	movement, situation
costume:	surface, color, movement (sometimes volume, when sculpture is used as part of the costume)
poetry:	movement, word, situation

All the forms are characterized by the presence of two additional media, *experience* and *relationality*. *Experience* is that twofold property in the work of art which on the one hand is the subject-matter input, as it were, incarnated into the media and on the other hand is the totality of output informed by the special circumstances of media, subject, and perceptor. *Relationality* is not a property of the media but is a discriminating operation performed upon the media in terms of which experience is possible. All these media work within the frame of reference of certain cultural conventions at one level, and certain individual conventions at another, which describe given physical features or conditions within the work of art as constituting necessary and sufficient equivalents to given kinds of affective response in transaction.

The relevant study of each of the arts, then, will in the areas of the relevant media concentrate on efforts to ascertain those features of media which are distinctive, that is to say, those which are of affective import, seeking to identify *aesthemes*, which one may define as the physical least common denominators given affecting significance, as distinguished from those features which are non-distinctive. The researcher will conduct his inquiry in terms of structure on the one hand and style on the other, the former being defined as those spatial or temporal elements effective of development in continuity and the latter being defined as those spatial or temporal elements which extend in space or synchronically in time. In the final analysis, after having studied distinctive features of structure and style and after having generalized them for all the arts, the scholar will attempt to write a "grammar" of the art of the people, stating general physical conditions and feelings which, irrespective of the physical dissimilarities among the arts, will adequately state the case for the whole affective system in the arts.

It may reasonably be asked what presumably would be the characteristics of the knowledge that will be acquired from studies deriving from such a philosophical position and its logically derived methods. Would such knowledge be in any wise different from that which is now achieved? In answer to the latter question, I say simply, categorically, "yes," and I shall attempt to document my assertion by developing an answer to the more analytic first question.

In the first place it is clear that the view is of the work of art as a "non-symbolic, affecting, media-expressed, content-full, transactional entity" created to be precisely what it is and inalienably in its own terms, and that accordingly knowledge produced will at best relate to this total complex of factors and at least relate to one of its terms. It is also clear that these factors will be studied in connection with physical features determined to be distinctive in accordance with the extent to which they do or do not incarnate the features of this complex. They will also be studied in terms of the human inner half of the transaction. Knowledge derived from such studies will thus be of affecting-form-in-experience in one part and of the existential field of human experience itself in another part, for despite ontological differences, in one respect the work of art stands in a relationship to human feeling as the symbol does to the reason, in the sense that it is an externalization. It is, of course, an expressive and not a symbolic externalization.

Knowledge detailing something of the content and forms of feeling, the interorganization of those forms, and a grammar of their behavior is new and distinctively humane knowledge.

In short, the work of art is a special form of human existence. That it should be studied for non-significant things it is not, rather than for the significant fact it is, is an amazing situation that one hopes will find revocation during the next two decades. During this time, perhaps, we may hopefully expect to witness the burgeoning of a new humanism that will insist upon looking upon art for the humane, unique, and important event each work of art is. What one wishes to see, in order to guide and foster such relevant inquiry, is the rise of a new anthropology, a humanistic anthropology—or an anthropological humanism, for that matter—of which there are a few heartening signs in the growing influence of phenomenology upon American intellectual life. African studies present concerned scholars with unique opportunities to advance such knowledge, for the field is rich with art and is blessed with a wide spread of imaginative scholars from a wide range of disciplines, scholars who have seen new problems and have been hospitable to novel approaches.

DISCUSSANT'S COMMENTS

7

Edward Callan

In making a plea for proper recognition of the autonomy, even perhaps the aesthetic rights, of the work of art, Dr. Armstrong seeks a methodology that may be applied with equal validity to the art of all times and regions, including the art of Africa. In particular, he seeks a methodology that will have certain points of correspondence with the one devised by linguists for the description of languages, and in this connection he has supplied a term that constitutes an aesthetic equivalent of those basic measures of form and sound that linguists call *morphemes* and *phonemes*, that is, the term *aesthemes*.

I am reminded of my favorite line from W. B. Yeats: "For wisdom is a butterfly, and not a gloomy bird of prey." In pursuit of a methodology that will properly respect the autonomy of the art object, Dr. Armstrong seeks to liberate the realm of art from those "gloomy birds of prey" who tend to treat the work of art as a symptom of something else, and also from those "butterflies" who engage in undisciplined and undirected collection of data. While applauding Dr. Armstrong's purpose, my hope would be that a few butterflies might be spared. I would also hope that those who embark on the task of naming and classifying aspects of art in the service of the new methodology will seek also to supply adequate terms for the inherent element of joy that characterizes the artistic impulse, even when its subject is tragic—what W. B. Yeats calls "the shaping joy that kept the sorrow pure."

There is one thing we may say with some hope of certainty about the immediate future, and that is that it will closely resemble the immediate past. In looking ahead to the responsibilities of scholars in the field of traditional African art and folk-literature in the light of Armstrong's plea for respect for the central importance of the work of art itself, all we can hope for is increased care and more rigor. For if the work of art itself is our object, and if we are to put our new methodology to use, the task of the scholar will be to provide us with the *authentic object*. Where oral traditions are concerned, such authentication is frequently a long, arduous process.

On the other hand, the contemporary artist, whether he be

African, Asian, or European, lives in daily contact with horizons of experience and springs of feeling unthought of by his predecessors in any age or place. Within a few hours on an average day he may listen to both Bach and the Beatles on his phonograph or radio. He has at hand literature, music, and sculpture on a universal scale. It should be no surprise, therefore, to find the Nigerian novelist Achebe adapting a theme from the Irish poet Yeats: ''Things fall apart; the centre cannot hold''; or to find Gabriel Okara in his poem ''Piana and Drums'' declaring:

> And I, lost in the morning mist
> Of an age at a riverside, keep
> Wandering in the mystic rhythm
> Of jungle drums and the concerto.

These men and their successors would ask to be judged by no lesser norms than their fellow artists elsewhere, and it is important for scholars to re-examine those categories that may place undue emphasis on the ''divided'' or ''dual'' cultural worlds of these artists and to see them as inhabiting a unified, if complex, world of experience embracing great variety—''the jungle drums *and* the concerto''—within its horizons.

ETHNOMUSICOLOGY IN AFRICAN STUDIES: THE NEXT TWENTY YEARS

8

Klaus Wachsmann

However uncertain the future may be, it can be predicted that the engineering skills available for research in *sound* in music and speech will be considerable and that these skills will provide techniques leading to new methods of analysis and to new insights. And sound surely is an important angle of ethnomusicology. Also, the study of music as *human behavior*, another angle, is unlikely to remain static. Social and economic change and political direction will no doubt influence music and musicology. Political scientists and economists might well make forecasts that interest musicians.

These two aspects, sound on the one hand and human behavior on the other, have remained somewhat separate in the past, but the conviction is growing that the two approaches need integrating. For reasons that need not be considered here, the problem seems to be more pressing in African musicology than in any other musicology. It is a moot point whether such integration can be achieved by a single scholar without loss of competence in either of the two spheres, or whether it calls for cooperation between specialists, a skill that requires cultivating. In terms of university policy the question is whether the departments of anthropology and others not primarily concerned with music as sound and the schools of music can develop an integrated teaching program.

Musical sound has attracted more attention in recent years because of the interest that Africans are showing in the practice of their music. For African students, creative practice is a prerequisite of African musicology in the same way in which the Western repertoire is the foundation on which Western musicology stands. Strictly speaking, sound in this sense belongs to the schools for the creative arts, and therefore ethnomusicologists may feel excluded. However, from the point of view of African studies there is no problem: the *creative practice*, a third angle if you wish, is an essential part of the African reality. In these terms of reference I see a triangular relationship: music as sound, music as human behavior, and the living repertoire of music. The last, most of all, is within the special competence of our African colleagues.

Against the background of these general considerations, I propose to deal with my subject under ten more specific headings. I have refrained from detailed elaboration of any particular theme, and I do not claim that the list is complete. I think of the headings as pointers to the *pressures* and *responses* that will occupy us in the coming years. I have adopted this method because I do not think of ethnomusicologists as being free to choose their own themes, but rather as scholars and artists who are sensitive to the challenges of their times. Occasionally the headings overlap since the issues are interrelated:

Pressures	*Responses*
1. Distortion of idioms and values	Study of criteria
2. Western popular preferences	Africa-wide, comparative study in the universities
3. Impact of communication media	Focus on oral transmission
4. Show business	Scientific films
5. "Popular" music	Sociological analysis of musical fashions
6. Emphasis on social correlations	Inquiry, musical styles, and cultural systems
7. Emphasis on concepts	Exploration of texts, linguistics
8. Theory of cantometrics	Validity of parameters, nature of correlations

| 9. Denial of aesthetic values | Focus on canons of evaluation embodied in speech |
| 10. The rise of African "art" music | Analogy with neo-African literature |

Pressures and Responses

Distortion: study of criteria

The first Congress of Black Writers and Artists in 1956 resolved to put an end to the destruction of African art and furthermore to prevent the subtle damage of distortion of their idioms and values.[1] Presumably this issue will remain acute, but as knowledge of the criteria and parameters that are valid in the music increases, the distortion is likely to become correspondingly less. Little is known as yet of the complexity of values on the continent as a whole, and as a result the basic assumptions from which to approach a given piece of music are uncertain. For instance, we cannot always distinguish between collective and individual traits. Naturally, musical terminology is poorest when it comes to the intangible elements. The West does not have an extensive terminology, let alone scientific taxonomy, for voice quality and production, for the subtleties of attack in string playing and drumming, or for the quality of sound in general. The systematic literature regarding musical concepts in Africa is comparatively recent, and the dialogue between Western composers and their African colleagues that promises so much has only just begun.

Western popular preferences: Africa-wide, comparative study

One is tempted to declare dogmatically that African music is now popular in the West. But on close inspection the statement needs qualifying: it would be more to the point to say that West African percussion, rather than African music, has succeeded. If proof is wanted, it must be very rare that one finds concerts or performance groups for Bushman and

1. James Baldwin, "Letter from Paris: Princes and Powers," *Encounter*, VIII (January, 1957), 52–60.

Pygmy vocal music, for the harp music of Uganda, for the songs of Mauretania, to mention only a few of the neglected styles. In the minds of Western listeners, Guinea Coast percussion has become the image that must serve for all music from Africa. Rather than conclude that African music is not uniform, audiences will label other sounds as "Arabic" or "Oriental." It is extraordinary how little can be said with authority as to what is "exotic" in African music and what is not.

Fela Sowande often complains of this image.[2] Indeed, the preferences of the West may well affect taste in Africa. It may be too late to correct the image or even quixotic to try, but its existence strengthens the case for comparative studies and for studying an Africa-wide experience in the universities.[3]

Observations like that of A. M. Jones, "the music of the Western Sudanic-speaking Ewe people is one and the same music as that of the Bantu-speaking Lala tribe,"[4] are correct in their context but may mislead because they are based principally on only a few parameters. One could argue with equal justification that African Negro music and Persian music are one and the same because hemiolas occur frequently in both.[5] In spite of several well-informed attempts to locate distinctive stylistic areas,[6] the problem of "African music, one or many" is still far from being solved.

2. Fela Sowande, "Oyigiyigi: Introduction, Theme and Variations on a Yoruba Folk Theme for Organ" (New York: Ricordi, 1958).

3. For art historians, regional preferences are natural since large parts of Africa do not have sculpture, but musicians do not make a distinction that would be analogous to the difference between "sculpture" and "utensil." Thus, music can be said to exist anywhere.

4. A. M. Jones, *Studies in African Music*, I (London: Oxford University Press, 1959), 199.

5. Hormoz Farhat, "Hemiola in Persian Music," paper read at the Annual Meeting of the Society for Ethnomusicology, New Orleans, December 28, 1966.

6. Jones, *Studies in African Music*, I, 203–29; Alan P. Merriam, "African Music," in *Continuity and Change in African Cultures*, ed. by William R. Bascom and Melville J. Herskovits (Chicago: University of Chicago Press, 1959), pp. 76–80; Alan P. Merriam, "Characteristics of African Music," *Journal of International Folk Music Council*, No. 11 (1959), pp. 13–19; André Schaeffner, "La Musique d'Afrique noire," in *La Musique dès origines à nos jours*, ed. by Norbert Dufourq (Paris: Larousse, 1946), pp. 460–65; Marius Schneider, "Über die Verbreitung afrikanischer Chorformen," *Zeitschrift für Ethnologie*, LXIX (1937), 79.

Communication media: [7] oral transmission

It may seem overambitious to attempt to set contemporary African music in the perspective of the roles of all media of communication in a society—writing, printing, disc and tape, radio and television—but there are relevances and interrelationships that would make such an attempt valuable. To do so would involve, among other things, a survey of the programs of the radio stations since their inception, and of the cultural, commercial, and political influences bearing on the media (in Uganda, for instance, the disc trade is a matter of Indian enterprise). It is an education to leaf through the 78 rpm discs on sale in the local shops, to listen to the "top ten" announced in the local press, and to note the favorites in broadcasting. It would also be instructive to see how African program directors are trained, for instance by the Office de Cooperation Radiophonique (OCORA) in Paris for the French-speaking countries overseas, and to analyze the training syllabuses. Learning processes of any kind and the history of music are inextricably linked, and the manipulation of taste is an interesting phenomenon in all societies.

Of all the communication media, musical notation in contemporary Africa is the most difficult to handle. African music is oral; to apply a Euro-centric, and thus in the African context inappropriate, system of musical transmission would, in my opinion, be like trying to mix oil and water, and equally futile. One hopes that music-educationists will join forces with music-psychologists in tackling the problem of transmission. The most significant factor in oral transmission is the spoken word. I am referring to the role of speech as text—by far the largest part of the African repertoire is text-based [8]—and to the role of speech as a vehicle for stylistic criticism. Thus research in the verbal arts is likely to take a lead in the analysis of music.

7. One would automatically turn to Marshall McLuhan for the most recent statement of the problem. The text of McLuhan's address on "The Impact of Communication Media on Music," presented at the meeting of the International Music Council, UNESCO, on September 10, 1968, is not available at this writing. The paper and the discussions it no doubt provoked at the meeting should be of great interest.

8. Dr. N. England notes that Bushman and Pygmy songs are notable exceptions.

One observation might be added here with regard to the communication media and the writing of music history in Africa now and in the future. To project into the next twenty years, the accumulation of recordings from 1900 to 1988 will make excellent material. In a rapidly changing world four-score years of music do indeed represent "historical depth."

Show business: scientific films

Entertainment at home and abroad is taken seriously by several African governments. National dance troupes have official financial backing. The transition from the traditional setting to the stages of Broadway and the platforms of world exhibitions usually calls for a producer to "knock the show into shape." Will these productions release a chain reaction that will eventually reach the smallest village team? If so, this is the stuff of which music history is made. To trace the evolution of musical styles one needs documentation of the process itself. Expertly made scientific films would serve the purpose well. Films are primary source material for research; they have the advantage of embracing both the oral and visual, thus linking music with motion; and they can be entertaining. So far few films have exploited the research potential inherent in the medium, presumably on account of the thorny question as to who is to direct the production—an anthropologist, a film artist or technician, a choreographer, or a musician. Is not teamwork the answer?

Although scientific film is thought of mainly as a medium of teaching and research, such film could be edited for television entertainment as well.

"Popular" music: the sociology of musical fashions

The so-called popular genres have deeply impressed Africa. The result has been an amalgam of jazz, calypso, the Beatles, and other Western traits with local traditional elements. To African ears the local element is most noticeable; the texts are certainly local and topical. Can experts in art music afford to stand aloof from popular practice without losing touch with the forces that are so obviously at work in all societies? In my own experience, the answer in Africa is that they cannot. Atta Mensah's research in "Highlife," the Ghanaian version of this music, and David Rycroft's work in South Africa are examples of important studies of popular influence on local forms.[9]

From the assumption that ethnomusicologists are sensitive to trends, in this context popular preference in Africa, it would follow that sooner or later these musical fashions will be studied. In the meantime sociological analysis might prepare a frame of reference for musicologists, a foundation from which to start.

Since the "popular" style is universal, its study would be universal too, and would include the African contribution to American music culture. It need not necessarily aim at seeking the ultimate origins of jazz and of the blues, but it could attend to the history of the African influence in American music since the 1940's.

Emphasis on social correlations: inquiry, musical styles, and cultural systems

The social role of music is of particular interest to musicians, especially when the music belongs to a culture alien to them. In African musical circles the trend today is first to perform and only secondarily to explore social implications. Nketia even speaks of "artistic value," something that he can discuss out of social context.[10] But one finds exponents of an opposite view too. For Okot p'Bitek a piece of music is an empty shell if its social role has been recast artificially.[11] Frantz Fanon and Keita Fodeba resolve the argument in their own way: if the new role is vital to society, music will adapt and serve.[12] In their eyes, vitality is a matter of politics and revolutionary necessity. This attitude is also familiar to Westerners (see

9. Atta Mensah, "The Impact of Western Music on the Musical Traditions of Ghana," *Composer: Journal of the Composers' Guild of Great Britain*, XIX (1966), 19–22; David Rycroft, "African Music in Johannesburg: African and Non-African Features," *Journal of International Folk Music Council*, No. 11 (1959), pp. 25–30.

10. J. H. Kwabena Nketia, "Artistic Values in African Music," *Composer: Journal of the Composers' Guild of Great Britain*, XIX (1966), 16–19.

11. G. W. Kakoma, Gerald Moore, and Okot p'Bitek, eds., *Proceedings of the First Conference on African Traditional Music* (Kampala: Makerere University, 1964), p. 45.

12. Frantz Fanon, *Les Damnés de la terre* (Paris: Cahiers Libres, 1961), trans. by Constance Farrington as *The Wretched of the Earth* (New York: Grove Press, 1965), p. 182; Keita Fodeba, *Poèmes Africains* (Paris: Seghers, 1958), pp. 20–25.

Simone de Beauvoir's tortured questioning of musical experience).[13] It leads to a disregard of and even to hostility toward stylistic criticism.

However, new roles tend to affect style. For musicians there is a central problem here: how can they correlate a break in the continuity of a style with a break in the continuity of other human activities? The International Musicological Society discussed "Crisis Years in the History of Music" at its recent Congress, and the proceedings should contain material that is relevant to African musicology.[14] Helm, in reporting on the Congress, observed that "there is also a distinct trend away from the traditional approach which considers the development of music and musical styles primarily in terms of stylistic analysis."[15] In this context I would like to quote John Blacking, who for many years has championed the case for the sociological approach to music:

> More attention must indeed be given to the sociology of music; but useful discoveries will not be made until the organization of *sound*, which is after all an expression of social realities, is investigated with the same rigour and respect as the organization of the makers of sound.[16]

Emphasis on concepts: exploration of texts, linguistics

In the light of the discussion at the Third International African Seminar at Salisbury,[17] the difference between the emphasis on social correlation and the emphasis on concepts would be one of the differences in emphasis between British and French anthropology. This seems to be borne out by the

13. Simone de Beauvoir, *Force of Circumstance*, trans. by Richard Howard (Harmondsworth: Penguin, 1968), pp. 669–70.

14. This should be available in 1970.

15. Everett Helm, "Ljubljana Conference: Scholars of Music Break Tradition," *Christian Science Monitor*, October 6, 1967, p. 4.

16. John Blacking, in *Man*, III (June, 1968), 314, letter in response to Rodney Needham, "Percussion and Transition," *Man*, II (December, 1967), 606–14.

17. M. Fortes and G. Dieterlen, eds., *African Systems of Thought*, Studies Presented and Discussed at the Third International African Seminar at Salisbury, December, 1960 (London: Oxford University Press for the International African Institute, 1965), pp. 3–4, 43–44.

fact that Dampierre's, Rouget's, and Zahan's studies,[18] for instance, apparently have no counterpart in the English literature, with the noteworthy exception of Robert Thompson's data on the verbal aspects of the dance in Benin.[19] Linguistics also have an obvious stake under this heading, as in communication, in the development of research.

Concepts are elusive, even if they are verbalized. Horton pointed to a fundamental problem recently in essays that were written primarily for anthropologists but which also implicate musicologists.[20] What is the basis of inquiry to be? Do we look for differences between the musics of Africa, the West, and any other culture that we happen to draw into our investigation? (This was the stance that had been adopted early in the history of comparative musicology, as ethnomusicology was then called.) Or do we look for elements that are common to several or all music cultures? African music is now enthusiastically received, especially by the younger generation, perhaps because of the discovery, real or imaginary, of common features,[21] and one can sense a musical climate that favors Horton's suggestion. This widespread interest may have far-reaching consequences.

I look forward to seeing research in African music undertaken by Indian musicians. It would not surprise me if they interpreted African music in terms different from those that Western scholars have adopted, and projected into it their own concepts, which might lead us to new perspectives and lines of inquiry.

Theory of cantometrics: the validity of parameters, the nature of correlations

Alan Lomax correlated sound with subsistence complexity.[22] His method, cantometrics, is to identify a performance in

18. Eric de Dampierre, *Poètes Nzakara* (Paris: Julliard, 1963); Gilbert Rouget, ''Tons de la langue en Gun (Dahomey) et tons du Tambour,'' *Revue de Musicologie*, L (1964), 3–29; Dominique Zahan, *La Dialectique du verbe chez les Bambara* (The Hague: Mouton, 1963).

19. Robert F. Thompson, ''Dance Among the Yoruba'' (Paper read at the Colloquium on Critical Standards in the Arts of Africa, U.C.L.A., March, 1968).

20. Robin Horton, ''African Traditional Thought and Western Science,'' *Africa*, XXXVII (January, 1967), 50.

21. Bruno Nettl, *Folk and Traditional Music of the Western Continents* (Englewood Cliffs, N. J.: Prentice-Hall, 1965).

22. Alan Lomax, ''The Good and the Beautiful in Folksong,'' *Journal of American Folklore*, LXXX (1967), 312–35; and Alan Lomax, ed.,

terms of any of thirty-seven parameters he has selected and to map out their geographical distribution. The parameters refer to musical categories like polyphony, monophony, type of rhythm, nature of accent, treatment of text, and so forth. Lomax's theory is that the distribution patterns of parameters match perfectly the distribution patterns of distinctive levels of subsistence complexity.

A secondary question arises with regard to the nature of correlations: can they be reversed? That is, can deductions be made from a (known) specific level of subsistence complexity toward an (unknown) configuration of musical parameters that goes with it? Or to take a more concrete case, can a prehistorian, after having determined the subsistence complexity of an extinct society by the evidence from ancient sites, speculate as to the music of this society on the basis of Lomax's correlating parameters? The problem has a fascination of its own in Africa where no musical sounds from before 1900 have survived. It also touches on the methodological problems inherent in all correlation.[23]

Denial of aesthetic values: canons of evaluation embodied in speech

In *The Anthropology of Music*, Alan Merriam argues that the term "aesthetics" is inapplicable in African music because it has become compromised by its specific reference to Art, with a capital "A." [24] Yet the concepts embodied in African vernaculars permit speculation that there are aesthetic criteria for the response to music and dance.[25] Vocabularies do point to canons of evaluation by which performance is critically judged, and they are used as such. Furthermore, it seems that the distinction between craftsman and artist is feasible in certain societies.[26] The canons may change in the course of

Folk Song Style and Culture: A Staff Report on Cantometrics (Washington, D. C.: AAAS Publications, 1968).

23. See Needham, "Percussion and Transition," and subsequent correspondence.

24. Alan P. Merriam, *The Anthropology of Music* (Evanston: Northwestern University Press, 1964), pp. 259–76.

25. See, for example, Thompson, "Dance Among the Yoruba."

26. Warren D'Azevedo, "The Artist Archetype in Gola Culture," Conference on the Traditional Artist in African Society, Lake Tahoe, 1965. (Mimeographed.)

history; so do the roles of the senses. New thoughts have been expressed in a literature bearing on aesthetics, but their relevance to African systems of value remain to be tested.[27]

African "art" music: analogy with neo-African literature

The search for a "national" idiom led to remarkable experiments in Africa in the 1960's. The experiments took the form of composed music, in most cases derived from, and at the same time departing from, Western methods. There is a tendency in African studies to underestimate rather than overestimate the significance of such experimentation. Yet a neo-African musical opus is at least analogous to a neo-African novel or poem. If the composer should lean heavily on Western technique, his work is comparable to an African novel in English or French. The analogy may still hold even if he should succeed in creating a vernacular idiom in composition, which is in itself a Western procedure. Neo-African composers are—like Béla Bartók—composers and ethnomusicologists at the same time. One cannot assess their impact on Africa, or for that matter on the West, but the indications are that their work is going to occupy us increasingly.

Neo-African writing is accepted as a subject in African studies and by departments of English in certain universities, and one hopes that neo-African composition will receive similar recognition, especially on African soil.[28] In my experience, ethnomusicology has much to offer in the training of neo-African composers.

Conclusion

It is difficult to focus on a future that stretches so far ahead. Much is expected, but at times the expectations are overshadowed by uneasiness. Already we know the cost of the frightful changes that have come over the acoustic environment, especially in the larger Western cities. To be sure, George Orwell's

27. Leonard B. Meyer, *Music, the Arts and Ideas* (Chicago: University of Chicago Press, 1967); Anton Ehrenzweig, *The Hidden Order of Art: A Study in the Psychology of Artistic Imagination* (Berkeley: University of California Press, 1967).

28. Akin Euba, "In Search of a Common Musical Language in Africa," *Interlink, The Nigerian-American Quarterly*, Vol. III, No. 3 (1967).

Nineteen Eighty-Four falls within the span of time to be covered here. One also remembers Teilhard de Chardin's vision of a human evolution toward an almost entirely collective experience. One wonders how close the reality will come to the fantasy and the vision. However, it would be common sense to look at the problems of the future as a continuation of the past, and thus I conclude that the history of ideas in ethnomusicology will be worth studying.

I have two practical suggestions to make: (1) The need for an interdisciplinary program seems to me most pressing. This statement refers not only to those disciplines mentioned in the previous paragraphs but also to many others. There are few opportunities at present to practice what is being preached here. There is also a certain diffidence about the feasibility of this interdisciplinary approach. (2) Regular meetings are needed in which the dialogue with African colleagues can take place and the awareness of currents and trends heightened. Ideally, a consortium of the kind that met in 1966 at Bloomington could be arranged. As in Bloomington, such a consortium might consist of six members who would hold perhaps three, certainly not less than two, meetings a year. The discussions could concentrate on pressures and responses, on keeping in touch with music in Africa, and on research. Publication of the proceedings would help to give purpose and vision to African ethnomusicology in the years to come.

J. H. Kwabcna Nketia

I would like to comment briefly about how we in Africa may react to some of the pressures and responses that Professor Wachsmann has outlined in his paper and to indicate something of our view of the priorities for the next twenty years.

Professor Wachsmann is right when he suggests that we in Africa are not likely to respect the dichotomy between sound and behavior. Our music is so closely involved with dance and drama, with ceremony and ritual, that we cannot really isolate a musical study from its context. We are interested in both sound and behavior because music in Africa is a much more complicated thing than either of these elements. The solution may be in some kind of interdisciplinary approach.

One of the problems this question raises is that of the kind of training that the musician in Africa or the ethnomusicologist in African studies should have. Certainly from our point of view it would be wrong to give the musician in Africa a narrow conservatory training, which emphasizes only techniques of music. Our traditions emphasize poetry as well as music, and the musician is not only a performer of music but also a creator of words; his modern counterpart therefore should have an appreciation of the problems of language as well as an understanding of music.

I would also agree with Professor Wachsmann's comment that ethnomusicologists must be sensitive to the challenges of our time. But for us in Africa, this means working out some scale of priorities in our research. At this stage cantometrics will not be our first priority. We have neither the training nor the equipment to pursue these interesting problems at this time. Perhaps young African musicologists who are growing up, and who will have scientific training, may join hands with their colleagues in the West in the study of cantometrics—this probably will be one of the important contributions that this part of the world can make to our work on the continent.

But there will be some kind of geographical definition of priorities. For example, African musicologists are likely to be concerned with the study of small groups. Whatever has been done in ethnomusicology, you will find that people will go over the ground again because they want to know what their own people do. The results of this work may eventually enlarge our views of the distribution of any given parameter.

We may find that our scale of priorities will be influenced by national considerations as well. In Ghana, for instance, we are not yet a nation of one people, but we still have some kind of national identity, and we talk about ourselves as Ghanaians. This has some implication for research. In thinking about the selection of areas or groups, one may consider first the size of the people and their relative importance in the new culture of a country. Thus in Ghana, I am interested in knowing what each group offers to the total national heritage. When Professor Wachsmann talks about national dance companies, for instance, he is recognizing an exponent of what the people consider to be the heritage of their country.

Then there are regional studies which are bound to follow the purely national studies, because there are forms of interaction across national frontiers. To confine our studies to the Akan in Ghana, for instance, and not consider the group in the Ivory Coast, would seem to be a very limiting approach. And if we are interested in historical problems, which I hope will be the case, we will have to look across international frontiers to study the wider historical picture.

Beyond the regional studies, there is the continental, or Africa-wide, view. It is not only in the West that the rather narrow view of African music has to be corrected. People may not realize, for instance, that it is difficult for the Akan to appreciate Gogo music at first hearing. The traditions are different, and musically the structures are different. Even within the national context this is one of the problems we have to face. Teaching peoples of differing ethnic backgrounds to appreciate the music of one another, going beyond our own countries to take a continental view of African music, presents an enormous challenge to the musicologist in Africa.

I know that for many years to come generalizations about the music of Africa cannot be absolute because we have not finished the exploration. However, I do not think that this should prevent us from generalizing in terms of what we know now. The generalization is based on available knowledge, and when we expand the frontiers of our knowledge we will revise our view of the continent. Perhaps those of us in Africa are sometimes too concerned with our local problems, while those who are outside the continent may tend to sacrifice the unique perception to the broader view. But this is where we can complement one another.

Professor Wachsmann remarks on the issue of the distortion of idioms and values in the interpretation of African music. I expect that in the next twenty years we will find that we are more concerned with the material itself than with the correction of image. The kind of exchange that we are having now and the knowledge we are accumulating will enable us to be more objective about African music. The more we know, the less we will feel that we have to apologize for African music or be compelled to praise it. In accepting it for what it is worth, we will come to a point where we will realize that judgments about music will also apply to African music.

But the ethnomusicologist in Africa cannot just look at the material without also thinking about the use of this material. We are confronted with special problems in the training of musicians, and when we, as ethnomusicologists, study music, we have to be concerned with the use of music in traditional society. We will be interested in the relationships between music and ritual, and music and dance, and, arising out of this, the use of music in traditional forms of drama. We are interested in the relationship between music and life, and so we will want to explore all these traditional uses as bases for further musical development in terms of our culture.

The problem of show business which Dr. Wachsmann mentioned is an interesting one to us, but since the pressures are sometimes different in our environment, our response may take a slightly different form. The problem of presentation, for instance, has to be looked at, and the kind of research that the ethnomusicologist does may help the theater person in this respect. In my part of Africa, for example, the dancer dances toward the drummers. In a stage performance, then, the dancer may be dancing with his back to the audience. Now if you change this so that the dancer dances away from the drummer, a break in communication between the drummer and the dancer occurs. To give another example, I remember hearing a criticism of one dance that was being done by the Ghana Dance Ensemble. The form of the dance was correct, but the critic remarked that the person who was dancing was not a royal person. In other words, this was the dance of royalty, and there was an expectation that the character and the costume of the character would show this. This was a chance remark, but it helped the choreographer to think again. When we take performances to villages, we have always observed where people applaud and where they are quiet, in order to see if, in fact, we have been faithful to the tradition or whether we have failed somewhere.

The problem of music history is also very interesting. Professor Wachsmann mentioned the great possibilities of recordings gathered over a span of time. That things change so rapidly now is fascinating to me; even over an interval of ten years it might be worth looking at what has happened. For example, we have recordings done by a group in Kumasi fifteen years ago, and a new band has now been formed which includes some of the members of the earlier group. A colleague of mine is re-recording the group in order to find out what changes have taken place, and why. In addition to this, he is studying other groups which use the same musical form. In this process he is not only discovering the change but he is looking for the dynamics of change in this music.

Along with the study of music history, I think that we will be concerned with problems of music education. This is a part of how we see ethnomusicology, because the process of transmission is involved in music education. We will be interested in looking at techniques of performance in studying values in music—artistic values, social values, and other values—in order to seek out the bases of training in traditional society and determine what we, as musicians, should do in a newer kind of society.

Ali A. Mazrui

Nationalism in colonial Africa played two fundamental roles. The term "African nationalism" is used here in its original sense of a race-conscious, transterritorial, and anticolonial bond between Africans in relation to their land and their rights. In this sense it redefined the area of political activity and the boundaries of political loyalties. The two functions were, of course, closely related but could be analytically differentiated. There can be political loyalties even in situations where there is very little political activity. Yet a process of redefinition is a dynamic one, and loyalties can only be redefined in situations where politics is an active force.

Nationalism as a Politicizing Factor

In what way did nationalism in colonial Africa help to redefine the area of political activity? The question is partly related to the issue of whether tribal communities are political communities at all. It is possible to look at politics as a product of differentiation. In situations where the political, the administrative, the mystical, and the ritualistic are undifferentiated, politics as a distinct activity might not flourish. It might be argued, in fact, that politics would not even exist in such a community. Likewise it might be argued that politics presupposes a discernible class of politicians. Thus, in societies where no distinct class of people are identifiable as politicians, politics would have no autonomous identity. The society might indeed have a system of government, but that is not the same thing as a system of politics.

Those who hold this view would therefore insist that politics is essentially an aspect of modernization. It arises out of structural differentiation and functional specificity. A society develops a polity when political activity becomes more easily isolated from, say, magic or criminal proceedings.

On the basis of such a definition of politics, one might look at African nationalism as the breeding ground of modern politics in Africa. That is why so many observers during the colonial period regarded the growth of political consciousness as virtually the same thing as the growth of nationalism. It was assumed that communities which were completely tribalistic—like the Masai in Kenya and Tanzania or the Karamajong in Uganda—were by definition nonpolitical. But communities which were producing nationalist agitators—like the Ibo in Nigeria or the Kikuyu in Kenya—had *ipso facto* a high degree of political consciousness. The study of African nationalism was therefore the study of the beginnings of modern politics in Africa.

But there are alternative interpretations of the relationship between nationalism and politics during Africa's colonial period. One such interpretation would argue that African nationalism did not signify the birth of politics in Africa, but simply its nationalization. It can be argued that politics did operate within traditional communities in that the complex process of publicly determining *who gets what, when,* was something which went on all the time. Factions disputed resource allocation, and there were methods of resolving conflicting claims. If this is the essence of politics, it was as present in traditional communities as it might be anywhere else.

Under this broader definition of political activity, what African nationalism did was to nationalize politics in each of the African colonial territories. Going beyond intrigue within each ethnic community, nationalism released a consciousness of the territory as a whole as an arena of political argument, struggle, and discourse.

The initial stages of this nationalization of politics did not take the form of a direct struggle for independence but very often took the form of more limited extensions of African political participation at the national level. In British Africa particularly, the legislative council had a special meaning. Political struggle by Africans was initially designed to increase African influence within the legislative council. Political participation was conceived in terms of extending the franchise and increasing African representation within that colonial legislature.

In those countries which had a significant white-settler community, central politics developed quite early, but central politics was not the same thing as national politics. The former was the politics of a central legislative council and of elite activity between government administrators and settler communities, and the early thrust of African nationalism was directed at broadening African participation in this central system. Colonial Kenya was one example of this.

In Kenya the franchise was granted to the settlers quite early and was later extended to the Indian community and then to the Arabs. To the extent that this form of activity was focused on central legislative and administrative institutions of colony-wide significance, Kenya had centrally oriented politics quite early. But the nationalization of politics came only with the increasing involvement of Africans in the central system. The growth of African agitation for participation at the center entailed a growing involvement of indigenous people in national issues. The growing demands for increased African representation in central institutions later culminated in the cry for "Undiluted Democracy" and "One Man, One Vote." The full nationalization of Kenya politics was attained with the Africanization of power. When the reins of government were handed over to indigenous hands, the political system as a whole attained a special level of nationalness.

But the attainment of a transfer of power to African hands has been accompanied by a decline of that phenomenon which we used to call African nationalism. The nationalist movement, which was designed primarily to loosen the controls of alien power, had found sustenance in a particular type of colonial situation. The imperial withdrawal did not mean an immediate end to those emotions, but it has meant a gradual decline of their influence on everyday political behavior. Except in isolated cases, anticolonialism is a battle cry of the past in most African countries.

The decline of African nationalism in many of these countries also meant the decline of national politics. The political parties which captured the wave of nationalist agitation have in many cases now lost their cohesion and sense of purpose.

They have lost some of their old capacity to promote a sense of national involvement. In addition, the decline of political competition and the suppression of political rivals have curtailed the openness of debate and the pursuit of public support on which politics as an activity must inevitably thrive. In some cases, corruption and electoral malpractices have created widespread political cynicism in the populace, making it harder than ever to achieve a sense of real national involvement.

It would be true to say of many African states that the golden age of modern politics for their people coincided with the golden age of African nationalism. When the latter declined as a major determinant of political behavior, modern politics also declined as a national phenomenon. Angling for official favors or intriguing in clandestine ways has, of course, continued. So has some political activity in the villages and district councils. But in a quite fundamental sense, politics in many African countries has, in the last few years, been partially denationalized.

Be that as it may, it was not merely the boundaries of political activity which were redefined by the rise and then decline of nationalism; the boundaries of political loyalties were also affected.

The Retribalization of Politics

The most direct redefinition of loyalties which took place concerned the relative strength of ethnic or tribal loyalties on one side and broader national loyalties on the other. There was an assumption among analysts of the African colonial scene that nationalism got its recruits from the ranks of the detribalized. It was noted that from these ranks came the leaders of the anticolonial agitation, and that these agitators were the first distinct and definable class of politicians produced by modern Africa. The politicians were in the majority of cases Westernized or semi-Westernized, and it is partly this factor which tended to mark them in the eyes of the spectator as a detribalized group.

Yet this whole language of analysis did not adequately differentiate between tribalism as a way of life and tribalism as loyalty to an ethnic group. There were, in fact, two senses of membership of a tribe. One was the sense of belonging, and the other the sense of participating. The quality of belonging simply asserted that one's ethnic affiliation was to that tribe, but the quality of participating implied a cultural affiliation as well. It implied a sharing of the particular tribal way of life. When analysts talked about detribalization, they often meant a weakening of cultural affiliation, though not necessarily a weakening of ethnic loyalty. A person could become Westernized and adopt an almost entirely Western way of life, but he might still retain great loyalty to the ethnic group from which he derived.

An alternative formulation of this distinction is to distinguish tribalism from traditionalism. African nationalism took its leading recruits from the ranks of the detraditionalized, rather than the detribalized. The educated and semieducated Africans who captured leading roles in the agitation movement had indeed lost some aspects of traditional modes of behavior and adopted others under the influence of Western education and control. But the erosion of traditionality did not necessarily mean the diminution of ethnicity.

Among the most radically detraditionalized of all Africans must presumably be included African academics at universities. But the universities of Ibadan and Lagos before the Nigerian coup of January, 1966, were already feeling the internal tensions of conflicting ethnic loyalties. The University College, Nairobi, is currently experiencing comparable difficulties. The Luo as an ethnic group has produced more academics in East Africa than any other single community. This is not simply a matter of size, as there are other ethnic groups of comparable magnitude. No sociological or sociopsychological study has yet been undertaken to explain this phenomenon. Perhaps it is too early to see much significance in it, as the sample of East African scholars is still rather limited. But the simple fact that the number of Luo academics has been disproportionate within the University College, Nairobi, has caused some tension. The situation is not as acute as it must have been at the University of Ibadan before the first Nigerian coup when the Ibo were in disproportionate numbers among several categories of staff. But there is no doubt that at Nairobi, as was the case at Ibadan, even the most highly detraditionalized of all Africans, the scholars, have been feeling the commanding pull of ethnic loyalties.

If one insists on regarding the colonial phenomenon of nationalist agitators as an outgrowth of partial detribalization, one must look at some of the events following independence in Africa as illustrations of partial retribalization. In Nigeria the latter phenomenon attained tragic dimensions.

The Ibo, for so long part of the vanguard of African nationalism, have found themselves since early 1966 retreating into an
ideology of the paramountcy of ethnic interests. Their deepest
political passions were retribalized, and the painful drama of
conflict and civil war in Nigeria began to unfold.

In less stark terms, retribalization is also discernible in
other parts of Africa. In Kenya, Luo ethnicity has probably
significantly deepened since independence, partly as a defen-
sive reaction to some government policies. The political passions of Luo freedom fighters in the colonial struggle have
become to some extent denationalized. The retreat of African
nationalism has helped rekindle some earlier flames.

Implications for Research

The decline of nationalism in Africa has important implications for research, particularly in the field of political science.
We have argued that nationalism as a movement in the colonial period was a major politicizing factor. We have gone
further and suggested that the weakening of nationalistic
sentiments which has come with attainment of independence
has narrowed the area of political activity. There is less national political activity in many African countries today than
there was before independence.

The decline of politics has had ominous implications for
political science in those countries. This is partly because the
decline of politics has been due to a declining openness of the
polity, and political science is par excellence a discipline of
the open society. To take the example of Uganda, it is clear
that public articulation of grievances, as well as open debate
on matters connected with central government policy, was a
more recurrent phenomenon in the first three years of Uganda's independence than it has been since the crisis of 1966.
The Baganda, for so long the most articulate group in the
country, have become relatively silent. Uganda still has an
opposition party, the Democratic Party, and expression of
dissent has by no means been suppressed, but there can be
little doubt that the political system is less open now than it
was a few years ago. Many critical issues about the Baganda,
which might have been easily researchable in 1965, now present great difficulties of access. Yet the Uganda government
can defend itself by arguing that the Buganda area is still
under a state of emergency. Any curtailment of political

curiosity in Uganda has to be given a legal defense, challenge-
able in the courts. And the court system in the country
continues to enjoy unmistakable independence. The legal state
of emergency in Uganda is a device which is after all a
reassuring admission that suppression of dissent is an
abnormality.

There are other African countries where dissent is more
clearly suppressed, and where no opposition party is permitted. In countries where elimination of public articulation of
conflicting interests is so drastically circumscribed, the decline
of politics is more complete. And the decline of politics in this
sense is often also the decline of political science. For political
science, particularly since it is in part the study of sources of
power and its utilization, cannot exist in societies which are
too illiberal. The discipline, almost by definition, tends to be
interested in the more sensitive subjects of study in a society:
What influence does the military exert on political policies in
a country? How are political values and loyalties imparted by
the schools in some other country? What are the real causes of
a current cabinet crisis? What is the role of corruption in the
political system of a developing country? Even in the most
open societies these topics are not always available for investigation. They are, in fact, topics which require a high degree of
political toleration if they are to be glimpsed at all.

It is these considerations which have linked the fate of
political science in Africa with the fate of African nationalism. The decline of African nationalism as a broad anticolonial movement has carried in its wake the decline of political activity itself. And the decline of political activity has
narrowed the area of operation for political science.

Political science is affected not merely by the redefinition of
the arena of politics in developing countries but also by the
redefinition of political loyalties as a national crisis in many
of these countries. African nationalism in the colonial period
was on the whole a race-conscious nationalism which was often
transterritorial, uniting in sympathy Africans in one colony
with Africans in another. The task of nation-building in many
African countries today is a struggle to try to transform this
old race-conscious nationalism into state-conscious patriotism.
The decline of the race-conscious nationalism has, as we have
indicated, often been accompanied by a resurgence of ethnic
loyalties and ethnic antagonisms. The quest for nationhood
after independence is therefore a search for an alternative
intermediate loyalty. In Uganda, for example, loyalties must

be focused at a point somewhere between the transterritorial loyalty to the African race, on one hand, and ethnic loyalty to the Baganda on the other hand.

In the struggle to forge this new identity, the range of political access may be extremely limited for the academic researcher. This restriction of inquiry provides another meeting point between the destiny of African nationalism, the resurgence of ethnic loyalties, and the fate of political science. Gone are the days when leading African nationalists could be interviewed at will by one expatriate graduate student after another. African nationalism during the colonial period needed the publicity which came with political and social science research. But in the effort to develop and consolidate state-conscious loyalties, African leaders may for the time being regard the knowledge to be derived from academic investigation as forbidden fruit.

Conclusion

What of the future? We talk of the future, but African nationalism in its transterritorial and race-conscious form had its heyday in the past. A problem for future research, therefore, is documentation of a historical phenomenon. Considering the deep links that African nationalism has had with politics, communal identity, and research in Africa, there is a compelling case for as comprehensive a recording of this momentous period of African history as our contemporary resources might afford. Many of the participants in this period are alive today, although at the time they were playing their parts African political culture did not include meticulous keeping of written records and personal diaries. The resources of our technological era must now be called to the rescue. Extensive tape-recording of reminiscences and recollections of this period should be undertaken among those who witnessed or experienced some of the major moments of this historical drama.

Makerere University College recently played host to C. L. R. James, the Trinidadian social thinker and veteran Pan-Africanist. We attempted to record some of his reminiscences in a specially arranged seminar, but this was rather *ad hoc* and piecemeal. Here was a person who in the 1930's and 1940's discussed strategies and issues with people like George Padmore, Jomo Kenyatta, and Kwame Nkrumah. James is an enthusiastic writer in his own right, and he will undoubtedly record much of this material himself; but there are a number of other veterans in the story of Pan-Africanism and of African nationalism at large who do not have the same inclination toward keeping records of their memories. Further thought should now be given to the goal of preserving for Africa on tape what might be lost by the relative newness of literary culture in many African societies.

The directions taken by political science field research in the future will necessarily depend on new patterns of identity and of politics which might emerge in Africa. A return to the old form of African nationalism, deeply race-conscious and transterritorial, is not likely to be accomplished in entirety. Another way of expressing the essential goal of transforming this race-conscious nationalism into a state-conscious patriotism is to regard it as a transition from an African assertion of nationalistic feeling to an African creation of nationhood itself. At the moment many of the African states are having to cope with the problems of retribalization and the attendant tensions of instability and fragile legitimacy. These problems are themselves a challenge to political science as the discipline seeks to understand the causes of retribalization and the direction in which it is evolving. Some of the most exciting work in political science in the last ten years has been concerned with these issues of political development and national integration. But the very factors which make these investigations fascinating also make them difficult to carry out. A study of the cause of instability has tremendous potentiality for the understanding of human behavior in the sociopolitical context at large. Yet that very instability often militates against any attempt to put it under any systematic scrutiny. And faced with tasks of national cohesion, African governments are not often tolerant of academic investigations of such topics.

Perhaps there are rare occasions when knowledge should be "forbidden fruit," but to presume to judge which knowledge ought to be forbidden rests on a presumption of omniscience. On the whole there is probably greater risk in perpetuating a state of limited knowledge about a country than in permitting the possibility of accumulating too much knowledge. The process of national integration must in the end include a broad sweep of self-awareness in the country concerned. Such self-awareness should include an understanding of some of the political factors at play in the behavior of the people of that society. In a land badly torn and collectively disturbed by the tensions of faction, political science is certainly not a key to political sanity. But it can make a contribution to the greater sophistication of political consciousness in the country.

Hopefully, political science will be permitted to make such a contribution. A widening of opportunities for political knowledge in the days ahead should open the doors of reciprocity. Students of politics, in the very process of accumulating political data and augmenting the depths of political information and awareness, would help to redeem an old debt. The contribution which African political consciousness made to the emergence of an African political science would at long last be reciprocated through a process of cumulative political cognition in African societies.

REVISION AND UNIFICATION OF AFRICAN LEGAL SYSTEMS: THE UGANDA EXPERIENCE

S. Joshua L. Zake

There has been a very great rate of law formation in the new nations of Africa. The quantity of parliamentary legislation enacted in the post-independence period is in part a reflection of the rapid social change which is occurring in most parts of Africa with the resultant need for new laws to define uniformly the specific legal rights and status of individuals. But it is also a reflection of the process of transition of states from a colonial status to an independent nationhood. The colonial powers, which tended to divide and rule, often administered different ethnic groups as units whose legal systems were presumed to be foreign to one another. Thus political changes that at independence created national communities from various tribal units and ethnic groups dictated corresponding changes in the pre-independence legal systems.

The mere passage from the status of a subject people to that of an independent nation implied that certain legal situations and paraphernalia must also be changed in order to give effect to the political reorganization. In Uganda, for example, it would not have been possible to have an African as president, either executive or constitutional, without also changing the legal framework which had formerly provided for the status and the powers of the governor. A governor stood in a different relationship than would a national president to each of the various ethnic or territorial units of the country and to the several native-court systems. Similarly, when the colonizing community vacated the seat of power, the terms ''native,'' ''African,'' and ''European'' lost meaningful currency in the legal system. What was the exception became normal, and what was previously normal simply disappeared. Revision of the legal system was thus necessary to bring it up to date with the new normal state of affairs. Those who framed the Uganda Independence Constitution foresaw this problem and included in the Constitution provisions which enabled the necessary changes to be made.

Not all constitutional enactments have favored unification. In Uganda in the colonial period each of the various kingdoms had its own court system. At independence in 1962 the kingdom of Buganda insisted on perpetuating its court system, not only by maintaining a separate system, such as it was, but also by establishing a separate High Court of Buganda (as established by Uganda Constitution Instruments, Chapter 9, section 94). This High Court was to ''administer justice in the name of the Kabaka.'' With certain exceptions, the High Court for Buganda had ''within Buganda the same jurisdiction as the High Court of Uganda has within Uganda. . . .'' The Chief Justice and other judges of the High Court of Uganda were to be the judges of the High Court of Buganda. Here efforts to maintain the separate political identity of Buganda spread into the legal system. The result was the perpetuation of a dual system of law and law enforcement which continued to defy efforts to unify the nation after independence.

Customary Practice and the Developing Civil Law

With modernization the introduction of new activities and new practices which impinge on personal interests has made people more conscious of their legal status and more inquisitive of their legal rights. Legislation has been rendered necessary either to define the felt status or to spell out specific legal rights. Over the decades new attitudes toward property have solidified, and new relationships and statuses have developed. Increasingly, legal questions regarding property have been posed before courts of law, and new legislation has been called forth.

Doggedly and persistently a money economy has replaced other exchange systems except in very isolated communities. For instance, the cattle traditionally required of a man as a bride property has, in recent years, taken a cash expression in various communities in many African countries. Similarly, a man now has to work the land and sell his produce or work for wages in order to clothe himself and his family and to send his child to school. For many years people of a certain age have had to pay poll taxes. Governments have had to adopt coercive measures to make people pay taxes, and the tax net, requiring cash payments, has spread wider from year to year, involving more and more people. Now the income tax has arrived, and those with taxable incomes, especially those with sizable taxable incomes, are more conscious than ever of the need to account for their earnings. Whatever is done to affect their financial interest is now relevant.

In response, some of the changes which the government in Uganda has sought to introduce in the substantive law are of the most fundamental nature and often have had a profound influence on the authority of customary law. The law of succession is a good example, as succession is governed both by legislation and by custom. The Succession Ordinance was first introduced in 1906, but by a General Notice issued the same year the governor exempted the estates of all natives. Thus the disposition of these estates was left to the clan heads and the vagaries of customary law. But by the Exemption (Succession) Order of 1966, the whole of the Succession Ordinance is now considered to apply irrespective of race or religion to all estates in Uganda, with the one exception that in the event of intestacy the devolution of estates of persons subject to customary law is still governed by customary law. This application of the Succession Ordinance to all estates fundamentally affects the powers of the clan heads and the entire substratum of customary law.

In the related area of administration of estates, since 1933 the estates of natives were considered to be beyond the powers of the administrator general, who was the public officer entrusted with the administration of estates of persons who die intestate. The Administrator General's (Amendment) Act of 1967 abolished this exempting provision and by so doing left the administrator general as the only official with the power to administer the estate of any person who died intestate. Again the clan heads have been eliminated as administrators. The practical effect of two amendments is to render the clan heads powerless over the estates of deceased persons. Yet the mystic position of the clan heads in relation to the death of persons and the control of the burial and succession rituals has traditionally been the source of the clan heads' spiritual and temporal power. These amendments have therefore severely restricted the application of tribal law and the authority of the clan heads.

At the moment, the Uganda government has under active consideration four bills intended to regulate family law. These concern (1) the registration of births of all citizens, whereas previously the law covered only births of Europeans and Asians; (2) establishment of one law for all marriages of all citizens, including customary marriages; (3) introduction of a fresh law of matrimonial causes; and (4) revision of the act dealing with intestate succession which will set out rules to be followed by the administrator general in his administration of an estate of an African who dies intestate. These amendments represent the first instance in which such rules will have been set down in a written form, extracted as far as can fairly be done from what are believed to be the customary rules and practices. What is more, in each case there will be one act, with certain variations, for all citizens. These new acts will have far-reaching effects on the personal rights and statuses of individuals. It may be said that the sum of these new laws may indeed amount to a social revolution.

It should be noted that it is not the concern of the Uganda government to preserve any particular custom, but it is the government's concern that people's rights be clearly defined in the law, that people should know where they stand so that they can organize their lives and reasonably predict the legal consequences of their actions, and, finally, that for those who want it the law can easily be found.

Criminal Law and Integration of the Court System

One of the most immediate and challenging tasks which faced Uganda as an independent nation was the rationalization of criminal law. As in the case of civil law, there were until independence several systems of criminal law and criminal courts in the country. The criminal law which applied to non-Africans was contained in the Penal Code and Criminal Procedure Codes and in the Police Act. But a large body of unascertained, and in many cases unascertainable, customary criminal law was left to be applied to Africans by the local courts, which were presided over by lay magistrates and had jurisdiction only over Africans.

When Uganda achieved independence it became obvious that this arrangement could not be permitted to continue. We could not have a principle of equality before the law enshrined in our Constitution and then proceed to permit differential treatment for people of different ethnic groups. The unification of criminal law thus became an urgent task. Section 24 (8) of the Independence Constitution of 1962 provided as follows:

(8) No person shall be convicted of a criminal offence unless that offence is defined and the penalty therefor is prescribed in a written law:

Provided that nothing in this sub-section shall prevent a court of record from punishing any person for contempt of itself notwithstanding that the act or omission constituting the contempt is not defined in a written law and the penalty therefor is not so prescribed.

But the proviso to Section 3 of the Independence Order In Council suspended the operation of the above constitutional provision for a period of two years after independence. This was to enable the independent government of Uganda to examine and qualify the law relating to customary offenses.

During this period the national government carried out the widest possible consultations with all the local governments concerned. In the process a great discovery was made, namely, that the only criminal offense in all the land which was not already covered by the Penal Code was the offense of adultery between a man and a married woman. Out of the whole corpus of the so-called customary criminal law, all aspects, with this one exception, were found to be accommodated in the existing Uganda Criminal Law and Procedure. In other words, the unsatisfactory arrangement in the past of dual systems of courts for natives and non-natives existed simply because no one had ever ascertained the extent to which the customary criminal law coincided with statutory law. The colonial powers simply assumed that there was no coincidence whatsoever.

Before the end of the two-year period after independence the Penal Code was amended to include the one offense in customary law which had not been covered by the statutory criminal law. This amendment came into force on December 30, 1964, and on the same day the Magistrates Courts Act, which provides for an integrated system of courts throughout the country, was applied for the first time in one part of the country. By mid-1966 the entire court system was fully integrated.

Political Pressure as a Mechanism of Change

A look at the acts which have been passed since independence in Uganda and Kenya shows that, for all this intensive legislative activity, the number of acts which concern the legal system, either adjectively or substantively, is rather small. This may be a result of the conservatism of the law as well as the tenacity of custom. It might also be argued that in the revolutionary atmosphere which develops before independence and continues after independence, political pressure is a more effective mechanism for change than is the law. Those issues which affect large sections of the population collectively, or about which an articulate section of the population can agitate sufficiently to attract political support, can often be dealt with in a quick, if not a revolutionary, way. On the other hand, those issues which affect people individually or severally, although widespread, concern rights or claims which can be isolated and identified as enjoyable by individuals and so attract general attention slowly. Change in the law that affects the general public as a result of the cumulative complaints of individuals in the courts of law is usually carefully argued and slow to come about.

But the political processes of change operate within a system in which government and Parliament do have certain known and quite often effective sources, both formal and informal, of information about the needs of the people. These sources include political party conferences, District Council resolutions, government commissions, parliamentary group caucuses, and organized pressure groups.

Political party conferences are held annually to review the work of the party in the coming year. These conferences may also pass resolutions and give directives to the executive of the party and to the government in order to effect certain changes in the law.

The District Councils consist of delegates elected to represent people on a more local scale than the parliamentary constituency. These representatives live in the area, and so they are often in a position to discuss issues directly with the people. They may in their District Councils pass resolutions concerning any aspect of law or law enforcement. If several District Councils were to pass a resolution on the same issue this would obviously become sufficiently forceful to attract the attention of the cabinet or the parliamentary group and hence to move Parliament to act.

The government quite often appoints a commission to examine a certain area of government service and to advise on it. The government is, of course, not bound by the advice, but the reports from the commissions are very useful, and often the advice that is given guides the government as to what form of legislation is required. In this connection I would like to mention two commissions which have been very useful in examining certain aspects of the law in Uganda.

The Kalema Commission was appointed in January, 1964, to report on marriage, divorce, and the status of women. This commission had the most interesting terms of reference:

> To consider the laws and customs regulating marriage, divorce and the status of women in Uganda, bearing in mind the need to ensure that those laws and customs while preserving existing traditions and practices, as far as possible, should be consistent with justice and morality and appropriate to the position of Uganda as an independent nation and to make recommendations.

The report of the commission was presented in July, 1965. It was so strongly supported by some and so fiercely opposed by others that when it was published the government had to be very careful in proceeding on the basis of the report.

The Law Reform Committee is a permanent commission charged with the duty of reviewing any law of Uganda from time to time and making any necessary recommendations to the cabinet. The cabinet is not bound by these recommendations but must give them the most serious consideration. It was this committee which reviewed the Kalema Commission's report. As a result of the review, the four bills I have referred to above (those on registration of births, marriages, matrimonial causes, and intestate succession) were prepared and put before the cabinet.

The parliamentary group of the government party is another source of information. The cabinet and the back benchers meet before Parliament sits and also whenever they are called upon by the government chief whip to discuss impending parliamentary business. Bills that are to be introduced at the next parliamentary session will be discussed. Members of government and representatives of the people do come to these meetings with certain views, some of which are their own and some those of their constituencies. Recently, we have introduced the death penalty for robbery and attempted robbery with aggravated violence. This law received the widest support throughout the country, but the parliamentary group gave very careful consideration to it as each member of Parliament had with him evidence to support its introduction.

In every community there are pressure groups which make representations to the government and to members of Parliament to try to effect changes in existing law. In Uganda some of the most vocal pressure groups are the Uganda Council of Women, the Wet Coffee Processing Association, the Trade Unions, the Uganda Law Society, the Uganda Teachers' Association, and the Farmers' Unions. These pressure groups are generally concerned with a specific problem, and they attempt to change the law only insofar as their particular interest is affected.

Usually the type of information that comes from these sources tends to be of a general nature. This information helps the cabinet and members of Parliament to isolate problems, to identify the areas where these problems exist, and to recognize possible lines of action. More specific recommendations may come from the commissions, such as the Kalema Commission and the Law Reform Committee. (The Kalema Commission itself did not go far enough in its recommendations for supplementing its report, and it was necessary to call in the Law Reform Committee to actually work out the legislative details of what had been reported and recommended by the Kalema Commission.)

Research into Law in Africa

There are, and will continue to be, forces which will press for changes in legal systems in new nations, and there are sources which provide a certain amount of information about the needs of the people. But it is clear that general information about these needs is not enough and that a more concentrated research effort is necessary in order to define the dimensions of the required new laws or amendments to the existing law. The work of the Law Reform Committee referred to above clearly indicates the value of close examinations of the law and points to the need for research in certain areas. We must, however, examine how we should proceed if research is to be of value.

Legal research in Africa has not attracted many students, either as lawyers or anthropologists. There have been a few outstanding works in this field, such as Max Gluckman's *Judicial Process Among the Barotse of Northern Rhodesia* and Paul Bohannan's *Justice and Judgment among the Tiv.* There is a considerable body of descriptive or documentary work setting out what a system is and what rules are being applied in it. Rather than the documentary work, however, I would like to see analytical examinations of the effect of a particular rule of law in a community. If funds are available, research should be undertaken to evaluate the efficacy of a chosen law and to sound the reactions of people to laws and their enforcement. Much valuable information would be obtained from such research, and this information could be very useful to the lawmakers.

Unfortunately, much of what has been written reflects prejudices or preconceived ideas of African law. People talk about "African law," and teach it, but over the years little attention has been paid by scholars to the law in its reality. The London school of thought on African law became fashionable at an early date, and, ironically, a number of Africans have gone to the Inns of Court in London to be taught "African law." Just how static and unresponsive to reality this concept of African law has been is well illustrated by the ease with which the court system in Uganda was integrated once the content of customary law was actually analyzed. There was previously supposed to be a great difference between the Penal Code introduced by the British and the customary law in Uganda. Until this supposition was examined it was responsible for the continuation of the so-called customary law and the native criminal courts. A very great number of actions for which people were punished simply were not illegal. They were merely actions which provoked the displeasure of a chief or his underlings or were acts of disobedience which at most required only some disciplinary measure, not criminal punishment.

It is clear that a new and progressive approach in research into African law is necessary. The forces which influence ideas in any community in any part of the world also work in Africa. Customs are not static, and in modern Africa transition is occurring faster than in most areas of the world. If a fresh and progressive approach is not brought into research work, scholars may continue to talk out of historical context and to follow a phantom which has little substance in the living reality of the law.

Although the need for research is enormous, priority might be given to one area rather than to another. Looking at the broad spectrum of peoples' rights and statuses, it would appear, for example, that there are signs of strain in relations between landlord and tenant in Uganda. A research priority, then, might be land law. In Buganda the basic types of title, namely, freeholds, leaseholds, and the customary *kibanja* (meaning a large unsurveyed plot), are beginning to be inconsistent with realities as commerce brings its influence to bear on land as a source of income. The present Basulu and Nvujjo law provides simple rules of customary occupancy: as long as a *kibanja* tenant pays 8.50 shillings a year, he and his successors are entitled to stay on the *kibanja* plot in perpetuity. This provision has had an adverse effect on the development of African-held land, which forms by far the largest portion of freehold land in Uganda. The law has produced a situation where the tenant has little incentive to develop his *kibanja*. He is secure in his tenure, and his rights are inexpensive, although vague, since the same law which provides for his occupancy does not permit him to sell the *kibanja* or in any way alienate it. The law has prevented the more progressive landlords from carrying out improvement schemes on their land because of the expense involved in compensating these perpetual *kibanja* rights which cannot under the present law be changed, even as a contribution toward a general land-improvement scheme. Furthermore, the law provides that a *kibanja* tenant will be required to pay an annual due of about four shillings in respect of any economic crops grown and harvested on the land. This sum was fixed some forty years ago at a time when the only crops grown were cotton and coffee, and it is now a general nuisance both to landlord and tenant. Today, of course, there is much more economic activity on the land, such as dairy farming, poultry farming, and intensive market gardening. The law in this regard operates in favor of the *kibanja*-holder as against the landowner.

It will be seen from this brief analysis of the Busulu and Nvujjo that the time is more than ripe for a complete reappraisal of land-law provisions to bring them into line with modern land usage. It is also clear that customary practices with regard to land tenure are now irrelevant, but it would be equally inappropriate to apply English law in its entirety to this question.

The task before us is to determine what rules of occupation are now most fitting, that is to say, what rules would release both the tenant and the landlord from the tyranny of archaic customary practices of land tenure. In order to determine these rules we must go to the land market and to those people who live on the land, whether they be tenants or landlords, and who therefore have to bargain for their rights and claims. We want to know what is actually happening between landlord and tenant or between seller and buyer, whether of the land itself or of the *kibanja*. These are live problems and, regardless of what the courts may say, many dealings are carried on in the countryside over land rights, land holdings, and immovable properties. Most of these transactions are quite foreign to English land law and are probably peculiar to tenure in Buganda. Research is necessary to indicate what types of revisions are necessary in the law.

There must, however, be two guiding principles for researchers: (1) Whatever inquiry is made must be in relation to some practical problem. Considerable research has been done and many papers are hidden away in the archives of university libraries, but research that cannot treat of a problem that is of immediate relevance to us now would in my judgment be unnecessary and a waste of good time and useful funds. (2) There must, as far as is practically possible, be effective coordination of research projects with new developments and research programs. Nation-building requires that the issues which are related to the problem that is being examined should be understood by the research student, and he should, if possible, make it clear that these issues do exist, even if they do not constitute part of his study. This will help in pointing out possible lines of research in other areas and also in reminding those concerned with policy-making that examining one area of the social service of a community and finding solutions in that area does not exhaust their duty to continue research for the overall development of their country. These principles for research are of a general nature, applicable to legal as well as to other types of research.

In conclusion, I would like to say that we in Uganda believe that our legal system, like any other aspect of our national service, must be developed thoughtfully. We must pay attention to it, for example, as we pay attention to the development of education or commerce or communications or public health services. We feel, therefore, that to develop the courts and the agencies of law enforcement to an optimal usefulness we must proceed along guidelines determined by informed opinion. We are thus convinced of the need for sustained research. To this end, the Uganda government has decided to set up what is going to be known as the Law Development Center.

Before establishing this center, the solicitor-general of Uganda and myself carried on quiet discussions with various people in East Africa as well as in the United Kingdom and in the United States. We are still carrying on consultations, so I cannot at this moment discuss the constitution of the Center. However, certain principles have been agreed upon and certain sections of the work to be done there have been finalized so that the Center could be unofficially opened in the fall of 1968.

The Law Development Center will, among other activities, offer facilities for legal research. There will be no limitation to the scope of inquiry except that such inquiry be in accordance with the guiding principles mentioned above and, of course, within our financial ability to maintain such facilities. I hope that those interested—whether in private practice, or at the bench, or in the attorney-general chambers, or at Makerere, or even those who are not lawyers so long as they are interested and can contribute through research—will take advantage of the facilities we propose to offer. The Law Development Center will be working in close cooperation with Makerere University College. Already some of the people who will be members of the staff at the Center are lecturing in law at the new Law Department at Makerere. I must, however, underline the point that at the Center emphasis will be placed on the practical approach, which will be the best way to insure a fresh attitude toward legal systems in the new nations of Africa.

DISCUSSANT'S COMMENTS 10.

Alexander Nekam

I would like to speak briefly about one of the topics Mr. Zake has raised in his paper, the modernization of law in Africa. Within the last few years I have been twice in Uganda, studying in the field the workings of customary law of the traditional type. What I am going to say is based on these experiences, even though I cannot here attempt to document my conclusions.

There is one task which, it seems to me, by far outweighs in importance all the other problems African governments at present have to face: the task of making a nation out of their country, of fusing into one single community all those who live within the geographical limits of their power. To achieve this these governments must encourage and develop new loyalties which will be shared by all and which thus will facilitate the emergence of a unified viewpoint. At the same time they must try to diminish and, if possible, rechannel the centrifugal, disruptive loyalties of the past, those traditional loyalties which attach themselves to the tribe and the clan.

This, I feel sure, is how the African governments themselves evaluate their problem. It seems to me therefore that when they attempt to modernize their law, they do this not so much in order to achieve a new social order, to introduce socialism or a local variety of capitalism, or to implement some revolutionary experiment—important though such purposes might appear to some of these governments—but, above all, in order to create a state-wide community: to develop, through the creation of a uniform legal system, new loyalties of a unifying kind.

It is, I suppose, quite inevitable that much of this new, more uniform legal system should be Western-oriented: the changes came through the West, the West alone seems to have the easy know-how and the ready-made answers to cope with these changes. Still, here again, the main purpose can hardly be said to be Westernization; it is simply to establish, in the quickest possible way, a uniform system which applies to all within the state and which demands loyalty to nothing but the state.

The greatest obstacle in the path of unification is customary

law of the traditional type. Tribally oriented, the breeder of
parochial loyalties, it has to be subdued and reoriented if
unity throughout the state is to be achieved. All African
governments agree on this. They all try to neutralize customary law and to appropriate it for their own purposes.
They attack it directly, through legislation by revamping
procedure and diluting substance, by codifying what they declare to be the common essence of all customary law, and by
applying it everywhere in the same way. More importantly,
they attack customary law in an indirect way. They re-
educate the magistrate, cutting him off from his tribal roots
and indoctrinating him with Western patterns and imported
solutions. Traditionally, the magistrate is the mouthpiece of
his community; the law he dispenses is the customary law.
Once the magistrate is won over and his thinking is made to
reflect what the government wants to achieve, a new, uniform
system will emerge, changing the past without the outward appearance of change.

It is not easy to evaluate how successful these efforts are
likely to be and how they will influence the future of African
societies. Studying communities more remotely placed, where
the traditional ways still are strong and the challenge of the
outside world still is weak and intermittent, one might judge
these methods ineffectual and the attempt to harness customary law doomed to failure. On such people the efforts of the
government hardly seem to have an impact at all. The settled
order continues; the official courts are bypassed; the new
dispensation ignored. The government and its ways are felt to
be alien, the law by which the people live and the law officially
declared do not seem to meet at all.

Yet, on reflection, one's conclusions should be different.
Strong as many such communities still appear to be, their
strength is deceptive and is bound to fade away. Isolation
alone protects them and isolation cannot much longer be maintained. The outside world moves closer every day. Economic
changes and alien ways of life intrude all over. New tastes and
new values, new bases of comparison appear. People become
restless, they go away to school, they leave to find work, they
meet and marry outside. Their loyalties are weakened and
tend to disappear; the same values which a short time ago
were accepted as self-evident and natural are now felt to be
confining, artificial, unacceptable.

Change is the general pattern all over Africa: swift-moving,
pervasive, irreversible. The changes come too fast and go too

deep for these communities to assimilate them. Thus circumstances achieve what the government alone could hardly have done, they disrupt from the inside what a direct attack might never have succeeded in destroying.

In spite of all its difficulties and frustrations, the government is actually battling an enemy already defeated, one which may soon disappear altogether. Thus the main problem should no longer be how to achieve victory, but what to do once victory is achieved.

These traditional communities, as disruptive and antiquated as they have become, are alone in keeping alive much of what is distinctive and irreplaceable in the African way of life. Saving from this tradition whatever can be redeemed means saving the very fiber of these nations, their past, their personality.

It is easy to become overly enthusiastic about the new, to belittle one's own, and to overvalue what has been successful abroad. This is what is happening today in Africa in connection with the changing and modernizing of the law. Much that could have been saved has already been destroyed, even more seems immediately threatened.

To mold a unified nation still remains the first duty of an African government—we are all agreed on that. We must also admit that, for better or worse, Africa has by now been exposed to Western influence to the point where the Western pattern must remain dominant in the law. All this inevitably involves not only change, but much destruction and waste. Because so much will have to go in any case, what can be retained should be doubly protected. A most discriminating appraisal of what remains is needed, as is a careful attempt to blend the past with the needs of the future and a dedicated determination to save the African roots of the law in Africa.

Only the government can do this and only if it decides to act at once. Mistakes cannot be corrected once the past has gone. Everything unnecessarily discarded will one day be regretted. It will be a loss not only to Africa but to the whole world as well.

PROBLEMS IN THE CONSTRUCTION 11.
OF VIABLE CONSTITUTIONAL STRUCTURES
IN AFRICA

Kwamena Bentsi-Enchill

In considering the theme, "the next twenty years in African research," the task I have set myself is to delineate one broad and difficult area of research, namely, the need to confront that vast group of problems that surround the establishment of sound constitutional governments in African states. This is perhaps the most important and pressing of the many research needs that clamor for attention; and the challenge to the researcher is great, as may be indicated in a preliminary fashion by a series of questions.

What are the institutional problems in the establishment—the stable and solid establishment—of the political kingdom in Africa? Are there any peculiar features of the African situation which must engage the attention of the institution-builder seeking to solve these problems? Above all, what can research scholars, in Africa and abroad, do to assist in the solution of these problems?

Research in this area is, in my opinion, urgently needed. In Ghana today the launching of a new constitution is the central question. This has been true of Sierra Leone and Uganda, and it will be the case in Nigeria when peace is achieved. Just beyond the horizon in Kenya the same questions are hovering. Both at the attainment of independence in the several African states and since, the fleeting opportunity has arisen—sometimes, with the recent coups, more than once—to make a new beginning, to refashion the institutions of government and establish enduring commonwealths suited to local needs and circumstances. The challenge thus presented to Africans to respond with acts of creative wisdom is one that must be met with success, and the question of the day, I repeat, is this: What can research scholars in Africa and elsewhere do to assist Africans in the making of this creative response?

The justification for urging sustained research in this difficult area can be advanced on various grounds. The first is suggested by the biblical injunction, "Seek ye first the Kingdom of God and its righteousness and all these things shall be added unto you." Kwame Nkrumah, it may be recalled, substituted "political kingdom" for the words "Kingdom of God"; but he seems to have been saying much the same thing and promising much the same rewards. Be that as it may, the argument that a stable and responsible political order is essential for the attainment of other goals of community living would seem to be unanswerable.

Secondly, I would argue, it matters very much how a nation is launched. As in the boxing arena, it helps greatly if a useful set of rules is agreed upon before the start of a match, especially when the referee enforces these rules with skill. Though social forces will affect and mold any constitution, the constitution may itself become a social force generating instruction and habits of support for its successful functioning.

This line of reasoning may seem to risk falling into a fallacy of eighteenth-century naivete, that is, the facile supposition that all one has to do to achieve a viable, stable, and effective system of representative government is to enact a well-conceived formal constitutional structure. Such a criticism, however, would be unfair, for the contention here is not that this is *all* one has to do but rather that this is one of the things that must be accomplished and that it is an inexcusable waste of opportunity not to make every effort to achieve this kind of beginning. Indeed, the question must be asked: How can anyone concerned with the achievement of national unity, or the study of the factors making for national unity, legitimately ignore the constitution-making process or overlook the potential function of a constitution as the most effective symbol of the unifying forces operative in a community? Can one study the factors making for national unity in Nigeria, for instance, and ignore the institutional factors that have linked the Hausa with the Ibo?

My line of reasoning may also expose me to the accusation

that I am calling for Western research workers to go and lecture the Ghanaians or Nigerians on how to settle their institutional problems. Such a criticism is unnecessary because obviously the final decisions will be taken by the Ghanaians and the Nigerians themselves, and mostly by their political decision-makers. But this fact does not exonerate scholars in Africa and elsewhere in the relevant fields from a certain responsibility to these decision-makers. Where sifted information and knowledge are needed for the wise determination of issues upon which may depend a nation's success or failure, scholars can be accused of having failed their nation if they do not make the necessary effort to review the required information and acquire the necessary knowledge and to communicate it effectively to the decision-makers. This comment is, of course, addressed primarily to the scholars of the nation in question, but foreign scholars do not completely escape a certain responsibility, especially where their researches have also been focused on the problems of that nation. And the very nature of African institutional objectives dictates a further consideration for scholars, both African and foreign. The search of each of these African countries for a more perfect union and the pressure for rapid development on all fronts pose a need for basic knowledge about the comparative efficiency of different systems of institutions for the achievement of their complex and various goals. As no nation can claim to have achieved a complete solution, there is a need for institutional studies which show up the weaknesses as well as the strengths of different institutional configurations and expedients. In a world of conflicting ideologies some scholars operating within each ideological system can reasonably be expected to make objective comparative studies of the merits and demerits of their institutional systems as contrasted with others, and to make such information available to interested countries. In a world groping toward peace, settled order, and development, there is surely a need for a sustained questing after institutional devices that can assist in the attainment of these goals.

Brief notice must now be taken of one other line of criticism which may be advanced regarding the research I am advocating. I could be accused of urging my fellow Africans to copy a foreign example at a time when their proper endeavors should be toward original thinking based on the historic experience of their countries and the imperatives of their own cultures and aspirations. The short answer is that I am not only calling on my fellow Africans to do some original thinking, but I am proposing some of the steps that we must take to liberate ourselves for this endeavor. Conditioned as we are by our education and experience to think institutionally in terms of French or British models, my call is for the comprehensive and eclectic scrutiny of foreign systems and a hard, objective look at the realities of our domestic situation and the provisions of our traditional laws and customs. Only in this way can we begin to do some independent thinking.

Independent thinking, however, does not exclude deliberate borrowing and adaptation. We in Africa have no need to apologize if in our mature judgment we decide to borrow institutional arrangements from one or several foreign systems. Nor need anyone entertain the notion that by borrowing we will cease to be a distinctive people. Differentiation has an ineluctable persistence, and we shall not cease to be different from the peoples from whom we may decide to borrow an institution, or even a language!

So much by way of justification for the proposed area of research. I must now turn to a closer delineation of the area of inquiry. But first of all, some indication of my own involvement in the matter may be in order. Here is the description I gave of my chosen theme for a research seminar that I conducted at Northwestern University when I visited in 1965–66: "The seminar will investigate some specific problems of African political organization, the philosophies behind some of the solutions that have been attempted, the factors conducive to political instability, and will attempt a critical appraisal of various remedies proposed or proposable." The concern to bring an organized and informed discussion by leading scholars in the field to bear on the thinking that was going on in Ghana and Nigeria was my main theme of discussion both here and elsewhere at the time I was leaving the United States for Zambia. And in January, 1967, it proved possible for me to assemble at Freetown an informal gathering of Ghanaian and Nigerian lawyers and political scientists, including one sociologist and one economist, for an informal seminar on the problems of institution-building in our two countries. Unfortunately my duties in Lusaka have since interrupted plans for similar meetings and for the launching of an all-African Action Group for African Reconstruction and Institution-Building. It is certainly gratifying to return to Northwestern in 1968 and find a major project afoot for research into the problems of national unity in Africa. I would wish to see included in this program, however, a research concern in the techniques of social engineering in the nation-building task. In my opinion a major research endeavor can and must be focused on the system of formal and informal institutions and procedures called the constitution as well as on the component materials and techniques which the constitutional engineer must employ.

The concerns that led to the summoning of the Freetown seminar were described by me as follows:

> To the peoples of Ghana and Nigeria an unusual oppor-
> tunity has presented itself. This is the opportunity to re-
> organize our political life, to refashion the institutions of
> government, and to create enduring modern common-
> wealths suited to the needs and conditions of our diverse,
> but freedom and progress wanting, peoples.
>
> Opportunities of this kind do not often occur; nor do
> they last forever, as is shown by the crises we have recently
> passed through. A quick contrast between the hopes and
> enthusiasms of the immediate pre-independence phase and
> the malaise of the immediate pre-coup period suffices for
> illustrations of this point.
>
> Somehow the present opportunity must be used with the
> keenest sense of local realities, the most exhaustive con-
> sultation of the teachings of our experience as well as that
> of others elsewhere, and all our resources of wisdom and
> foresight. And on this basis must be mounted a supreme
> effort of original creative thinking and the systematic de-
> velopment of a broad consensus regarding our social and
> political institutions.

Our Freetown seminar singled out twelve critical questions or problems for discussion as being among the central issues to which attention must be paid in any attempt to fashion institutions to fit conditions in Ghana and Nigeria. These were (1) the importance of clarifying fundamental objectives; (2) the problem of the harnessing and controlled release of social and political power; (3) the problem of diverse populations and multiple cultures; (4) the need to foster national unity and the use of evolutionary methods of government; (5) the importance of making use of relevant elements in traditional political ideas, institutions, and processes; (6) economic devel-opment; (7) social and economic justice; (8) the need for legitimizing the authority of new institutions; (9) the prob-lem of political parties and representation; (10) fundamental liberties; (11) the problem of effective communication and the use of the media of mass communication; and (12) the assessment of specific institutions and machinery in terms of their appropriateness for use in these countries.

These topics point to research needs that must be met as part of an organized inquiry into the conditions for successful constitutional engineering in Africa. In any effort to meet these needs various research designs and methods will have to be adopted, including historical studies, institutional studies, process studies of public-policy decisions, attitude studies, and case studies of communities. Quantitative methods may find little scope here, and other methods will have to be employed, including a skillful use of comparative methods and of simulation techniques. Important work has been done in each of these spheres for Western countries, and one of the immediate needs is to assemble and sift all the relevant work as an aid to formulating new questions.

The discussion at the Freetown seminar was fruitful in deciding some controlling assumptions or considerations for constitutional engineering. Two of these may be mentioned here. To the first question calling for a clarification of basic objectives the answer was this: effective democratic government compounded with the highest possible and compatible rate of economic development firmly reflected in higher standards of living for the individual citizen and within a framework of respect for fundamental liberties. Was this a realistic conclusion? At least the objective is squarely proclaimed in the newly proposed draft constitution for Ghana. There can be little doubt that this is what the Nigerians will want. And one can add that the recent Czechoslovak crisis and the facts leading to the destalinization campaign in the Soviet Union all provide support for research into the conditions for effective and stable democracy based on the supposition that this is what people want.

Another topic that was isolated was the problem of diverse populations and multiple cultures. There was agreement about the fundamental importance of this problem and about the challenge to create a nation out of heterogeneous peoples. In this connection it was noted that British and French presuppositions have not been helpful. The African states do not have the time at their disposal for achieving the cultural unity which has come to France and England and countries like Holland, Denmark, Sweden, and Norway through long and arduous processes. If anything, the persistence of significant elements of ethnic cleavage, for example, in the United Kingdom, is suggestive. There would seem to be no basis for distinguishing the ethnic problems in Canada, Belgium, Yugoslavia, or Czechoslovakia from those encountered in other states. A careful scrutiny of these foreign situations was seen to be important, and attention was drawn to factors contributing to the triumph of the Swiss over the problem of cultural disunity. It seemed evident to the seminar that the facts of cultural diversity must be accepted instead of being dismissed under terminology such as tribalism or retribalization, and that room should be made for the expression of specific cultures in their various areas. These factors were seen to argue strongly in favor of regional and local devolution of authority, though that need not mean the total insulation of one culture from the other. The systematic promotion of cross-ethnic organizations—ranging from schools and national universities to professional and trade associations and various branches of the public service—was seen as a method of keeping open avenues of interaction between the different cultures.

These two examples should suffice to show that major areas of investigation clamor for willing laborers. Another important area of political action to be considered in constitutional engineering is the question of political parties. None of the independence constitutions made any provision for them. Constitutions of the eighteenth century had not provided for parties; it was only after these constitutions came into being that modern political parties emerged as vital elements of the democratic process. But today failure to attend to the engineering problem of regulating the emergence of parties and the permissible modes of their operation is inexcusable. Notwithstanding all the talk of freedom of association, it is clear that political effectiveness in any of the viable modern democracies compels every serious political aspirant to operate through one or another of a limited number of political parties. In fact, it might even be argued that under optimal conditions a democratic polity should have not more than two political parties. Those who seek to establish a modern democracy may be confronted with the important engineering problem of arranging institutions in such a way as to achieve the two-party system.

The challenges to constitutional engineering are multiple, and all require research and synthesis of knowledge and experience to the desired end of informed decision-making at critical junctures in political history. Among these challenges might be included the problem of reorganizing the civil-service machinery to cope with the requirements of the modern welfare state, and the organizing of the electoral process in such a way as to minimize the influence of wealth.

There is one plausible line of criticism to which I lay myself open in pressing for sustained research in the area of constitutional engineering. The question may be asked: Are you not aware of the great difference between constitutional forms and political reality—that governmental institutions in their actual practice deviate from their formal competences? If so, why then should not the main resources be applied to the study of the political reality?

My proposal, however, is not to ignore social reality but rather to take the fullest possible account of it in social and legislative engineering. The only striking fact about the perceived divergence between formal governmental institutions and their practical working is that this divergence reveals the nature of law and of politics and dramatizes the problems of effective lawmaking. So too with constitutions, which are fundamental law. A constitution is a control mechanism, a regulatory device that channels conduct, whether of the government or of the populace, in directions which otherwise might not be followed in its absence or without enforcement. It provides facilities for peaceful collaboration and processes for conflict resolution. It is necessarily distinct from the social reality in which it operates. Yet it must be close and sensitive to the social milieu which it regulates, and it must be substantially acceptable to that society if it is to function satisfactorily. Between a constitution and the community for which it is the regulatory mechanism a gap must necessarily exist. Whether the gap is wide or narrow will depend on many factors, including its acceptability to the community and its enforcement machinery. These many factors must be fully comprehended by the would-be constitutional engineer. Successful engineering could enable a constitution to function as the most effective symbol of the unifying forces operative in a community, and broadly based researches in applied social science would seem to be essential to such successful social engineering.

GEOGRAPHY, SPATIAL PLANNING, 12.
AND AFRICA: THE RESPONSIBILITIES
OF THE NEXT TWENTY YEARS

Peter R. Gould

Introduction: The Academy and the State

In view of the great surge of activity bordering upon a
renaissance in geography during the last decade,[1] a person has
to possess considerable temerity or gall to predict "the next
twenty years in African research." Few geographers in the
late fifties would have predicted the way in which geographical problems in Africa are being examined today,[2] or the way
in which a number of African geographers are influencing the
methodological and conceptual revolution that characterizes
contemporary work in the behavioral and social sciences.[3]
With training programs at both the undergraduate and graduate levels that are radically different from a decade before,
with increasing emphasis upon more formal modeling and

1. Peter R. Gould, "Methodological Developments in Geography Since
the Fifties," in *Progress in Geography 1*, ed. by P. Haggett and R. Chor-
ley (forthcoming).

2. Edward W. Soja, *The Geography of Modernization in Kenya* (Syracuse: Syracuse University Press, 1968); and R. Mansell Prothero, *Migrants and Malaria* (London: Longmans, 1965).

3. Enid R. Forde, *The Population of Ghana: A Study of the Spatial Relationships of Its Sociocultural and Economic Characteristics* (Evanston,
Ill.: Northwestern Studies in Geography, No. 15, 1968); and Akin L.
Mabogunje, "Urbanization in Nigeria—A Constraint on Economic Development," *Economic Development and Cultural Change*, VIII (1965),
413–38.

inquiry, and with the widespread availability of large computers for instructional purposes, it would be both foolish and impertinent to predict the course of geographical research in Africa to the year 1990. It is for these reasons that I chose to include and emphasize two words in the title of this paper: *spatial* and *responsibilities.*

The first word is *spatial,* qualifying planning. Implicit in the notion of planning is the concept of *time.* Indeed, common units for the measurement of time are contained in the title of those documents embodying the hopes and desires of so many African countries today. Three-year plans, five-year plans, ten-year plans—all of them sequence human aspirations upon a continuum of time. National economies are broken into sectors, which are then further disaggregated before all the pieces are reassembled to form a goal far along the temporal continuum. Few plans, however, emphasize the spatial dimension which is the geographer's particular concern. But as planning questions at the national level become more and more critical, it is clear that the dimensions of space may be ignored only at a considerable price. Those who have worked at the national,[4] regional,[5] urban, or micro level realize only too well that the sequencing of the "wheres" in space is as important as the sequencing of "whens" in time if a country is to make the most efficient use of its human and natural resources.

The second word emphasized is *responsibilities.* Such emphasis is directed mainly at academic colleagues engaged in African research, and it reflects two things: first, the lack of feedback from academic research to the governments and agencies of those host countries in which research was undertaken, and second, the seeming irrelevance of much scholastic inquiry by social and behavioral scientists in general, and geographers in particular. In our position of great, and rightfully guarded, freedom to inquire, what academic luxuries can we morally afford today? Every geographer will answer this question in different ways, but he who does not ask the question at all will find the answer being provided for him by his students—if he has any.

Despite the fact that the phrase "it's academic" has become

4. John Friedman, *Regional Development Policy: A Case Study of Venezuela* (Cambridge: The M.I.T. Press, 1966).

5. L. P. Green and T. J. D. Fair, *Development in Africa: A Study in Regional Analysis with Special Reference to Southern Africa* (Johannesburg: Witwatersrand University Press, 1962).

synonymous with "it's irrelevant," it will be clear from my later remarks that I am not implying that all geographers should immediately engage in the day-to-day regional planning problems that continually vex and dismay the responsible politician and government servant. Should we give up academic inquiries in the best sense, it would not be long before the well of conceptual insights with practical implications would dry up. Rather, I emphasize the geographer's responsibilities beyond the academic walls so that future research may at least consider the question of practical and educational pertinence, and so that relevant findings are communicated quickly to those faced with planning decisions. These decisions are frequently difficult to make because information of a factual or structural nature is lacking. Thus, if anything should characterize responsible geographic research to the twenty-first century in Africa, it is strong flows of information between the academy and the state.

Getting Down to Facts

In a recent review of contemporary aspects of geography and their ties to regional and national planning questions, Torsten Hägerstrand noted, "If we look away from certain rather new sorts of purely theoretical investigation which can be undertaken without very much of an observational base, geographical research almost by definition has to be founded on empirical data."[6] No geographer who has worked in Africa would deny the truth of such an observation, for much time and energy must be spent on the laborious and painstaking task of data-gathering. So obvious and so frequently pedestrian is the task of data-gathering that its fundamental importance is seldom discussed or emphasized. But given our present state of ignorance, it is only information in the form of relevant and reliable facts that can provide the sure base from which to build. As Blair Kinsman has noted in another but closely allied field, "When you know nothing a little data does wonders for locating the phenomenon."[7]

6. Torsten Hägerstrand, "The Computer and the Geographer," *Transactions of the Institute of British Geographers*, No. 42 (December, 1967), pp. 1–19.

7. Blair Kinsman, *Wind Waves: Their Generation and Propagation on the Ocean Surface* (Englewood Cliffs, N. J.: Prentice-Hall, 1965), p. 450.

Peter R. Gould

Information: What facts do we want?

Given the high cost of obtaining reliable information, we should be able to assume that it is collected to some purpose by governments and geographers. The collection of information, whether for scholarship or planning, implies a theoretical framework, however weak, on the part of the former, and purposeful, goal-directed inquiry on the part of the latter. But in Africa, as elsewhere, those basic assumptions often do not hold, and much money and human energy are expended each year to collect information that is never used.[8] Statistical abstracts and reports from most African countries are loaded with irrelevant and unreliable figures whose collection was started in colonial times but which today are virtually worthless. In the meantime, information that could sharpen both spatial planning decisions and academic research goes uncollected for lack of funds and proper direction. An example, which African research workers could multiply a distressing number of times, emphasizes this point.

This example relates to an origin-destination survey, which is one of the most valuable types of information for geographers and planners since it informs them what moves from where to where, and when, within a region or country. Forming the basis for many geographical studies with any pretense to structural or dynamic insights, and serving as the fundamental data input for many transportation, agricultural, industrial, and social-planning decisions, the origin-destination survey is perhaps *the* most essential data source for spatial research. While such data sources hardly exist in Africa today, a reasonably large-scale survey was started in Ghana as early as 1956–57. Costing thousands of pounds, and engaging the time and energy of hundreds of men for one week during every month of the year, it took six men a further year to compile and sort the preliminary returns from the individual checkpoints. Unfortunately, except for those engaged directly in the survey, no one seemed to know it was going on. Wheels that started turning at the end of the colonial period continued to turn under their own momentum during the first days of independence, and no use was ever made of the information either by transport or other planners.

Too much information-gathering is characterized by such

8. Peter R. Gould, *Data, Decisions and Development in Transportation: Some Lessons from the East African Experience* (report submitted to the Brookings Institution, 1963), pp. 61–63.

lack of coordination, as well as by extreme delay in getting the compiled facts into the channels of decision-making. It is here that geographers, together with their colleagues in regional planning and other academic fields, must take on the responsibility of advising statistical departments as to which facts are the truly relevant ones. Geographers, perhaps more than members of any other single academic discipline, have a tendency in their spatial and synthetic overview to use information of many different kinds. Providing their intellectual sympathies lie with the task of the regional planner, they and the economists are probably in the strongest position to urge revision upon government statistical departments which appear to continue the data-gathering tasks of the colonial period in lieu of thinking through the new national requirements brought about by independence.

Information: How shall we get the facts?

Data-gathering methods have expanded greatly during the past five years and hold great promise for the future. Nevertheless, for the next decade we shall still be in an interim period during which traditional ways of gathering information will continue to be used throughout much of the developed and underdeveloped world. The most important agency engaged in such tasks is the national census, and here the role of the geographer in Africa is clear. That the last census of Ghana is the finest in Africa is, in large measure, a result of the degree to which academic geographers were involved in its planning and execution. Given a degree of map coverage that many other African countries have yet to aspire to, Ghanaian geographers were able to devise a well-delimited set of enumeration areas so that detailed population maps could be prepared from the census returns for planning purposes. Such meticulous preparation seldom constitutes a glamorous task, but it is a truly important and fundamental one to which geographers must contribute if advances are to be made in social and spatial planning.

While the preparation and execution of a census is laborious, the most serious delays frequently occur at the compilation and publication stages. It is here that modest advances in remote-sensing hold great promise for census-taking.[9] In Swe-

9. A general statement of potentialities is contained in NAS–NRC, *Spacecraft in Geographic Research*, National Academy of Sciences Pub-

den, experimental projects may start soon to test the feasibility of recording census data by remote-sensing methods, and there is the possibility that such work will be extended to a small area of India during the 1971 census. Data will be recorded by field workers in the traditional way, but the information will be punched on large cards which will then be prominently displayed, surrounded by a white target circle, on the roof of a family dwelling or in the adjacent courtyard. Planes will fly over the area recording the census information and its actual geographic location. Both social and locational information will be either transmitted directly to computers on the ground or stored on tapes in the aircraft for computer processing upon landing. Within hours, the data should be compiled, sorted, classified, tabulated, and mapped so that the results of the census will be made available immediately for planning purposes—rather than languishing in statistical offices for months, or even years, after the census has been taken.

More advanced remote-sensing methods hold further promise for the gathering of geographic information in the spatial, as well as the more usual time, coordinates. Land use, agricultural, forest, and soil surveys may well be undertaken in Africa by remote-sensing methods before another decade is past. Already experimental work is going forward to establish the spectral signatures of different types of land use—characteristic patterns that are established by splitting the recorded radiation into a number of components and noting the characteristic variations in each of them. While such sensors are being carried by aircraft today, they will eventually be contained in earth satellites. Thus geographers and planners can look forward to the day when many forms of spatial information are gathered by these methods.[10] Linked to large computing facilities, such observational satellites could provide a monthly crop survey for an African country within an hour, or a map showing the density of traffic on every road within minutes!

Information: How shall the facts be handled?

The facts should be handled, of course, by computer. In Africa, as in the rest of the world, geographical research, no

lication 1353 (Washington, D. C., 1966), but the geographic literature in this area is large and growing rapidly.

10. D. S. Greenberg, ''Space: Vienna Meeting Examines Value for Developing Nations,'' *Science*, CLXI (1968), 992–94.

matter where it is placed upon the pure to applied continuum, will increasingly require large and fast computing facilities. Already the pinch is being felt, and there is hardly a geographer engaged in African research work in this country who has not felt frustration at the lack of computing facilities in Africa or who has not had pleas from African colleagues to make small amounts of computer time available in this country. To my personal knowledge, geographic research in Sierra Leone, Uganda, and Tanzania is being held up by the lack of computer facilities, and the demand, and frustration, will increase as more and more contemporary departments of geography and regional planning are established. Such departments in American and Swedish universities are already among the heaviest users of computers in the academic world.

The availability of modern computing facilities thus lies at the root of the question as to whether spatial planning and geographic research can truly "take off" in Africa. Not only are such facilities essential if geographical and planning data banks are to be set up, but, as Hägerstrand has noted, they will also be required for efficient descriptive mapping, the analysis of geographical data, and the running of process models with immediate practical implications.[11]

But computers are expensive, and few African countries can afford the millions of dollars that most major American universities spend every year for such facilities. On the other hand, an increasingly good case can be made for the view that few African countries can afford *not* to invest in such information-gathering and processing machines. The acquisition of computing facilities is not a question of prestige. African nations must plan with great efficiency to make the optimal use of their physical and human resources; efficient planning requires the acquisition and manipulation of large quantities of information; the acquisition, storage, and manipulation of information can be undertaken effectively only by computing machines. But what about the question of expense—let alone all the other problems, such as fluctuating electricity supplies and the need for highly trained personnel? Recent advances indicate that an interim answer will be the transmission of information from African universities and government agencies via satellites to the large, high-speed computing facilities of Europe and the United States. Today telephone hook-

11. Hägerstrand, "The Computer and the Geographer," pp. 1–2.

ups to regional computing facilities are familiar in the United States, and it will not be long before such facilities will be available to African governments and scholars via satellite transmission. Making large computer facilities available to African universities and governments in this way will be an essential intermediate step on the way to building an information-processing center for the whole of Africa. Surely in this area lies one of the greatest hopes for international cooperation in and with Africa.

Getting Down to Ideas

To speak of *African* geographical research can be somewhat misleading if the phrase implies something set apart and quite distinct. The fact that such research takes place in, and is concerned with, Africa by no means divorces it from the major intellectual thrusts characterizing the discipline the world over. On the contrary, the continent offers an important laboratory for the testing of very general ideas, concepts, and theories which, if they do not melt in the empirical crucible of Africa, will have profound practical implications for national planning purposes. Thus, it is almost impossible to conceive of geographical research in Africa divorced from the major lines of research elsewhere.

The map as a model

In a very fundamental sense, mapping characterizes most scientific inquiry. But rather than seeking the perfection of isomorphisms, we seek those homomorphic, or many-to-one, transformations where certain structural relationships of our own choice are preserved to suit our own particular purposes.[12]

Such pattern-preserving and pattern-seeking activities are familiar tasks to the geographer as he abstracts, compresses, and simplifies reality to construct his simplest and most fundamental of models—the map. Geography has just gone through an unfortunate period of map depreciation, as the mathematically inclined forgot it temporarily, and the rest

12. Stafford Beer, *Management Science: The Business Use of Operations Research* (New York: Doubleday, 1968), pp. 62–67.

were never trained in its use; the map is not a toy, to be regarded condescendingly as something extremely simple, but an analytical tool whose power stems from its very simplicity and familiarity. Just how crucial it is to geographic research and regional planning will be attested by any worker in Africa who has had the misfortune to attempt research in an area that was not thoroughly surveyed. I make this obvious point to emphasize, once again, the responsibility of the academic geographer in Africa, for he must still advise, pressure, cajole, and beg the politicians to assign scarce national resources to the basic task of mapping Africa. He also bears the responsibility of demonstrating the utility of all forms of mapping to the regional planner, the politician, and those major foreign-aid agencies whose spatial spectacles so frequently need cleaning. Only a few African countries, for example, have a national atlas, and, while they are well ahead of the United States in this respect, much can be done by geographers to supplement existing efforts. In the United States, William Bunge has proposed an atlas portraying the social health and condition of the nation, and such a project might well be emulated by other geographers as they conduct their African research.

The problem of compiling imaginative and useful national atlases also emphasizes the educational task that the geographer in Africa, as elsewhere, must face. Spatial information, relationships, and juxtapositions are frequently best displayed in cartographic, as opposed to mathematical, form. Nor are the educational tasks confined to the schoolroom, for the map often becomes the most valuable way of conveying pertinent information to decision-makers at the highest levels. Two examples at different scales illustrate the point. In East Africa the geographer Fair, by the simple juxtaposition of cartographic patterns, which in essence are Venn diagrams on the surface of the earth, outlined the very limited areas that could plausibly be considered as industrial regions for the future.[13] Similarly, an economist in Ghana, investigating the structure of staple food marketing and its associated costs, was forced to model geographic space by constructing his own map of a limited area. By careful field work, during which information on transport costs was transferred to maps of small feeder roads converging upon a major market center, well-supported

13. T. J. D. Fair, "A Regional Approach to Economic Development in Kenya," *South African Geographical Journal*, XLV (1963), pp. 55–77.

recommendations were made for the assignment of limited financial, and overabundant labor, resources.[14] In both examples, however, the map was an essential tool in the formulation of policy decisions involving the spatial assignment of resources.

Increasingly, the use of somewhat unusual map transformations will be required or desired. The ideas of administrators may frequently be clarified when they are shown what "spaces" they are actually dealing with. Hunter has already demonstrated the utility of simple, but effective, map trans formations for the sequential plotting of epidemics,[15] but the use of geographic map transformations need not be confined to the area of medical geography. Civil servants in ministries of education should be provided with maps of their country transformed to "education space," in which educational districts are shown in proportion to the school population to be served. Similarly, industrial planning must take place within an "industrial space," which is the result of a transformation expanding favorable, and shrinking unfavorable, areas displayed on the conventional map.

The theory of central places

Born in southern Germany, and extended in central Iowa, the major body of geographic theory is essentially a Western European and American construct. Progress in recent years has been slow, for the direct confrontation of theory and reality has been difficult to achieve. Such difficulties have virtually forced the theory to remain geometric and static in nature. In Europe, the present patterns of central places are the outward expression of long processes acting over centuries, and even in the United States the dynamics of central-place development are difficult to unravel. Not that many have tried, for there seems to be a perverse focusing upon static structural patterns whose explanation will be achieved only when the dynamics of central-place theory are understood.[16]

14. Douglas A. Scott, "Asesewa Market and Feeder Road Study" (Accra: USAID, September, 1966). Mimeographed.

15. John M. Hunter, "1957 Pandemic of Asiatic Influenza: A Geographic Study of England and Wales" (paper delivered to the Association of American Geographers, Washington, D. C., August 18–22, 1968).

16. Evon Vogt, "On the Concepts of Structure and Process in Cultural Anthropology," American Anthropologist, LXI (1960); also Emmanuel

There is no question, however, that information about the dynamic aspects of central-place systems is difficult to obtain in areas where change takes place slowly (as in Western Europe), or where the investigative difficulties are compounded by having other large-scale processes acting over the space simultaneously (as in the United States with its pioneer settlement taking place on a continental scale).[17] But while data problems are severe in Africa, the time scale is greatly compressed. With the exception of Western Nigeria, with its traditional and special urban forms, Africa experienced little in the way of central-place development until quite recently, except at the lowest levels of the hierarchy in the form of extended family dwellings and villages. With some obvious exceptions, which need not be enumerated here, such a situation held until approximately the turn of the century. Today, only seventy years later, central-place systems, dominated overwhelmingly by primate cities, have emerged in the respective national spaces of Africa. It is because the time scale has been so compressed, and the concomitant development of central places so rapid, that Africa may well become a major laboratory for geographic research into such spatial systems. Not only do geographers have a chance of observing the first and middle stages of increasingly stable and well-articulated central-place systems, but such fundamental structures underlie many other phenomena investigated by the geographer. There is evidence demonstrating that when we speak of modernization we are really considering the urbanization process; but then the urbanization process is itself simply an intense aspect of central-place dynamics.[18]

On the grounds that there is nothing so useful as good theory, it is worth noting that theoretical work on central places represents geographical research with important practical applications. While it is clear from a few case studies that central-place systems in Africa are converging to stable patterns from a state of considerable ''spatial flux,'' there is still

Mesthene, ''How Technology Will Shape the Future,'' *Science*, No. 3837 (1968).

17. Fred Lukermann, ''Empirical Expressions of Nodality and Hierarchy in a Circulation Manifold,'' *The East Lakes Geographer*, II (August, 1966), 17–70.

18. Peter Gould, ''Problems of Structuring and Measuring Spatial Changes in the Modernization Process: Tanzania 1920–63'' (paper delivered to the American Political Science Association, Washington, D. C., September 3, 1968), pp. 1–23.

time to make decisions that will shape such patterns and structures in a developing nation so that these intense nodes of human activity serve the goals of administrative as well as economic efficiency. Regional planners in Ghana have already demonstrated the way in which basic central-place information can point up gaps in the spatial lattice; and with only crude theoretical notions to support them, they have made recommendations for the establishment of regional service and administrative centers.[19] But Ghana is relatively well ahead of many other African countries in which the central-place systems are still in embryonic form. Thus, well-informed and theoretically sound planning decisions in this area can shape and affect the efficiencies of many locational decisions in the future. The key phrases here are *well-informed* and *theoretically sound*. Clearly the provision of relevant information and the development of sound theory are major geographic tasks ahead in Africa.

The diffusion of innovations

Questions regarding the diffusion of innovations frequently arise when African development problems are considered in their spatial context. Thus another major area of geographic research appears to have considerable implications for development policy. As has been repeatedly noted, diffusion processes take place at varying geographic scales,[20] although it is only recently that some analytical, as opposed to descriptive, attention has been paid to processes at scales larger than the individual or micro-level.

While it is unnecessary to review the Swedish studies on the diffusion of agricultural innovations,[21] it is worth noting that as yet no comparable work at the micro-level has been com-

19. David Grove and Laszlo Huszar, *The Towns of Ghana: The Role of Service Centers in Regional Planning* (Accra: Ghana Universities Press, 1964).

20. Torsten Hägerstrand, "On Monte Carlo Simulation of Diffusion," in *Quantitative Geography: Part I: Economic and Cultural Topics*, ed. by W. L. Garrison and D. Marble (Evanston, Ill.: Northwestern Studies in Geography, No. 13, 1967); and in the specific African context, Peter Gould, "A Note on Research into the Diffusion of Development," *Journal of Modern African Studies*, II (1964), 123–25.

21. Torsten Hägerstrand, *Innovation Diffusion as a Spatial Process* (Chicago and London: University of Chicago Press, 1967), a translation of *Innovationsforlöppet ur korologisk synpunkt* (Lund: C. W. K. Gleerup, 1953).

pleted in Africa. Such paucity must be lamented, for quite apart from the advantages accruing from comparative or cross-cultural research, the knowledge provided by such studies would have immediate application at the planning level. How, for example, do agricultural innovations such as cocoa sprayers diffuse in Western Nigeria? How will transistorized, battery-operated TV sets diffuse in the same area? How does membership in a cooperative society in Uganda spread? And how would such knowledge enable other desirable innovations to be spread more quickly and efficiently? Such questions and subjects for inquiry are frequently undertaken elsewhere; they are needed in Africa.

In the near future, geographical research in Africa will have much to contribute when it focuses upon the diffusion of contraception and family planning. At the present time we have no studies on the spatial diffusion aspects of such innovations, and even in India no studies exist of the way in which the use of the intrauterine devices has spread through a region. Yet it is in this area that data sources are relatively good, for the medical history, date, and home location of every woman are recorded upon the first visit to the family-planning clinic. Despite such good data, it is important for geographers to be associated with the establishment of family-planning clinics so that the process may be observed from the very beginning and so that simple questionnaires can be designed to elicit additional information at the time of each visit. With a body of empirical studies on the diffusion of contraceptive information, and building upon the basic Monte Carlo simulation work already undertaken in the field of agricultural diffusion, it should be relatively easy to construct good predictive models so that family-planning information can be diffused much more quickly and effectively than before.

At the regional level there are still very few studies of geographical diffusion. Yet since it is precisely at this level that many planning questions are considered, research in this area would have both theoretical and practical consequences. At this scale, geographers are concerned not so much with the diffusion of information from one individual to another as with the manifestations of such information flows in the form of institutions such as cooperative societies or schools. The few studies we have of the diffusion of schools and education come from Western Europe,[22] and the developing patterns appear

22. C. Arnold Anderson, ''Patterns and Variability in the Distribution

to display considerable regularity through space and over time. In Africa, however, school locations will be planned to a considerable extent in the future, and it is possible that studies of institutions diffusing more "naturally," like cooperative societies, will yield greater insights.

The question of cooperative diffusion is an interesting one, and what little evidence we have from Africa suggests that the "waves of innovation" operating at the micro-level do not describe diffusion processes operating at the regional scale.[23] As cooperative societies, considered as very simple, virtually one-function central places, diffuse through an area they are clearly space-competitive innovations tending to push themselves away from one another up to distances determined by the average threshold size. For the diffusion of such space-competitive innovations, interesting planning problems arise involving efficiency questions over long- and short-term planning horizons. If a new cooperative movement is allowed to take its own course, it may diffuse very quickly but may leave behind it inefficient spatial "gaps" which are difficult to fill later because of the space-competitive nature of the innovations. If the short-run goal is to get the "cooperative idea" throughout the region quickly, however, then the cost of such spatial inefficiencies (the duplication of cooperative offices, physical facilities, etc.) may be worth paying. On the other hand, if a long-term planning horizon rules the process and the diffusion is controlled (by government license or other means), then cooperative societies may be placed in planned locations to completely pack the space to the threshold levels required. Thus, under a free-diffusion process, the cooperatives are likely to go through the regional central-place hierarchy, while the planned diffusion might appear to operate as a wave leaving behind closely packed "cooperative regions" without any inefficient gaps to be filled in at a later date.[24]

Finally, the process of diffusion can be considered at the

and Diffusion of Schooling," in *Economic Development*, ed. by C. Arnold Anderson and May Jean Bowman (Chicago: Aldine, 1966), chap. 17; and Torsten Hägerstrand, "Quantitative Techniques for Anaylsis of the Spread of Information and Technology," *ibid.*, chap. 12.

23. Preliminary trend surface analyses by the author on the 1,200 cotton cooperatives in Lake Province, Tanzania, indicate little overall regularity, though space-filtering to reduce noise has yet to be attempted.

24. Peter Gould, "Problems of Location and Accessibility in Local Agricultural Development (paper presented at the Seminar for International Studies, Lund, Sweden, June, 1967).

national level. Indeed, the whole process of nation-building and modernization may be considered one in which successively greater areas of national space arc brought into closer contact with the core area. For many parts of Africa the task of nation-building is the primary one to which all other goals may be subsumed if necessary. It seems clear that the political geographer has much to contribute to this task, providing his studies are always informed in the last resort by questions of policy and application.[25] The process of modernization and nation-building appears to involve a convolution of two diffusion processes; namely, a rapid hierarchical process through the system of central places and a slower contagious process outward from the major nodes to their surrounding areas. But in many African countries today isolated nodes still appear quite detached from the main core areas. If the task of nation-building involves the successive linking of such regional growth poles, then clearly geographical research on nation-building, in space and over time, has direct policy implications for the construction of those linkages that will bind the pieces of a nation more tightly together by increasing the interaction between all the parts.

Normative models in a spatial context

While normative, or optimizing, models appear to be drowning today in a sea of footnotes to probability models, their apparent inadequacy to *describe* spatial behavior should not blind us to the fact that they still have great value if the aim is to *prescribe* optimal behavior under a set of carefully stated requirements and assumptions. Nowhere is such prescriptive power more relevant than in Africa, where development budgets are being stretched to the utmost limits and where every penny must be forced to do the work of two. Thus normative models make excellent sense in many spatial planning areas, as does geographic research that would support them by its relevance to real questions with considerable humanitarian overtones. If, for example, education is considered important and there is evidence that attendance and learning readiness decline with distance from the school,[26] the question

25. Soja, *Geography of Modernization in Kenya.*

26. Terrence Lee, ''Psychology and Living Space,'' *Transactions of the Bartlett Society,* II (1963), 9–36.

of optimally locating schools to minimize the distances of school journeys is no longer an esoteric one to be considered only by the operations research worker. Similarly, if national plans for a developing hospital system do not consider the question of optimal locations carefully, considerable waste may occur as some regions are oversupplied to the detriment of others.

The location-allocation problem has yet to be solved entirely, but useful advances have been made as larger computers have become available to geographers. By linking the classical transportation problem with an efficient algorithm to solve the Weberian extremum problem, Goodchild and Massam have illustrated the way in which multiple facilities converge to stable and optimal locations under the equal capacity constraint.[27] While the example they chose was the assignment of administrative centers in Canada, the implications for policy-making in Africa are obvious, for it is in the consideration of such locational questions that the interplay between the geographer's laboratory and the politician's office can be most fruitful. It is also worth noting that by clearly laying out alternative solutions to the politicians, there is probably less chance that locational decisions will be made upon purely political, selfish, and therefore wasteful, grounds. Thus, the optimizing model provides a normative bit in the politician's mouth to check excessively inefficient policies. In this way, some of the wasteful cross-haul patterns that characterize raw material and finished commodity flows in certain regions of West Africa might have been eliminated.

While not strictly normative, the notion of spatial assignment may also be extended to government personnel. There is a considerable tendency for government servants, administrators, and teachers to try to obtain assignments in the capital or the larger cities of the country. Yet, at the same time, there is great need in many African nations to get well-trained, well-educated, and properly rewarded government personnel into the more rural areas to serve and catalyze them.[28] Geographic research on the perception and space-utility surfaces of newly entering government servants has raised the question

27. M. F. Goodchild and B. H. Massam, ''Administrative Areas on a Non-Uniform Population Surface'' (McMaster University, 1968), p. 13. Mimeographed.

28. Peter Gould, *On Mental Maps.* Michigan Inter-University Community of Mathematical Geographers, No. 9 (1966), p. 50.

of transforming the surfaces to smooth "assignment planes" by relating salary differentials inversely to perception scores. In this way, greatly desired locations would subsidize those perceived as less desirable where the need for trained personnel was judged an important national priority.

Systems of spatial behavior

Given the complex and multivariate nature of most social phenomena acting over space and time, it is hardly surprising that the social and behavioral sciences are becoming more and more concerned with such general analytical frameworks as systems analysis. Thus we may expect during the remainder of the century that geographical research in Africa will be increasingly characterized by such approaches. Geographers are now facing the fact that mathematical intractability characterizes much of their work, and consequently their present concern for elementary simulation methods and process models will develop and expand rapidly in the years to come.

While there is presently little to show in the way of research results generated by a systems approach to spatial problem-solving, a number of examples are available which demonstrate the utility of decomposing complex and interlocked systems into smaller and more readily understood pieces.[29] Furthermore, as we consider the role of the geographer in African regional planning, it should be noted that the systems-analysis approach is valuable simply for the patterns and habits of thought it engenders. The geographic research worker operating within a cybernetic or systems framework brings to bear analytical approaches in which such general notions as feedback, feedforward, and homeostasis are implicit.[30]

If spatial systems are generally characterized by a number of nodal subsystems and linkages, then the task of the geographer is to describe such systems accurately so that prescriptions may be made for the more effective and efficient linking of the separate pieces. Whether the research focuses upon nodes of export production and linkages to the ports, or nodes of modernization linked by surface or electronic communica-

29. Christopher Alexander, *Notes on the Synthesis of Form* (Cambridge, Mass.: Harvard University Press, 1966), especially Appendixes 1 and 2, pp. 136–91.

30. Richard L. Meier, *Developmental Planning* (New York: McGraw-Hill, 1965), pp. 64–102.

tions facilities, the general prescriptive problem is to increase the flows that bind and articulate the nodes into a coherent system. Meier, for example, has noted how the development of education in an underdeveloped area represents a force to increase the flows of information which appear to measure, and set limits to, the level of development that may be achieved.[31] A recent call to develop a geography of education has considerable implications for developmental planning in Africa,[32] for locational, diffusion, and planning questions are inextricably intertwined and are best approached through a systems framework that brings to bear very general ideas and models upon the problem of increasing information flows through education.

The systems approach to geographic research that is allied to regional planning also engenders an attitude of flexibility to the planning process in that thinking takes place within a probabilistic, rather than deterministic, framework. Contemporary planning has frequently been likened to the flight of a rocket on a space mission. Initial efforts are made to define the target and direction as clearly as possible, but the ability to make adjustments in flight, even to the extent of selecting a different target, are explicitly provided for in the initial planning stages. There are few experienced planners who do not explicitly or implicitly try to build such flexibility into plans at all levels. Thus it is obvious that research geographers, who are willing and able to work with and advise on planning in Africa, must bring to bear habits of thought that provide for such flexible and self-correcting planning schemes. Such habits of thought should not be difficult to acquire, for general systems notions characterize many phenomena of traditional interest to geographers. Road development in Africa, for example, may be considered as a flexible, space-searching instrument, so that a road network may be considered conceptually as a self-correcting mechanism constantly influenced by feedback information.[33] Roads may be built initially at low standards, but if commodity flow is generated from the regions they tap the road traffic itself may be considered feed-

31. *Ibid.*, p. 95.

32. Shannon McCunne, ''The Geography of Education,'' guest editorial in *Economic Geography*, XLIV (January, 1968).

33. Peter Gould, *Space Searching Procedures in Geography and the Social Sciences*, Working Paper No. 1 (Honolulu: Social Science Research Institute, 1966), pp. 25–38.

back information to the decision-makers who subsequently upgrade the road to gravel standards. Should more feedback develop in the form of increased commodity flows, decisions may be made to further upgrade a road to tar, or even concrete, highway standards. On the other hand, if a road is built and no feedback occurs it may be allowed to deteriorate back to bush. Thus road development may be considered as a space-searching and space-organizing system with considerably more flexibility than rail development, which requires much larger lumps of investment.

In the area of transport development the geographer's spatial viewpoint may be particularly valuable to the national and regional planner. National development plans are often considered only from the sectoral point of view, and despite discussions about articulating and linking the sectors together, too frequently they go their own independent ways under the auspices of various ministries. Thus modern geographers, trained in more general and powerful approaches to problem-solving, should be able to play an increasingly important advisory role in planning at all levels.

The establishment of priorities is normally of prime importance in planning, and such questions raise the concomitant problem of the evaluation of plans and various sub-projects contained within them. While the evaluation of social planning is still at a rudimentary level,[34] it will become increasingly important as nation after nation in Africa makes a commitment to planned spatial change. We still know very little about the geographic forces and changes that result from such planned spatial investment as the building of a new road. Studies of road impact are virtually nonexistent in Africa, yet evaluation of such projects is essential in situations characterized by extremely limited resources. Increasing the density of a transportation network in Africa by adding new linkages and upgrading and improving old ones sets in motion a whole sequence of tightly interlocked social, economic, cultural, and political changes.[35] Such changes must be recorded and evaluated objectively so that planning in the future can take place on a surer footing.

34. Edward A. Suchman, *Evaluative Research: Principles and Practice in Public Service and Social Action Programs* (New York: Russell Sage Foundation, 1967).

35. Edward Taaffe, Richard Merrill, and Peter Gould, "Transport Expansion in Underdeveloped Countries," *Geographical Review*, LIII (1963), 503–29.

Research and Training: Opportunities and Responsibilities

The academic and applied relevance of geographic research in Africa during the latter part of this century will ultimately be rooted in the training programs of university geography departments. In Africa there is already considerable recognition that contemporary training is essential if geographers are to make their full impact upon the two worlds of scholarship and practical affairs. At the University of Ghana, the involvement of geographers with census planning is well known, and at the University of Kumasi the Department of Regional Planning has done much to engender a feeling of responsible involvement on the part of its students. This is a refreshing change, for too often African university students cling to a mandarin-like bibliographic dilettantism that neither they nor their countries can afford. Contemporary training programs also exist at the University of Ibadan, and rapid changes appear likely at the universities at Ife and at Fourah Bay in Sierra Leone. Geographers are also deeply involved in the Bureau of Resource Assessment and Land Use Planning at the University College, Dar es Salaam; and at the new University of Zambia, the Department of Geography has made a strong commitment to applied work in the national interest. In many of these cases, the influence of contemporary American training is obvious, and the impact of such a small group of African scholars highlights the responsibility of modern departments of geography in the United States and Europe for training African geographers and regional planners over the next decade. Such responsibilities should be easy to grasp provided major geographic departments are prepared to meet them with imagination and with a clear sense that training programs for African scholars must be relevant to the research and teaching tasks that they will face upon their return to their home countries.

It should not be necessary for the African (or American) student today to waste time on traditional factual, but now esoteric, portions of the geographical curriculum. Rather, attention should be paid to those bodies of theory and methodology which provide more general, and therefore more powerful, approaches to problem-solving situations. Such training programs should also provide greater opportunities to work in adjacent fields, for the African geographic scholar, like his

American and European counterpart, should be able to work closely with members of allied social and behavioral sciences, as well as with regional and national planners who carry the day-to-day burden of planning efforts. Brazilian government authorities are planning to expand pre- and postdoctoral work in contemporary geography, and it is difficult to think of any investment in human resources that would pay greater dividends for Africa than a steady flow of a score of well-trained geographers and regional planners each year over the next two decades. In many African countries the patterns and locations are still in a state of considerable spatial flux, and there are opportunities for geographic planning which will never come again. Decisions approaching optimality, if they can be made today, will shape and influence the efficiency of African economies for decades to come. Normative decisions, well-buttressed by meticulous geographic research, can save substantial investment funds which can be programmed for further development. And such development, though scientifically based, is concerned in the deepest sense with the human condition. Money saved by an efficient decision in one area may be used for new schools, new hospitals, overseas scholarships, and support for those cultural activities that preserve, enhance, and develop the great artistic heritage of Africa.

Finally, the contribution of American geography to Africa must be greatly strengthened. At a time when there appears to be greater interest in Africa than ever before, there are threats to major support programs for doctoral students. The Foreign Area Fellowship Program, whose long-term impact on American scholarship is virtually incalculable, needs long-range support. So do government-financed programs. At the postdoctoral level, also, research support must be increased, particularly for those research projects with immediate relevance to the host governments. Greater flexibility must be built into research programs of senior scholars, for experienced research personnel, in contact with African colleagues and with well-focused projects, may well accomplish in two properly supported summers a year's work of the type supported by traditional research programs.

Should such support for field research be reduced, both America and Africa will pay a price in the future for uninformed and inexperienced advice to national and international development agencies. ''Experts'' who bring an attitude of mind to bear on African problems that may be summarized by the phrase "This is the way we did it back home in Utah" do more damage than good. Only by continuously building and strengthening a cadre of scholars with the experience of African field research will such advice be improved. Such support, it seems to me, must come from agencies, such as the National Science Foundation, which lack the propensity to attach strings, because the academic scholar working in Africa must maintain that independence of questioning and inquiry that has always characterized sound scholarship. As the academic geographer increasingly takes on an advisory role, he must have the courage to give his best opinion even though it may be unpalatable to the agencies concerned. Too frequently agencies seeking academic help appear to want their preconceptions confirmed and legitimatized by an outsider, rather than seeking solutions in an open way. The best advice may frequently require unexciting, but vital, information-gathering projects that do not lend themselves to the grand ambassadorial gesture and a ribbon-snipping occasion. Since it is difficult for men in a government bureaucracy to give advice beyond unspoken, but all too clear, limits, the independent and experienced scholar must take on such difficult, and sometimes unpleasant, responsibilities.

To give a concrete example in closing, there is little use in supporting new road-building activity when there is no conceivable base for accurate cost-benefit studies beforehand, and when the refurbishing and upgrading of existing facilities are clearly the major priorities. Cost-benefit, evaluative, and predictive studies require sound data bases for their execution. Yet it is precisely the unexciting, but fundamental, establishment of such data bases for which it is difficult to find international development support. A new road, even though it proves to be an ineffective and low priority investment, brings the ambassador with his scissors, and produces glowing "clasped hands" speeches that appear in newspapers and reports to home governments. Origin-destination surveys, and other careful and patiently devised sources of hard data that underlie truly rational planning decisions, receive little publicity and cause few ripples in the news media. Yet, in the long run, investment in such seemingly pedestrian activities may well produce payoffs far beyond the more glittering projects.

Thus, from facts at the beginning of this paper, we have come back full circle to the factual base upon which scholarly research and rational spatial planning in Africa must ultimately be founded. Over the next twenty years, as always, the task of the African geographer, in both his scholarly and his applied role, will be to bring the hard facts and powerful ideas together for the further development of geographic theory—for there is nothing so useful as good theory.

Akin L. Mabogunje

Among the many studies of the problems of national unity in Africa, the question of mal-location of development during the colonial period is one which is seldom considered. The colonial administrations in Africa had as a primary objective the easy exploitation of local resources to supply the raw material needs of the metropolitan country. In consequence, there gradually evolved in Africa a disproportionate concentration on export activities and an inordinate concentration of development in the coastal areas. The result is the phenomenon common in most African countries where a single primate city on the coast serves as capital, port center, social, educational, commercial, and industrial headquarters, and alone contains 10 to 20 per cent of the total population of the country.

Such over-concentration immediately points up the inequality of developmental opportunities in most African countries at independence. When combined with the ethnic problem, this fact emphasizes a major obstacle to national unity. Yet any government, to be stable and successful, has to balance the need to distribute development projects widely (in order to meet the legitimate demand of its population and achieve greater national cohesion and unity) against the equally important objective of locational efficiency and growth.

The main burden of Peter Gould's essay is, therefore, to identify the major elements which need to be appreciated in trying to strike or reach such a happy balance. In particular, the paper reviews the role which a space-specific discipline such as geography can play in Africa in the realization of this objective. Briefly, Gould identifies three major areas needing greater research or institutional attention. These are data-collection, the formulation of more rigorous theories to guide policy decisions and planning, and the institutionalization of personnel exchanges between African and American universities.

We, at the African end, regard and have found these exchanges both vital and valuable. What Africa offers in exchange for the trained manpower it receives from the developed countries are opportunities for theory-formulation and theory-testing in communities which are in a state of considerable spatial flux. Few would deny the immense importance of such a payoff.

Gould reviews geography's greater concern with static structural patterns and its current weakness in understanding the dynamics of central-place systems. In particular, he points out the close interrelation between modernization and urbanization and the fact that the urbanization process is itself but an intense aspect of central-place dynamics.

One example of contemporary theoretical weakness in the area of central-place dynamics is the bewilderment and dismay which so far characterize the work of social scientists and their attitude toward the phenomenon of rapid urbanization in Africa. The rate at which Africans have moved into the cities in the last ten years has been unprecedented in the history of the continent. Most social scientists seeing this phenomenon seem preoccupied with the problem of unemployment which it creates. Few have tried to understand it as part of a dynamic process necessary for the structural transformation of any developing area. Such a different perspective, if theoretically motivated, could lead to greater research concentration on the identification of those elements in the situation making for the attainment of a higher order of spatial equilibrium.

Gould suggests that greater insight into these spatial aspects of developmental processes in Africa can be gained through the conceptual framework provided by normative models and systems analysis. Normative models, he believes, still enable us to prescribe optimal locational decisions under a set of carefully stated requirements and assumptions. I would also add that these models make it easy to indicate to the decision-makers the social or opportunity costs of wrong locational decisions. Systems analysis in particular has tremendous possibilities in geographic research work in Africa. Apart from the fact that it helps to emphasize the need for searching for the feedback and feedforward of various spatial processes, as well as emphasizing the linkages among the nodal structures that constitute human occupancy of the earth's surface, it has the added advantage of engendering attitudes of flexibility which facilitate self-correction of planning activities. Gould illustrates this fact by briefly considering a systems approach to the spatial problems of road development in African countries. In a paper which I presented last year at the African Studies Association in New York, I have also tried to show how this conceptual approach allows us to gain new insights into the rural-urban migration process in Africa.

One major area of priority which, to my mind, has been unfortunately neglected in this paper is that of rural settlement and land-use development. In the last ten years, the creation of various man-made lakes in many parts of Africa has led to the displacement of large numbers of people and to programs for resettling them in new villages and hamlets. In the same period, plans for agricultural development in many countries have been predicated on the establishment of new patterns of rural settlement. Questions have invariably been asked by policy-makers as to what principles and concepts should guide these developments. To answer these questions requires an awareness and understanding of the dynamics of rural settlement and land-use development in the same way as we try to comprehend the dynamics of central-place systems.

Yet it is true that in terms of theoretical formulation, geography has not advanced in this particular field much farther than the work of von Thunen. The reason in part is that in the highly urban, industrial societies of Western Europe and America problems of rural settlement and land-use have lost much of their urgency and therefore pose little challenge to academic research workers. But these problems remain crucial in most underdeveloped countries. What are the land-use and settlement implications of the development from a subsistence to a commercially oriented economy? How do these affect the planning and locational decisions for amenities and utilities in rural areas? What aspects of the dynamics of the situation are relevant for further promoting and stimulating efficient utilization of resources? What are the relationships between these dynamic systems and that of central places? These and many other equally important questions seem to me to define some of the major priorities in geographical research in Africa in the next twenty years.

Gould emphasized quite rightly that any valid theoretical system which can illuminate our understanding of these problems must be based on adequate and well-organized data systems. It is an agonizing fact that leaders in only a very few African countries see the immediate relevance and supreme importance of data-collection to their development efforts. Gould, of course, sees the problem as due also to the bureaucrats who have not succeeded in shaking off the colonial attitude to the issue. In most African countries, the best statistical data available are those, collected at the ports, of monthly exports to and imports from Europe. Data are grossly lacking on the internal configuration of the economy, on the distribution and characteristics of the population, on production and internal trade, and on various other transactions within the national area. To solve this problem requires an awareness by both the political leaders and the bureaucrats that such data are crucial to the task of nation-building. More than this, both groups need to be aware that the unit for such exercise should be the individual settlement, locationally identified, and not large aggregations like the division, the province, or even the region.

For African countries facing the great stresses of political instability and fragile national unity, concern with the locational dimensions of policy decisions is clearly an imperative for successful nation-building. Gould has made a major contribution by indicating the responsibility of research scholars, especially geographers, working in Africa for bringing this fact home to the decision-makers.

SOCIETY, POLITICS, AND ECONOMIC DEVELOPMENT IN AFRICA

13

Irma Adelman, George Dalton,
and Cynthia Taft Morris

In recent years economists, anthropologists, sociologists, and political scientists have studied development and modernization in Africa in order to analyze and suggest policy guidelines for the changes occurring throughout the continent. To understand modern African economies it is necessary to have a knowledge of their economic history as well as of their present structure and performance. The first section of this paper therefore describes traditional village-level African economies before they became part of politically independent nation-states and began their deliberate efforts to modernize. It is a descriptive account concerned mainly with the mutual dependence between economy, social organization, and culture in the traditional setting. The second and third parts of the paper constitute an empirical and statistical survey concerned with macro-development—the transformation of African national economies in the years since political independence.

Traditional African Societies

It is impossible to understand the economic organization of traditional Africa without understanding its cultures and

The discussion of traditional African societies in the first section of this paper is elaborated by George Dalton in ''Traditional Economic Systems,'' in *The African Experience,* ed. by E. W. Soja and J. N. Paden societies. The economy was "embedded" in society in the sense that underlying social relationships provided the rules and channels for the allocation of land and labor, for work organization, and for the distribution of produce. It is this "organic" or "*gemeinschaft*" nature of traditional society that leads anthropologists to analyze religion, polity, and the rules of kinship (marriage, descent-reckoning, lineage) in such detail.

For those familiar with Western societies and economies it is probably easiest to appreciate the distinctive features of traditional African economies by contrasting them with our own economic system.

Any economy may be regarded as a set of systematic arrangements to provide its society with material goods and specialist services. In performing these functions, all economies make use of (1) natural resources, such as land, minerals, forests, and waterways; (2) human labor; (3) tools and technical knowledge; and (4) organizational procedures that are called institutions: division of labor, rules of land tenure, forms of money, marketplaces. Developed economies such as the U.S. and U.S.S.R. as well as traditional African economies such as the Tiv of central Nigeria [1] differ with regard to the quality, quantity, and diversity of the natural resources and human labor at their disposal; the quantity and quality of tools and technical knowledge they have; and the kinds of structural arrangements or institutions they use.

The most important differences between traditional Africa and present-day Europe and America (particularly in structural arrangements and institutions) were in size and effective integration. African societies did not have that set of mutually reinforcing, large-scale, integrative institutions which characterize modern economies—institutions through which are expressed socioeconomic interaction, cultural identity, and common awareness, by millions of people.[2] African societies

(Evanston: Northwestern University Press, forthcoming). Other sections of this paper are reprinted, with minor changes, with the kind permission of Johns Hopkins University Press, from Irma Adelman and Cynthia T. Morris, *Society, Politics, and Economic Development: A Quantitative Approach* (Baltimore: Johns Hopkins University Press, 1967).

1. Paul and Laura Bohannan, *Tiv Economy* (Evanston: Northwestern University Press, 1968).

2. See Godfrey and Monica Wilson, *The Analysis of Social Change* (Cambridge: Cambridge University Press, 1945), chap. 2, "Scale."

tended to be small and self-contained. Poor transport and communication prevented economic and cultural interaction and exchange among societies that were also separated from one another by language, religion, tradition, and polity. Differences in language and religion were particularly common. Traditional Africa spoke hundreds of languages. With the important exception of Islam, traditional African religions tended to be idiosyncratic. African polities were not organized along the lines of modern nation-states and did not provide the range of public services that modern governments do. Along economic lines, traditional Africa lacked not only machines and applied science but also nationally integrated resource and product markets and their accompanying monetary systems.[3] Their small size and primitive technology meant low productivity and extreme dependence on physical environment; and the absence of market integration and commercial money meant local social dependence (the need for household, lineage, or tribal cooperation and mutuality) in production processes.

In these small, locally contained communities, in which almost everyone knew everyone else and in which many activities and relations were shared, custom was tenacious. Traditional practices and values were transmitted intact, and children grew up to lead much the same lives as their parents. Cultural and physical isolation meant the absence of knowledge of different, alternative ways of doing things. Choice was narrowly constrained by what was known. Under such conditions, innovation was difficult.

Deviation from traditional practice was also risky. To experiment with new crops or new techniques of production was to risk hunger if the innovation failed.[4] Where social rank was sharply defined, moreover, for the lowly to be overly ambitious was to risk punishment by social superiors for attempting to rise above their station and thereby threaten the highly placed persons. But even where social rank was not sharply stratified and the boundaries of permissible action not clearly

3. See Karl Polanyi, *The Great Transformation* (New York: Rinehart-Winston, 1944); George Dalton, "Economic Theory and Primitive Society," *American Anthropologist*, LXIII (February, 1961); Paul Bohannan and George Dalton, "Introduction," in *Markets in Africa*, 2d ed. (New York: Doubleday, 1965); and Irma Adelman and Cynthia Taft Morris, *Society, Politics, and Economic Development* (Baltimore: Johns Hopkins University Press, 1967), chap. 5.

4. See W. Allan, *The African Husbandman* (London: Oliver and Boyd, 1966).

circumscribed, sanctions for doing the traditional were strong. Mutual dependence meant mutual obligation. To fail to appear at a work party to clear a cousin's land, to fail to pay first-fruits to a chief, or to fail to contribute to a younger brother's bridewealth would have been to invite retaliation by people upon whom one depended to reciprocate when needed.

If we contrast the organization of agricultural production in a traditional African subsistence farm and a U.S. commercial farm, we can point up some distinctive features of African economies. Typically, the African farmer acquired land at no cost to himself as an inalienable right of membership in his lineage or tribe.[5] He had the right to use the land, but not to dispose of it or leave it unused. By contrast, in U.S. agriculture rights of acquisition or use of someone else's land are acquired by money purchase or rental, and no previously existing social relationship between buyer and seller, or landlord and renter, is necessary.

So too with tools and farm labor. The African made his own digging stick or hoe, and he and his family supplied the ordinary farm labor. For tasks requiring an unusual amount of labor, such as clearing land or harvesting, the African relied on his social relationships—neighbors, friends, agemates, clients, kin—whom he thanked by feeding or by hosting a beer party, and with whom he reciprocated by helping them clear land and harvest crops. This is very different from the Iowa wheat farmer who purchases his tools and equipment and hires most of his labor at a money wage.

The African farmer's activities were an integral part of his local community only. He depended on local social relationships and typically relied on no person or agency external to his community for factors of production. The Iowa farmer in contrast is utterly dependent on strangers outside his local community: on chemical firms in Pittsburgh to provide him with pesticides, on factories in Detroit to provide him with tractors and other farm machinery, on banks in Iowa City to lend him money. Indeed, the institutional transformation of traditional subsistence economies may be characterized as a movement from dependence on local social relationships to dependence on distant impersonal markets.

There are striking differences in the methods of disposition

5. Bohannan, *Tiv Economy;* and I. Schapera, *The Bantu-Speaking Tribes of South Africa* (London: Routledge and Kegan Paul, 1937).

of produce in the two systems as well. In the American economy, market exchange is the dominant and integrative, but not the only, mode of distribution. It is dominant because the greater portion of the economy's total output is disposed of by market sale (the Iowa farmer sells almost all he produces). It is integrative because the basic resources—labor, land, minerals, and technical equipment—are channeled to production processes through market sale, and output is distributed similarly. However, a minor portion of goods and services is transacted differently: gift-giving on ceremonial occasions (Christmas, birthdays, weddings), obligatory military service (the draft), and the free provision of elementary education (regardless of the taxes, if any, paid) are obvious examples.

In Africa, where most of the produce was consumed by the farmer and his family, there were economies in which reciprocity (gift-giving) was the dominant and integrative mode of transaction. Reciprocity may be defined as an obligatory two-way transfer (gifts and counter-gifts) of resources, goods, and services, induced by a social relationship between the gift partners. The proper ratio of exchange (what is an adequate return gift) [6] is determined by social criteria such as the social distance between the two, their age and status. Reciprocity is a socioeconomic transaction in the sense that it characterizes material transfers induced by social relationships. And just as there are many variations of the general transactional mode we call market exchange—pure competition, oligopoly, monopoly—so too there are varieties of reciprocal transactions. [7]

"Redistribution," that is, the upward and downward transactions between the political center and its village-level constituencies, [8] was another transactional mode in traditional societies. In chiefdoms and kingdoms, rank and file persons paid tribute—ordinary goods, labor for roads, and military service—upward to central political authority, which used the

6. Marshall Sahlins, *Tribesmen* (Englewood Cliffs, N. J.: Prentice-Hall, 1968), chap. 5.

7. Marshall Sahlins, "The Sociology of Primitive Exchange," in *The Relevance of Models for Social Anthropology*, ed. by M. Banton (London: Tavistock, 1965).

8. Karl Polanyi, "The Economy as Instituted Process," in *Trade and Market in the Early Empires*, ed. by K. Polanyi, C. M. Arensberg, and H. W. Pearson (Glencoe, Ill.: The Free Press, 1957); and Karl Polanyi, *Dahomey and the Slave Trade* (Seattle: University of Washington Press, 1966).

receipts for its own maintenance and to provide public services, such as defense and religious ceremony.

In traditional Africa, the close connection between economy and social organization was also expressed in what anthropologists call the prestige sectors of the economy. These refer to a special set of valuables or treasure items (for example, cattle or blocks of camwood) which were highly prized. The conditions under which an individual acquired and paid out treasure items were carefully prescribed. The items were paid out in a special set of transactions (for example, bridewealth or bloodwealth) involving honorable fulfillment of obligations, social prerogatives, and rank. These treasure items and the social situations in which they served as necessary means of reciprocal payment were charged with emotion and moral fervor. They were symbols in the sense that wedding rings, sports trophies, and crown jewels are symbols. They played socioeconomic roles, however, that have no close counterparts in Western societies. They were, indeed, a kind of "social money" for a circumscribed set of reciprocal transactions in the prestige sector.[9]

The Modernization of National African Economies

Most African economies are now pursuing development policies deliberately, consciously, and quickly. Except for Japan and Soviet Russia, this deliberate drive to develop and modernize is outside the experience of the developed nations. The United States and Britain developed less consciously, less as a matter of deliberate national effort, and less as an urgent responsibility of governmental initiative. There is great pressure on African governments to formulate development programs which will increase incomes rapidly. Too often, however, the programs are based on fragmentary data and unrealistic expectations.[10] To add to the difficulties and tensions, these countries are in the process of structural transformation politically and culturally as well as economically and technically—they are building their nations and societies as well as their economies.

9. George Dalton, "Primitive Money," *American Anthropologist*, LXVII (February, 1965); and Mary Douglas, "Raffia Cloth Distribution in the Lele Economy," *Africa*, XVIII (April, 1958), 109–22.

10. See Wolfgang Stolper, *Planning Without Facts* (Cambridge, Mass.: Harvard University Press, 1966).

Many other countries outside Africa may be described as underdeveloped. It has been shown that the large set of underdeveloped countries can be divided into three groups: low, intermediate, and high.[11] Such a separation is analytically useful because the socioeconomic structures and the socioeconomic problems of development for each sub-set are markedly different.

At the lowest level of development are countries principally, but not exclusively, in sub-Saharan Africa.[12] A typical country in this group shares many characteristics with the traditional village-level economies described in the first section of this paper: it is characterized by the occupation of an overwhelming proportion of its population in traditional subsistence agriculture where production takes place in largely self-contained units and the marketing of surpluses is of only incidental economic importance. Such a country also has a small but growing market economy characterized by either cash-crop peasant agriculture or foreign-owned modern plantation or extractive activities. Often there are significant differences in levels of social and cultural attainment as well as in levels of technology between the market and non-market sectors.

Throughout the traditional agrarian and pastoral sectors, where typically more than 80 per cent of the population lives, economic, social, and political relationships are largely confined to closely integrated village or kinship groups. Tribal allegiances are extremely important since tribal organization binds a sizable number of villages into larger ethnic, religious, and political complexes. These tribal ties derive strength from their convergent religious, political, and economic character, for it is the tribe that provides the religious bond of belief in a common ancestor—the seat of political leadership and the ultimate authority concerning rights to land. At the same time, the cooperative village group continues to dominate people's daily existence and to provide the focus for traditional social and economic activity as well as to constitute the principal administrative unit. These small-scale preindustrial communities are almost completely independent of the nation-state economically and politically and have an internal system of organization based on face-to-face relationships and structure in terms of kinship roles and other social institu-

11. Adelman and Morris, *Society, Politics, and Economic Development*.

12. See *ibid.*

tions. Only the most tenuous ties link them with the national polity.

In the traditional sociocultural setting typical of the non-market sector of these countries, economic activity tends to be a subsidiary expression of predominantly communal relationships.[13] The principles governing economic activity are not separate from those regulating overall social behavior. On the contrary, the economic system of tribal societies tends to be embedded in the economic system. For example, barter and exchange are usually expressions of long-term reciprocity relations implying trust and confidence rather than bilateral transactions in which articles of value are exchanged.[14] Since production for market exchange is merely a marginal source of livelihood for the traditional sector, the price mechanism does not serve an important function. It tends neither to stimulate improvements in productive efficiency nor to reallocate factors of production among various activities. Economic specialization of tasks occurs almost exclusively as a differentiation of age, sex, and kinship status rather than as a designed method to exploit market opportunities.

The allocation of factors of production in the traditional economy is largely determined by social custom and does not involve a separate economic calculus. Where produce is not destined for market sale, the allocation of labor is governed by traditional practices rather than by market considerations such as wages. Rights to property are vested communally and are acquired by a prescribed system based on status and lineage within the kinship group; in particular, rights to cultivate land cannot be purchased by payment of rent. For these reasons, capital invested in the various combinations of labor and land cannot readily flow from one branch of production to another as it must if the market mechanism is to perform its allocative function. As a result, techniques of production do not change in response to market forces, and therefore they tend to be quite primitive and static.

The sociocultural climate of the countries in this group is characterized by marked cultural, ethnic, and religious differences among the various tribal groupings, as illustrated by the fact that typically less than 60 per cent of the population

13. See George Dalton, ''Traditional Production in Primitive African Economies,'' *Quarterly Journal of Economics*, LXXVI (August, 1962), 360–78.

14. Polanyi, *The Great Transformation*, p. 61.

speaks the same language. The lack of economic, social, and political integration in these nations persists not only because of the diversity of tribal allegiances but also because of the self-sufficient nature of homemade technology, the prevailing illiteracy of the population, and the absence of mass communication media. In all but six countries, more than 85 per cent of the adult population is illiterate; in most instances newspaper circulation is below 10 per 1,000 population, while radio licenses are less than 50 per 1,000 population. The lack of transportation facilities within the rural sector and the prevailing inadequacy of connections between the countryside and urban centers, as well as the physical ruggedness of jungle or mountain terrains, are also important contributors to the persistence of a diversity of small-scale local cultures.

As a result of both the geographic and cultural isolation of the typical small community in these countries and the strength of traditional social organization, there is little experience with modern practices that alter environment. Attitudes toward birth, health, and death have in most instances remained those instilled by inherited wisdom and convention without awareness of real alternatives. Birth rates are rarely under 40 per 1,000 and in a number of countries are over 50 per 1,000. Modern medical practices have made little headway; generally there is only one physician per 10,000 population, and infant mortality rates are often over 150 per 1,000. In addition, the populations of more than four-fifths of the countries in the sample suffer from malnutrition or poorly balanced diets, and from significant incidence of tropical, infectious, and parasitic food- and water-carried diseases. While death rates are generally declining, this is primarily the result of nationally organized environmental measures to eradicate diseases, such as malaria, rather than the outcome of local adoption of modern standards of sanitation and hygiene. In general, man's outlook in these small rural communities is strongly traditional, and programs of modernization have hardly begun to affect the attitudes of the majority of the populace.

Adjacent to the traditional sector, there exists in all countries of this sample a small cash economy which is generally oriented toward production for export markets. In the countries of West Africa and British East Africa the cash economy has for the most part developed as a supplement to subsistence farming through the expansion of indigenous small holdings in which production of rubber, cocoa, coffee, etc., for export is increased by means of conventional techniques and familial labor. In other countries, such as Libya and several countries of central Africa, the origin of the market sector has been the foreign development of export-oriented plantations, farming estates, or extractive industries; the use of hired migrant labor from the traditional sector and the application of modern technology characterize these commercial ventures.

The extent of influence of the commercial sector upon traditional social organization varies with the nature of the market sector. Where successful indigenous cash-cropping has evolved, the impact upon customary attitudes and practices tends to be greatest, and the modernizing influence upon communal and tribal relationships the most marked.[15] On the other hand, where large-scale foreign development has occurred in an essentially independent enclave, the economic and social dichotomy between the market-oriented and traditional sectors is considerably greater. The migrant laborers, even while involved in the modern sector, maintain a close attachment to the villages in which their kin reside and to which they intend to return, with the result that they do not act as agents of modernization within their traditional setting.

The urban centers of the countries in this group generally include less than 10 per cent of the population. Their major economic activities are the commercial and banking services associated with foreign trade, some limited small-scale industry oriented toward the domestic market, and the performance of the bureaucratic functions which nation-states in the modern world require. Modern industry plays only a small part in the economy of these towns. In about half of the countries in the group, industry is primarily of the artisan handicraft type; in the rest, while a limited number of technologically modern industries have evolved, these are usually characterized by small-scale production for domestic consumption. The traditional agricultural economy is still important in the life of these urban communities since many town dwellers continue to engage in subsistence farming and regard their traditional rights to land in the tribal sector as their only source of material security. Furthermore, the majority of the indigenous urban population has recently emigrated from the vil-

---

15. Aidan Southall, ed., *Social Change in Modern Africa* (London: Oxford University Press, 1961), p. 4.

lage and a considerable number of these migrants intend to return to their rural homes.

Even though the primary social and cultural ties of the indigenous urban population remain those of the village and tribe, the towns are nevertheless major centers of change. New types of social relationships are formed there; the distinctive characteristic of these relationships is that they are often based on common economic status, place of work, or other mutual interests rather than on ethnic or familial ties. The formation of these new social relationships arises in part because in the towns economic activity originates largely in response to market stimuli and therefore tends to be differentiated from the kinship system. In addition, the all-embracing social bonds of traditional community systems are less easily maintained in an urban setting in which key members of the kinship group may be absent. These new relationships are more fluid and subject to change than their rural counterparts and they constitute a solvent for eroding the particularistic tribal loyalties. A further characteristic of towns which accounts for their modernizing influence is the concentration of mass communication media and educational facilities, both of which are important instruments for disseminating new ideas. Finally, the towns provide employment for the small number who have been educated in the West and who seek the wider national roles created by independence.[16]

It is the small educated middle class that is the driving force behind the modernizing influences exerted by the towns. The middle class, which typically consists of less than 5 per cent of the population, is the focal point of political life and of economic modernization efforts. Its composition reflects the absence of those occupations characteristic of large-scale industry; government employees, clerical workers, and those associated with the commercial life of the country form an unusually large proportion of its membership. In those towns where an important part of economic activity is related to the export of cash crops, the indigenous educated component of the middle class tends to be considerably more significant than in the mining towns of more recent origin. In the latter towns, entrepreneurial and commercial roles are performed almost exclusively by expatriates, and as a result the indigenous

---

16. For discussion of the role of towns in the process of change in newly independent nations, see Lucy Mair, *New Nations* (Chicago: University of Chicago Press, 1963), chap. 5.

population is relegated almost completely to unskilled and semiskilled occupations.

Social mobility, in the sense of opportunity to enter a growing middle class, is of necessity limited at this level of development both by the extremely small size of the middle class and by the very narrow base of the educational system. A typical country in this group has less than 15 per cent of its school-age population in school. At the same time, social mobility, in the sense of the absence of purely social barriers to mobility, does exist in most of these countries since their societies tend to be quite egalitarian with respect to a man's class origins.[17] This is true partly because there are no important differences between the traditional culture of the villages and the culture of the sociopolitical elites, although there may be great differences in education.[18]

Politically, the nations in this group tend to adopt autocratic solutions to the problems of rapid change. As of about 1960, significant freedom of political opposition and press existed in only a handful of the countries in this group. Almost half of them had only one national unity political party with all other parties banned, or no political parties at all. Furthermore, in the remaining countries, while no significant restrictions were placed upon political organization, only about half a dozen of them had two or more reasonably effective political parties in operation. These parties tended to be based on ethnic or religious groupings rather than on class or ideology. The choice of authoritarian types of central government in this group of countries stems at least in part from the need to devise political forms that facilitate the political integration of diverse, heterogeneous, and atomistic traditional units. The great need for political integration is emphasized by the fact that in some of these countries the adoption of Western-type parliamentary institutions at the time of independence led to struggles for national power among different tribal, regional, and religious groups. In several instances these power contests were so sharp that they posed serious threats to the stability of the new national polities. As a

17. Exceptions are countries such as Afghanistan, Nepal, and Ethiopia, in which traditional social hierarchies include a ruling hereditary aristocracy to which access is closed.

18. See L. A. Fallers, "Social Stratification and Economic Processes," in *Economic Transition in Africa*, ed. by M. J. Herskovits and Mitchell Harwitz (Evanston: Northwestern University Press, 1964), pp. 113–30.

result, parliamentary forms were soon replaced by strong executive governments.[19]

An additional factor contributing to the tendency toward authoritarian solutions to problems of political integration is the general ideological orientation of the elite. The recent colonial experience of most of the countries in this group has made their leaders more desirous of political and economic equality with other nations than of internal freedom and democracy. Faced with a scarcity of experienced indigenous entrepreneurs and businessmen and with the lack of a sizable indigenous private industrial base, the leaders, in their intense desire for rapid economic modernization, have tended to resort to central government dictation of economic development efforts.

The use of the government as a vehicle for carrying out nationalist aspirations for rapid modernization and industrialization is, of course, severely impeded by the inadequacy of the government apparatus. Another significant obstacle to government efforts to act as a modernizing agent stems from the tensions and instability created by the process of nation-building. As efforts at political integration proceed, heterogeneous regional and ethnic groups are brought into rivalry with each other; the outcome is increased racial and cultural tensions on the one hand and, on the other hand, increased tensions between the majority, which remains attached to traditional small-scale societies, and the minority, whose primary attachments are to the nation as a whole. The result is that in all the countries in this group there have been at least occasional outbreaks of violence between tribes, between regions, or between modernizing elites and traditional authorities.

In all the countries in this group, economic institutions are at a very rudimentary stage of development. Financial institutions are of course limited to the cash economy; with few exceptions, they attract a negligible volume of voluntary indigenous private savings. Investment in the traditional sector is almost entirely self-financed or financed through unorganized money markets. Investment in the technologically advanced sector, where it exists, is financed almost completely by private foreign or expatriate capital. One should note, how-

19. See St. Clair Drake, ''Democracy on Trial in Africa,'' in *Africa in Motion, Annals of the American Academy of Political and Social Science* (July, 1964), pp. 118–19.

ever, that in a small number of countries characterized by peasant cash-crop agriculture, government-controlled financial intermediaries obtain a significant flow of compulsory savings, at least part of which they channel into medium- and long-term credit to industry and agriculture.

Tax institutions tend to be quite underdeveloped, as indicated by ratios of tax revenue to GNP, which are generally less than 12 per cent, and/or by heavy dependence upon a single foreign-owned mineral sector for taxes. Physical overhead capital is in the majority of cases still grossly and pervasively inadequate. At best, transportation and power facilities suffice to satisfy limited current needs only in those geographic regions in which the market sector is relatively advanced. Even in economies with well-served market sectors, however, the inadequacy of the infrastructure still constitutes a major economic bottleneck to further growth.

In view of the social, political, and economic characteristics of the countries in this group, it is hardly surprising that their investment and growth rates have been quantitatively small. In over half the countries, the ratio of net investment to national income for the 1957–62 period was less than 10 per cent, the rate specified by Lewis as the minimum required for the initiation of sustained economic growth.[20] Annual rates of growth in per capita GNP for the great majority of the countries in this group were less than 1.0 per cent per capita during the thirteen-year period 1950/51–1963/64. The remaining countries were of two types. In some, the increase in monetary income per capita was due largely to the income created in a dynamic foreign-owned mineral sector and did not involve significant rises in the average income of the indigenous population; several of these countries registered monetary growth rates of 3 per cent or more. In others, particularly a few countries of East and West Africa, growth rates were between 1 and 2 per cent per capita; in these countries the expansion of peasant cash-crop agriculture has initiated a more wide-spread improvement in standards of living which presages the possibility of a cumulative growth process.

Even though quantitative evidence suggests that little

---

20. W. Arthur Lewis, *The Theory of Economic Growth* (Homewood, Ill.: Richard Irwin, 1955), chap. 5. A ratio of net investment to national income of 10 per cent is equivalent to a ratio of gross investment to GNP of about 13 per cent, on the assumption that for countries in this group net investment is approximately three-fourths of gross investment.

growth has taken place in the majority of these countries, this fact should not be interpreted to indicate that they are entirely static. Significant changes are taking place in the social and political lives of the people. The expansion of mass communication, education, and transportation is widening the range of individual experience for a growing number of the populace. More and more families are turning to cash-crop production, thereby extending their involvement in the larger society. Urban centers are growing and the movement of labor from agriculture to the cities has increased. Finally, efforts on the part of leaders to create a national identity and to increase the sense of national unity have to some extent been successful in changing the small-group outlook of the indigenous population.

As for economic institutions and physical overhead capital, almost all these countries have experienced some improvements in the past fifteen years. Transportation and power networks have expanded considerably, and tax collections have in most instances increased. Monetization of the economy is proceeding rapidly in practically all the countries in this group; however, in most cases this has not been translated into significant expansion of central financial institutions. Almost one-third of the countries have experienced improvements in agricultural productivity through the use of better tools and knowledge; in most of the remaining countries agricultural production has kept pace with population growth as a result of the cultivation of additional lands with existing techniques. While the social, political, and economic transformations taking place in these countries are quite striking, it should be noted that their quantitative impact upon growth rates and levels of overall development is as yet small.

In summary, a typical country at this stage of socioeconomic development is characterized by a predominant tribal subsistence sector in which economic activity is embedded in social structure, most people live in small-scale hinterland communities, and mass participation in the national polity is virtually unknown. Bordering upon the subsistence sector is an expanding market sector from which all social, economic, and political change emanates.

The Technique of Factor Analysis

The interdependence of economic growth and sociopolitical change is generally recognized by social scientists. Development economists, in particular, are aware that key economic functions used in analyzing advanced economies may take quite different forms in less-developed countries for reasons which are largely political, social, and institutional.[21] However, efforts to extend growth analyses to include non-economic factors are hampered by the absence of empirical knowledge about the manner in which they operate.

The analysis of sociopolitical and institutional influences upon development contained in the rest of this paper is an attempt to gain more precise empirical knowledge about the extent and nature of interdependence of economic and non-economic aspects of the development process, with special reference to Africa. Such an analysis, undertaken by economists, may serve two purposes. First, it may suggest hypotheses relating non-economic to economic variables which are both suitable for testing by more intensive analyses and relevant to the central concerns of development economics. Second, it may underscore the need felt by economists for more exact knowledge about the interrelationships of the development process and thus stimulate joint research efforts by economists and members of other disciplines.

More specifically, an attempt is made in the rest of this paper to gain some semiquantitative insights into the interaction of various types of social and political change with the rate of economic development. For this purpose, the techniques of factor analysis [22] are applied to a large number of indexes representing the economic, social, and political structure of twenty-eight less-developed countries in the period 1957–62.

The results of the analysis show that a remarkably high percentage of intercountry variations in the rates of economic development in Africa (66 per cent) is associated with difference in non-economic characteristics. Thus it would appear that it is just as reasonable to look at underdevelopment as a social and political phenomenon as it is to analyze it in terms of intercountry differences in economic structure. The results

21. See, for example, B. F. Hoselitz, ''Non-Economic Factors in Economic Development,'' *American Economic Review*, XLVII (May, 1957), 28–41; and Benjamin Higgins, ''An Economist's View,'' in *Social Aspects of Economic Development in Latin America*, II (UNESCO, 1963), 141–251, esp. 178–82.

22. For a detailed treatment of the technique of factor analysis, see Harry H. Harman, 2d ed. rev., *Modern Factor Analysis* (Chicago: University of Chicago Press, 1967); and L. L. Thurstone, *Multiple Factor Analysis* (Chicago: University of Chicago Press, 1961).

of the factor analysis neither demonstrate that economic growth is caused by sociopolitical transformations nor indicate that variations in development levels determine patterns of social and political change. Rather they suggest the existence of a systematic pattern of interaction among mutually interdependent economic, social, and political forces, all of which combine to generate a unified complex of change in the style of life of a community.

Since factor analysis can use as data inputs a relatively large number of intercorrelated variables, a broad selection of indicators of the social and political structure of twenty-eight less-developed countries during the period 1957–62 was included in our study of differences in levels of economic development.

The social characteristics included were selected to depict important aspects of the social changes associated with urbanization and industrialization, such as the modernization of communication, education, and outlook. The choice of political indicators for our study was designed to capture leading aspects of the growth of modern nation-states. In addition, several characteristics represent the quality and orientation of political administration and leadership and the importance of key interest groups within a nation.[23] The economic indicators were chosen to portray those changes in economic structure and institutions typical of industrialization and economic growth. The complete list of the social and political and economic characteristics included in the final version of the factor analysis can be seen in Table 1.

Definition of variables and method of classification

The procedures used in defining indicators and in ranking countries differed somewhat for various types of country characteristics. Three different types were distinguished: (1) those for which classification could be based solely on published statistics; (2) those for which it was necessary to combine statistical and qualitative elements; and (3) those which were purely qualitative in nature.

23. We were obliged at an early stage in classifying countries to reject several indicators which we found could not be formulated with sufficient concreteness to permit unambiguous country classifications. The importance of achievement motivation and social attitudes toward economic activity were indicators which appeared desirable a priori, but which we were obliged to reject on this score.

With respect to indicators defined by published statistics, classification of countries was relatively simple. Four to six brackets were established into which countries were grouped. Where data permitted, gradations within categories were also differentiated. The classification scheme for the extent of literacy illustrates the methods used for this type of variable.

Sometimes more than one statistical series was used to describe a characteristic. For example, the variable describing the extent of mass communication is based upon a composite index of newspapers in circulation and radios in use. The principal categories were set in terms of newspapers in circulation and gradations within brackets based on radios in use or licensed.[24]

A second type of country characteristic is distinguished by a blend of important judgmental elements with statistical elements. The derivation of the variable describing the extent of social mobility illustrates the procedures employed for this type of characteristic. Since social mobility proved too broad a concept to be described by published statistics alone, two qualitative aspects of mobility, access to leadership elite and extent of ethnic barriers to advancement, were combined in this variable with a statistical measure of educational opportunity.

A third and important type of country characteristic included in our study was the purely judgmental one. Even for qualitative indicators, it proved possible to arrive at category descriptions which were sufficiently precise and inclusive to permit unambiguous classification of most countries. Cross-checks to preliminary classifications were obtained by consulting AID and other country experts and by referring to published country and regional studies.

Once the classification of countries according to the various characteristics was complete, each of twenty-eight less-developed countries was given a letter score—A, A−, B+, B, etc.—with respect to thirty-five social, political, and economic indicators.

Since the use of factor analysis requires that the variables be specified numerically, the final task in preparing data inputs was to assign scores to the letter classifications. The scale chosen was a simple linear one. It is obvious, of course, that the choice of a numerical scale for qualitative indicators

24. These data are published in Bruce M. Russett et al., *World Handbook of Political and Social Indicators* (New Haven: Yale University Press, 1964).

is arbitrary. However, the use of an arbitrary scale does not appear to seriously invalidate the results. For inasmuch as the raw material of factor analysis consists of the correlation matrix among the various social and political characteristics, and correlation coefficients are unaffected by linear changes in scale, the results are invariant with respect to linear transformations of the scale used.

Several non-linear changes in scale were also tried (such as a log transformation and the use of reciprocal), but it was found that the results of these transformations either yielded similar results or made less sense and varied more with changes in sample size than the simple linear scale chosen.[25]

The factor analysis: results and interpretation

The results of the factor analysis are summarized in the matrix of common factor coefficients presented in Table 1. Each entry a_{ij} of the matrix shows the importance of the influence of factor j upon sociopolitical indicator i. More specifically, the entries or "factor loadings" indicate the net correlation between each factor and the observed variables.

The interpretation of factor loadings may more easily be made in terms of the squares of the entries in the factor matrix. Each $(a_{ij})^2$ represents the proportion of the total unit variance of variable i which is explained by factor j, after allowing for the contributions of the other factors. If the first row of the table is examined, it can be seen that $(.41)^2$ or 16.8 per cent of intercountry variations in rate of change per capita GNP are explained by Factor 1, an additional $(.27)^2$ or 7.3 per cent by Factor 2, and another $(.18)^2$ or 3.2 per cent by Factor 3; the net contribution of Factor 4 is only $(.03)^2$ or .1 per cent, and of Factor 5, $(.65)^2$ or 42.2 per cent.

The right-hand column of the table gives the sum of the squared factor loadings, or the "communality" of each variable. The communality indicates the proportion of the total unit variance explained by all the common factors taken together and is thus analogous to R^2 in regression analysis. The communality of per capita GNP, for example, is:

$$(.41)^2 + (-.27)^2 + (.18)^2 + (-.03)^2 + (-.65)^2 = .699$$

That is to say, 70 per cent of intercountry variations in rate of growth of per capita GNP are associated with the five common

25. See Thurstone, *Multiple Factor Analysis*, chap. 2.

TABLE 1: Rotated Factor Matrix for Change in Per Capita GNP (1950/51–1963/64) Together with Thirty-five Political, Social, and Economic Variables [a] (Low Sample)

Political, Social, and Economic Indicators		Rotated Factor Loadings				h_i^2
	F_1	F_2	F_3	F_4	F_5	(R^2)
Rate of Growth of Real Per Capita GNP: 1950/51–1963/64	.41	−.27	.18	−.03	−.65	.699
Importance of the Indigenous Middle Class	.76	.36	−.10	−.03	−.15	.744
Extent of Social Mobility	.57	.50	−.03	−.04	−.28	.662
Level of Effectiveness of Financial Institutions	.71	.12	.23	−.28	−.31	.744
Level of Effectiveness of the Tax System	.71	.33	.24	.01	−.12	.691
Level of Modernization of Techniques in Agriculture	.46	.44	.35	−.21	.02	.568
Character of Agricultural Organization	.51	.11	.10	−.04	−.25	.347
Degree of Improvement in Financial Institutions since 1950	.73	−.28	.33	.11	−.16	.764
Degree of Improvement in the Tax System since 1950	.68	.15	.43	.33	.03	.777
Change in Degree of Industrialization since 1950	.67	−.01	.27	.04	−.06	.532
Degree of Improvement in Agricultural Productivity since 1950	.89	−.03	−.07	−.04	−.08	.809
Strength of Democratic Institutions	.21	.83	.11	−.06	−.08	.758
Degree of Freedom of Political Opposition and Press	.10	.87	.07	.10	−.04	.791
Predominant Basis of the Political Party System	−.03	.76	.17	−.16	.12	.654
Degree of Competitiveness of Political Parties	.10	.82	.04	−.43	−.12	.889
Strength of the Labor Movement	.13	.77	.12	−.04	−.33	.730
Political Strength of the Traditional Elite	−.25	−.57	.33	−.24	−.10	.561
Political Strength of the Military	.11	−.67	.07	−.42	.28	.732
Degree of Administrative Efficiency	.42	.54	−.06	−.18	−.42	.682
Degree of National Integration and Sense of National Unity	.04	−.21	.68	−.03	.48	.740
Degree of Cultural and Ethnic Homogeneity	−.12	−.26	.56	−.02	.41	.564
Extent of Urbanization	.11	.02	.70	−.29	−.14	.603

TABLE 1: (Continued)

Political, Social, and Economic Indicators	Rotated Factor Loadings					h_i^2 (R^2)
	F_1	F_2	F_3	F_4	F_5	
Extent of Mass Communication	.08	.27	.75	.18	−.26	.739
Rate of Improvement in Human Resources	.26	.01	.85	.14	.03	.818
Level of Modernization of Industry	.27	.28	.59	−.03	−.46	.710
Level of Adequacy of Physical Overhead Capital	.31	.29	.68	−.13	−.33	.768
Extent of Political Stability	.12	−.04	.02	.87	−.19	.816
Degree of Social Tension	.05	.06	−.11	−.80	−.12	.678
Extent of Leadership Commitment to Economic Development	.56	.16	−.33	.47 [b]	.09	.672
Extent of Literacy	.19	.30	.37	−.45	−.19	.502
Character of Basic Social Organization	.22	.07	.45	−.49	.40	.659
Extent of Dualism	.59	.17	.34	−.04	−.60	.866
Structure of Foreign Trade	.12	.22	.06	.00	−.55	.371
Abundance of Natural Resources	.03	.23	.47	.30	−.61	.738
Gross Investment Rate	.15	−.02	−.05	.03	−.71	.532
Degree of Modernization of Outlook	.55	.24	−.08	−.23	−.57	.743

[a] Boxed figures indicate the factor to which each variable is assigned. Variable omitted because of insignificant correlation: extent of centralization of political power. Variables omitted because of low high loadings: size of the traditional agricul·rural sector, degree of improvement in physical overhead capital since 1950, and crude fertility rate. Percentage of overall variance explained by factors: 68.5. Percentage of variance explained by last factor included: 6.5.

[b] A variable having loadings on two factors which are not significantly different is assigned to that factor to which it is judged to have the closest affinity.

factors which are extracted from the thirty-five economic and sociopolitical variables incorporated in our analysis.

The matrix of factor loadings, in addition to indicating the weight of each factor in explaining the observed variables, provides the basis for grouping the variables into common factors. Each variable may reasonably be assigned to that factor with which it shows the closest linear relationship, i.e., that factor in which it has the highest loading. Where loadings of a variable in two factors are very close, the variable has been assigned to the one with which it is judged to have the closest affinity.[26] Table 1 lists, first, indicators which have their highest loading in Factor 1, then those with highest loadings in Factors 2, 3, 4, and 5 successively. Boxes indicate the loading in that factor to which each indicator is assigned.

Once variables are assigned to common factors, the factors need to be "identified" by giving a reasonable explanation of the underlying forces which they may be interpreted to represent. To quote Thurstone, who pioneered the use of factor analysis in psychology: "The derived variables are of scientific interest only insofar as they represent processes or parameters that involve the fundamental concepts of the science involved."[27]

A study of the interrelationships among the social, political, and economic forces which influence the growth process at the lowest level of development (Table 1) produced several important conclusions. First, it is evident from this table that the development process in this group cannot be understood without reference to both social and economic phenomena. The reader will note that there is no sharp separation between indexes of social structure and those of economic organization. This outcome reflects the fact that once the forces leading to economic development have been set in motion, economic and social progress tend to go hand in hand. However, while there is no clear delineation between economic processes and their social counterparts, a detailed study of the statistical results suggests, as we shall see below, that economic forces exogenous to the subsistence sector play a leading role in the initiation of

26. This is accepted procedure for combining variables into common factor groups. See, for example, Robert Ferber and P. J. Verdoorn, *Research Methods in Economics and Business* (New York: Macmillan, 1962), p. 105. Unfortunately, no tests for the significance of differences in factor loadings exist; however, it is evident that small differences in loadings cannot be considered significant.

27. Thurstone, *Multiple Factor Analysis*, p. 61.

the transition from stagnation to some modicum of dynamic activity.

The second important conclusion that can be inferred from the factor analysis is that the significant dynamic processes at this level of development are the *growth of the market sector* and the increasing dualism of the economy brought about by the development of a distinct modern market sector alongside the traditional subsistence sector. Both the social and economic aspects of these processes are evident in the factor analyses. Thus, in the sociopolitical results (Table 2) the dominant factor (Factor 3) represents the primarily social transformations involved in these processes, while in the economic analysis (Table 3) the important factors reflect those economic changes that provide the motivations and opportunities necessary to stimulate the social transformations.

A third conclusion suggested by our results is that *the primary impediments to economic growth for countries at this lowest level of socioeconomic development reside in the inhibiting character of the traditional social structure within which economic life tends to be embedded.* This conclusion is suggested by the extent to which the social concomitants of the growth of the modern sector, in and of themselves, account for differences in economic performance. (In the sociopolitical analysis, Table 2, they ''explain'' 79 per cent of intercountry variations in rates of growth of per capita GNP.) Finally, we must note that political forces exert but a weak quantitative influence upon the rate of development of economies at this level. This can be seen from the fact that the most important political variables, which appear in the factors representing the strength of participant political institutions and the nature of political leadership in both the combined and the sociopolitical analyses, account for less than 10 per cent of intercountry variations in growth rates. In the next few sections we shall examine these conclusions in greater detail.

The important social processes

Inherent in both the growth of the market system and the expansion of the modern sector are two social processes represented in Factor 3 of Table 2. The first of these is a *process of differentiation of economic activity from the social life of the community through which the rules that govern economic activity within the society tend to become separate from those*

TABLE 2: Rotated Factor Matrix for Change in Per Capita GNP (1950/51–1963/64) Together with Twenty-three Political and Social Variables [a] (Low Sample)

Political and Social Indicators	Rotated Factor Loadings				h_i^2
	F_1	F_2	F_3	F_4	(R^2)
Rate of Growth of Real Per Capita GNP: 1950/51–1963/64...........	—.23	.11	—.85	.05	.790
Strength of Democratic Institutions..	.86	—.05	—.19	.08	.792
Degree of Freedom of Political Opposition and Press................	.90	.09	—.09	.07	.827
Predominant Basis of the Political Party System....................	.77	—.26	.11	.05	.678
Degree of Competitiveness of Political Parties......................	.80	—.45	—.19	—.13	.896
Strength of the Labor Movement....	.78	—.05	—.22	—.15	.684
Political Strength of the Traditional Elite...........................	—.54	—.29	.02	.33	.479
Political Strength of the Military....	—.66	—.40	.09	.10	.620
Degree of Administrative Efficiency..	.56	—.01	—.50	—.23	.612
Extent of Political Stability........	.01	.86	—.12	.15	.779
Degree of Social Tension............	.02	—.68	—.18	—.29	.583
Extent of Leadership Commitment to Economic Development..........	.17	.54	—.19	—.21	.397
Extent of Literacy	.32	—.47	—.38	.24	.524
Character of Basic Social Organization...........................	.09	—.63	—.07	.29	.499
Size of the Traditional Agricultural Sector.......................	—.13	.35	.66	—.15	.591
Extent of Dualism................	.22	.05	—.90	.04	.857
Importance of the Indigenous Middle Class.........................	.44	.14	—.57	—.19	.574
Extent of Social Mobility..........	.55	.04	—.57	—.16	.659
Degree of Modernization of Outlook..	.22	—.12	—.78	—.38	.830
Degree of National Integration and Sense of National Unity.........	—.16	—.18	.07	.80	.705
Degree of Cultural and Ethnic Homogeneity	—.22	—.15	.10	.77	.669
Extent of Urbanization	.05	—.43	—.41	.47	.575
Extent of Mass Communication	.31	.04	—.39	.61	.623
Crude Fertility Rate	.04	—.21	—.15	—.57	.395

[a] Boxed figures indicate the factor to which each variable is assigned. Variable omitted because of insignificant correlations: extent of centralization of political power. Variables omitted because of low high loadings: none. Percentage of overall variance explained by factors: 65.1. Percentage of variance explained by last factor included: 9.7.

which underlie the social organization. One aspect of this process of differentiation is the breakdown of the sway of traditional organizational structure and the accompanying increased separation of economic activities from their conventional social context. This aspect shows up in the dominant explanatory factor of the sociopolitical results as a direct

TABLE 3: Rotated Factor Matrix for Change in Per Capita GNP (1950/51–1963/64) Together with Seventeen Economic Variables [a] (Low Sample)

Economic Indicators	Rotated Factor Loadings h_i^2			
	F_1	F_2	F_3	R^2
Rate of Growth of Real Per Capita GNP: 1950/51–1963/64	.43	.65	−.10	.626
Level of Effectiveness of Finanical Institutions	.68	.25	−.43	.708
Level of Effectiveness of the Tax System	.58	.17	−.46	.583
Character of Agricultural Organization	.52	.32	−.12	.381
Degree of Improvement in Financial Institutions since 1950	.69	.08	−.34	.592
Degree of Improvement in the Tax System since 1950	.59	−.11	−.60	.714
Change in Degree of Industrialization since 1950	.69	.05	−.28	.560
Degree of Improvement in Physical Overhead Capital since 1950	.52	.46	−.08	.494
Degree of Improvement in Agricultural Productivity since 1950	.90	.06	−.05	.817
Extent of Dualism	.51	.53 [b]	−.56	.845
Structure of Foreign Trade	−.04	.57	−.25	.387
Abundance of Natural Resources	−.08	.57	−.59	.679
Gross Investment Rate	.16	.81	.07	.692
Size of the Traditional Agricultural Sector	−.36	−.25	.49	.435
Level of Modernization of Industry	.22	.34	−.74	.713
Level of Adequacy of Physical Overhead Capital	.19	.27	−.82	.783
Level of Modernization of Techniques in Agriculture	.38	.04	−.53	.431
Rate of Improvement in Human Resources	.22	−.11	−.74	.616

[a] Boxed figures indicate the factor to which each variable is assigned. Variables omitted because of insignificant correlations: none. Variables omitted because of low high loadings: none. Percentage of overall variance explained by factors: 61.4. Percentage of variance explained by last factor included: 8.6.

[b] A variable having loadings on two factors which are not significantly different is assigned to that factor to which it is judged to have the closest affinity.

relationship between decreases in the size of the traditional agriculture sector and faster economic growth.[28] Another aspect of differentiation is reflected in this same factor by the

28. The relevance of some of the differentiation aspects of the growth of market economies in a Western historical context has been pointed out by Karl Polanyi, who writes in *The Great Transformation*: "A self-regulating market demands nothing less than the institutional separation of society into an economic and political sphere. Such a dichotomy is, in effect, merely the restatement, from the point of view of society as a whole, of the existence of a self-regulating market"; see Adelman and Morris, *Society, Politics, and Economic Development*, p. 71.

positive association of the extent of dualism. This indicator represents the transformation of a predominantly agrarian society into one in which a modern industrial, plantation, or estate sector with its own specialized socioeconomic structure and institutions evolves side by side with the traditional subsistence sector.[29] Finally, the growth of an urban class of entrepreneurs, businessmen, and bureaucrats performing specialized economic functions outside the context of traditional kinship relationships and the concomitant increase in opportunities for social mobility are further indicators of the process of differentiation of the economic from the social roles and activities within the society.

The corollary social process associated with the growth of the modern sector and the expansion of the market system is *the process of social integration through which the members of small-scale traditional communities are integrated into the larger national economy and society.* The attitudinal aspects of the integration process are reflected in part in the dominant factor of Table 2, by the indicator of the degree of modernization of outlook. The integrative force of the rise of the market economy is depicted in this same factor by the negative relationship between the size of the traditional non-monetized sector and economic growth rates.[30] These dynamic processes of differentiation and integration are the crucial social concomitants of the growth of market-oriented economic activity and are particularly important in the early phases of economic development. Together they account for more than 70 per cent of intercountry differences in growth performances at this lowest level of socioeconomic development. The fact that such a large proportion of the variance is related to those differences in social structure characteristic of the expansion of the market economy and the growth of a distinct modern sector serves to emphasize the importance of transforming social organization in a manner that can permit substantial

29. It should be noted that the indicator of the extent of dualism is scored in such a manner that at the end of the scale a positive change represents the increase in dualism which occurs as the expansion of a distinct modern sector imposes itself upon a predominantly agrarian society. At the upper end of the scale, a positive change with respect to this indicator consists of reduced dichotomies between the traditional and the modern as elements of both eventually become intermingled throughout the society.

30. See Ragnar Nurkse, *Problems of Capital Formation in Underdeveloped Countries* (New York: Oxford University Press, 1953), chap. 1. As indicated above, this variable also reflects the process of differentiation.

increases in the extent to which economic considerations govern economic activities.

The critical importance of enlarging the sphere within which economic considerations govern economic activities in countries at the lowest level of socioeconomic development is perhaps not surprising. After all, most textbooks in elementary economics start out by underlining the role of economic principles of exchange and production in determining the choice of output, the apportionment of output among consumers, the allocation of factors of production among competing uses, the distribution of income, and the rate of capital accumulation in the economy. In fact, economic principles of exchange and production play such a basic role in the functioning of most advanced societies that Western economists tend to take their existence for granted and often devote their efforts to the analysis of ways in which the functioning of the economic system can be improved in the interest of community welfare and to the examination of areas in which economic criteria must, for various reasons, be supplemented or even supplanted by other allocative principles.

Let us consider in more detail the importance of enlarging the area of activity in which strictly economic motivations predominate. First of all, in order for a modern extractive, plantation, or estate sector to develop in a country at the lowest level of socioeconomic development, it is evident that the force of economic incentives must increase, not only among the foreign or expatriate elements but also in the indigenous traditional society. In particular, a continuous supply of labor to the modern sector can only be assured over a period of years if members of traditional small communities begin to view their labor as exchangeable for material gain. This change in outlook, to be effective, requires a considerable social transformation within the tribal subsistence society.

To appreciate the extent of the transformations required to enable economic motivations and market-oriented activities and behavior to develop within the indigenous economy, let us look at the operation of a society in which the application of economic criteria to production and exchange is either completely absent or else has only marginal significance. In traditional tribal societies, long-established social customs and norms tend to govern both the production and exchange of goods. As was pointed out in the first part of the present discussion, practically all the movement of material goods and services in such societies is governed by the social principles of reciprocity and redistribution. Since these principles of exchange are clearly social in character, it is evident that the bulk of goods and services in societies in which markets have at most a peripheral influence are transferred in accordance with social, not economic, rules. Moreover, it is characteristic of these non-market principles of exchange that (1) the terms of trade are not determined in accordance with demand and supply but rather are regulated by tradition; (2) they have a social and generally a moral content, as well as an economic function; (3) participation in these exchanges rarely extends outside a particular kinship and lineage group; (4) different rules of exchange usually govern the transfer of different kinds of goods and services (e.g., luxury or "prestige" versus subsistence products); and finally (5) markets for factors of production are nonexistent.

As one might infer from this very abbreviated description, the economic life of a society in which market principles play only a minor role is inherently static and fragmented. The prevalence of traditional barter ratios, reinforced by the ethical and social content of the exchange process and by the absence of factor markets, tends to insulate the system from both exogenous shocks and internal change.[31] The almost exclusive limitation of the bulk of exchanges in these non-commercialized economies to the kinship groups and the separation of transactions into different "multicentric" spheres of activity, which results from the fact that different transaction principles generally apply to different classes of goods and services, combine to generate fragmentation and isolation among the several realms of exchange. Furthermore, the absence of factor markets tends to preclude positive responses to new technological opportunities in agricultural production. It is therefore not hard to see how the limited extent of market-oriented behavior hampers the development of an economy characterized by a very large non-market sector. For such a society only the transformation to an exchange economy dominated by market considerations and cash transactions offers even the possibility of a certain amount of dynamism and economic integration.

31. The long-term persistence of these barter ratios, incidentally, suggests that they very likely represent equilibrium ratios (in the economic sense of satisfying the usual marginal conditions), not because they have evolved in response to economic forces but because they have undoubtedly conditioned the values of the society to conform with the traditional rates of exchange.

The discussion of the preceding paragraphs explains why our factor analyses for the nations in this group indicate so close a relationship between success in raising economic growth rates in the short run and those social changes that are necessary in transforming the traditional subsistence sector into a commercialized arm of society.

The economic forces

The incentives for the social transformations of the subsistence sector which are necessary for economic growth at this level of development are provided by economic forces. More specifically, the economic mechanism by which social transformations are induced is the expansion of the modern sector. This expansion proceeds in a dualistic manner by means of the creation of a modern export-oriented extractive, plantation, or estate sector. The significant economic forces inherent in this dualistic expansion are illustrated in Factor 2 of the economic analysis (Table 3), and Factor 5 of the combined analysis (Table 1), and they account for over 40 per cent of variations among countries in economic growth rates in the combined and economic analyses. In both sets of results the factor representing the important economic forces combines the extent of dualism, the structure of foreign trade, the abundance of natural resources, and the gross investment rate. The inclusion of the extent of dualism reflects the key role of the expansion of the modern sector in providing economic stimuli to social change within the subsistence sector. The export orientation of the modern sector, which is typical of countries at this level, is indicated by the inclusion of the indicator of the structure of foreign trade, which, at the lower end of the scale, represents the great concentration of exports characteristic of the early stages of growth of the modern sector. The incorporation of natural resource abundance depicts the extent to which the growth of the modern sector at this level is based upon the exploitation of natural endowments, particularly agricultural and extractive resources. The unimportance of manufacturing production in modern sector growth at this level is indicated in the economic results by the association of the indicator of industrial modernization with a factor that contributes little to the explanation of economic growth rates (Factor 3, Table 3). Finally, the growth of the modern sector is of course limited by the extent to which investment can take place. The critical role of this constraint is reflected in the inclusion in the important economic factor (Factor 2 of the economic analysis) of the gross investment rate.

As one might expect, for countries at the lowest level of economic development the strongly inhibiting nature of the traditional social structure and of the associated value system militates against the ability of changes in economic institutions (other than those that directly affect the everyday lives of the members of the society) to generate further change and to lead to economic growth. In particular, we find that none of our indicators of improvements in economic institutions and techniques (changes in tax systems, improvements in financial institutions, increased modernization of industry and of agriculture, and improvement in human resources) contributes to the explanation of intercountry differences in economic growth at this stage. Nor does the level of development of financial and tax institutions appear to be relevant. The unimportance of all of these forces is indicated by the fact that their complete omission from both the economic analysis of Table 3 and the combined analysis of Table 1 does not reduce the proportion of the variance in rates of growth of per capita GNP explained by the analysis.[32]

That this imposing array of economic variables makes such a small contribution to explaining overall economic performance for countries at this low level of development is due in part to the fact that only relatively small differences in the extent of improvements in these aspects of economic performance characterize the countries in this group. Before these more advanced economic forces can move significantly and have much impact, the socioeconomic processes involved in the rise of a modern sector and the expansion of the market economy must lead to a higher level of socioeconomic development than that which exists today in even the most developed countries of this group. The social and economic transformations that stimulate the growth of market-oriented behavior and activities thus constitute prerequisites for the implemen-

32. Indeed, the omission of all these indicators from the economic and the combined analyses raises the communality of rates of change in average income from 63 per cent to 73 per cent for the economic analysis and from 70 per cent to 75 per cent for the combined analyses of Tables 1 and 3, to associate in factors with which they are not closely related. The possibility that the inclusion of additional variables will reduce some communalities is discussed in Adelman and Morris, *Society, Politics, and Economic Development*, chap. 3.

tation of improvements in economic institutions, which will in turn affect the pace of economic growth in the short run.

The unimportant social forces

For countries at this lowest level of development, the extent of purely sociocultural integration and cohesiveness appears to be a relatively unimportant determinant of economic growth, as can be seen from the results given in Tables 1 and 2, in each of which the factor containing measures of the extent of national integration, cultural and ethnic homogeneity, mass communication, and urbanization (Factor 3, Table 1; Factor 4, Table 2) has a negligible weight. This is not surprising on an a priori basis. Clearly, before the social and economic structure of these atomistic hinterland societies has been sufficiently transformed so that a minimal amount of contact and interdependence among fragmented kinship and lineage groups can be established, it is unlikely that the absence of national integration and the presence of sociocultural heterogeneity per se will operate as a significant barrier to development. Furthermore, because of the strength of the divisive social forces at this level, there exist only relatively small differences among these countries in the extent of breakdown of tribal allegiance and the degree of ethnic and cultural homogeneity.

The political forces

The nature of the political approach to nation-building has only a small effect upon the rate of economic growth for countries at this low level of development. Factor 2 of Table 1 and Factor 1 of Table 2, which represent these political influences, account for only 5 to 7 per cent of the intercountry differences in the rate of growth of per capita GNP for these societies. Among the forces that are associated in this factor with better economic performance are more centralized political systems, less effective democratic institutions, greater restrictions on freedom of the press, and more severe limitations on the activities of the political opposition. There is also some tendency for the more rapidly developing of these countries to be controlled by a single national-unity party and to possess only very weak voluntary associations such as labor unions. In addition, at this level, those nations characterized by traditionalist leaderships—in particular, those with more control by traditional elites, greater strength of the military, and less rationalization of bureaucratic structures—tend to some extent to have higher rates of growth. Thus, the analysis suggests that there is a weak but positive relationship between more autocratic, less representative forms of government and more rapid growth rates within this group of countries.

The direction of these associations is due, by and large, to the fact that at a low level of socioeconomic development the conditions necessary for the establishment of democratic institutions are almost entirely absent. Illiteracy, poverty, and the predominantly animistic character of the established communal religions all combine to hinder the development of individuality and personal independent status within the polity. Furthermore, the particularism and traditionalism typical of small-scale tribal communities pose strong barriers to the development of a sense of national identity and unity. As a result, wherever political mobilization for economic and social modernization does occur, it generally takes the form either of an autocracy buttressed by traditional concepts of legitimacy or of an autocracy characterized by a charismatic leader brought to prominence in the struggle for independence. These systems of political mobilization, as discussed above, tend to emphasize the strengthening of the national image vis-à-vis other nations rather than the promotion of the internal development of participant political systems. The leaders of these systems, who are usually strongly desirous of industrialization and economic development, typically seek more rapid solutions than would be feasible under representative government and, in addition, are often antagonistic toward colonially instituted parliamentary systems. Thus, the tendency for less democratic systems to accompany higher rates of economic growth is to an important extent a reflection of the positive association between more effective systems of political mobilization and better economic performance; at this low level, where the essential conditions for institutions based on widespread participation are generally absent, the more effective political systems tend to be those in which the centralization of political power has advanced farthest. However, the weakness of the association implies that the effectiveness of measures for political mobilization in overcoming the bottlenecks to growth posed by the strength of traditional social organization is quite limited.

Actually, there appears to be little correlation between the form of government and the extent of leadership commitment to economic development at this level, as indicated by the fact that the variable representing leadership commitment, in both the sociopolitical and the combined results, associates with a factor different from the factor describing the strength of representative political institutions. In the sociopolitical results it is the factor depicting the extent of social and political stability that includes leadership commitment to development (Factor 2, Table 2). In this factor, higher literacy rates and weaker tribal organization are combined with increased social and political instability and less effectiveness of political leadership in the economic realm. These associations are indicative of the social and political constraints that reduce the effectiveness of governmental actions at this level of development. The relative unimportance of differences in the extent of political mobilization for development in explaining inter-country variations in short-term economic growth is evident in the negligible explanation (less than 1 per cent) of rates of growth of per capita GNP offered by the factor incorporating this force (Factor 4, Table 1). Of course, this does not mean that a national mobilization effort much greater than is typically permitted by the divisive forces characteristic of countries at this level would have insignificant results. Ghana, for example, which a decade and a half ago would have belonged in the low group, has developed over a relatively short period to the level of the intermediate group by means of an extent of political mobilization considerably greater than that which typifies the countries in the low group.

Summary

The analysis in this paper makes it clear that at the lowest end of the socioeconomic scale the nature of the growth process requires both economic and social transformations. It is apparent that for this group of countries the extent to which the sway of tribal society has been reduced and the degree to which the modernization of social structure has proceeded are important determinants of the rate of improvement of purely economic performance. These social transformations are required for the enlargement of the sphere within which economic activity operates independently of traditional social organization. It is also apparent that the economic process by which growth is induced involves the dualistic development of a modern, foreign-trade-oriented sector based on the exploitation of natural resource endowments. This economic process provides both the opportunities and the incentives for the social changes that are essential for the initiation of economic growth at this level of development. The successful permeation by the market economy and the continuous expansion of a technologically advanced sector entail significant transformations of social structure because of two concurrent phenomena. First, within the traditional agricultural economy the spread of production for the market inevitably involves a decline in the control of tribal institutions over economic actions. Secondly, the expansion of a distinct modern sector augments the importance of market transactions within a traditional society by increasing wage payments to members of indigenous villages as well as by increasing their cash purchases of consumer goods. Therefore, it is the appearance and growth of opportunities for the exchange of goods and for the sale of labor which stimulate the requisite social transformations rather than social changes internal to the traditional society. Political forces do not exert a particularly strong systematic effect on rates of economic growth, even though there is a slight tendency for authoritarian governments to be more effective economically.

A FORMALIST VIEW OF AFRICAN ECONOMIC ANTHROPOLOGY

14

Harold K. Schneider

In order to assess the current state of economic anthropology in Africa one must decide what economic anthropology is. Those who are familiar with the sometimes bitter disputation among students of this subject realize the primacy of this question. Put simply, the Polanyi-Dalton-Bohannan position, generally referred to as substantive,[1] amounts to a review of studies of systems of distribution conducted in a structural-functional framework of thought. The substantive view seeks to understand how the system of production and distribution serves the society. In contrast, the Cook-Burling position,[2] generally referred to as formal,[3] is a deductive approach that seeks to determine how allocation of resources is decided by the individual or the firm, which is assumed to be attempting to maximize utility.

The extent of divergence between the substantive and formal approaches to economic anthropology is suggested by a

1. Karl Polanyi, Conrad M. Arensberg, and H. W. Pearson, eds., *Trade and Market in the Early Empires* (Glencoe, Ill.: The Free Press, 1957), p. 243.

2. Scott Cook, "The Obsolete Anti-Market Mentality: A Critique of the Substantive Approach to Economic Anthropology," *American Anthropologist*, LXVIII (April, 1966), 323–45; and R. Burling, "Maximization Theories and the Study of Economic Anthropology," *ibid.*, LXIV, (October, 1962), 802–21.

3. Polanyi, Arensberg, and Pearson, *Trade and Market.*

comparison of articles reprinted in Dalton's *Tribal and Peasant Economies: Readings in Economic Anthropology* and those in LeClair and Schneider's *Economic Anthropology: Readings in Theory and Analysis*.[4] There is only one duplication despite the rather large number of readings contained in each book.

The reason for this difference is not hard to find. In the revised introduction of the second edition of *Markets in Africa*, Bohannan and Dalton write:

> In marketless communities and those with peripheral markets only . . . it is kinship or tribal affiliation within constraints imposed by technology and physical environment that dictate how land, labor and products are produced and allocated.[5]

By contrast, the formalists' economics is not the study of how kinship or tribal affiliations dictate production and allocation but of choice between alternatives seen in a framework of assumed desire to maximize utility. To quote Robbins' famous *Essay on the Nature and Significance of Economic Science:*

> When time and the means for achieving ends are limited *and* capable of alternative application, *and* the ends are capable of being distinguished in order of importance, their behaviour necessarily assumes the form of choice. Every act which involves time and scarce means for achievement of one end involves the relinquishment of their use for the achievement of another.[6]

Formalist economic anthropology is the study of choice-making. For substantivists to deny the applicability of formal techniques to Africa suggests that choice in African societies does not amount to very much. Substantive economics assumes, that is, that the alternatives open to Africans are so limited that Africans can be considered to be tradition-directed, and that if choice then is not significant in African behavior, Africans do not have to economize. To a formalist,

4. George Dalton, ed., *Tribal and Peasant Economies: Readings in Economic Anthropology* (Garden City, N. Y.: Natural History Press, 1967); and E. E. LeClair and Harold Schneider, *Economic Anthropology: Readings in Theory and Analysis* (forthcoming).

5. Paul Bohannan and George Dalton, eds., *Markets in Africa*, 2d ed. (Garden City, N. Y.: Doubleday, 1965), p. 1.

6. Lionel Robbins, *An Essay on the Nature and Significance of Economic Science*, 2d ed. (London: Macmillan, 1952), p. 14.

this approach has puzzling implications. If the allocation of wealth is determined by kinship or tribal affiliations, if distribution is simply a matter of reciprocity and redistribution in the altruistic sense that Polanyi seems to mean, then it logically follows that resources are unlimited, which is hard to believe, or that wants are severely limited, which I also find hard to believe, or that the locus of choice-making is removed from the individual or family to the lineage or tribe. If this latter is so, then the allocation process is still amenable to formal investigation. It makes little difference to economic analysis whether a lineage council or an individual is seen as the decision-maker about how much is to be planted, what labor is to be allotted to agricultural production, or how the product is to be distributed. The point is that choices must be made; formal theory seeks to understand the basis for choice-making and thus to predict and explain behavior.

For some reason both substantivists and formalists tend to focus on exchange or distribution, probably because of the empirical predominance or high visibility of these processes. But a formal investigation does not require this emphasis. As Hoselitz has noted for Indian peasants, "production for subsistence and for the market are real alternatives,"[7] hence, the distinction between production for home use and for the market is not significant. Thus, a situation can be imagined where no exchange ever takes place, simply because it is more rational in terms of maximization of utility for the producer to consume his own products. Therefore, even though there is no market in the physical sense, there is a market system in the sense that choices must be made with respect to how limited resources are to be used to achieve satisfaction.

If it is allowed that African behavior can be analyzed from the point of view of choice-making, it can also be claimed that the structural parallels between Western and African societies are greater than is generally assumed. I have argued that in Africa cattle, or rather livestock in combination with certain other things, function as money does in our economy. I also believe that Africans are to an appreciable extent economic men in the literal, as well as in the theoretical, sense. They invest, seek to accumulate profit, bank, capitalize, innovate, and so on. I also feel that there is nothing wrong in concen-

7. Berthold Hoselitz, "Capital Formation, Saving, and Credit in Indian Agricultural Society," in *Capital Saving and Credit in Peasant Societies,* ed. by Raymond Firth and B. S. Yamey (Chicago: Aldine, 1964), p. 371.

trating on the economizing of material means, although I think the greatest advances in economics in general will come with a realization that material and non-material wealth should be treated together. Most anthropologists who have taken a formal approach, Pospisil, for instance,[8] have looked at their societies with a view to seeking parallels with our economy. They are not sophisticated in economic theory, but they sense in the lives of the people they study economic behavior which parallels our own but which is not specific to capitalist economy.

To explain why a focus on decision-making characterizes formal economics carries us one step further. In a truly deductive theoretical social science, in Knight's words, one "uses inferences from clear and statable abstract principles, and especially intuitive knowledge, as a method."[9] In the case of economics, if one assumes that the actors are motivated to maximize utility, rationality is defined as behavior which most efficiently moves in that direction, and predictions about behavior are based on this model. If one predicts behavior thereby, all to the good. If one does not, also all to the good. In both cases a scientific advance has been made. Such an approach does not demonstrate whether people are rational or irrational. Rationality is a way of describing decision-making behavior in a structured model. Further, the assumption that all men are economic men follows the line taken by Friedman when he writes that "unless the behavior of businessmen in some way or other approximates behavior consistent with the maximization of returns, it seems unlikely that they would remain in business for long."[10] Similarly, unless the economic behavior of Africans is in some way consistent with the resources available in relation to their goals, they would not survive. Thus formalists seek to understand the process of choice-making in order to predict behavior and thereby understand it.

There are those who feel that even if formal economics can be employed as suggested, economics has not been as successful in predicting behavior as might be expected, but formalists

8. Leopold Pospisil, *The Kapauku Papuans* (New Haven: Department of Anthropology, Yale University, 1963).

9. Frank H. Knight, "Anthropology and Economics," *Journal of Political Economy*, XLIX (April, 1941), 247–68.

10. Milton Friedman, *Essays in Positive Economics* (Chicago: University of Chicago Press, 1953), p. 22.

nonetheless believe that the best strategy for dealing scientifically with African economic behavior is to approach it deductively rather than purely inductively, historically, or descriptively. The failure of the social sciences to predict human behavior to any significant degree may in part be due to a failure to use methodology deductively.

Formal analyses of African indigenous economies are not common, but they are present and increasing. Probably the first to try a formal approach is Goodfellow, whose attempt in *Principles of Economic Sociology* to apply formal economic concepts to South African Bantu is in my opinion underrated. As Goodfellow puts it,

> The greater part of the apparatus of economic theory may be evolved without going outside a single household. This being so, it would be surprising if modern economic theory failed to apply to the peoples known as primitive.[11]

He then writes that

> The principle of economic disposal is an essential part, or aspect, of any cultural scheme. One of the basic facts to be observed in any culture, however primitive, is that it has mechanisms whereby the individual is taught not to waste, to acquire values in consonance with those of his fellow-beings, and to manage his affairs according to those values. Even if the savage, therefore, could be said to be "dominated by custom," this, far from meaning that he did not dispose economically of his resources, might mean just the opposite; for custom may best be regarded as the mechanism through which this essential aim is achieved.[12]

My own writing on the Turu is an example of a rather unsophisticated formal approach.[13] Like Pospisil writing on the Kapauku,[14] I worked more by instinct than by systematically applying formal economic theory. But this has an advan-

---

11. D. M. Goodfellow, *Principles of Economic Sociology* (London: Routledge, 1939), p. 6.

12. *Ibid.*, p. 16.

13. H. K. Schneider, "Economics in East African Aboriginal Societies," in *Economic Transition in Africa*, ed. by M. J. Herskovits and M. Harwitz (Evanston: Northwestern University Press, 1964), pp. 53–76; and H. K. Schneider, "A Model of African Indigenous Economy and Society," *Journal of Comparative Studies in Society and History* (1964), pp. 35–37.

14. Pospisil, *The Kapauku Papuans*, pp. 18–31.

tage. I see the use of livestock as money as an economic process, where more formally trained persons, bound by a specific conception of economy, do not. My view of Turu economy can be briefly summarized here.

Adult Turu men have a clear notion of what their own economic system consists of, although I would stress that what people conceive to be the system and what it is in formal terms are not necessarily the same. This is true of our own economy. The businessman "knows" what the economic system is and can verbalize rules of decision-making behavior that will lead to getting rich. For example, "A penny saved is a penny earned." But under certain circumstances, as in the present American economy, such a rule, in formal terms, is probably irrational. "A penny spent is a penny earned" would be more appropriate. Similarly, the Turu knows that one should increase the number of his wives in order to increase production and so to get rich. But under some circumstances multiple wives can be a deficit.

Granting, then, that there is not a one-to-one fit between the formal conception of an economy and people's notions of it, the Turu will tell you that the way to get rich (and "Everyone wants to get rich; how can it be otherwise?" said one graybeard to me) is to grow lots of bulrush millet, store it in the house, and then try to keep from eating too much of it while waiting for a famine to strike the land, during which time the grain can be converted to cattle, the most prized form of wealth. (One of my informants made a lot of money this way in 1938 when he exchanged grain for cattle at a rate of three to four *debes* per heifer. A *debe* is a four-imperial-gallon petrol container which holds forty pounds of millet. During 1959–60, a reasonably good production year, the price was twenty *debes* per heifer.)

In the Turu economy the variables associated with production of wealth are cattle to produce manure to fertilize the land; manured farmland; grazing land, particularly swamp land which can be used for reserve grazing; wives, who are the labor force; and a group of friends who can be called upon as a reserve labor force and as a source of low-interest loans. Another feature of the system is the practice of livestock loaning, which enables a wealthy man to increase to an indefinite number the cattle he possesses.

The critical thing to keep in mind in doing a formal study of an economy like this is that magnitudes must be produced for these variables (amount of grain produced, exchange rate for livestock, size of land holding, amount of production achieved by a single wife, and so on) in order to study how the variables relate to one another and to determine whether the economic decisions of the Turu are in fact theoretically rational. If they are rational, predictions can be made about economic behavior. If they are not rational, then we are warned to look further for important dimensions of the system. It does not, however, follow that if in terms of the theory one finds that behavior is not predictable, one can then conclude that the behavior of the actor is in some absolute sense unpredictable or economically irrational.

Comparative economics, which is what economic anthropology in my view is, would be well served by systematic study of groups of societies, such as the cattle people of Africa. When I began to investigate the literature in the wake of my study of the Turu, I found many parallels to the Turu system in other societies, not the least of which were revealed by tables of exchange rates (buried in footnotes and in appendixes of books) suggesting that a system of money like that of the Turu was widespread. But Turu society was also different from other societies (for example, few use manure, as do the Turu and a few neighboring tribes, with the result that the production system for grain is strongly affected, most notably by forcing nomadic behavior on cattle-owners). Hence we have the possibility of a large number of comparative studies.

Polly Hill is well known for her analysis of the migrant farmers of Ghana.[15] Briefly, she has argued that the apparently mysterious growth of cocoa production in Ghana is explained by recognizing that indigenous peoples can be capitalistic. The cocoa farmers, that is, seeing the profit possibilities of growing cocoa, began to move to new lands in order to better grow it. To me, a particularly appealing thing about this thesis is that it demonstrates a point I consider very important to the theory of culture change: people always have values which are not satisfied under a given system and which therefore can explain their switch, given the opportunity, to a new form of life. An extreme cultural relativistic point of view would predict that they would not change because any

15. Polly Hill, *Migrant Cocoa Farmers of Southern Ghana* (Cambridge: Cambridge University Press, 1963).

cultural system is self-contained. Recently Polly Hill has published a "plea for indigenous economics," [16] by which she means the study of the relationship between the "cash and subsistence sectors." She urges that Africans are basically "rational," but that the structure of this rationality must be studied in the field. I take this to mean that each system is differently structured and that rationality is defined by how the system is conceived and is not absolute. She goes on to say that the economic lives of "primitive" people are not simple, and economists therefore should not be reluctant to apply their theories to them.

In my view one of the most subtle and productive of formal thinkers in the African area is Mary Douglas. In her paper on the Lele in *Markets in Africa* she contrasts the Lele and Bushong, asking why the Bushong are "richer" than the Lele.[17] She describes the Lele as starting with poor soil but also as being less inclined to produce goods because the older men have the system tightly under control, whereas the Bushong obtain wealth and status by stressing the production of material wealth, their system being a more open one. In terms of the goals of these two peoples, low production is rational in one society but not in the other. My reservation about Douglas' thesis is in her tendency to equate high productivity with good in some absolute sense. But this is not a dominant idea. While Douglas does not give many figures or magnitudes in her paper, it is noteworthy that magnitudes are implicit in the analysis; the question that focuses the study requires some knowledge of the magnitude of wealth in each of these two societies. Still I would have welcomed the publication of her figures for the simple reason that one of the values of a formal approach is that it allows replication of analysis.

Mary Douglas has published a paper on "primitive rationing" which illustrates well the probable future of formal comparative economics in Africa. Abandoning the substantivist approach, which claims that "primitive" money is not money because it does not mediate supply and demand in a market, she accepts that money can exist in African indige-

16. Polly Hill, "A Plea for Indigenous Economics: The West African Example," *Economic Development and Cultural Change*, XV, No. 1 (October, 1966), 10–20.

17. Mary Douglas, "The Lele—Resistance to Change," in *Markets in Africa*, pp. 183–213.

nous economies and that it can operate as money does in our economy.[18] But she argues that in many indigenous economies, such as the Lele, social factors intrude to affect the free flow of money. The money is more analogous to coupons in our society, impeding movement of wealth and controlling it. She writes that coupons when spent return to an issuing point and their acquisition is continually under survey and control. The main function of these coupons is to provide the necessary condition for entry to high-status positions, or for maintaining rank, or for countering attacks on status.[19] The approach manifested in this article, while original and interesting, still shows some tendency to maintain the social-economic dichotomy that to my mind confuses economic thinking.

Recent papers by Barth and Joy on the economy of the Mountain Fur in the Sudan are sophisticated and impressive.[20] Working from a basic characteristic of a formal analysis, viewing behavior in terms of choices, Barth develops a system of alternatives for a Fur management unit which he presents as a flow-chart depicting the main forms of goods and services in the economy, how they are produced, and how they can be exchanged. That is, "it depicts the flow of value through the system":

> From the point of view of each individual unit of management, the central purpose of economic activities must be to direct the flow of his own assets in these various channels in such a way as (i) to achieve maximal increase in them while (ii) obtaining a balanced distribution of value on the various consumption items of market goods, porridge, beer, housing, *Haj*, and feasts.[21]

Joy builds on Barth's model and recommends the results as indicative of the value of collaboration of anthropologists and economists:

18. Mary Douglas, "Primitive Rationing: A Study in Controlled Exchange," in *Themes in Economic Anthropology*, ed. by Raymond Firth (London: Tavistock, 1967), p. 124.

19. *Ibid.*, p. 133.

20. Fredrik Barth, "Economic Spheres in Darfur," in *Themes in Economic Anthropology*, pp. 149–73; and Leonard Joy, "An Economic Homologue of Barth's Presentation of Economic Spheres in Darfur," *ibid.*, pp. 175–89.

21. Barth, "Economic Spheres," p. 162.

A matrix presentation can be made to represent exactly the properties of the flow system outlined by Barth. When this is done so as to incorporate the full information included in the paper it includes much that does not appear in Barth's diagram (e.g., the distinction of sub-periods for labor supply and crop-input requirements). . . . Conceptually, [the matrix approach argues] that the attempt to formulate a matrix requires one to ask analytically significant questions.[22]

I would endorse Joy's proposal, pointing out that Benton Massell, using multiple regression analysis, analyzed my Turu data in order to test my claim that Turu act rationally in their allocation of resources. His provocative conclusion was that there is support for this claim in the pricing of women relative to cattle and the refusal to sell cultivable land at the institutionally fixed price:

However, it is worth noting that this "rationality" applies to the aggregate while not to the individual farmsteads. For, given the relative factor prices, those producers with a high capital-labor ratio could increase profits by acquiring more wives, whereas producers with a low capital-labor ratio would do well to acquire more cattle. In other words, all households could improve their performance by moving closer to the point at which the relative marginal productivities equal the relative factor prices.[23]

Since the aggregate here was a localized lineage, this might provide support for the claim that lineages are corporate; a lineage, that is, acts like a firm.

Other examples of the use of formal thought occur in the writings of Victor Uchendu on the Igbo,[24] and Judith Heyer with respect to linear programming in the analysis of peasant farms in Machakos, Kenya.[25]

22. Joy, "Economic Homologue," pp. 187–88.

23. Benton F. Massell, "Econometric Variations on a Theme by Schneider," *Economic Development and Culture Change*, XII (October, 1963), 34–41.

24. Victor C. Uchendu, *The Igbo of Southeast Nigeria* (New York: Holt, Rinehart and Winston, 1965).

25. Judith Heyer, "Linear Programming Analysis of Peasant Farms in Machakos District, Kenya," paper presented at E.A.I.S.R. Conference, Kampala, Uganda, 1966.

Conclusion

In considering the future of African economic anthropology, then, two legitimate techniques of analysis seem to be open to us: the substantive and the formal. A substantive approach is essentially a sociological orientation focused on how the exchange system of material means fits the status system and serves to maintain the social system. In short, it is concerned with social stability. The formal approach leads to an orientation which sees societies as complex games composed of the following elements: (1) rules or laws and conditions limiting the actions of players, (2) goals or values for which the players are striving, and (3) strategies, the plays of the contestants who are attempting to reach the goals within the framework of rules and who are further governed by the conditions or setting of the play. In a sense, the substantivist is concerned with the rules of the game and how players are kept in bounds and the game maintained. The formalist is concerned with the strategies used by the players and how these relate to achieving the desired goals.

I conceive of the formal approach in economic anthropology as differing from Western economics in being much more explicitly concerned with how the rules condition strategies, although most scholars taking a formal approach to African economics have focused on what constitutes rational strategy. My study of the Turu, Barth's analysis of the Fur, and Hill's account of the growth of cocoa farming are all strategy oriented. Only Douglas in her study of the Lele has chosen to stress how the cultural setting has affected the system of decision-making.

One of the problems that arises in the quest for a formal economic anthropology of indigenous Africa is the question of what constitutes an indigenous economy. One is tempted to answer that it is *any* economy ordinarily not thought of as a market economy, or what Bohannan and Dalton refer to as marketless economies. The problem is the same as that facing the sociologist attempting to identify his unit, society. I do not feel it is a serious problem at this point. A system of allocation of resources which can be perceived in a framework of non-Western customs may be regarded as an indigenous economy. The importance of focusing on such exotic economies is simply that such a stance is likely to be theoretically edifying as well as valuable for studying economic development or change.

The value of such an approach for studying economic change can be illustrated from my own experience with destocking among the Turu of Tanzania. Working from the assumption that the Turu are not economically motivated, the government began in 1952 to destock the area with the aim of reducing erosion. The plan was to remove one animal in every 10 from each homestead. It was calculated that this would result in a net livestock decrease of 10 per cent. In fact, it resulted in a decrease of only about 6 per cent because most Turu had less than 10 head and so were not required to give up any animals. Consequently, in 1957 the rate was increased to 1 in 6. This led to a very substantial reduction of livestock but also to great unrest among the Turu, so much so that by 1959 the destocking program was discontinued.

Looked at in formal terms, the across-the-board reduction of livestock had far-reaching functional consequences. If livestock are money, in the sense of being media of exchange and repositories of value, and if they are eliminated at a constant rate, this can be seen to be a reduction in the supply of money with deflationary consequences. By deflating the money by a constant applied evenly to the population, the effect seems to have been to cause a decrease in the flow of livestock to grain-holders and of grain to livestock-holders as a function of the increase in value of the livestock. That is to say, people everywhere were affected immediately and in similar ways by this method of destocking, resulting in a general state of unrest and failure of the program.

In a formal approach, I think special stress should be placed on the need for quantification of variables. It is easy to demonstrate the importance of being able to indicate the quantities involved. If we were to compare the ways in which Masai and Mbundu utilize their cattle, we could say of the Masai that they slaughter cattle for meat and live very extensively on milk. In contrast, the Mbundu, who are also cattle people, do not eat their cattle and do not even milk them. To what are we to attribute the great difference? Murdock seems to think it is explained by a difference in cattle customs diffused to the Mbundu plateau before milking was invented. Perhaps this is so, but one would have to admit that a new light is cast on the problem when one realizes that the ratio of cattle to people among the Masai is perhaps twenty cows to one person, while among the Mbundu it is one cow to every ten persons. A formal approach, in contrast to the substantive, is characterized by its focus on magnitudes. It is assumed that people enumerate their wealth and seek to arrange it to achieve maximum value. Magnitudes are necessary to measure this process and to build theory which is predictive.

When urging the adaptation of formal economic modes of analysis, I do not mean that we should abandon the traditional anthropological framework. I foresee a growing together of the two fields, economics contributing the structure of formal thought necessary for what I believe would be the most fruitful analysis of decision-making, anthropology contributing knowledge of the social and cultural parameters that condition how choices are made by the actors.

DISCUSSANT'S COMMENTS 14.

Simon Ottenberg

Professor Schneider's paper is in keeping with the recent trend in anthropology to move away from a strong emphasis on social structure and social relationships, seen in an organizational framework, toward a view of man as a person choosing among alternatives and as a decision-making individual. Similar developments have recently occurred in other subfields of anthropology, such as kinship studies and political anthropology. Thus the view Schneider espouses is a logical extension of these, albeit he is drawing ideas from economics. The view is most welcome as an alternative to the Dalton-Bohannan-Polanyi approach, not necessarily because the latter is not of value, in my view, but because it has tended to dominate African anthropological thought to the exclusion of other approaches.

Nevertheless, I believe that Schneider distorts the substantive economics view. The substantive approach is concerned with many more things than the question of how the system of production and distribution serves the society. It is concerned with developing an anthropological economics in its own right and with the question of the relationship of social structure to economic behavior. The substantive approach is, according to Schneider, concerned with social stability. I consider this a misreading of the aims of Dalton, Polanyi, and others. The typology of economic systems that they have developed, and which is explored briefly in the introduction to the second edition of *Markets in Africa,* edited by Dalton and Bohannan, is particularly adapted to viewing growth and change in economic behavior and relating these to other changes in the society. Polanyi's study of the Dahomean slave trade is certainly a case in point. One may not agree with the particular typology chosen, but it does afford a view amenable to studies of change as well as comparison of African economics in different societies.

Schneider implies that the substantive approach is more concerned with viewing the constraints on economic behavior than with seeing it as a choice among alternatives. This is probably correct for some writers and incorrect for others. I feel that he has raised a false argument. Schneider is interested in alternatives and decision-making. But when we begin to ask what alternatives are open to the individual or group in the economic sphere we must deal with the question of constraints, since it is within the framework of constraints, cultural rules and values, that alternatives are placed; there is no question of totally free choice. Therefore, Schneider himself, in any analysis of alternatives, cannot escape something of the view that he criticizes.

This brings me to my essential argument about the paper. Schneider has distorted and extended the two views—the substantive and the formal—to the point of an overpolarized dichotomy. I do not see that the two views are essentially in opposition, and, indeed, there would be some profit in combining them. For example, it would be interesting to take the typology of economic systems in the substantive approach and see whether each type has characteristic patterns of economic choice for individuals or groups. Whether this was to be found or not would be quite revealing. Further, economic choice has to be seen within the framework of some sort of social system. It is not possible to totally escape the analysis of structure, the relationship of economic behavior to political styles, and so on. Schneider represents a rather abstract model of decision-making, of alternative-selection, which gives little indication of how he, or others, will go about the process of analysis, how they will evolve patterns of decision-making, and what the relevance of such patterns may be. The formalists have a very good point, but it does not seem to me that they have yet demonstrated how it operates in analysis. Further, the view leaves undefined the question of differentiating economic factors in choice and alternatives from political or other factors. This makes for a looseness of definition of what economics is that the substantive approach avoids. I do not think this definitional problem is insoluble.

In short, I would certainly encourage the formal approach as potentially of great value, but there is no reason that it should hamper itself by a distortion of other views or claims to a type of analysis which it is still in the process of working out.

COMMUNICATIONS MEDIA IN AFRICA: 15.
A CRITIQUE IN RETROSPECT
AND PROSPECT

Hamid Mowlana

The mass media, as they come to the emerging African nations, are regarded by some to be "the great hope of democracy," while others consider the press, radio, and television to be "insidious devices that would capture and enslave helpless masses."[1] There is no right or wrong to these opposing viewpoints—the facts of media development in Africa can argue for both. There is general agreement, however, that improvement of mass communications in Africa is imperative. This paper will review the state of the mass media in sub-Saharan Africa today, exploring its general development and pointing out significant gaps in this progress. The predominantly Arab countries of North Africa have experienced different patterns of development and so are not considered in this paper.

With adequate and effective communication the pathways to change can be made easier and shorter. A developing nation must have an adequate flow of information if it is to educate its people and modernize its economy. Communication is a basic element in the process of change, and the communications media have a vital role to play in economic and social development and in the building of nation-states and social institutions.

1. Melvin L. DeFleur and Otto N. Larsen, *The Flow of Information: An Experiment in Mass Communications* (New York: Harper, 1958), p. xii.

The process of modernization and the acquisition of a true "nation" status involves a threefold development: education, communication, and economic development. These three areas, which I believe to encompass the realm of social development, are interrelated and interdependent. Thus an adequate flow of information is essential to the growth, both economic and social, of a developing country.

Just how "adequate" is Africa's flow of information? At the 1962 meeting of exports on development of information media in Africa it was found that the mass media were powerful educating tools, but that these tools were not easily accessible to the entire population.[2] UNESCO, the organization that called the meeting, decided that for a country to be considered adequately supplied with information media, at least ten copies of a daily newspaper, five radio receivers, and two cinema seats must be provided for every one hundred persons in the population. But in 1964, for every one hundred persons in Africa there existed only one copy of a daily newspaper, two radio receivers, and one-half a cinema seat.[3]

Developmental Factors

The sporadic nature of both media and literacy development within regions and within the African continent as a whole is clearly discernible. Media and literacy seem to cluster in the urban or more industrialized centers, leaving vast areas of the countryside untouched. Media and literacy usually occur together, and they feed from one another.[4] Media increase awareness to the point where awareness becomes literacy. After that point literacy must forge ahead of media development to keep the demand for information rising. As the demand rises, the media will expand to take care of that demand and will in the process increase literacy by providing more information. And so the circle goes.

But Africa does not have time to wait for that circle to eventually embrace the entire continent. Africa's newly inde-

2. UNESCO, *Developing Information Media in Africa,* Reports and Papers on Mass Communication, No. 37 (Paris; UNESCO, 1962), p. 7.

3. UNESCO, *World Communication,* 4th ed. (Paris: UNESCO, 1964).

4. Daniel Lerner, *The Passing of Traditional Society: Modernizing the Middle East* (Glencoe, Ill.: The Free Press, 1958), p. 43.

pendent states have stepped into a rapidly spinning twentieth century, and they face the problem of unifying their people as nations. A significant gap is in the fact that the media are not providing an adequate and effective flow of information to all the people.

One can doubtless provide some explanations of why the mass-media systems in Africa are still rudimentary. Education is a point where the development of the media can be accelerated. A lack of instruction and literacy in the people and a lack of training throughout the media are limiting the development of the communication media in Africa.

The International Press Institute at its annual meeting in June, 1968, in Nairobi, Kenya, reported that "illiteracy remains a major problem in all African nations, ranging from 70 to 90 per cent or more." [5] The highest rate of literacy, by UNESCO figures, is 25 to 30 per cent in Uganda. In the countries once gathered under the umbrella of French West Africa, this figure drops to a literacy rate of less than 5 per cent. Considerable variation in literacy rates exists within a given region. It is thought that 85 per cent of the population in English-speaking West Africa cannot read and write, but the figure drops to about 50 per cent in Lagos, the capital of Nigeria.[6]

All such figures must be constantly revised because of the tremendous educational strides being made in many African countries. In recent years some forty thousand Africans have studied abroad. About eight thousand have gone to Communist countries, with an almost equal number going to the United States. A recent report indicates that about ninety-eight thousand students have studied in Africa's fifty-six institutions of higher education, but almost half of these are from the Republic of South Africa.[7]

5. "African Overview," a report by the International Press Institute committee to the 17th annual assembly of IPI, Nairobi, Kenya, June, 1968.

6. UNESCO, *World Illiteracy at Mid-Century*, Monographs on Fundamental Education, No. 11 (Paris: UNESCO, 1957).

7. IPI, "African Overview." According to this IPI report, only nineteen of the fifty nations or territories have local provisions for higher education. The total African enrollment is near 120,000, but only 11,500 of them are south of the Sahara. Some gifted students do go abroad to study, but the total equals only about 18 per 100,000 inhabitants. Conversely, it has been estimated that some 100 million African adults cannot read or write. Allocations for education range from $0.50 to $2.00 per person annually.

Another important shortcoming in the communication process is the economic gap, which lies at the root of various attacks launched against the media. Financial problems occur on both sides of the two-way communication process. On the transmission, or media, side, much of the equipment must be imported because of the lack of production facilities on the continent and the general low level of the economy. Also, government taxes raise this cost considerably, in spite of the fact that many restrictions on educational equipment have been lifted.

Newsprint, vital to publishing, must be imported by Africa. This poses additional cost factors. According to a *Newsweek* survey in 1965, the cost of a ton of newsprint in Nairobi was $230, compared to $134 per ton in New York.

Poor telecommunications networks make distribution both costly and haphazard. Charges that the press is influenced and largely controlled by the world agencies, post-colonial ties, and governmental organizations and departments stem largely from the fact that the developing media, due to lack of capital, are forced to rely on outside sources for their news supply rather than obtaining their own news agencies and news-gathering facilities. This situation has been an important reason for the clustering of news facilities in urban areas and a reason for the dearth of upcountry coverage. Media do not have the money to finance a staff of correspondents to cover the rural areas, nor can they afford to expand their production or distribution systems.

On the other side of the communication process is about 70 per cent of the population with average annual incomes of less than $100.[8] Relative to this low income, the new mass media are expensive. For example, the *Togo Press,* one of the better quality papers, costs 250 Togo francs (about $1.00) per month, but this represents 20 per cent of the average worker's monthly income.

Lack of money in the population prohibits any large-scale production facilities for the media. Film production is virtually nonexistent in Africa, both because of the economy and because of the lack of trained personnel. The low economic level of a country inhibits the expansion of the media for another reason: where there is lack of industry there is a lack of advertisers, who could possibly help the new media get on

8. UNESCO, *Developing Information Media in Africa,* p. 11.

their feet financially. The cost factor is a great one for the television medium, since its facilities are more expensive than those of either the press or radio. In planning a television station, therefore, great care is necessary. Failures cannot be afforded.

These two main gaps—education and economics—need to be filled before the media can provide an adequate information flow to all parts of Africa's population. Several steps have been taken to close these gaps, and many more are in a theoretical stage.

Important in the study of communications media in Africa is a double-edged question about the effects of the media on sociopolitical development, both for the present and from a long-range perspective. Most of the states of Africa view the mass media as instruments of national policy, devices by which the goals of the national state or the government can be furthered. Such a theory of the role of the media demands control over its content. This question of the role of the mass media in national development is basic to a conception of the future of the media in Africa.

Today, leaders in the independent African states devote a major part of their energies to communicating with one another, with the general population, and with the world at large. Most African governments have official information services which constitute in large part their communication resources on a day-by-day basis. The importance that African leaders attach to the foreign media has been noted. African presidents would often give more personal interviews to foreign correspondents than they would give to the local press. This is illustrated in the report given by an African journalist to the International Press Institute conference in June, 1968:

A few years ago the former president of my country wrote a lengthy rejoinder to a British newspaper's editorial comment on his role as a constitutional head of state. I said at the time that the President of Nigeria could not be a busy man if he would become a correspondent of the letters to the editor column of an overseas newspaper. On hindsight, I think that the reason he took the step is that our African leaders will subconsciously look to the press of the former colonial power for approval. This is perhaps human failing; it is one for which I have no sympathy. But if we are seeking the reasons why African leaders are touchy with the foreign press, this is one of them.[9]

As the media get more steady on their feet in Africa, the problems of media control and press freedom are bound to arise, creating a triangle of friction: media wanting to freely direct their own programming, government wanting to control and influence these powerful means of reaching the population, and the population demanding leadership as well as free information flow.

Today the trend is toward more, not less, government press control in Africa. The 1968 International Press Institute study of the world-press systems concluded that "it is quite possible that unless the economic situation gets better in the near future, a large number of African nations will have government-owned and government-controlled printed media as well as electronic media of mass communication." The report noted, among other things, that the press of African republics more and more is becoming one that (1) espouses nationalism; (2) sides with one of the nation's political factions; (3) creates internal tension; (4) criticizes colonialism; and (5) rejects a respect for objectivity.[10]

A survey of press freedom in Africa was conducted by the Freedom of Information Center (University of Missouri) for the year 1966. Called the Press Independence and Critical Ability (PICA) Index, the survey gave the 15 African nations measured a −0.42 rating on a scale that ranged from +4 (absolute freedom) to −4 (absolute control). Kenya ranked fortieth (with a +1.20 rating) among the 94 nations in the world survey, and first among the 15 African nations (Algeria, Libya, Morocco, Sudan, and United Arab Republic were classified under the Middle East).[11] An earlier world freedom classification published in 1965 by Raymond Nixon had assigned Kenya a 5 rating on a 9-point scale, indicating an "intermediate or mixed system with no clear tendencies toward either more freedom or more control at the time."[12] Of

9. Peter Enahoro, "Reporting Africa," a paper read before the IPI Conference, Nairobi, Kenya, June, 1968, p. 4.

10. IPI, "African Overview," p. 4.

11. Ralph Lowenstein, "World Press Freedom, 1966," Freedom of Information Center Publication, University of Missouri, No. 166, August, 1966.

12. Raymond Nixon, "Freedom in the World's Press: A Fresh Appraisal with Data," *Journalism Quarterly*, XLII (Winter, 1965), 3–14.

Nixon's twenty-five points characteristic of free-press countries, Kenya clearly revealed only four: (1) non-Communist country; (2) constitutional government; (3) working constitutionalized democracy, committed to development as a national goal; (4) bureaucracy as post-colonial transitional. Other characteristics indicated that Kenya had a poor climate for press freedom: (1) substantially a one-party system; (2) very low per capita gross national product; (3) high agricultural population with low industrialization; (4) little urbanization; (5) low literacy; (6) low media usage; (7) lack of privately owned news agency; (8) strong leadership charisma.

Communication Network and Flow of News

There has been a trend in recent years for the newly independent nations of Africa to establish their own news agencies. According to the 1964 UNESCO survey, there were twenty-four news agencies serving in Africa, whereas in 1956 there were only three. These countries, however, still rely heavily on world agencies for information. One study in 1965 found that the information received from these world agencies is neither adequate nor very effective in serving the needs of the new African nations.[13] This study referred to the situation as a "news flow imbalance between the rich and the poor nations," and agreed with a previous survey which stated that "it tends to ignore important events and to distort the reality it represents."[14]

Today one finds the influence of colonial relationships in the use of the wire services in African nations. There seem to be wire service "spheres of influence," Reuters, for instance, in English-speaking and Commonwealth nations and AFP in French-speaking Africa. Each of these "spheres" is dominated by news from the respective news capital, London or Paris. Some observers have warned of the harmful effects such

13. William A. Hachten, "The Flow of News and Underdevelopment: A Pilot Study of the African Press," paper read before the International Communications Division of the Association for Education in Journalism at the annual convention, University of Iowa, Iowa City, August 30, 1966, p. 3.

14. Wilbur Schramm, *The Role of Information in National Development* (abridged version of *Mass Media and National Development*) (Paris: UNESCO, 1964), p. 65.

world news agency domination may have on nations struggling
for economic and political independence, believing that the
hopes of the "have-not" nations for the development of their
own individually effective mass-communication systems are
being dashed in their infancy by their dependency on foreign
news flow.

The outward flow of news from African nations is further
limited by high communication charges. Except in the Republic of South Africa, telecommunication facilities are une-
venly developed and very expensive throughout Africa. In
addition, the rates charged for world news agency service are
high, and the equipment costs are great when compared with
the rather meager finances of the developing countries.

News-gathering facilities determine the relative emphasis
news from different regions within Africa will get in a particular nation's press.[15] The picture that the population of a
state gets of itself, of other states, and of the continent as a
whole will be influenced in part by the political and economic
links within the news-coverage chain. Because of the lack of
technical facilities, news moving across the continent and that
moving to and from other countries tends to be of the "catas-
trophe" or "hard" type.[16] Africa thus appears to be a trou-
bled continent both to its own people and to peoples throughout the rest of the world.

The pattern of newspaper press in Africa is often surprising. There are at least four distinctly different types of newspapers circulating in Africa today.[17] First are the foreign
newspapers and magazines, such as *Le Monde* and the *Times*
(London), published in Europe. The educated elites look to
these papers, which are available in every African capital, for
news and comments on international affairs. The second type
of press comprises the newspapers published locally but
owned by foreign interests. These papers, which were first
edited for Europeans, are now to some degree edited and read
by Africans. An example is the Nigerian *Daily Times,* bought

15. John C. Condon, "Nation Building and Image Building in the
Tanzanian Press," *Journal of Modern African Studies,* V (November,
1967), 344.

16. Hachten, "The Flow of News," pp. 4–12.

17. William A. Hachten, "The Role of the Press in a Developing
Country," a paper read before the IPI conference, Nairobi, Kenya,
June, 1968.

by the *Daily Mirror* group of London. The *Mirror* group gave the paper a tabloid format and raised its circulation from 25,000 in 1951 to 120,000 in 1965.[18] But such papers have come under a good deal of suspicion in the years since independence. The third kind of press comprises those independent newspapers supported neither by foreign capital nor by government. The *West African Pilot* was an example of such a journal. These papers are in the position to provide the kind of news coverage that the new nations need, but unfortunately, outside of the Republic of South Africa, due to lack of resources and financial base few are able to do so. The fourth kind of press in Africa is completely government-owned and marks the most significant trend in African journalism today.

The four Tanzanian papers published in Dar es Salaam—two ruling-party organs and two privately owned enterprises—were surveyed by John Condon, and his findings may be considered illustrative of the press in Africa.[19] The most popular daily, *Ngurumo*, is described by Condon as "a blotchy, bold-typeface tabloid of four pages." It carries stories of domestic quarrels, swindles, and so forth. *Ngurumo* is privately owned, written in Swahili, and sells for ten cents. The *Standard*, the other private paper, is written in English and is the largest in number and size of pages. The *Standard* is served by Reuters, Kenya News Agency, and the *Financial Times* (London) clipping agency. *Ngurumo* has no wire services. The *Standard* is the only daily with a Sunday edition, the *Sunday News*. Its readers are 60 per cent African, while nearly all of *Ngurumo*'s readers are African. The most widely distributed daily, *Uhuru*, is owned and controlled by TANU, Tanzania's ruling party. *Uhuru* is written in Swahili, while the *Nationalist*, the other party organ, is an English-language paper. These "voice of the party" papers together have a staff of about sixteen editors and reporters. Reuters and AFP serve them.

All four dailies use "stringers" to cover the upcountry, but none has full-time roving reporters in that area which comprises over 95 per cent of the country's population. Each paper sends half its copies upcountry and distributes the

18. See Rosalynde Ainslie, *The Press in Africa* (London: Gollancz, 1966).

19. Condon, "Nation Building and Image Building."

other half in the capital. This means that about 12 million people in the upcountry have to make do with the same number of copies as go to only 325,000 in the capital. This situation, along with the bad roads and uncertain transportation networks, accounts for the fact that dailies are seen by relatively few people outside the larger cities. Church publications, such as the *Kiongozi,* and some monthly government pamphlets give the rural people a little taste of information here and there. But by and large the country as a whole is starved for information. Newspapers are prized very highly, even among the illiterate, since they are both expensive and hard to come by, and papers are often used as a status symbol.

Condon found the relative absence of Zanzibar news (only 1 to 2 per cent of total news) rather surprising in view of the political importance of Zanzibar to Tanzania. He attributes this finding to apparent restriction of "hard" news from Zanzibar by that country's government.

Condon writes:

> The Swahili reader receives a very limited view of the world outside Tanzania. The reader of *Ngurumo . . .* receives less world news (by word count) in fifteen days than *The Standard* reader receives in one. Thus the clearer world image which the reader of English is more likely to begin with (for knowledge of English is an index of schooling) is increased and sharpened through his reading *The Standard* and *The Nationalist.* But the Tanzanian, who is literate only in Swahili, does not greatly sharpen his image of the world through reading *Uhuru* and *Ngurumo.*[20]

While most of the newspapers in Africa are concentrated in a few large urban areas, 80 per cent of Africa's people live in rural districts. Statistics gathered by UNESCO on the African press show that in 1964 there were 200 dailies in Africa with a total circulation of only about 3.4 million. In fourteen African countries, there was no daily general-interest newspaper at all. Progress and expansion of the press in Africa has been slow. Since 1952 the number of dailies has only increased by ten, and the circulation per 1,000 inhabitants has barely moved at all. However, the rural press is in its infancy and there has been a sizable increase in the number of publications

20. *Ibid.*

directed toward the newly literate in rural areas.[21] Governments have been encouraging the growth of the vernacular press and have been waiving customs and duties on educational communications materials and equipment.

Importance of Electronic Media

To keep the demand for the information media rising, a rapid means of education, especially adult education, is needed. Radio is believed to be a good answer to the immediate communication needs of African nations. Radio can make potent improvements in the media situation.

Radio broadcasting has advanced more rapidly than the press in Africa, and the radio is the primary source of news. Although the cost of radio is substantially lower than other media, broadcasting facilities are still largely beyond the means of private ownership. In most African countries broadcasting services are either government-controlled, or partially government-controlled and partially privately controlled. The expansion of these services has been actively encouraged by governments. UNESCO figures show that in 1950 the total number of radio broadcasting transmitters in Africa was 140, and the total number of receivers was 1.4 million. Between 1950 and 1960 the number of radio receivers in the world doubled, and Africa, with the lowest number of sets in 1950, almost quadrupled its total.[22] The development of low-cost transistors, which free radio reception from dependence on a power source, has revolutionized radio in Africa. UNESCO figures for 1964 world communications show 550 radio transmitters for Africa and 11 million receivers. Although these figures are still below the recommended minimum of five per one hundred inhabitants, it is apparent that radio has made enormous advances in the past few years in Africa. In Tanzania today the UNESCO radio minimum of five receivers per one hundred inhabitants has almost been reached, although newspapers, television, and film still lag far behind the UNESCO minimum standards for information media.

21. ''Mimeo Newspapers—A New Kind of Journalism,'' USIS feature, No. F–65–323, September, 1965. A pioneering experiment in producing mimeograph newspapers, successful in Liberia, is of interest to developing nations in Africa.

22. UNESCO, *World Communication*, p. 45.

The rapid expansion of radio services in Africa can be attributed in part to the fact that radio is a flexible medium, capable of reaching broad audiences, urban and rural, literate and illiterate. Propaganda agencies—both domestic and foreign—are glad to provide tapes and other facilities. Governments often choose to use radio as a medium of national policy.

With the rapid expansion of radio broadcasting services in Africa, the educational potential of the medium is beginning to be tapped. Radio Madagascar, for instance, broadcasts continuously throughout the day, alternating its focus between an urban and a rural audience. City and country dwellers have different needs in terms of both time and interests, and Radio Madagascar meets both needs by sandwiching five- to fifteen-minute educational programs, appealing to the rural population, in with its regular programming. Plans were also made in Madagascar to launch ninety "Clubs Radiovision," or centers where the educational broadcasts could be discussed. These programs have been successful and have proved the value of linking radio broadcasting with visual-aid materials in the area of adult education.

A far-reaching development in radio for Africa has been the rural radio forum plan, which had already proved to be an effective boost to rural development in Canada and in India. The forum program, a combination of mass media and group discussion, was first attempted in Canada in 1941. An essential ingredient to the success of such programs is "participation." In 1964 a similar project, the Farm Radio Forum, was launched in Ghana by UNESCO and various organizations sponsoring the project on behalf of the government of Ghana.[23]

The educational uses of radio point up the problems of language multiplicity in Africa.[24] Often the same program is broadcast in the European language of an area and then rebroadcast in the vernacular language. Radio broadcasters, in attempting to match their programs to the needs of a particular audience, must often decide what is to be the language of transmission.

23. UNESCO, *An African Experiment in Radio Forums for Rural Development*, Reports and Papers on Mass Communication, No. 51 (Paris: UNESCO, 1958), p. 11.

24. Oliver Litondo, "Mass Media and Linguistic Communication in East Africa," *East Africa Journal* (May, 1967), pp. 16–18.

Another problem of radio in Africa is that of atmospheric interference. The transmissions are severely affected by solar interference from October to April, and improvement can only be made by the introduction of FM broadcasting, combined with medium-wave "booster" service. The feasibility of FM radio broadcasting was discussed by UNESCO at the 1962 meeting of experts on development of information media in Africa. While FM was effective in reaching dense population areas, the meeting noted certain drawbacks, such as the limited range of reception and a greater receiver expense. The higher quality of sound of FM was, however, considered valuable for educational purposes. But the development of FM radio broadcasting served as Africa's steppingstone to the development of television reception.

Although the cost of television broadcasting limited its earlier development, the medium is now beginning to grow out of its infancy in Africa. In spite of extensive poverty and low living standards, several factors favored the introduction of television. Governments of the new nations had seen the successes of radio in education, and they considered the addition of sight to sound a valuable help both to formal and to adult education. Also, they knew that development of national unity, loyalty, and pride was extremely important to the future of the new nations. Television stations carry with them a certain status, and could be as capable of evoking national pride in Africans as could the development of modern national airlines or industrial plants.

In spite of the short transmitting signal, which tended to limit television to the major population centers, it was felt that the expense of establishing transmitting facilities could be justified largely through the use of the medium in teacher education. The need for qualified teachers was great, and the teachers were to be found in the urban centers, as was the medium itself.

When the 1962 UNESCO meeting on media in Africa convened, there were already regular television stations in operation in Algeria, Nigeria, the United Arab Republic, and the Federation of Rhodesia and Nyasaland. Also at that time, there were approximately 150,000 receiving sets in use. Commercial television appeared in Kenya in the fall of 1962 and in Uganda in the fall of 1963. By 1964 Africa had a total of fifty-eight regular television transmitters. The number of receivers was estimated to be 490,000. Medium figures for the African states are still lower than those of any other nations, but further progress in television is almost assured, especially since the medium's use in education has become apparent.

The 1962 UNESCO meeting recommended that film production be integrated with radio and television, since the demand for audio-visual aids to education was steadily rising. At that time the only African nation producing feature films regularly was the United Arab Republic, although Tunisia and the Republic of South Africa were making a few. The UNESCO report said that about a dozen countries were making newsreels and documentaries, but that the "production of educational or instructional films . . . was sporadic and often local." [25] Audio-visual centers for schools and adult education programs have since been set up throughout Africa. At present, a pilot project testing the effectiveness of the audio-visual media is being conducted with the help of UNESCO in Dakar, Senegal.[26] The project was launched in July of 1964 and is scheduled to last until the end of 1969.

Media Research and Training

In recent years the leaders of the new nations of Africa have realized the importance and value of cooperation and coordination among governmental agencies, media personnel, and educators within their respective nations, among other nations of Africa, and among other nations of the world as well. This cooperative theme has been continued and enlarged since the 1962 UNESCO meeting. The problem of education in media development has received much attention in recent years.

In 1967 a seminar on mass-media communications was organized at Makerere University College, Uganda, by the East African Academy. It recommended that national broadcasting stations give more and better time to adult educational programs. In addition, periodic audience surveys by the stations were suggested, as well as more research, better training for radio and television teachers, and more attention to reception problems. To aid the education problem faced by the media and to close the gap of cultural diversity between the media operators and the population of Africa the seminar recommended that "in the interests of nation building, mass com-

25. UNESCO, *Developing Information Media in Africa*, p. 30.

26. Owen Leeming, "Senegal: Adult Education Experiment," *New Africa*, X (January–February, 1968), 1–2.

munications media should offer increasing proportions of locally planned and produced indigenous programmes.''

The Makerere seminar also discussed the problem of language diversity and expressed the need for a Linguistic Communications Research Center ''to remove linguistic, psychological or sociological barriers to communication through publication of the facts and improved educational enterprises of all kinds at all levels amongst children and adults.'' The seminar felt further that this research center should provide audio-visual courses for the cinema, television, and radio; research; and training for translators.

The development of Eurovision and Intervision, linking European countries with a means for direct relay of television broadcasts, is considered to be a possible answer to Africa's telecommunications problems. The creation of relay facilities in African nations, recognized as an ideal of international broadcasting, is becoming a reality through the use of space satellites.

The need for development in Africa of national and regional facilities for program production is also being recognized. Programs are presently imported from the more advanced countries, but there is a need for development of the industry in Africa in order to draw more local people into the field of mass media. Training facilities must be expanded, and international exchange programs for trainees need to be revamped in the light of the needs of the developing country.

Three organizations are at present working in this direction: The International Press Institute in Switzerland has organized two journalist training programs, one specifically for East and central Africa to which the Ford Foundation has contributed considerable support. The Thomson chain of newspapers is conducting both on-the-job training and in-England training for African members of its newspaper staffs. And the Foreign Journalists Project, sponsored by the United States State Department and directed by Professor Floyd Arpan of Indiana University, has been arranging a four and one-half month study-work-travel program for journalists and communication specialists of various nations, including those of Africa.

The bulk of the training programs has been offered by the two former colonial powers most active in Africa—Great Britain and France. The Overseas Training Program is run by the BBC in London, and the Studio-Ecole is run by the Office de Cooperation Radiophonique in Paris. Upon observation of these programs in 1963, one American specialist recommended that since American programs cannot offer as extensive an education in elementary-level training as these long-established programs, the American programs should be centered around advanced studies, such as audience-research methodology and educational television.

Over the last few years AID has sponsored twenty-five to thirty students in mass communications per year, but as the "communications revolution" continues many more students will be clamoring for knowledge of the media. To know what these trainees need in the way of media education, more research on mass-communications problems in Africa is required. Africa is a rapidly changing continent—its needs and its problems are constantly shifting, and the demands put upon the media are tremendous in view of the state of constant mobility and the urgent need to educate the population. If the media are to do an effective job, they must be completely in tune with the African people. This is the task for research—an ever-growing and demanding task that must be met if Africa is to have a free and adequate flow of information.

AFRO-AMERICAN INDIANS AND AFRO-ASIANS: CULTURAL CONTACTS BETWEEN AFRICA AND THE PEOPLES OF ASIA AND ABORIGINAL AMERICA

16

Peter B. Hammond

It is time Africanists began to direct more scholarly attention to Africa's influence, or *presence*—past and present—beyond the confines of the continent itself. Particularly deserving of such attention is a series of so far almost totally neglected subjects related to the processes and consequences of nearly five centuries of culture contact between the peoples of West Africa, their descendants born in the New World, and the aboriginal inhabitants of the Americas, the Indians. Exploration of a parallel series of subjects is contingent upon study in ethnohistorical depth of what has happened during more than a thousand years of culture contact between central and East Africa and the peoples of Southwest Asia.[1]

Afro-American Indians

West African–American Indian culture contacts have been ignored as a research field by Africanists and Americanists alike, perhaps as a result of the overspecialization of scholars in each field. Students of the American Indian, even those who have directed their attention to acculturation, have concen-

1. I am grateful to the National Science Foundation and to the Institute of Southern History, The Johns Hopkins University, for support of the research described here.

trated almost entirely on Indian-white contacts.[2] Africanists interested in the destiny of West Africans forcibly resettled in the Americas have been primarily concerned with Negro-white acculturation.

For those reasons, and perhaps for others as well, there is an empty place in the ethnohistorical and ethnographic record of the New World where there ought to be information on what has happened in the centuries since millions of West Africans were first placed in geographic and cultural proximity to large populations of American Indians.[3]

Important questions in history, in physical and cultural anthropology (especially in the study of acculturation), in linguistics, and in other fields as well, will remain unanswered until the work of Africanists, Afro-Americanists, and American-Indian specialists is appropriately synthesized and modified in accordance with the results of new research on Indian-African and Indian-African-European culture contacts.

Questions such as the following require exploration and clarification: What specifically different factors affected the historical and cultural circumstances under which West Africans and American Indians first came into contact with one another? How did such circumstances vary in differing regions of the New World? What important variations, areal and temporal, were there in the patterns of accommodation

2. To cite some representative recent instances in which the subject of Indian-Negro contacts has been ignored: Harold Driver's *Indians of North America* (Chicago: University of Chicago Press, 1961) makes only one reference to Negroes, and that is to Negroes in Mexico; Fred Eggan in delivering the Morgan Lectures at Rochester University, published as *The American Indian: Perspectives for the Study of Social Change* (Chicago: Aldine, 1967), ignores the question of Indian-Negro contacts as completely as Morgan himself did; Owen *et al.*, editors of *The North American Indian: A Sourcebook* (New York: Macmillan, 1967), similarly ignore Indian-Negro contacts, as does E. H. Spicer in his *Perspectives in American Indian Culture Change* (Chicago: University of Chicago Press, 1961).

3. The work of Frank G. Speck, from his early "The Negroes and the Creek Nation," *Southern Workman*, XXXVII (1908), 106–10, must be excepted. And more recently the subject has been reopened, if somewhat obliquely, by A. I. Hallowell in his fascinating article, "American Indians, White and Black: the Phenomenon of Transculturation," *Current Anthropology*, IV (1963), 519–31. For work outside the U. S., the classic exception is the monograph of Douglas Taylor, *The Black Carib of British Honduras*, Viking Fund Publications in Anthropology, No. 17 (New York: Viking Fund, 1951). Aspects of the work of Gonzalo Aguirre Beltran, particularly his *La Población Negra de Mexico* (Mexico, D. F.: Fondo de Cultura Economica, 1946), must also be excepted.

developed as a means of regulating relations between the two groups? What were the relevant demographic variables— where the aboriginal population was sparse, for example, as it was in the lowland Circum-Caribbean region, or where the density of the indigenous population was higher, as it appears to have been in the Mexican interior and along the Pacific coast? Were technological and economic relations between the Negroes and the Indians competitive, symbiotic, or mutually exclusive? And how did this factor impede or facilitate racial and cultural assimilation?

Similar variations in the social organization of the two groups need to be considered. It seems likely that the family level of social integration characteristic of the coastal Circum-Caribbean tribes and those of parts of the southeastern coast of North America might have facilitated racial and cultural assimilation, in contrast, for example, with the more complexly organized, more highly stratified social systems of Indians in the interior regions of both areas.

The presence or absence of political centralization, especially as this might have facilitated or impeded the incorporation of alien individuals and groups, would also need to be taken into account. What were the relevant differences in status accorded by the dominant Europeans to Indians and to Negroes? We know that such differences varied both regionally and in time. In some instances, during the early stages of contact in the Caribbean, apparently few significant distinctions were made between the status of Africans and Indians. Later, however, especially in the northern part of what was to become the United States, there were important differences in the economic, social, and political positions of the two groups. In the United States the slightly superior position usually accorded to Indians by the dominant whites was undoubtedly a determining factor in structuring relations between the blacks and the aboriginal population.

What have been the consequences, both biological and social, of ''racial mixing''[4] between the two groups? In much of Latin America a *mestizo* population, varying in the specifics of its genetic legacy from region to region, is now often demographically and culturally in the majority. In striking

4. The term ''race'' is used throughout this paper with full awareness of the scientific impression of the word and of the errors in the concept it is used to define.

contrast, there is neither a comfortable descriptive term nor a comfortable social structural niche for persons of mixed Indian-African or Indian-African-European ancestry in Anglo-Saxon-oriented North America, either in the United States or in English-speaking Canada.[5]

Physical anthropologists need to ask how the infusion of Indian "blood" has affected the gene-pool of black Americans. Where and in what ways have the phenotype and genotype of American Indians been modified as a result of the now partial African ancestry of many of them?

The linguistic consequences of West African–American Indian culture contacts also need to be examined. Most of the work on Creole languages has been done by scholars more attuned to the detection of Africanisms than to consideration of the role of American Indian languages in the development of the patterns of linguistic behavior characteristic of culture-contact situations in the Americas.

Afro-Asians: Afro-Arabs and Afro-Aryans

Moving to the eastern side of the African continent, a parallel subject presents itself: the history and results of an even longer period of contact between Central and East Africa and the peoples of Southwest Asia.

With several exceptions—principally Islamic studies of various sorts and some work on the linguistic and cultural affinities between the Eastern Horn and the Southwest Arabian Peninsula—the subject of the processes and consequences of more than a thousand years of contact between the peoples of East and Central Africa and the cultures of Southwest Asia has been almost equally neglected.[6]

5. Some such persons and groups used to be referred to as "mustees" (from *mestizo*), "breeds," or "half-breeds"; others, as "half-niggers." Now the census records list them as Negroes, or relegate them to some newly invented category such as "other non-white," "Spanish," or "Puerto Rican," compounding the confusion such terms are devised to dispel. The ambiguousness of the position of persons so designated can hardly be overstated. Sometimes they are accorded the status of whites to their face, referred to as "colored" behind their backs, and listed on the census roles as Indians.

6. The work of such scholars as Middleton and Prins on the Swahili-speaking peoples of East Africa are exceptions: John Middleton, *Zanzibar, Its Society and Its Politics* (Oxford: Oxford University Press, 1965); and A. H. J. Prins, *The Swahili Speaking Peoples of Zanzibar*

A roster of research questions similar to the one I have suggested for the study of West African–American Indian culture contact might be tried. Who were the first Southwest Asian and Central and East African peoples to come into contact with one another? What factors precipitated this contact—warfare, the search for slaves, trade? What were the principal characteristics of the initial contact situation? To the extent that slavery was a factor, what were the specifics of the Southwest Asian economic situation which created the need for slaves? Did anything analogous to New World plantation slavery develop? If so, what were the relevant temporal and geographic variables in its operation? How, for example, did African slavery work along the arid coast of the Arabian Peninsula where most people have for centuries made their living as herdsmen, fishermen, or seafaring traders? How was slavery organized further up the Persian Gulf where the environment was more conducive to the development of agriculture—from Bushir eastward through Baluchistan?

What, if any, were the qualitative distinctions between the economic, social, and political status of the blacks and other, non-African, slaves? Here both Islamic and pre-Islamic ideas on the institution of slavery need to be taken into account. For instance, were differences between the Shiite and Sunnite interpretations of the slaves' personal and moral rights comparable to the significant distinctions made by Protestants and Catholics in the New World? If so, how did such differences affect the structuring of the blacks' relation to the rest of society, their chances for manumission, and the position ascribed to them and their descendants once they were free?

Where, if anywhere, and when historically did the blacks form separate communities? The fact that there are today no socially or culturally separate Afro-Asian communities in Southwest Asia, despite the centuries during which the African slave trade flourished in the area, requires an explanation. To my knowledge Negroes as a racial group in Southwest Asia were never assigned a social position so rigidly distinctive as the separate castelike status which for centuries has been imposed upon blacks in the Americas, especially in North America. The intrinsic interest of questions related to understanding the apparently much more rapid cultural and racial

and the East African Coast (London: The International African Institute, 1961). Also to be excepted is J. E. G. Sutton's The East African Coast (Nairobi: East African Publishing House, 1966).

assimilation of Africans in Southwest Asia is complemented by the critical relevance of such understanding for the achievement of a comparative perspective on problems of racial amalgamation and acculturation in the Americas where the blacks have so far had a very different fate.

Again there are questions for the physical anthropologist. What has been the effect of African genes upon the essentially Caucasoid peoples of Southwest Asia? The cultural anthropologist needs to ask related questions about how "racial" differences are perceived by the peoples of the region, and about what physical distinctions are regarded as significant. To what extent has the concept of a causal linkage between race and behavior—an idea essential to the justification of African slavery in the Americas and basic to the perpetuation of racism—been prevalent in Southwest Asia?

Almost everything remains to be learned about the cultural impact of African slavery upon the indigenous cultures of the Southwest Asian region: upon traditional technologies; upon economic systems; upon family organization and systems of social stratification; upon the organization and operation of the political process, particularly as it was related to control of the slave population; upon religious and magical beliefs and practices, Islamic and pre-Islamic; and upon art, especially music, dance, and oral literary forms.[7]

In linguistics, extensive work has, of course, been done on Swahili. But attention might also be given to the development of functionally similar languages on the coast of Southwest Asia itself, and to the impact of central and East African linguistic patterns upon the indigenous Afro-Asiatic and Indo-European languages of the area.

Afro-American Indians Again

The preceding discussion is intended to draw attention to an area of study which has been generally neglected. The questions raised certainly are not exhaustive, but hopefully they are suggestive of potentially fruitful directions for research. I

7. The United States of America can trace to the history of its contacts with Africa both a major source of its wealth in the past and, currently, its most compelling domestic problem. The effects on aboriginal American cultures may have been equally profound. It is possible that the parts of Asia in prolonged contact with Africa were similarly affected. If not, why not?

would like to turn now from the general to the specific, taking some research I have just begun on the subject of Afro-American Indians in the southeastern United States as a means of identifying, within the context of a particular instance, some of the problems and some of the potential payoff of conducting research along one of the two major lines of inquiry I have suggested. While my own research is substantively most closely related to the first of the two general subjects I have so far discussed, that of the processes and consequences of West African–American Indian culture contact, I see Afro-American and Afro-Asian studies as conceptually related aspects of a single major dimension of African studies which entails the search for a clearer understanding of the two-way results of Africa's contacts, past and present, with the Americas, Asia, and other parts of the world. In this sense I hope that what I have to say about a particular variant on the theme of Afro-American Indians may ultimately have some relevance for research on Afro-Asian culture contacts as well.

The specific subject of my current research has been briefly described elsewhere:

By the early seventeenth century there had begun to emerge throughout the Southeastern region of what was to become the United States separate, culturally and biologically distinguishable communities of persons of mixed Indian, African, and European descent, the result of unions between Indians, ''settlement'' and ''savage''; Negroes, slave, free, and runaway; and whites, indentured servants, soldiers, traders, trappers and other frontiersmen.

As the population of European settlers and African slaves increased and the plantation system spread, the dominant social structure became polarized between blacks and whites. The position of persons of ''tri-racial'' origin became increasingly ambiguous. They were not accepted as whites, avoided categorization as Negroes, and when classified as Indians were subjected to persecution and efforts at forced ''removal.''

Their response was and continues to be withdrawal from a larger society in which their status is invariably uncertain and often a source of serious contention. Today there may be as many as twenty-five communities of such persons, all sharing a distinctive subculture, each inhabiting a different but almost always isolated region of the Southeastern United States. Their total population probably exceeds 100,000. [If this estimate is correct, they are more numerous now than were the Cherokee, the Seminole, the Choctaw, and the Chickasaw combined.[8]] A few have begun to migrate to the cities of the region where their communities form separate, small enclaves in the Negro ghettos.[9]

The particular groups selected for study are the Pocotcoke of Delaware, the Wehatan of Maryland, the Mustee of Virginia, the Manteo of North Carolina, and the Black Creeks of South Carolina. (I have altered slightly the names and the specific locations of these groups.)

The Pocotcoke are a tri-ethnic population of some five or six hundred living in southeastern Delaware. Most reside in an isolated rural area known as Angola River Hundred, part of an early plantation site. They regard themselves as the descendants of the Indians of the region, but recognize that they are now a racially mixed group. However, they do not acknowledge the partial African ancestry which is evident from their appearance, but describe themselves as the result of intermarriage several hundred years ago between local Indians and Spanish and English sailors. Today the Pocotcoke make their living as small farmers. Their dispersed rural community is split internally between those who have insisted on their Indian identity and refused to use schools and other public accommodations provided for blacks, and those who have acquiesced to being categorized as "colored."

As is characteristic of the history of most such communities in the southeastern United States, government policy toward the Pocotcoke has been inconsistent. At times they have been provided separate Indian schools. At other times they have been required to attend Negro schools. Pocotcoke army recruits have occasionally been inducted as whites. At other times they have been forced to serve as blacks. As a result of such experiences, they shun contact with government agencies and also avoid close relations with both local whites and Negroes. They live apart, marry only among themselves, are

8. Eggan, *The American Indian*, p. 17.

9. Peter B. Hammond, "Factors Contributing to the Cultural Isolation of Communities of Mixed Indian-Negro-White Ancestry in the Southeastern United States," unpublished ms., Institute of Southern History, The Johns Hopkins University, 1968.

politically inactive, and maintain their own churches. Occasionally they try to reinforce their identity as Indians by wearing feather headdresses or holding Indian dances. But the Pocotcoke do not look like Indians. And despite their occasional efforts to revive what they regard as their aboriginal cultural heritage, what is known of their present-day way of life suggests that it more closely resembles that of their poor black neighbors.

The Wehatan constitute a population of several thousand who live in the rural areas of Prince Edwards and Arundel counties in southern Maryland. They work principally on tobacco farms, live in scattered country neighborhoods, marry among themselves—thus perpetuating a number of congenital anomalies—and they resist the tendency of local whites to categorize them as Negroes by minimizing social contacts with all outsiders.

The Mustee are one of more than a dozen tri-ethnic communities in Virginia whose status has been made especially difficult because of the rigidity of a Virginia statute which defines as non-white any person who has any "trace whatsoever of any blood other than Caucasian." They work principally as share-croppers, farm laborers, and fruit-pickers. Like other tri-ethnic groups, the Mustee endeavor to avoid social contacts with both whites and blacks. They face the added problem of avoiding identification with other separate "non-white" communities in Virginia—principally those of descendants of freedmen—which do acknowledge their partial African ancestry but carefully remain socially separate from darker skinned Negroes whose ancestors are presumed to have remained slaves until Emancipation. The Mustee also live apart in scattered rural communities. Often they remain illiterate because of their refusal to attend "colored" schools. Although they are endogamous their young women have a reputation for promiscuity with whites, who believe Mustee girls prostitute themselves to "lighten their strain."

Of the several tri-ethnic communities in North Carolina—the Laster Tribe, the "Portuguese," the Smilings, the Cubans, and the Person County Indians—the largest, in fact the largest of all the tri-ethnic communities in the Southeast, is that formed by a group previously known as Roanokes but now, as the result of a successful petition to the state legislature, as Manteo Indians. Totaling nearly 30,000 in Roxboro County alone, more live in adjacent rural areas and in other parts of the state. However, most Manteo live in the countryside around Manteoton and in the small town of Pinemont where they constitute the majority of the population.

As with many of the larger and more stable tri-ethnic communities, the Manteo, assisted by some romantically inclined outsiders, make much of the mysteriousness of their history. Often they are purported to be the descendants of Sir Walter Raleigh's "Lost Colony" established at Roanoke Island in 1587 and wiped out, presumably by Indians, in 1591. The earliest records describe free non-white farmers living in the region of what is now Roxboro County when the first English and Scots settlers arrived there in the 1730's. As a white-dominated planter society was established, African slaves were brought in, and most "pure" Indians were killed, driven out, or enclosed in reservations in the eastern part of North Carolina, the ancestors of the Manteo found themselves isolated in a society in which almost everyone else was either white or black.

They have persisted as a separate community ever since, fighting in and out of the courts for clarification of their status, alternately insisting they are Indians and demanding to be treated as whites, but steadfastly resisting categorization as blacks. From time to time and place to place special schools have been provided for them. Occasionally they have been granted privileges otherwise reserved for whites, but as with all such groups they have found the response of the larger society and its government unpredictable and their principal adjustment has been withdrawal.

Most Manteo work as tobacco farmers or as farm laborers, but a small group of middle-class professionals has grown up around Pinemont. Many are employed at Pinemont State College, originally the Roanoke Normal School, where until 1945 only "Roxboro County Indians" were eligible for admission.

Like other poor Southerners, many Manteo are now losing their jobs as a result of the spread of large-scale mechanized farming. For the past several decades they have been migrating to Baltimore where several hundred now occupy a neighborhood known locally as the "reservation," which is on the periphery of the black ghetto. In Baltimore, as in North Carolina, the struggle over their status goes on. They are set apart from blacks, neighboring poor whites, Gypsies, and Puerto Ricans by their appearance, by differences in their cultural behavior, and by the recurrence among them of distinctive family names soon recognized by others as peculiar to them.

In its general outlines the culture history of the Black Creeks of South Carolina appears to resemble that of the Manteo of North Carolina. But as a consequence of the greater social and economic stagnation of the region in which they live, and because of the greater rigidity of the traditional color bar in South Carolina, their cultural setting has been least affected by the relatively rapid rate of change which marks the other regions of the rural Southeast in which tri-ethnic communities are found. The precariousness of the Black Creeks' status as "Indians" is increased by the presence of neighboring racially mixed groups, such as the Catawba, whose right to recognition as Indians is given greater credence by local whites because they have retained their tribal name and some tribal land. Also, they show less physical evidence of African ancestry and have a reputation for antipathy toward the Black Creeks.

A primary dimension of the research will require the development in historical perspective of a balanced ethnographic picture of the contemporary subculture of these communities of mixed West African–American Indian–European origin. It will thus be necessary to collect and analyze three interrelated sets of data: (1) documentary records and orally transmitted accounts concerning the development of such communities in the southeastern United States from the early seventeenth century to the present; (2) ethnographic materials on the communities as they exist today; and (3) information on the present status of their relationships with the white, black, and Indian communities with which they co-exist.

Determination of the parallel or shared historical origins of these communities requires the identification of the particular groups of whites, Indians, and blacks from which they are descended. What segment of the white population mixed socially and/or sexually with blacks and Indians during early colonial days? Under what circumstances? What was the status of the blacks involved? Were they primarily freedmen, runaways, or slaves? Who were the Indians, "settlement" or "savage"? From what tribal groups did they come? What can be learned from early accounts about the cultural position of the first offspring of "mixed" unions? What regional variations were there in the status of tri-ethnic individuals and their communities? And how did their position change through time?

To answer these questions, not only standard works on the history of the southeastern region and on colonial America need to be consulted but local, state, and federal archival materials must also be examined. For example, much is to be learned from legislative records which document changes in the legal position of such groups—their classification and reclassification as "Free Issue," as "Free People of Color," as blacks, as Indians, as "Other Non-Whites," and occasionally, and usually only temporarily, as whites—especially as these changes have affected their rights to hold property, to vote, to defend themselves in the courts, to be educated, and to seek by legal means to improve their position. Newspaper accounts are also useful in tracing the shifts in status which have always been a principal source of the social disequilibrium and lack of cohesion characteristic of such communities in the Southeast.

Much also needs to be known of the different indigenous cultures, or subcultures, of Indians and blacks in the same region, and of their constantly shifting status in relation to the dominant white community. Attention must be given as well to those aspects of the Indians' traditional culture which facilitated or inhibited racial and cultural borrowing from blacks and whites. Significant differences in technology and economy, in the organization of Indian social and political systems, and in religion all must be examined as they may have affected the cultural context in which contact between Indians, whites, and Africans occurred. The status of Indians in relation to the white community must also be taken into account. For example, in some parts of the Southeast, Indians were used as slave-catchers and enjoyed an appreciably superior status so long as they avoided contact with Negroes. In other areas and at other times Indians shared the same status as white and Negro indentured servants. Indians were also enslaved.

Both the West African cultural heritage of the blacks and the characteristic aspects of their way of life as slaves, as runaways, and as freedmen must also be examined. The ethnographic data on West Africa is relatively rich. Information on the Afro-American subcultures of the Southeast has so far been less well developed. But much can be learned from historical accounts of the status and role of black bond servants; of plantation slavery; of slavery in the cities of the Southeast; of the status of non-whites, slave and free, during the Civil War and Reconstruction; and from ethnographic observation of the patterns of black subculture which prevail in the area today.

A second principal research dimension entails identification of the distinctive aspects of the contemporary subcultures of tri-ethnic communities in the Southeast with special attention to those factors which contribute to their continued cultural isolation. The nature of their relation to the particular type of natural environments in which such communities are most often found needs to be understood—in most areas they are isolated in pine barrens, swamps, or on tidewater islands—especially as this affects their means of livelihood, their settlement patterns, and their ability to improve their living standards and alter their socioeconomic position. The characteristics of their technology—both farming and hunting techniques and craft specializations—require study, as they provide a means of supplementing cash income and of reducing dependence on the market. Attention should also be given to the operation of alternative bases of work organization and of distribution, especially to kinship-based systems of redistribution and reciprocal community-wide economic systems, such as mutual-aid societies.

Evidence on the family organization characteristic of the core membership of tri-ethnic groups suggests that the endogamous segment of the community is built up from ambilocal, frequently matricentric, extended families which collectively constitute a deme. If so, this factor must be considered as it affects community organization and inhibits cultural and biological assimilation. Internal social stratification is apparently based on differences both in economic position and in physical type. Those who are better off materially and more nearly "white" in appearance frequently occupy positions of superior social status and have greater opportunities for the achievement of further mobility through migration, "passing," and marriage with whites. At the other end of the color continuum characteristic of such communities are poorer, darker skinned individuals and families whose position is often very close to that of local Negroes.

It appears that political organization within such communities is almost nonexistent. Leadership operates within the context of the kinship system only. The potential for internal conflict is somewhat reduced by the economic semi-autonomy of family groups—like blacks in the same region, most are economically dependent on whites, rather than upon one another—and by the scattered patterns of settlement. Disputes among community members are most often settled among themselves, by recourse to the mediating role of some senior kinsman of both disputants, or by feuding.

Examination of the principal components of the subculture characteristic of tri-ethnic communities should be complemented by study of the interplay between their subcultural situation and their personality development. Usually they are described by blacks, whites, and Indians alike as dishonest, dirty, hopelessly stupid, untrustworthy, totally lacking in ambition, and generally "sorry"—qualities ascribed to the deleterious effects of inbreeding and/or "race-mixing." While such descriptions are largely to be explained as manifestations of prejudice, it will be important to consider the extent to which certain such character attributes are, in fact, representative, to be explained as an adjustive response to persecution, deprivation of various sorts, and uncertainty, shame, and confusion concerning their identity. Feelings of worthlessness appear to be further reinforced by their typically unsuccessful efforts to improve their status. Given the stressfulness of their situation, listlessness and passivity—alternating with occasional outbursts of violence—and avoidance of contact with those who question their necessarily fragile self-image, may actually be adaptive.

The third principal dimension of the research on these communities of mixed West African–American Indian–European origin requires explicit identification of the external circumstances which reinforce the continued tendency toward cultural isolation characteristic of nearly all such communities in the United States. Here the quality of contact with the white-dominated culture is critical and requires detailed attention. Typically the relation of the members of tri-ethnic communities to the technology and economy of the majority culture is marginal. The relative technological and economic stagnation characteristic of most areas where they are found is complicated both by lack of skills and the difficulty of fitting into a biracial work organization. Often they have received practically no education, and as they refuse to work with blacks and are usually not permitted to work at "white" jobs, they are frequently unemployable. As farm laborers, sharecroppers, or subsistence farmers, their relationship to the market economy is typically dependent and precarious. Like poor whites, blacks, and Indians in the same region they are often further immobilized by debt or the lack of the cash reserves necessary to travel in search of better work elsewhere.

Socially excluded by whites and the few remaining ''real'' Indians, and shunning contact with blacks, they are almost totally cut off socially from the larger community. In any encounter with persons outside their own group there is always the likelihood of a challenge to their insistence on being identified as whites or Indians. In most rural areas where they live, segregation is still the rule. They must either avoid places of public accommodation or risk a humiliating dispute. In a few areas, in Roxboro County, North Carolina, for example, separate facilities are often provided for them. Elsewhere they are occasionally permitted to use accommodations otherwise set aside for whites. But frequently they are segregated with blacks. The pattern of their treatment may vary from county to adjacent county and even from individual to individual within a single family depending on differences in appearance, class position, or upon the degree of prejudice of the particular whites with whom they come into contact. The uncertainties in their situation encourage withdrawal and contribute to the reputation of members of such communities for ''clannishness.''

In Delaware and in North Carolina separate ''Indian'' schools have from time to time been provided for members of such communities. Occasionally these schools have been supported by the state, but more often the tri-ethnic groups have been required to support them themselves and to supply and pay their own teachers. More often, however, they have been expected to attend school with blacks. Rather than do this, many have preferred to allow their children to remain illiterate, thus creating and perpetuating a major obstacle to their mobility.

The uncertainty of these peoples' social status and racial identity has affected their relation to the white-dominated political system as well. Often they have been denied the franchise along with all other non-whites. Occasionally they are permitted to vote, but they are almost invariably excluded by tradition from holding political office. Most try to minimize all contact with government agencies where the question of their racial identity might arise. Tax-collectors, census-takers, licensing bureaus, welfare agencies, public health facilities— all are equally to be avoided.

Persons identified as members of tri-ethnic communities are

even more completely excluded from participation in white and Indian religious organizations. And they are unwilling to attend church with blacks. With the exception of the Catholic converts, the majority are nominally Baptists and Methodists, and in accordance with the prevailing pattern in the Southeast, most tri-ethnic congregations are small and independent. In their religious organization, as in all other aspects of their way of life, they follow a separate way.

Conclusion

Many of the questions raised in the initial stages of the research described here cannot yet be answered. When they can be, I hope we may better understand at least this particular variant of the several possible consequences of centuries of culture contact between West Africans, American Indians, and Europeans in the southeastern United States, elsewhere in the country, and, perhaps, in other parts of the Americas as well.[10] In addition, an old-stock American ethnic group will have been more fully identified; a wider perspective for the study of culture history in the southeastern United States will have been suggested; some new problems in ethnic stratification may be more explicitly recognized, especially problems related to the peculiarities of the status of that growing and increasingly important population of Americans—and Africans and Asians—whose mixed racial and cultural origins have resulted in the emergence of intermediate ethnic groups whose identities defy efforts at neat categorization as either red, white, or black.[11]

10. The linguist William Stewart tells me that he has recently encountered Gullah-speaking Seminole in West Texas.

11. The absolutistic black-white or black-white-red biases of the social structure of most of the English-speaking areas of the Americas reflect the fact that there is no word in English synonymous with the Spanish term *mestizo* or the french *métis*, nor is there any concept or category analogous to that of *mestizaje* or *métissage*. When Americanists speak of racially mixed peoples in the New World, they are invariably referring to Indian-European ''mixtures'' and usually borrow the Spanish *mestizo* to describe their physical type and the word *ladino* to define their culture. In contrast, in categorizing anyone of partially African ancestry, they use designations which strikingly parallel the doctrines advocated in such benighted statutes as the Virginia Racial Integrity Law, which defines as Negro anyone with any ascertainable quantum of ''non-caucasic'' blood—excepting only those with less than one-sixteenth ''Indian blood.''

AFRICAN AND AFRO-AMERICAN RELATIONSHIPS: RESEARCH POSSIBILITIES

17

Sterling Stuckey

The issue of African survivals among Afro-Americans has generated heated confrontations between some of the leading authorities on the black experience in America. Melville Herskovits, who did so much to advance African and Afro-American studies, and E. Franklin Frazier, the distinguished black sociologist, were notable representatives of the opposing views. These differences over the question of African survivals have long been debated. Lorenzo Turner and Robert E. Park, while teaching at Fisk, argued frequently but genteelly over the extent to which black people in this country had retained ties with African cultures. Turner and Park were representative, though in a lower key, of the debate which raged among a number of scholars during the 1940's. Subsequent efforts were to compile considerable evidence in support of the Herskovits-Turner position. Thus not only Herskovits and Turner, but DuBois and Carter Woodson, first among trained American historians to contend that Afro-American culture was significantly influenced by Africa, have in large measure been vindicated.

Despite the studies which have been conducted since the 1940's, historians have, with very few exceptions, given insufficient attention to the work of those scholars who addressed themselves to the issues of African survivals raised by Du-Bois, Woodson, Herskovits, and Turner. It is quite possible that the notion of Afro-American cultural deprivation, which has long influenced the thinking of most Americans toward black people, militates against historians using findings from those studies which affirm the presence of Africanisms in American culture. This trend is not confined to the issue of African survivals but extends beyond it, covering as it does a reluctance to deal with a wide range of African and Afro-American relationships. Such ignorance among historians has made the effort to understand the black experience in America from its beginnings to the present time far more difficult than it might have been.

The field of African and Afro-American relationships has been neglected for so long by the academic establishment that, despite some outstanding work completed in this area, a host of possible topics remain to be researched. It should be asserted at the outset that many of these problems cannot be researched without taking into consideration another dimension of the interaction between Africans and Afro-Americans: the ways in which West Indian blacks have influenced Africans and Afro-Americans, and in turn have been influenced. The role of West Indians in this system of relationships would carry us beyond the scope of this paper, but the researcher must keep this wider setting in mind.

The initial task of the American historian who would explore the significance of contact between black Americans and Africans is to submit himself to a questioning review of work originating in other disciplines on the topic. If he is to understand Afro-American personality and cultural developments, for instance, and how these relate to Africa, he must first go back to the slave era and seek to understand how Africanisms were used to enable slaves to endure in American slavery. Since historians have not yet begun to deal with the slave as artistic protagonist (as the creator of the largest and most original body of American folklore), they must rely on the cultural findings of other disciplines in their attempt to reconstruct the slave ethos. Historians must understand something of the methods and materials of anthropology, folklore, ethnomusicology, and linguistics. Otherwise, much will continue to escape them. Similarly, the anthropologist, the political scientist, the psychologist, and the student of art and literature will have much to learn from the historian. It is clear that the complexity and the comprehensiveness of the research problems before us will demand a reciprocity of scholarship and a multidisciplinary view.

Historians have recently begun to give appreciable attention to comparative studies of slavery, and it is evident that considerably more research into slavery, involving scholars from several disciplines, is required. The far-reaching questions of the strategy and psychology of oppression and resistance demand the attention of scholars today. As Ralph Ellison has suggested, we simply need to know much more about how people under various forms of oppression in different parts of the world cope with their situations.

Cross-cultural studies of the responses of Afro-Americans in slavery and of Africans under colonialism should provide considerable insight into these questions. In undertaking such studies we must not allow our research to become arrested at the point of comparative analysis of structural similarities or dissimilarities of systems of slavery and colonialism. To be satisfied by such a survey would be to blunt our insight into the deeper significances of the situations of both oppressor and oppressed. Studies of slavery in the Americas and colonialism in Africa may prove an especially fruitful area for research insofar as we are able to investigate in these situations affective and cognitive aspects of relations between black and white.

The range of possible focuses for such studies is broad. One might treat forms of physical resistance to slavery and colonialism. Another might cover more covert methods of resistance, that is, those ranging from work slowdowns and malingering to other forms of subtle sabotage. These studies of resistance raise important questions about the nature of informal organization among slaves and colonial subjects. We do know that in America a man of religion frequently emerged as the underground leader on Southern plantations, commanding respect and allegiance from a significant number of his fellows. Can an analogue to the Afro-American slave exhorter be found in response to colonial rule in West Africa? If so, to what extent were these informal leaders congruent with authorized leadership in their communities, and to what extent were they carriers and representatives of the cultural traditions of their people? How did their power compare qualitatively with that of the overlord and with that of the established authority in their societies?

Studies of the effects of paternalism on the personality development of the Afro-American and African during and following slavery and colonialism should reveal much about the limitations of black political and intellectual leadership. In this regard, a comparative study of Belgian paternalism in the Congo with the paternalism of the slave South might prove especially fruitful. There is, however, a much greater need for studies of the effects of slavery and colonialism on the personality development of the slavemaster and the colonial overlord. Special attention needs to be given to ways in which racism affected the personalities and the institutions of those who ruled in slavery and colonialism. We particularly need studies which will reveal more about manifestations of psychopathology in ruling groups. More specifically, we must be prepared to test the thesis that excessive power in the hands of oppressors very likely stretched the sense of self-esteem of many to dangerous proportions.

One way of increasing our knowledge of aberrations within oppressor groups would be by examining and comparing at critical points the lore of the overlords in slavery and segregation together with the lore of colonialists. For instance, there is reason to believe that the sexual views of whites in Rhodesia and in the United States, as they relate to oppressed blacks, are very similar indeed. Are there other related stereotypes about blacks which these overlords entertain? Is there a tendency among oppressor groups in slave, segregated, and colonial societies to rationalize their behavior by creating myths, and are such myths similar or very closely related? How great a role has race played in the creation and maintenance of stereotypes during and following oppression?

Some first-rate work has already been done on segregation practices in both South Africa and the United States, and we can expect to see, before long, comparative treatments of segregation in, for example, Rhodesia, South Africa, and the United States. In particular we need to know to what extent parallel behavioral traits and rationales have developed in these societies and how concepts of segregation, apartheid, and the rhetoric of partnership in fact are used. Comparative studies of segregation in cities, say, Johannesburg and Birmingham, Salisbury and Montgomery, Dakar and New York, might be undertaken. Small cities or areas should not be ignored by those researching racial practices and theories. Already we are beginning to get comparative studies of closed societies in the United States and Africa. Though political scientists are pioneering in this research, it is likely that historians, necessarily more concerned with the evolution of such societies, will turn increasingly to this line of investigation, benefiting from the work which has been done. Comparative institutional studies ranging over such subject areas as legal systems, schools, churches, police, labor unions, and political organizations should tell us much about the workings of racist ideologies and their impact upon the development of institutions.

Scholars in America and Africa need to initiate research into the ways in which Africans and Afro-Americans have perceived the workings of the color line. Though the role of color has not been the same throughout Africa, it is likely that there is a general pattern of responses to racism there which can be compared and contrasted with its counterpart in America. The writings of intellectuals and politicians would be of considerable value in such a study, though other approaches would doubtless be worth pursuing. While recent or current attitudes on this question would logically fall more within the purview of the sociologist or social psychologist, an examination of the views which have been taken on this subject over time would be firmly within the bounds of the historian.

Several studies of Afro-American thought on Africa are now under way. At least one scholar is covering the period from 1880 to 1919, and a study of emigration movements between 1890 and 1910 was recently completed. But there is need for an overall history of Afro-American thought on Africa. Afro-American newspapers and church journals, together with the records of the Negro Convention Movement, are among the indispensable sources for the nineteenth century, where the materials tend generally to be more fugitive. Researching Afro-American thought on Africa in the twentieth century will be much easier, for the sources are more abundant. Research on the manifestations of African consciousness and Back-to-Africa movements prior to and following the Civil War needs to be done. An examination of evidences of African consciousness among Afro-Americans during the 1850's, and of how this consciousness related to the desire of many to emigrate to Central America, must be initiated. A full-length study of Martin Robinson Delany's attitudes toward, and activities in, Africa is long overdue, as is a comprehensive study of Alexander Crummell's ideas on Africa. Fortunately, at least two historians are now working on Crummell's vision of Africa and his activities there. Another great but neglected black missionary, William Henry Shepperd, merits thorough treatment. A biography of Bishop Henry M. Turner, perhaps the most outstanding proponent of

African consciousness in the nineteenth century, should tell us much about the nature of white oppression and black disaffection in America.

Whenever possible, the researcher must attempt to discern the African response to various Afro-American expressions of interest in Africa. A focus for research might be the images of Afro-Americans which Africans have entertained over a period of several generations, especially during that period extending from the mid-nineteenth century to the emergence and decline of Marcus Garvey. In addition, the deep concern which Afro-American interest and activity in Africa caused in South, East, Central, and West Africa during the late nineteenth and early twentieth centuries needs to be researched. The excellent treatment which Professors Shepperson and Price gave to the Nyasaland native uprising in 1915 might serve as a model for scholarly works treating this dimension of Afro-American and African relationships. The impact of the emergence of independent African states upon Afro-American thought, though already examined by Harold Isaacs, is surely in need of further exploration.

The separatist church movement of South Africa, which Bishop Turner did so much to inspire, might fruitfully be compared with religious separatist movements in the United States. A study of nativist religious movements in Africa generally might reveal certain common denominators with their counterparts in the United States. Though creditable studies have been done on Elijah Muhammed's Nation of Islam, a more thorough exploration of the religious views of this movement should be undertaken. It is clear that reinterpretations of black religion in America must be completed before comparative studies with black religions in Africa can be undertaken. Again, research on Negro American folklore should be of considerable help in making the necessary reassessments as well as comparisons.

A careful study of the history of Pan-Africanism has yet to be written. We need a work which will place this important movement in proper perspective, that is, against the backdrop of nineteenth-century Pan-Negroism. In addition, the more traditional approach to Pan-Africanism—treating it almost exclusively in political terms—should be set aside in favor of a serious effort to show how Pan-Africanism relates to the theories of negritude and African personality. We are still waiting for a biographer capable of catching the spirit of the chief architect of Pan-Africanism, W. E. B. DuBois. The DuBois papers, which are not yet available to scholars, probably will reveal much concerning his attitudes on a great variety of subjects relating to Africa. A study of DuBois's cultural views on Africa might disclose that he was an early and sophisticated proponent of negritude. Such a study should seek, among other things, to determine how the DuBois variant of negritude differed from that projected by the Harlem Renaissance writers, and anticipated the views of Césaire and Senghor.

For the students of history who possess the requisite literary insights, a study of the place and meaning of Africa in the New Negro movement would fill a gap in our knowledge. It would be important for the scholar to consider, among other things, the relationship of images of Africa and Africans projected by Harlem Renaissance writers to the social, economic, and political milieu in which these men were writing. While we know that the poetry of Sterling Brown and the work of Langston Hughes influenced Léopold Senghor, we know all too little about the manner in which Afro-Americans and Africans from French West Africa related to one another. Work on this topic should answer important literary as well as historical questions.

A comparative study of D. D. T. Jabavu and Booker T. Washington would be a valuable contribution to our understanding of the manner in which Afro-American and African moderates have sought to wield influence. One scholar is now working on this topic. Though we already have a creditable study of Marcus Garvey, there is certainly room for additional ones, especially one which will seek to give proper emphasis to the role which Mrs. Amy Garvey played in her husband's movement. The Garvey brand of black nationalism, together with the nationalist thought of DuBois and Booker T. Washington, are in need of reassessment, perhaps in a single work. A substantial contribution to our understanding of black nationalism and the place of Africa in the thought of the three most important black nationalists of this century would result from a first-rate study of this type. An investigation of the less-known views on Africa of John Edward Bruce, Bishop Alexander Walters, Benjamin Brawley, William H. Ferris, and James Weldon Johnson, as Professor Shepperson has suggested, would add much to our knowledge of what important members of the black intelligentsia thought of Africa. Carter Woodson's attitudes toward, and influences on, Africans and their history merit special attention.

A number of Afro-Americans who rose to prominence in this century also merit the attention of scholars. Ralph Bunche, Alpheus Hunton, William Leo Hansberry, Paul Robeson, and Malcolm X are among these leaders. Robeson and Malcolm easily merit individual treatment. A study of Robeson may well reveal that this man played a far more important role in furthering African independence than is usually known or imagined. As with DuBois, the biographer of Robeson must himself be a man of no mean gifts. A study of Malcolm X's thoughts on, and experiences in, Africa will be necessary before students of Africa are prepared to treat adequately those black leaders who followed him there: Robert Moses, John Lewis, James Farmer, Floyd McKissick, Wilfred Ussery, and more than a score of other civil-rights activists, many of whom were from the deep South. Interviews as well as newspaper and personal accounts will be useful for pursuing this research. How Malcolm's experiences in Africa affected his vision of racial conditions in America would be an important aspect of any study of his African experience. In this vein, the relationship between Malcolm X and the current widespread interest in Africa and things African among black people suggests itself for investigation.

We also need a thorough investigation of contact between Afro-Americans and African students in the United States who later became leaders in the new nations of Africa, although such research hopefully would be part of a broader investigation of the experiences in America of African students as a whole. This line of inquiry should be complemented by one which treats the experiences of African dignitaries in this country. Indeed, interaction between Afro-Americans and Africans in a number of world capitals needs to be examined. We still do not know enough about the extent to which, for instance, Jomo Kenyatta and Paul Robeson influenced each other during their long years of association in London. We are equally interested in the experience of Afro-American expatriates living in Africa. Key questions in these researches would be: what expectations are brought to the new situation, and what changes take place when blacks, separated by centuries, rendezvous in distant lands?

Eventually studies of attitudes and positions taken toward Africa and Africans by organizations and groups such as the American Society on African Culture (AMSAC), the Phelpes-Stokes Foundation, and the American Negro Leadership Council on Africa might be undertaken. Similarly, an examination of the positions taken on Africa by the Student Non-Violent Coordinating Committee (SNCC), the Congress of Racial Equality (CORE), and other civil-rights groups, national and local, should repay effort.

A word of caution is in order: more time must elapse before scholars can with confidence gauge and interpret recent manifestations of interest in Africa. There is, however, little doubt that this interest promises to be long-standing and widely influential. To be sure, before long the historian will be asking new questions about the influence which Africa has exercised over large numbers of black Americans. Not only are our judgments relative to slave personality and experience likely to be in for some revision, but we may well discover that African consciousness, though heightened by crises, has been so persistent and powerful a force in the lives of black Americans as to merit consideration as a relatively normal, rather than an aberrant or occasional, state of mind.

I want now to suggest that the value of further research, especially that of a cross-cultural and multidisciplinary nature, may well be to move us closer to an understanding of the historical reality of the situation of black people in America. We may revise the traditional perspective which views blacks, since slavery, as second-class citizens to a perspective which places them in the context of people caught up in a situation that is essentially colonial or worse. It should be noted here that it would be unwise to project more research topics than past and present needs seem clearly to call for. New research problems will doubtless grow out of accumulating research in the field together with the continuing relationships of Africans and Afro-Americans.

Meanwhile, black students are calling for black instructors to teach courses in Afro-American and African history, areas of study in which there are not many qualified scholars, white or black. The request of the students is legitimate: there are very few black teachers of any kind in northern universities, and practically none working in African history. This situation is compounded by the alarmingly small number of black students in graduate schools, a state of affairs which is directly linked to the failure of the American educational system to educate well more than a relatively small number of black people. Numerous universities, attempting to compensate for past indifference, are now feverishly recruiting black undergraduate students. But it will take a long time before even successful recruiting campaigns can produce a significantly larger proportion of black teachers and even more time before they can be expected to make important scholarly contributions in the field. Whatever happens with regard to recruitment and development, one thing is certain: scholarship in Afro-American and African history will not come into its own until black scholars emerge to play leading roles as interpreters of the history of their people in America and Africa.

One aspect of the current interest in Africa is the demand for Afro-American or black studies programs in which African history and cultures would occupy places of prominence. Black-student organizations in many parts of the country are also calling for cross-cultural courses in which people of African descent in the New World would be studied as well. These students are requesting a curriculum which, hopefully, will help them understand the experiences of people of African ancestry over the centuries. In a word, they would like to see the kind of scholarly treatment of Afro-Americans and Africans which pioneers in the field, especially Woodson, DuBois, and Herskovits, projected decades ago. It is likely that now they will be accommodated.

COOPERATIVE RESEARCH
IN PROGRESS
THROUGH THE PROGRAM
OF AFRICAN STUDIES

THE MADINA PROJECT:
SOCIOLINGUISTIC RESEARCH IN GHANA 18.

Jack Berry

Greenberg, in reviewing the present state of African linguistics, says that "the work already accomplished in the study of African languages, extensive as it is, is thus hardly more than a preliminary sounding into the depths that remain to be penetrated in the vast world of African languages."[1] And he gives a list of major desiderata for further linguistic research in Africa which includes almost every area of traditional concern within the discipline. It is not the purpose of the present paper to reproduce Greenberg's inventory or even to comment on it. (His whole statement is in any case a reasonable and conservative assessment of the situation with which few of us would wish to quarrel.) Rather my intention here is briefly to consider one area of linguistic and associated research mentioned by Greenberg in which it seems safe to predict a considerable expansion of activity over the next few years. Sociolinguistics has only recently developed as a subject of interdisciplinary study in the social sciences, but it is already seen as a subject in which the challenge to creative thinking is great and in which African problems can play an essential role.[2]

The term "sociolinguistics" is not easy to define precisely,

1. Joseph H. Greenberg, "Linguistics," in *The African World*, ed. by Robert Lystad (New York: Praeger, 1965), p. 441.

2. *Ibid.*, p. 440.

and I shall not attempt to do so here. For the immediate purposes of the present paper it will be sufficient if we say generally, albeit somewhat vaguely, that sociolinguistic studies for the most part deal with the systematic relationships that obtain between language and society. In sociolinguistics are included such topics as "the relation of language differences to social class; the differential social roles of different languages coexisting in the same society; the development and spread of lingua francas as auxiliary languages in multilingual situations; the factors involved in the differential prestige ratings of languages; the role of language as a sign of ethnic identification; language in relation to nationalism; and problems of language policy, e.g., in education."[3] Clearly, such problems have a special relevance in Africa and other developing areas of the world.

The Madina project of my title is an example of one type of sociolinguistic inquiry. Though it is still very much a matter of research in progress (the first set of questionnaires has only recently been assembled), a description of the project may be of interest, if only as an illustration of the possibilities of this kind of study. In what follows, I have tried to give some indication of the aims and purposes of the project and of how these aims relate to the broad concerns of sociolinguistic theory as I understand them at the present time.

The project is a joint undertaking of the Department of Linguistics, Northwestern University, and the Institute of African Studies, the University of Ghana. Its field director is Dr. Gilbert Ansre, a Senior Research Fellow of the Institute and one of the leading Ghanaian linguists. The project was originally planned and has been carried out at all stages in the closest cooperation with the Department of Linguistics at Northwestern, for the most part in liaison with its chairman.

The immediate purpose of the project, as it is defined in the records of the preliminary discussions between the Director of the Institute of African Studies, Professor Nketia, and myself in Legon in October, 1966, is quite briefly to assemble a description of the language situation in Madina. The term "language situation" is to be understood as referring to the total configuration of language usage at a given time and place, including such data as how many and what kinds of languages are spoken by how many people, under what circumstances, and what attitudes and beliefs are held by the

3. *Ibid.*, p. 427.

community about their languages. It is an assumption of sociolinguistics that a full-scale description of a language situation along these lines constitutes a useful and important body of data for social scientists of various interests.

That such full-scale descriptions do not exist anywhere as yet—least of all in Africa—is a subject of repeated comment in the literature. A recent conference, sponsored by the African Research Committee, in surveying the field of sociolinguistic research in Africa noted everywhere a lack of even the most fundamental linguistic-demographic information (only first-language data is available in the obvious sources, and it is the common experience that even national censuses are most inaccurate in matters of language). The drafting committee of that conference urgently called for descriptions of language situations according to the various approaches described in the literature, and the committee itself considered, by way of example, one possible approach to a sociolinguistic study of the Swahili situation in East Africa.[4]

In a sense, the Madina project can be considered a direct response to the committee's appeal. For some time the Department of Linguistics at Northwestern had been seeking an opportunity to experiment in a meaningful way with such surveys and hoped especially to acquire experience in organizational matters for which there were no precedents, such as training of personnel to administer questionnaires and field tests. The Ghanaian linguists, for their part, were acutely aware of the urgent need for such surveys. A new interest in local languages was being expressed on all sides in Ghana, especially by educationists in their demands for an official statement of language policy at the national level. (These demands have since been formalized in the fifteen resolutions of the recent planning conference held in Legon in May, 1968.) [5]

At the October, 1966, meeting it was agreed that rather than seeking outside support a beginning could be made using the limited financial resources available to fund a small pilot sociolinguistic survey. Presumably the survey could be justified later not only in terms of the data collected but also on

4. Jack Berry and Joseph H. Greenberg, "Sociolinguistic Research in Africa," *African Studies Association Bulletin*, IX (September, 1966), 7–9.

5. *Proceedings of Conference on the Study of Ghanaian Languages in Schools and Higher Institutions in Ghana* (Accra, forthcoming).

the grounds that it would have provided valuable experience for mounting other such surveys in the future and would have created a trained cadre to administer them. And should increased funds become available, it might well serve as the prototype of a series of similar smaller- or larger-scale surveys in different parts of Ghana that could be useful for comparative purposes. (Madina is, of course, assumed to be a "representative situation" paralleled in many multilingual urban and suburban communities in modern Ghana.) Finally, the real possibility that Madina could be resurveyed easily at regular intervals proved very attractive.

The choice of Madina for the pilot survey was determined largely by the need for economy. In the case of Madina a survey in depth at reasonable cost was feasible because of the small size of the settlement and its proximity to Legon (two miles), which made for easy access and low transport costs in conducting the survey and maintaining effective control and supervision of it. Further, Madina had already been the subject of a preliminary demographic study, the Quarcoo-Addo-Peil survey, which had been carried out in 1966 by the social studies section of the Institute of African Studies. The authors promised their cooperation in the linguistic survey, and their very comprehensive questionnaires have in fact been made available to us and have been used in our own survey.

The Quarcoo-Addo-Peil survey was important not only for the considerable savings in time and labor it effected but also in that it guaranteed at the outset a situation of considerable interest in which ethnic, sociocultural, and economic heterogeneity was matched linguistically by pronounced individual and social multilingualism. (Only 4 per cent of those questioned in the Quarcoo-Addo-Peil survey had said they knew only one language; 73 per cent had claimed to know three or more.) The following few paragraphs will summarize briefly those parts of the Quarcoo-Addo-Peil survey that seem immediately relevant to this paper. For those who wish more detail, the study is now available as a publication of the Institute of African Studies.[6]

Madina, as its name suggests, was founded by Muslims from northern Ghana and outside. The settlement is less than ten years old. (There is no mention of it as a unit in the 1960

6. A. K. Quarcoo, N. O. Addo, and M. Peil, *Madina Survey* (Legon: Institute of African Studies, University of Ghana, 1967).

census.) The foundation stone was, in fact, laid on October 22, 1959, and at the same time the village was officially named Madina at the suggestion of its founder, Alhaji Seidu Kardo, and with the approval of Nii the La Mantse and his elders.

Over the past few years Madina has grown rapidly. Migration of course has been the largest single factor in this growth. Madina appears to be developing as a mixed suburb and has attracted a very broad range of residents of all income levels. The majority come because of good job opportunities either in Madina itself or on nearby building projects, for the most part on university sites. Two-fifths of all males and four-fifths of all females earn their living in Madina. Others, mostly non-manual workers from Accra who continue to work there, originally came to Madina to establish homes because of available "litigation-free" land or for other reasons. It was found that 29.0 per cent of the males and 11.3 per cent of females travel daily to Accra to work.

Nearly all the investigators observed—and responses to relevant questions in the schedules would appear to support their view—that cultural heterogeneity is taken for granted in Madina. There is an impressive amount of ethnic mixing in neighborhoods and even in houses. Some neighborhoods have attracted more Muslims, while others have more skilled workers or homeowners, and some have more Ewe or Akan; but there is no neighborhood which could be termed exclusive, no group which could be said to be segregated from the rest. And "rich" houses (according to interviewers' ratings) are scattered throughout the town.

Heterogeneity nevertheless is the single most significant fact about Madina from the survey's point of view. Residents come from all over West Africa, although the majority are from southern Ghana. Birthplace and former-residence statistics show that one-third of the heads of households, for example, were Ewe, about one-fourth were Akan, and somewhat fewer are from neighboring countries (if Togolese Ewes, for whom the political boundary has no cultural meaning, are counted as southern Ghanaians). About one in ten was Gã. Non-Ghanaians who did not grow up in Accra tended to have migrated to Accra, usually without other stops in Ghana, and to have moved from there to Madina. These constituted about 16 per cent of the total population. Of all tribes represented in Madina, 80 per cent are from southern Ghana and Togo. Ewes and related Togolese form the one single majority group, followed first by Akans, Kwahus, and Akwapims, and second by Gã-Adangbe/Krobos.

There is also a very wide range of socioeconomic statuses represented in the population of Madina. Of all persons over fifteen years old, only 6 per cent were unemployed at the time of the survey. Farming, trading, crafts, clerical, and teaching are the major occupations. The professions are represented by 0.8 per cent of the population. The majority of the working male population are craftsmen: masons, carpenters, builders, and cabinetmakers. These come mostly from the tribes of southern Ghana, especially the Ewe and related Togolese. The professional and teacher-clerical occupational groups are similarly almost wholly restricted to southern Ghanaians, especially Ewes (and southern Ghanaians constitute the majority of students at the secondary, teacher-training, and university level). There is a conspicuous absence of northern Ghanaians and non-Ghanaians in these occupational groups. Males of northern or external origin for the most part work as laborers, and for them the illiteracy rate is significantly higher than for southern Ghanaians. Of all northern Ghanaians, 80 per cent were illiterate, for example, while 67 per cent of the Hausa, Fulani, Dahomeans, Potokoli, Moshi, and others from the Upper Volta had no education. This is against a 45 per cent illiteracy rate for southern Ghanaians.

Turning now to the sociolinguistic questionnaire drawn up originally by Nketia, Ansre, and myself and since elaborated by Helaine Minkus of Northwestern University, it might be useful first to indicate briefly the main goals of our inquiry, discussing each separately against the theoretical background of the "language situation" considered as the basic topic of sociolinguistic investigation.

The main aspects of a language situation would seem to be (1) purely linguistic, (2) purely demographic, (3) sociocultural, (4) social-psychological, and (5) political. It has become fairly standard practice to discuss a language situation under these five headings.[7]

The purely linguistic aspect needs no consideration in this paper. It is assumed that basic descriptions exist for all languages spoken in Madina and that on the evidence of these descriptions there is fairly general agreement about the struc-

---

7. See, for example, Joseph H. Greenberg, "Urbanism, Migration and Language," in *Urbanization and Migration in West Africa*, ed. by Hilda Kuper (Chicago: University of Chicago Press, 1965), p. 59.

tural and/or functional classification of these languages (for example, pidgin/ creole/ vernacular/ standard/ marginal,[8] etc.; Kwa/ Chadic/ Gur, etc.) and about the degree of linguistic complexity and dialectal diversity involved in each case.

The purely demographic aspect of a language situation concerns the distribution of speech-forms, the extent of multilingualism, and the extent of literacy in one or more languages. The distribution of these speech-forms either as first or other languages in relation to factors such as occupation, social status, ethnic origin, and religious affiliation constitutes the sociocultural aspect. Here also might be included questions of types and frequency of language choices for offspring from mixed marriages. These two aspects of the language situation in Madina, together with the closely related set of problems centered on language attitudes—value judgments on the basis of potency, aesthetic evaluation, and assumed usefulness; prestige ratings of the various languages; the motives for learning them and the manner in which they are learned (Greenberg's "social-psychological aspect")—constitute the main areas of concern of the Madina project.

As to the fifth and last aspect, under which would be subsumed such questions as language in relation to political parties, national aspirations, and the language policies of government and private agencies, a decision was taken early in the planning of the project that these topics were best considered outside the scope of the survey; they might more effectively be made the topic of a separate investigation, preferably on a wider scale.

The full linguistic schedule, as it is presently conceived, divides conveniently for discussion into two main parts: a first part which follows the well-established pattern of bilingual censuses, and a second part which is more specifically addressed to some of the problems mentioned above as constituting the social-psychological aspects of a language situation. The information which is normally sought about the learning and use of languages other than the mother tongue can be summarized under five categories of questions: (1) the order of learning and age at which learned (e.g., infant/ child/ adult bilingualism); (2) the persons from whom learned (e.g., language usage in the home along the lines of the

8. See, for example, W. A. Stewart, "An Outline of Linguistic Typology for Describing Multilingualism," in *Study of the Role of Second Languages in Asia, Africa and Latin America*, ed. by F. Rice, (Washington, D. C.: Center for Applied Linguistics, 1962), pp. 15–25.

Hoffman or other bilingual schedules); (3) the type of learning and mode of use (oral, written, reading); (4) the proficiency achieved; (5) motivation and functions served (function in social advance, usefulness in communicating, cultural value, etc., as revealed by details of family descent, education, occupation, church affiliation, visiting habits).

Of these five items, only the question of proficiency requires extended comment. The discrepancies between what people say and what they actually do in language usage have repeatedly been noted in the literature.[9] Serious discrepancy between claimed and actual bilingual or multilingual competence has been the subject of some conjecture over the past few years. For example, in the account of a recent conference on multilingualism in Africa the difficulties of testing language competence are stressed:

> A certain amount of relevant discussion ensued when questions were raised concerning attempts to measure degrees of bi- or multilingualism. It was suggested that some of the techniques of dialect geography might prove useful; that reliable interview techniques could elicit the extent to which a given person not merely could speak the language but did, in fact; and that criteria such as the ability to take and operate a message might serve as useful indications of bilingualism. On the other hand it was pointed out that many emotional and political factors, possibly at the subconscious level, tended to vitiate the use of questionnaires or types of interview, though this did not mean that experiments along these lines should not be made.[10]

In the Madina survey it is intended that proficiency be measured, in the first instance, impressionistically by native-speakers who have received detailed instructions on rating as part of the training program for interviewers. Interviewers will all be undergraduate students of the University of Ghana who have been selected by Dr. Ansre on grounds of interest, aptitude, and proven native-speaking facility in two or more of the languages listed in the schedule. During a two-week training period (which, it is hoped, will include instruction in the purposes and background of the survey, interview techniques, translation into the vernaculars of the English version

9. Berry and Greenberg, "Sociolinguistic Research in Africa."

10. *Symposium on Multilingualism* (Brazzaville: CCTA/CSA, 1962), pp. 157–58.

of the schedule, and methods of assessing language competence) interviewers will be divided into teams in such a way as to insure that in each team the major languages of Ghana are represented with native-speaking competence. In conducting interviews (the language to be used throughout will be the first language of the respondent) bi- or multilinguals will be asked to assess their competence in the second or other language in terms of a crude scale of partial vs. full. *Ad hoc* proficiency tests will be conducted *in situ* by a native-speaker of the language in question, and a rating will be assigned on a scale ranging from I (minimal) to IV (near native-speaking). Throughout the survey, these ratings will be the subject of spot-checks to test consistency in grading between teams, and of individuals and teams, over time. A reasonable scatter of respondents will then be subjected to intensive testing by normal foreign-language proficiency testing methods in an attempt to assess the validity of the earlier impressionistic judgments. It is hoped that further tests can be conducted on selected true bilinguals to obtain relative proficiency scores and, possibly, bilingual indices.

The remainder of the schedule is designed to elicit stereotypes of the language or languages used by the respondents and of other local languages not spoken by the respondents. It is assumed that these stereotypes will correlate with general attitudes to the relevant culture. They are seen as an important aspect of the sociolinguistic situation, since they materially affect questions about mutual intelligibility as well as attitudes toward the teaching of the languages concerned and also toward their use.

It is intended that the total schedule be administered in three phases. Phase I, which has recently been completed, has provided basic information about what languages are represented in Madina and the extent of claimed individual multilingualism. Some 2,000 questionnaires have been completed in which respondents have listed their first language together with those other languages in which they claim full or partial competence. These questionnaires also elicited certain preliminary data about language attitudes. On the basis of a cursory examination of this data it is possible to make the following observations with some degree of assurance.

1. Very few of the 2,000 or so respondents admitted to being monolingual; in many cases, some competence was claimed in at least three languages and a good few respondents claimed competence in five or more languages.

2. There was little evidence of language shift; for virtually all respondents the mother tongue was still the first language.

3. Respondents for the most part expressed an eagerness to learn additional languages and to improve performance in languages in which they already claimed some competence. The languages people most often said they wished to learn were English, French, Arabic, Hausa, Twi, Gã, and Ewe. The reasons given for wishing to learn or to improve performance in these languages patterned significantly: economic and social advancement (particularly in the use of English and, to a lesser extent, French), for use in trade, for purposes of travel, for religious reasons (Arabic), for more effective communication, or less specifically because the respondent "liked" the language. A number of respondents, somewhat unexpectedly, stated that they wished to learn a language so as to know when its speakers were insulting or plotting against them.

4. For the same reason, a number of respondents said they would conceal knowledge of a second language on certain occasions. Fear of ridicule was the other most common reason advanced for not wishing to speak some languages publicly. In most of these cases the languages concerned were second languages imperfectly acquired, but with a number of speakers of Guang languages, it was the mother tongue about which they were sensitive.

5. Answers to questions which asked which language respondents liked best and which they liked least yielded the following results: The mother tongue was rarely disapproved of and was frequently the language liked best. English, French, Arabic, Twi, Ewe, and Hausa were often cited as languages liked best and very rarely as languages not liked at all. A few languages were regarded negatively by a significant number of respondents: Gã, Nzema, Guang, and some or all of the languages of northern Ghana and Nigeria. In almost every instance those who disapproved of Gã did so on grounds of "its profanity." The reasons advanced for dislike of the other languages mentioned were less clear and merit further investigation, but in a good few cases disapproval of the language was clearly a reflection of a dislike of its speakers.

6. The most common answers to the question "Which language do you think will be the main language spoken in the future in a) Madina b) Accra c) Ghana" were a) for Madina—Gã, Hausa, and Twi (in that order); b) for Accra— Gã, English, Hausa (in that order); and c) for Ghana—Twi, English, and, less frequently, Hausa.

The above observations are necessarily to be considered tentative in the extreme, since they derive only from a hasty and superficial scanning of the completed questionnaires. They would not be presented at this time except as an example of the sorts of information it is hoped will accrue from the Madina survey. It is clear that such information has an immediate relevance to many of the problems mentioned, for example, under the fifth, or political, aspect of a language situation.

It is expected that Phase II of the survey will be implemented soon. A sample of the population of Madina will be rigorously tested to determine their actual competence in all languages of which they claim knowledge. In addition, they will be intensively interviewed concerning language acquisition, language usage, and language attitudes.

In Phase III of the survey, interviews and tests of language competence will be supplemented by techniques of participant observation designed to study respondents' actual language behavior in everyday situations and by other methods suited to elicit the more subtle aspects of language attitudes.

Remi Clignet

The notion of increase in scale is particularly appropriate for a study of national integration. Indeed, it corresponds to a spatial, temporal, and functional extension of the control systems prevailing in a particular society.

Researchers concerned with this notion have proposed that the increase in scale of a society is accompanied by the emergence of crucial forms of social differentiation in the composition of its major urban centers. Thus, it has been demonstrated that the higher the scalar position of a particular society, the more its urban subpopulations are differentiated in terms of social rank and life-style, factors which operate independently of one another. It has also been demonstrated, however, that life-style begins to operate only after the society under investigation has reached a critical threshold of scalar development, whereas the intensity of the discriminative power exerted by social rank increases regularly with scale. For example, life-style is neither a powerful nor an independent differentiator of African urban subpopulations in the way in which it would discriminate, for instance, between the subpopulations of an Italian city or, even more, an American metropolis. Similarly, the role performed by education and occupation (as components of social rank) becomes more manifest as one moves from African to Italian to American major urban centers.

Evidences concerning the influence exerted by other determinants of social differentiation, such as migratory status and ethnicity, remain equivocal. It is difficult to decide whether the power and the independence of these two factors depend on the scalar position or on the scalar slope of the nations investigated. It is equally difficult to determine whether the relationships between scale and these two determinants of social differentiation are linear or discontinuous. An examination of African urban centers should help us in our effort to ascertain the real nature of the association between scale and social differentiation.

In considering the relationship between the scalar characteristics of African societies and the social differentiation of their centers, it should be noted that all contemporary African nations are presently characterized by a low scalar position, although they demonstrate a high slope of scalar development. The proportions of educated individuals and of persons engaged in non-agricultural or in non-manual occupations remain quite moderate, but school enrollments are rising rapidly. Similarly, the proportions of urbanized subpopulations remain low, although cities are experiencing a fast rate of growth and are attracting a large number of migrants from a variety of regions and neighboring countries.

Under such conditions, we can apply the method of controlled comparisons in African cities to determine whether similarly low scalar position and similarly high rates of scalar development are accompanied by the emergence of similarly powerful and similarly independent determinants of social differentiation. A first comparative strategy consists in specifying the nature and the extent of the association between scale and social stratification. A comparison of Accra and Abidjan suggests this association to be influenced by both the nature of their experiences and the distribution of cities by size. Indeed, in spite of similarities in the scalar characteristics of these two countries, there are variations in the significance of the role played by social rank, life-style, migrant status, and ethnicity in the differentiation of the subpopulations living in their respective capital cities. The social area analysis of Douala and Yaounde should enable us to undertake another type of specification and to identify other variables likely to affect the association between scale and social differentiation.

First, we can analyze whether this association varies with the size of the urban center investigated. Thus Douala has a population of over 200,000 inhabitants, whereas Yaounde is only half as large.

Secondly, we can analyze whether this association varies with the dominant functions served by the center under study. Thus, Douala is the main port of Cameroon, and its population is active in a variety of export-import concerns as well as in industrial activities. In contrast, Yaounde is the federal capital of the country, and its population is predominantly represented in the tertiary sector of the economy.

Thirdly, we can make comparisons not only between Cameroonian cities but also between such cities and their counterparts elsewhere in West Africa. For example, given the fact that Douala and Abidjan are of approximately the same size, serve the same economic functions, and have been subjected to the same colonial model, we can expect their subpopulations to be differentiated along similar lines. Should differentiation differ as between these two cities, we may speculate about the relative impact of cultural factors on the one hand, and city-size distribution on the other, that is, on the association between scale and social differentiation.

Data to be included in the analysis of Douala and Yaounde will be derived from the tapes on which the census materials of these two cities have been transcribed. These censuses were taken for Douala in 1964 and for Yaounde in 1962 under the direction of the Services de la Statistique du Gouvernement Camerounais. They covered the entire population of the two cities, and the raw data that originated from them has been locally "cleared" through various computer programs.

One clear asset of the two census tapes of Douala and Yaounde is the richness of the information that they contain about the occupational status of the adult population. First, accurate descriptions of the nature of the occupations performed by individuals are given, and this facilitates a clear distinction between manual and non-manual active persons. Secondly, meaningful distinctions are made as to the position occupied by individuals in their occupational category, and it is therefore possible to distinguish persons in terms of their independence and the relative income that they enjoy. Thirdly, it is possible to analyze and classify wage-earners in terms of the characteristics of their employers and thus to distinguish between individuals working for large-scale concerns and their counterparts employed by small-scale local firms or individual employers. Fourth, we are given some information, although only for Douala, about the amount of time during which unemployed persons have been out of the labor market. This type of data should enable us not only to have a better appreciation of unemployment throughout urban space but also to reach a better understanding of the determinants of this increasingly significant social problem.

The second quality of these censuses is that they include a variety of measures pertaining to the modernization of the individual. For example, we are able to discover how many women have been "officially" married, that is, married by modern authorities. Similarly, in the case of Douala, we are able to determine the distribution of children whose births have been reported at the office of vital statistics.

Thirdly, the censuses contain a number of important information items on public health. For the two cities analyzed, we have the distribution of various types of diseases by census tracts. For Yaounde we have information concerning the total number of births and infant deaths in the year preceding the census, and reports of the number of births which occurred in hospitals. We are also able to determine the ratio of occupancy of the city's dwelling units and its variations throughout various neighborhoods.

With regard to analyses to be generated from the data, our first goal is to examine the forms and determinants of social differentiation prevailing in the two major urban centers of Cameroon. Following the suggestions of Janet Abu-Lughod in her paper, "A Critical Test for the Theory of Social Area Analysis: The Factorial Ecology of Cairo, Egypt," I will conduct a factorial analysis to identify the nature of the determinant or determinants of social differentiation.

Yet, social area analysis is not an end in itself. The identification of distinctive subpopulations in urban centers should facilitate a more accurate approximation of the forces underlying the adjustment of individuals to a modern setting. For example, in a forthcoming publication Joyce Sween and I have examined how exposure to modernizing forces and social structures of origin interact to affect the type of marriage contracted by the adult male and female populations of Abidjan. We intend to go one step further and examine how, in Douala and Yaounde, the distribution of polygyny is affected both by ethnicity and socioeconomic status in a variety of neighborhoods with distinctive social rank, life-style, migrant status, and ethnic characteristics.

This type of analysis is useful not only in determining

whether urbanization is associated with a nuclearization of the family and hence with a greater availability of individual actors to participate in larger scale organizations, but also in helping us to reach a better comprehension of the interaction between individual personalities and their environment. We have suggested elsewhere that meaningful distinctions should be entered between the modernization of means used by individual African actors and the modernization of the ends to which they aspire. The extent to which these two forms of modernization coincide or differ, which is of relevance for the development of national integration, depends on the form of interaction between personality and environmental characteristics.

TRANSACTION FLOWS AND NATIONAL UNITY: THE NIGERIAN CASE

20

Edward W. Soja

The communication and preservation of information within a community of people, be it a family, an ethnic group, or a modern nation, provides the integrative glue which enables the community to survive as a cohesive, organized unit. Human communications is the very basis of social and political organization. It creates through the dynamic exchange of information between the component parts of a system the bonds of mutual awareness and interdependence which promote integrative behavior. Any attempt to understand the problems of building national unity in Africa, therefore, must involve an examination of the structure, content, and flow of information through space and time.

My research within the framework of the National Unity Project has focused upon the analysis of communications systems in East Africa and Nigeria. The basic objective of this research has been to develop methods for evaluating quantitatively the patterns of territorial integration, both in terms of interregional communications and with respect to interurban linkages. In this paper, I will review briefly some of the work that has already been completed on this subject and outline, equally briefly, some work that is currently under way.

As a geographer, my major interest has been in spatial interaction, that is, the degree to which areas and places are linked together by the flow of people, goods, and information, and the nature of these linkages. This interest, however, creates a major problem of data collection, particularly when one is concerned with large areal coverage and two-way flows of communication. If one wishes to examine the relative degree of connectivity between, for example, the major towns of Kenya, there are few dependable indicators for which quantitative data can be collected.

Railway traffic, both for goods and passengers, provides one possible source of data, but its use would restrict coverage to the areas served by railways, even if accurate origin-destination data were available. There are some flow data for road traffic, but it is virtually impossible to disaggregate these data to provide measures of interregional or interurban linkage on a national basis. Newspaper circulation and other forms of mass media are helpful in examining connectivity with the focal centers from which they originate, but these indicators are of little use in determining the linkages between smaller cities or regions. Postal traffic would be an excellent data source, but statistics for origin and destination simply do not exist.

On the aggregate and large-scale level, therefore, only telecommunications data and data on such economic indicators as interregional trade and money flow appear to provide the types of measures necessary to evaluate spatial patterns of integration on a national basis. And of these two groups of measures, telephone traffic alone has the extensive data base suitable to statistical analysis over periods of time and covering a large number of points and areas within the state. Nearly every African state has surprisingly abundant and detailed accounts of telephone traffic, since these data are essential for the planning and operation of a telecommunications network. Moreover, the data involve actual flows from place to place, unlike postal statistics, which are primarily concerned with volumes at particular points rather than with the flows between them.

Each year, for example, the East African Posts and Telecommunications Administration in Nairobi conducts a census of trunk calls between twenty-four exchange regions in Uganda, Kenya, and Tanzania. In recent years, these censuses have been based on a thirty-hour sample of periods of peak traffic flow during the working week. In addition, more intensive surveys of selected exchanges have been made over a full month, thus giving a detailed account of telephone traffic between such important centers as Dar es Salaam, Kampala, Nairobi, and the rest of East Africa.

In another paper, I have analyzed these data for the period 1961–65 in an attempt to examine the changing patterns of spatial integration in East Africa as a whole, and within Kenya and Tanzania separately.[1] The study used the techniques of transaction-flow analysis and was based on an indifference model developed and modified from earlier models by Steven Brams in a doctoral dissertation in political science at Northwestern University.[2] The idea behind the model is relatively simple. It assumes that a degree of interaction which suggests a close behavioral linkage between two units, whether they are cities or human beings, can be reached only when the transaction flow between these units is significantly greater than expected, given the relative size or importance of each unit within the overall communications system. This greater than expected relationship has been termed "salience."

The relative size measure used most frequently in this model is the proportion of total transactions in the entire system that is received at a particular point. Thus, to give a specific example, if Nairobi receives 10 per cent of all telephone calls made in East Africa, the model assumes that all other centers will be expected to send approximately 10 per cent of their outgoing calls to Nairobi. When actual flows, in both directions, exceed the expected by an arbitrarily chosen proportion, the units are considered salient. In another context, the units could be considered "close acquaintances."

The application of this model to the twenty-four exchange regions of East Africa produced some very revealing patterns of salience, particularly with respect to their changes over the critical time period when each of the three territories achieved independence. The most powerful factor affecting the pattern was the existence of international boundaries, which acted to compartmentalize transaction flows into distinct national systems. Moreover, this inward-looking national focus became accentuated over time. The Arusha-Moshi area, for example, was very salient with Nairobi in 1961, but much less so in 1965. During the same time period, the salience of this area with Dar es Salaam increased dramatically, thus marking a

1. Edward Soja, "Communications and Territorial Integration in East Africa: An Introduction to Transaction Flow Analysis," *East Lakes Geographer*, IV (December, 1968), 39–51.

2. Steven Brams, "Flow and Form in the International System" (Ph.D. dissertation, Northwestern University, 1966); see also Steven Brams, "Transaction Flows in the International System," *American Political Science Review*, LX (December, 1966), 880–98.

distinct reorientation of this region after Tanzanian independence. Also interesting was the progressive isolation of Uganda; in 1965, Uganda had no salient link with any region outside its borders, although internally it was quite closely interconnected.

I was able to collect even more detailed telecommunications data during my recent stay in Nigeria. The Nigerian Telecommunications Department has been conducting detailed telephone traffic censuses for nearly 160 urban centers since 1961. These censuses have been based on two twenty-four hour surveys conducted on the same days at each center, and they provide an intriguing indication of the patterns of interurban linkage throughout the federation.

As might be expected, political events in Nigeria have led to many significant gaps in the data. But these gaps are in themselves interesting and revealing. First of all, the entire file for the former Eastern Region disappeared. Only the existence of a handwritten sheet of tabulations for the entire country enabled data for the East in 1965 and 1966 to be collected. The 1965 data also completed the set of statistics covering all of Nigeria, the only year for which complete data are available. In 1966, the rioting and unrest prevented any data from being collected in the Northern Region; and for the Northeastern Region (the telephone exchange regions are not exactly coincident with the former administrative regions) the data are incomplete. Attached to the data which did exist for 1966 in the Northeast was the following note, an understated reflection of the internal turmoil going on at the time.

> (Dated January 26, 1967)
> Records were not taken at other exchanges in this area due to protracted trunk circuit faults and shortage of trained staff as follows:
> a) Trunk circuits faulty and exchange cut off: Maiduguri, Gombe
> b) No trained staff to take record at: Barakinladi, Keffi, Mubi, Potiskum, Vom, Yola.
> (Signed) Acting District Commercial Manager, Jos.

The data which have been collected are currently in the initial stages of processing. The various types of analyses being planned include (1) a restructuring of the 1965 data according to the boundaries of the twelve new states proclaimed by the Federal Government in 1967, and a transaction-flow analysis of these data similar to the ones conducted in East Africa (this should provide some interesting information on the patterns of intraterritorial connectivity prior to the secession of Biafra); (2) an analysis of the changing patterns of connectivity through time for those areas which have sufficient data (a case study will be made of the Midwest Region, for which data exist both before and after its separation from the Western Region); and (3) an overall analysis of interurban linkages in Nigeria and an attempt to subdivide

SALIENT LINKAGES: 1965 (preliminary estimates)

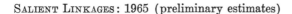
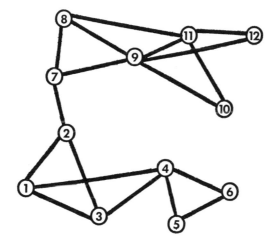

the country into a hierarchy of communications regions (this analysis would also identify important focal centers of communication at various levels in the hierarchy).

These studies have not progressed far enough for any substantive conclusions to be presented here. The following table, however, is presented to indicate some of the preliminary work that is being done and perhaps to suggest some of the patterns that may emerge with further analysis. The table shows all calls made in 1965 between what are today the twelve new states of the Nigerian Federation and are thus based on a restructuring of the 1965 data to conform to the new boundaries.

A very rough calculation of the pattern of salient linkages for 1965 is shown in the sketch map. The pattern is not particularly unexpected. The six states which composed the

Interstate Telephone Traffic in Nigeria: 1965 Sample

(Figures represent average of two twenty-four hour samples, December 7 and 9, 1965)

States	1.	2.	3.	4.	5.	6.	7.	8.	9.	10.	11.	12.	Totals
1. Lagos	—	*475	191	395	121	11	42	24	214	63	174	8	1718
2. West	*525	—	229	86	8	1	95	8	68	15	25	1	1061
3. Midwest	258	303	—	157	32	2	18	1	3	3	3	0	780
4. East Central	517	89	135	—	607	296	11	7	53	57	46	2	1820
5. Rivers	157	13	25	533	—	65	3	1	8	5	5	0	815
6. Southeast	13	3	4	330	107	—	0	0	1	2	0	0	460
7. Kwara	94	122	16	19	1	0	—	36	99	17	25	4	433
8. Northwest	20	14	3	12	0	0	32	—	343	21	125	6	576
9. North-Central	363	77	6	74	6	3	94	188	—	173	452	60	1496
10. Benue-Plateau	99	19	7	55	5	0	16	9	214	—	84	79	587
11. Kano	381	71	19	113	19	2	52	123	585	104	—	88	1557
12. Northeast	18	6	0	2	0	0	1	3	105	149	78	—	362
Total	2445	1192	635	1776	906	380	364	400	1693	609	1017	248	11,665

* Does not include direct-dialed calls

former Northern Region are tightly interconnected and are focused primarily on what is now the North Central State, which is in turn salient with all other states in the north. The North Central State includes such important centers as Kaduna, the former capital of the Northern Region; Katsina; and Zaria, site of Ahmadu Bello University. Southern Nigeria, in turn, forms an almost entirely separate communications subsystem, but has no single state which dominates the pattern of salience as the North Central State does in the north. Only Kwara, with its large Yoruba population, is linked to both the northern and southern subsystems, a position which clearly reflects its history.

The sketch map is offered only as a simple illustration of the type of analysis being done. There are obvious problems which arise with the use of telecommunications data and these must be recognized and dealt with if interpretation is to be reliable. For example, there is little indication as to who is making the telephone calls. It is likely that most are administrative or business calls, although the full twenty-four hour sample makes this less true for Nigeria than for East Africa, where only peak traffic periods are sampled. Further complications arise with direct-dialing systems, for which no data are available. But the only direct-dialing system in Nigeria which crosses state boundaries at present is that between Lagos and Ibadan, which are in states that are salient even if only operator-placed calls are considered. And as all who have spent time in Nigeria will recognize, there is, of course, the problem of inefficiency in the telecommunications system. Many have probably heard the story of the businessman in Apapa, the main port for Lagos, who, after many discouraging trials with the telephone, was forced to depend on a messenger to convey information between the Apapa office and Lagos, just across the bridge.

Nevertheless, the advantages of telecommunications data far outweigh the disadvantages. They provide much-needed information on interregional and interurban communications, and their widespread availability also permits comparative analyses to be made. Although other relevant measures of interaction could be developed, the detailed telephone traffic census taken at regular time intervals supplies one of the best sources of statistical data existing in Africa and one of the best frameworks for measurement and interpretation of patterns of territorial integration. There have been relatively few attempts made anywhere in the social science literature to develop methods of quantitatively measuring the various dimensions of national unity, particularly with respect to identifying the patterns of connectivity between the subregions of a state. It is within this context that transaction-flow analysis can hopefully make some major contributions.

NATIONAL INTEGRATION AND STABILITY IN AFRICA

21.

Robert Cameron Mitchell, Donald George Morrison,
and John N. Paden

The transfer of political institutions and the politics of nation-building have occupied much of the recent attention in
political science with reference to Africa. Yet, with the breakdown of political systems in many states, it may be necessary
to reassess both the sociopolitical complexities involved and
the modes of analysis which have been used to interpret these
complexities. Whether our analytical approaches have been
legal-institutional, neo-Marxist, structural-functional, or jour-
nalistic, we have not been able to anticipate the particular
patterns of instability which have emerged, nor do we yet
know the crucial mechanisms in the process of political integration. The "work-in-progress" represented in our research,
as summarized in this essay, is an experiment. It is an attempt
to assess the merits of an empirical multivariate approach to
the issues of national integration and stability. It is dedicated
to the younger generation of African "social engineers" who
will carry partial responsibility for constructing truly African solutions to the problems of a vast continent. In our own
research we have dealt only with "diagnosis" and not with
"prognosis."

Terms of Reference and Project Development

Our research project originated as an attempt to bring together scholars from the disciplines of applied mathematics,

sociology, and political science to deal with a complex and politically sensitive topic. Two of the researchers had dissertation field experience in Africa, and the third worked in Latin America. Both the Program of African Studies and the Council for Intersocietal Studies at Northwestern seemed to encourage multidisciplinary research, yet actual instances of such research were less than common. In this case, the idea of such an investigation was initiated without funding expectations. The funding from the Council for Intersocietal Studies and the Program of African Studies allowed a much more comprehensive attack on problems of instability and integration than the original modest goals of the unfunded project.

The purpose of the project was to examine the substantive aspects of instability and integration within the African context and to assess the methods appropriate to such a study. On the substantive side, integration theory seemed to fall into four categories of analysis: transaction-flow analysis, functional-interdependence analysis (e.g., institutions), value congruence, and identity analysis. Due to the limitations of data sources, we selected the second and third types of analysis. We selected four units of analysis: urban, ethnic, elite, and country. The universe selected was the sub-Saharan independent African states, thirty-two in number. On the methodology of analysis, we initially employed the technique of step-wise multiple discriminant function analysis, which normally requires at least a nominal dependent variable and interval (or ordinal) independent variables. By this method, we can discover those independent variables which best account for the difference between groups as defined by the value of the dependent variable. We have proceeded to a multi-method approach whereby important conclusions can be checked with the use of several statistical methods, especially causal modeling. This will aid in checking the validity and reliability of the model.

Initially, the three researchers were given funding for a secretary and several graduate-student assistants. The initial grant began in April, 1967. An extension of this grant allowed us to proceed during the academic year 1967–68 and to concentrate heavily on the project during the summer of 1968, again with the assistance of several graduate students, including many of the African graduate students at Northwestern. The project will terminate in August, 1969.

Data Gathering

One of the initial tasks was to develop a propositional inventory of definitions, hypotheses, and theories regarding integration and instability. We generated a two-hundred-page inventory of propositions arranged by topic. From this inventory we constructed our initial variables. Much of this inventory has subsequently been computerized.

Having formulated variables, we tried to assess whether appropriate data were available on the African states. Using the facilities of Northwestern University's Africana library as well as published and unpublished bibliographies, we created a bibliographic referencing system which was keyed into our units of analysis and our variable categories. All references (approximately 20,000) were put on machine-readable IBM cards, using a KWOC format, so that retrieval could be handled easily by our coders. This format will allow continual additions to the bibliography, which will become a permanent part of the Northwestern Intersocietal Information Center (IIC), directed by Professor Kenneth Janda.

By far the largest portion of our time and resources has gone into the coding of the variables. To date, we have approximately twelve hundred variables, with little or no missing data on our set of thirty-two countries.

Perhaps the most fundamental deterrent to more effective cross-national studies of Africa is the lack of data. It became clear during the course of our project that this problem could be partially resolved if a wide array of sources, some quite obscure, were used. The expenditure of human resources for this undertaking has been considerable, but it was felt that no adequate quantitative work could be done that did not put considerable resources into collecting data and cross-checking the reliability and quality of that data.

The results of this data-collection effort can be summarized as follows for our thirty-two independent sub-Saharan countries.

Individual political actors: Biographical data has been coded on over one thousand individuals, including age, ethnicity, education, occupation, and parental background. This data was gathered entirely from public sources, although ethnic coding was often possible only through consultation with scholars from particular countries. There is missing data on the background variables with many of the lesser known individuals.

Ethnic units: We have selected 154 ethnic groups for analysis, which represent all units of over 5 per cent total population in each country. These ethnic groups were coded on 24 social, cultural, and political variables, largely based on our ordinal scaling of categories suggested in Murdock's *Ethnographic Atlas.* An intensive effort on our part has filled in all missing data on these groups, and this information will be an important aspect of our analyses of elite and communal instability.

Urban units: We have selected for analysis the four largest urban units in each country. Population rates of change and ethnic data on these urban areas have been gathered. The four largest urban units in each country were selected because patterns of urban primacy and ethnic imbalance enter into some of our theoretical work. There is no missing data, and preliminary publication of our data in *African Urban Notes* has elicited some very helpful information from experts on various cities.

National systems units: At the national level, we have gathered data on over twelve hundred variables across the thirty-two countries. These include both structural and flow information. Some of the categories covered are political structure, communications, transportation, education, religion, demography, ecology, military structure, international relations, social welfare, economic resources, trade and commerce, standard of living, and language patterns (as well as urban, ethnic, and elite composite measures). Missing data as well as data reliability vary considerably, but in general only variables with little or no missing data will be included in our final analysis. Furthermore, since development over time is central to our analysis, we have collected data for many variables by decades, beginning in the 1920's. For variables which change considerably from year to year, such as balance of payments, we code the data for every year over the last decade.

This collection is one of the most extensive comparative data-gathering efforts yet made for the full range of African states. Hundreds of sources have been used, and we hope the product will prove useful to a wide range of scholarly interests. It is expected that the Intersocietal Information Center (IIC) will eventually act as distributor for this information. We are already cooperating with the broader academic community, and have recently turned over magnetic tapes of our data and code books to the Harvard University Data Center. In the near future we will be supplying these same materials to University College Ibadan in Nigeria and to the African Data Bank at Columbia University.

All data has been punched on IBM cards to allow statistical processing. Furthermore, the codebook is machine-readable. Hence, the codebook can be corrected, changed, or added to with a minimum of difficulty. The codebook is structured so that information-retrieval programs can search it for variables pertaining to any desired subject. This is an enormous advantage in light of the explosion in amount of data available in punched-card form.

Analysis

Preliminary analysis was conducted during the summer and fall of 1967, and the summer of 1968. At present, we are engaged in two major efforts of analysis which we consider "final."

The broad range of data gathered will allow the empirical analysis of hypotheses derived from our own model as well as from the literature. Unfortunately, much of the literature on national integration and instability is vague and very difficult to operationalize. This is perhaps basic to many of the disagreements in the literature, for example, the relationship of political instability to economic development.

Our basic techniques of analysis include discriminant-function analysis, causal modeling (path analysis), and factor analysis.

To give a brief indication of our preliminary findings, we noted, among other things, that the similarity of ethnic cultural patterns within a country seemed to be a prime determinant of stability. Secondly, among the highest correlations with patterns of instability were the various dimensions of "modernization," such as educational level, role of women, rate of urbanization, degree of technology, etc. The implications of both these results are considerable.

We have tried to generate two separate models of stability /integration: (1) a model of elite instability, and (2) a model of community instability. In the first model, we are analyzing the relationship between ethnic balance within cabinets and patterns of cabinet instability. We are considering as intervening variables different patterns of legitimacy, coercive potential, alternate elite structure, and mass social pressures. In the second model, we are analyzing the relationships between different types of community instability (especially irredentism and civil war) with patterns of ethnic proportionality, urban systems, and stages of national system development.

Externalities of the Project

The project seems to have stimulated and reinforced members of the Northwestern academic community in their attention to both substantive matters of integration/instability and methodological aspects of analysis. We held a one-day working conference in May of 1968, at which we presented and distributed twenty-five working papers on various aspects of the project. Faculty colleagues and graduate students were invited to participate in these sessions.

At least a dozen graduate student M.A. theses have been (or are being) developed out of close association with the project. All of these students have utilized the data resources of the project, as well as the time resources of the coresearchers. In turn, they have contributed their results to the project data bank.

At least five graduate students who have worked extensively on the project are currently in Africa doing field research on topics dealing with national integration which grew out of their work on the project.

During the academic year 1968–69, an advanced level graduate seminar on integration has been established within the political science department. One of the co-instructors of the seminar is also a co-researcher on our project. Outside experts on integration, such as Professor Karl Deutsch and Professor Henry Teune, have been brought into the seminar.

In May of 1968 the Ford Foundation extended a grant to the Northwestern University Program of African Studies for programs related to problems of national unity in Africa. The interactions between our pilot research project and other aspects of the African National Unity project have been close and mutually reinforcing.

Publication Plans

We are in the process of preparing three separate volumes, which represent our efforts on (1) data patterns and methods of analysis, (2) analysis of elite instability, and (3) analysis of ethnicity and community instability.

We are preparing for publication a volume to be entitled *Black Africa: A Handbook for Comparative Analysis*. The first portion of the book will present comparative data on approximately 175 select variables in 16 categories, such as political systems, economic systems, pluralism, and urban patterns. The second portion will present select data by country. For each of the thirty-two nations we will include a map and ethnic, language, political, and urban profiles. The final portion of the book will consider some of the crucial methodological problems of cross-national analysis in general as well as special problems relating to the validity and reliability of data for Africa.

We are currently engaged in data analysis which will test our model of cabinet instability. We are arranging our analysis in book form, tentatively entitled *Ethnic Balance and Cabinet Instability in Africa*.

We have also collected data and will undertake the analysis during 1969 of theories related to secession and irredentism in Africa. We are arranging our analysis in book form, tentatively entitled *Ethnicity, Modernization, and Community Instability in Africa*.

THE FIRST TWENTY YEARS: HISTORY OF THE PROGRAM OF AFRICAN STUDIES AT NORTHWESTERN UNIVERSITY

The Program of African Studies at Northwestern University celebrated its twentieth anniversary in 1968. In these two decades from 1948, the first formally established program of African studies in the United States developed from a few courses and a multidisciplinary faculty–graduate student seminar into a large, well-rounded series of African offerings in the social sciences and humanities. By the time of the anniversary conference some 25 faculty members, over 125 American, African, and European graduate students, and more than 1,000 undergraduates were involved in a wide range of formal and informal academic concerns on the Northwestern campus stimulated and coordinated by the Program of African Studies from its center at Africa House. Another 10 to 15 advanced graduate students were undertaking field work in Africa, much of it linked to faculty research. Institutes for secondary school teachers and curriculum development for the basic college course on Africa were only some of the activities that Northwestern University's African Studies Program was also undertaking as it extended its activities in the national and international spheres. The transformation had been rapid and reflected the sound foundations originally laid.

The leadership in creating the Program, and the subsequent development of Northwestern University as a major center for African studies, was provided by Professor Melville J. Herskovits, Professor of Anthropology, who served as Director of the Program from 1948 until his death in February, 1963. A pioneer in African studies, Herskovits' thesis was on the role of cattle in East Africa. This research stimulated his thinking on the influence of economics on cultural values, one of the many facets of his wide-ranging concerns. Already in the 1930's Professor Herskovits combined his own rich research and writing with courses presented at Northwestern University that centered on African content.

Professor Herskovits' concern for African studies had both academic and practical motives. He believed that American social scientists did not take sufficient account of cultural differences; that generally accepted social theories were chiefly applicable, in fact, only to Western experience; and that many social sciences were thus "culture-bound." He was also concerned that so few Americans possessed any comprehensive knowledge of Africa—indeed it was sometimes said in the 1940's that the few African experts in the United States could hold a convention in a telephone booth.

This paucity of experience and knowledge received prominence as Africa became increasingly important in American strategies and actions in World War II. The national need for information and for training in local languages quickly gave rise to crash programs (such as the Army Specialist Training Program and the Army Civil Affairs Training Service). At the same time, Professor Herskovits and other academic specialists on Africa, like Professor William O. Brown (subsequently of Boston University) and Professor William Hance of Columbia University, kept to the fore the scholarly implications of non-Western studies and sought ways in which a more academic orientation could be given to them. The American Council of Learned Societies and the Social Science Research Council stimulated conferences during the 1940's to reflect on, plan, and evaluate area studies other than the crash programs of the army. The World Areas Committee, a joint committee of these two organizations established in 1945–46, played a positive and important role in providing guidelines for the development of African studies.

A major step was taken in 1948 when the Carnegie Corporation provided the first basic external support which enabled Professor Herskovits to fashion courses with African subject matter into the core of a formal Program of African Studies. Subsequent grants from the Carnegie Corporation and the Ford Foundation, coupled with generous university support, have helped this pioneer Program—the first of the African Studies Programs in the United States (established five years before that at Boston and eleven years before the large and comprehensive Program of African Studies at the University of California in Los Angeles)—to maintain its momentum and growth. That there are now some forty formally organized college and university programs dealing with African studies, some twenty of them at major centers, reflects the significance of Professor Herskovits' early initiative as well as the steadily growing awareness of the importance for Americans of knowledge and understanding about Africa.

The original focus of the Program of African Studies was on "Africa South of the Sahara," a term at first interpreted so as to exclude not only the northern tier of the African states but also the Horn of Africa, i.e., Ethiopia and Somalia, and South Africa. Each of these areas has subsequently been added to the scope of the Program, which now includes courses, seminars, and research on all parts of the continent.

The scholarly assumptions on which the Program of African Studies at Northwestern University was founded were implicit in its structure. These provided a unifying element for the scholars from various disciplines who have participated in the Program of African Studies and helped to stimulate widespread academic interest in Africa. These assumptions can be briefly summarized as follows:

(1) that Africa is a significant area within which the social sciences and humanities can explore their own particular "problems";

(2) that departments must provide the major academic focus both for teaching and for degrees but that interdisciplinary seminars and research are also needed; and

(3) that the primary emphasis of the Program should be placed on training scholars at the graduate level, and should lead to advanced research.

Obvious as these assumptions may now appear, major problems have been faced not only in developing more comprehensive knowledge and searching understanding of Africa and its culture but also in fitting this knowledge into the orbit of established academic disciplines. An examination of college catalogues of twenty to thirty years ago reveals the scant academic interest in African culture and development of that period. This interest, where it was evinced at all, was often confined to a few departments: anthropology, sometimes geography, and also to a limited degree history; but African studies were commonly taught merely as an extension of European history. To persuade departments of the academic respectability of courses with African content, to overcome the suspicion that area studies might involve the watering down of disciplinary standards, and to attract the best graduate students whose skills and dedication were so much needed both to undertake the basic research on which sound conclusions could be based and to provide the scholars and teachers capable of training the next generation of African specialists—these were the pressing and omnipresent problems with which American Africanists had long to battle.

Particularly in the early years of Northwestern's Program of African Studies, it was extremely difficult to find adequate staff to join Professor Herskovits. The faculty–graduate student seminar established at Northwestern in 1948 was one means of enabling faculty members to develop competence in African studies and ultimately to offer courses in their own field. The seminar became famous for its ability to attract such informed observers and participants as Lord Hailey, Dr. Nnamdi Azikewe, Dr. Van Eck, and colonial governors and ambassadors, who spoke ''off the record,'' answering questions with an openness all too rare today.

Faculty members were also provided with firsthand experience in Africa through the assistance of interested foundations. Professor and Mrs. Herskovits made many extended trips through Africa both for research and to pave the way for less experienced scholars. The Carnegie Corporation enabled a number of social scientists from different universities, including Professor Roland Young of Northwestern University, to visit Africa in 1951 as part of the first of several group research teams. Professor Gwendolen Carter, who became Director of the Program in 1964, acquired her first African experience in 1948 through a grant from the Rockefeller Foundation.

Both Professors Young and Carter are political scientists, and it was this field that most closely followed anthropology and geography in attracting specialists, particularly as the widespread drive for African independence and the variety of responses to its achievement provided unparalleled comparative data. Still more recently, there has been an acceleration in the systematic work in African history, archaeology, linguistics, sociology, economics, law, education, and, to a lesser extent, psychology. (Of approximately 700 Fellows of the African Studies Association in 1967, some of whom were from outside the United States, approximately one-fifth were anthropologists, another fifth were political scientists, a slightly lower ratio were historians, one-tenth were economists, and there were 36 sociologists and 47 geographers.) Even now there has not been a great deal of systematic study of African art, music, literature, drama, philosophy, and religion.

The number of staff members at Northwestern University with major concerns for African studies has increased rapidly in the past few years. This increase has been greatly aided by the substantial support extended by the Ford Foundation for the period 1961–71, which followed an earlier five-year grant. Since 1965, when the Program of African Studies became a Language and Area Center, the United States Office of Education has made annual support grants.

The second Ford grant made specific provision for appointments in African history and African sociology, and both places were filled in 1964. Student demand made it necessary to add a second African historian in 1965, and the Sociology Department has had a second staff member with broad African experience since 1967. Staff members have also been added in political science, anthropology, economics, and geography through departmental support.

Northwestern University's Program of African Studies has been weakest in the humanities, but recent appointments are remedying this situation. The Departments of Art and English now include African specialists, and the joint appointment by the School of Music and the Department of Linguistics of Professor Klaus Wachsmann in 1968 brought to the campus a noted ethnomusicologist.

The most spectacular advances have been made in linguistics. In 1964, at the same time as the appointment of Professor Carter as Director of the Program, the Department of Linguistics (originally known as the Department of African Languages and Linguistics) was established with two outstanding Africanist linguists, Professors Jack Berry and Hans Wolff. Since the Program of African Studies became a Language and Area Center of the Office of Education in 1965, this additional support has been concentrated on building the African component of the Department of Linguistics into one of the strongest in the United States. A mark of the importance now placed on African languages and linguistics is that competence in one or the other is a requirement for the Certificate of African

Studies, inaugurated in 1965 to provide an addition to, but not substitute for, a graduate academic degree.

The number of African specialists associated through the Program has thus increased impressively in recent years. In 1963 there were eleven; in 1968, twenty-four. Some of these faculty members, like Professor Franklin Scott in history, Professor Roland Young in political science, Professor Paul Bohannan in anthropology, and Professor George Dalton in economics, have, with Professor Herskovits, provided the long-term core around which the Program has evolved. Other faculty members no longer at Northwestern, like Professor Alan Merriam (Chairman of the Department of Anthropology at Indiana University) and Professor John Middleton (Chairman of the Department of Anthropology at New York University) have aided greatly in the Program's growth.

Distinguished visiting professors have made great contributions to their departments and to African studies, notably Professor Roland Oliver of the School of Oriental and African Studies, University of London; Dr. Kenneth Dike, formerly Vice-Chancellor of the University of Ibadan; Professor Akin Mabogunje, Geography Department, University of Ibadan; Professor K. Bentsi-Enchill, Law Department, University of Zambia; Professor Jacques Maquet, Ecole Pratique des Hautes Etudes, University of Paris; Professor Kofi Busia, Department of Sociology, University of Ghana; Dr. Lucy Mair, Political Science, London School of Economics; Professor Kenneth Little, Department of Anthropology, Edinburgh University; Professor Margaret Read, Education in Tropical Areas, London University; Professor Thomas Hodgkin, Balliol College, Oxford; Professor Peter Bauer, London School of Economics; Dr. Audrey Richards, formerly Newnham College, Cambridge University; Professor Lyndon Harries, School of Oriental and African Studies, London University; Dr. Leo Silberman, Balliol College, Oxford; Professor Jeff Holden, University of Ghana; Dr. Thomas Melone, University of the Cameroons; Dr. Sheila van der Horst, South African Institute of Race Relations; Dr. Elizabeth Colson, formerly Rhodes-Livingstone Institute, Lusaka; Professor Jan Vansina, History Department, University of Wisconsin; Professor Paul Wingert, African Art, Columbia University; Professor Harry Rudin, School of Oriental and African Studies, London University; Professor Vernon McKay, School of Advanced International Studies, Johns Hopkins University; and Drs. Leo and Hilda Kuper, Departments of Sociology and

Anthropology, University of California at Los Angeles. In two instances, the late Dr. Eduardo Mondlane and Dr. Pius Okigbo, African Ph.D.s, returned to Northwestern to serve briefly as visiting faculty members. The University and the Program of African Studies also value the recollection of their close association with the Assistant Secretary-General of the United Nations, Dr. Ralph Bunche, who spent a postdoctoral term with the Department of Anthropology in 1936.

Although associated most closely with the College of Arts and Sciences, the Program of African Studies also has close links with the other schools making up Northwestern University, through faculty members who are African specialists. Professor Alex Nekam of the Law School, who has twice made field trips to Africa on Program funds, teaches a course on African law. Professor Klaus Wachsmann has reintroduced courses in ethnomusicology formerly taught by Dr. Alan Merriam. Professor Ethel Albert holds a joint appointment in the School of Speech and the Department of Anthropology.

All faculty members associated with the Program are members of particular departments and thus perform dual roles, each enriching the other. This is the answer to the charge that area studies are a rival method of organizing knowledge to that of the disciplines. Area and discipline are two ways of approaching intellectual inquiry and are complementary, not competitive. This is particularly the case since the value of interdisciplinary interaction has been more widely accepted. The present historical academic division may be compared with the pluralistic nation-state where the interests of the people extend beyond the state and where old boundaries may divide those with mutual interests. It would be difficult and undesirable to attempt to redraw academic boundaries. The departments are essential for disciplinary training; they give the scholar an academic home; they provide stability, continuity, and tenure. However, they must not be allowed to circumscribe the scope of intellectual inquiry.

Area studies are a source of data from which the disciplines can be enriched, reshaped, and supplemented in the continual intellectual process of acquiring and organizing knowledge. The success achieved by the Program of African Studies in stimulating interdisciplinary training and in identifying significant fields of research has opened up new vistas. An African historian, for instance, whose primary interest may be in the content of documents will also be concerned with evidence provided by digging (archaeology); oral tradition (social psychology); social organization (anthropology and sociology); the dimensions of migration and communication (geography); language data (linguistics); cultural data (musicology); and sometimes such an apparently remote subject as botany.

The term interdisciplinary, or even multidisciplinary, does not fully describe the academic development that has taken place. Stimulated in part by area studies though still more by new methodologies and techniques, the disciplines themselves have been modified and the scope of their interest broadened. The results of this recent period of remarkable productivity have been as dramatic, in their spheres, as the impact of Western ideas has been on the character of African thought and planning. Disciplines have been shaken and revitalized; the significance of culture has acquired new relevance; and working relations have developed between scholars who were previously better acquainted with research in their particular geographical areas than with the work of many colleagues in their own disciplines. The overall effect has been to develop a more healthy and cooperative relationship between African studies and disciplinary inquiry.

The organization of the Program reflects its close working arrangements with the departments. The Committee on African Studies, appointed annually by the Dean of Faculties, represents the various participating departments and schools and is chaired by the Director of the Program. The usefulness and convenience of this type of loose organization has been recognized by other universities, which have adapted it for their own use. Lectures, seminars, and social interchanges between those with African interests have been facilitated by the new quarters provided for the Program in 1961 when Africa House was established at 1813 Hinman Avenue. The opening speech on that occasion was made by the Honorable G. Mennen "Soapy" Williams, the Assistant Secretary of State for African Affairs, whose own office had been established only that year.

The scholarly study of Africa and the reports and fruits of public policy have also much to contribute to one another. A special tribute to the competence of the Program of African Studies and, in particular, to Professor Herskovits' soundly informed view of public affairs came with the request in March, 1960, from the Senate Committee on Foreign Relations to prepare the basic document on United States Foreign Policy toward Africa. The hundred-page report, prepared almost singlehanded by Professor Herskovits, remains a major contribution to thinking about American policies toward Africa and came at a particularly important time when the African drive for independence was transforming the continent.

The Program of African Studies has always welcomed the Foreign Service officers sent by the Foreign Service Institute for a year of intensive reading and study. Their experience in the field, usually gained at least partly in Africa, adds much to the seminars in which they participate, while they, in turn, learn of new approaches to analysis. Program faculty members have also been lecturers at the Foreign Service Institute and the War College, and Professor Carter was a member of the Africa Bureau's Advisory Committee during its existence.

The prime goal of the Program of African Studies has always been to train scholars, and those who have been associated with it have gained pre-eminence in many areas in this country and abroad. The first three Ph.D.s at Northwestern University with African subject matter, all in anthropology, have been particularly distinguished. Professor William Bascom (1939) is an outstanding art historian; Professor Joseph Greenberg (1940) is a leading linguist; and Dr. Hugh Smythe (1945), formerly Professor of Sociology at Brooklyn College, City University, New York, has been United States Ambassador both in Syria and in Malta. This breadth of scope and interest has been reflected in the careers of a number of Northwestern's African specialists, although most of them are in university posts.

Not surprisingly, Northwestern has long had a strong preponderance of Ph.D.s in anthropology among those particularly concerned with African studies. Indeed, in the total picture of the 78 scholars (through August, 1968) in this group, approximately half have taken their Ph.D.s in this particular field. Among those with defined African interests, there have been 37 Ph.D.s in anthropology, 12 in political science, 10 in history, 7 in geography, 5 in economics, 3 in sociology, 2 in psychology, 1 in English, and 1 in linguistics.

The Program of African Studies has maintained its original concentration on graduate work with constantly accelerating numbers. Of those just described as receiving the Ph.D. degree with concentration on African subject matter, over half (39) belong to the period from 1963 to 1968, and of these, 8 were awarded their degrees in 1967, and 6 more in 1968.

Twelve of those awarded the Ph.D. in the years between 1948 and 1968 have been African, and their record is indeed distinguished. Sejjengo Zake (Anthropology, 1962) is Minister of Education and Acting Attorney-General of Uganda; Pius Okigbo (Economics, 1956), who wrote *Nigerian Public Finance* and *Africa and the Common Market,* has been Economic Advisor to the Government of Nigeria and conducted the negotiations which established that country's relations with the Common Market; the late Eduardo Mondlane (Sociology, 1960), on leave from his post as Professor of Sociology at Syracuse University, headed the Mozambique Liberation Movement (FRELIMO); Mrs. Abeodu Jones (History, 1962) is Vice-President of the Research Association of Liberia and Research Specialist of the Department of Education, Liberia. Almost all the other African Ph.D.s hold academic positions in their own disciplines in African universities: Enid Forde (Geography, 1966) at the University of Sierra Leone; Isaria Kimambo (History, 1967) at the University College, Dar es Salaam, Tanzania; Samuel Nwabara (History, 1965) and Obi Wali (English, 1967) at what was the University of Nigeria, Nsukka; Israel Ola (Political Science, 1963) at the University of Ibadan, Nigeria; and Fola Soremkun (History, 1966) at the University of Zambia. Victor Uchendu (Anthropology, 1966) is Assistant Professor at the Food Research Institute of Stanford University.

Many of Northwestern's African graduate students have had to end their studies with the M.A. degree because of the demands of their home countries for their skills. Many others have come only for undergraduate work. Over 70 graduates from African countries have been granted the M.A. degree up to August, 1968, and 19 have taken Ph.D.s. Throughout the past twenty years, nearly 200 students from African countries have studied at Northwestern, either as postgraduates, special students, or as candidates for the B.A. degree. Some at the undergraduate level have passed through the Schools of Business, Dentistry, and Law, and a number have followed their special concentration in the Traffic Institute. Many have returned to their home countries to follow distinguished careers. Dr. Augustus Caine (M.A. Anthropology, 1959) is Secretary of Education in Liberia; Ebun P. Brown, a special student of economic development planning in 1961–62, is Deputy Secretary in the Ministry of Development in Sierra Leone; Tesfaye Gessesse, a student of the School of Speech, is now director of the Ethiopian Arts Center; Oliver Musuka (M.A. African History, 1965) is Principal of the Amordine Methodist Center in Rhodesia; Wande Abimbola (M.A. African Linguistics,

1966) is at the African Studies Division, University of Lagos; while others have spanned out to fill jobs in education, local government, journalism, and law. Joseph Okpaku (B.S. Civil Engineering, 1965) later switched to Literature at Stanford University and is editor of the *Journal of the New African Literature and the Arts*.

Professor Eugene Webb, formerly of the School of Journalism, associated a number of students in his critical analyses of African material. One of the School of Journalism's Ph.D.s, Hamid Mowlana (1963), shared interests between the African and Middle East fields and is now Associate Professor of International Communication at the American University in Washington. Among other graduate students of the School of Journalism with keen interests in Africa is Mrs. H. El-Kirdany (1956–57) who, under her maiden name of Laila Rostrom, has made an impressive career in television in the United Arab Republic and in Lebanon.

Northwestern University's most formal association with an African university has been the twelve-year contract between the Engineering faculty of the Technological Institute and the University of Khartoum, which Professor John Logan, Professor of Civil Engineering (now president of Rose Polytechnic Institute, Terre Haute, Indiana), initiated and which was originally supported by the Department of State and subsequently by the Agency for International Development.

Under this far-reaching arrangement, Northwestern trained a large number of Sudanese graduate students, of whom 4 received the Ph.D. degree: Idris Ahmed Mahmoud (Civil Engineering, 1966); Beshir Ahmed el Abbadi (Mechanical Engineering, 1966); Adam Mousa Madibbo (Civil Engineering, 1967); and Mahmoud el Sharif Agabein (Civil Engineering, 1968), while of the total of 16 who took the M.Sc. degree at Northwestern University, 5 more completed doctorates at other schools in accord with the intention of the program that the graduates should return to the faculty of the University of Khartoum with the widest and most valuable experience of U.S. engineering schools. Five more Sudanese graduate students are working toward the Ph.D. degree. Professor Raymond Kliphardt of the Engineering faculty has taken responsibility for providing staff for the Engineering School at Khartoum, while Professor Dafalla Addulla Turabi (now Dean of Faculty of Engineering and Architecture at Khartoum), Professor Sayed El Nazeer Dafalla (Vice-Chancellor of Khartoum University), and Dr. O. M. Beshir (Academic Secretary) visited the Technological Institute at Northwestern under the program of cultural exchange.

In addition to those who carried out their studies under these cooperative programs, another Sudanese student, Abdul-Rahman Abdun-Nur, completed his Ph.D. in Chemistry in 1966, and two American students, Mathew Betz (Civil Engineering, 1962) and Paul Roberts (Civil Engineering, 1966), completed research for the Ph.D. dissertation on African or related subject themes.

The basic goal of the Program of African Studies as set by Professor Herskovits has always been to create a corps of research-oriented scholars. From the first, therefore, graduate students sought funds to support field research. With topics chosen by themselves, they entered national competitions and scored impressive successes. In the field they enjoyed excellent relations with local institutions and officials, thereby setting standards that present-day students seek to emulate.

In recent years the number of grants for overseas training and research has increased substantially. External support through the prized Foreign Area Training Fellowships (still commonly called Ford grants from their source of support), National Science Foundation and National Institute of Mental Health grants, and Fulbright-Hayes awards, among others, has made it possible for increasing number of PAS graduate students to pursue important research in Africa. Most recently, internal support through Northwestern University's Intersocietal Council and the Program of African Studies' National Unity Project (both established under grants from the Ford Foundation) has aided still other graduate students, as well as faculty members, to carry on their research projects.

Since 1966, when four advanced graduate students were sent to different parts of Africa to do preliminary field work during the summer between their second year of course work and the preparation of their dissertation proposal, eight or nine graduate students a year have been provided with planned and directed summer field-work experience in Africa. In 1967 and 1968, this program was carried on in Ghana under the overall direction of the Director of the Institute for African Studies of the University of Ghana, Legon, and with supervision by members of his staff and a Northwestern faculty member. A specially planned Northwestern seminar on local field conditions now precedes participation in the program, which was supported in 1967 by the Ford Foundation and in 1968 by the Foreign Studies Extension Program of the Office of Education. Experience has already shown that this provision leads to more intelligently prepared dissertation proposals and to a far better approach to long-term field work.

The National Unity Project, for which the Ford Foundation provided a three-year grant in 1968, is a multidisciplinary research scheme involving both faculty members and graduate students. Its objective is to identify those factors aiding and those impeding national unity. The Project involves a systematic analysis of various systems that affect state systems, in particular, language, legal, urban, labor, and communication systems. In addition, research is proceeding on mobilization belief systems. The interaction of these various systems and its effects are being studied in particular in Ghana, Nigeria, and the Cameroon Republic, but data is also being sought in other African countries. The project makes provision for visiting African professors to work with local staff and students, and one of the first to come was Professor Ali Mazrui of the Political Science Department of Makerere University College. Support can also be extended to African graduate students for work at Northwestern that contributes to the general goals of the Project.

Another innovative venture is the Inter-University Committee for Ethiopian Studies, established in 1967 by Northwestern University, the University of Chicago, the University of Illinois (Circle Campus), and Haile Selassie I University in Addis Ababa, to develop a cooperative program of graduate courses with Ethiopian content among the three neighboring institutions—which can exchange credits as part of the Committee on Institutional Cooperation—and to encourage faculty and graduate student exchanges with Ethiopia. Professor Abraham Demoz, a distinguished linguist from Haile Selassie I University, introduced Amharic at Northwestern University in 1968–69. Professor William Shack of the University of Illinois provided a seminar on Social Change and Urbanization at Northwestern in the fall of 1968, and Professor Donald Levine of the University of Chicago offered a course and seminar there in the spring of 1969 open, as are the other opportunities, to students from the other institutions. Professor John Beckstrom and two Northwestern Law School students went to Ethiopia in the spring of 1969 to undertake cooperative research.

A crucial aspect of scholarship is books, and the Program

takes pride in the Africana Collection, now housed in a separate room in Deering Library and soon to occupy the top level of one of the towers of the new library. Such a decentralization of resources runs counter to correct library doctrine, by some views, but despite contemporary overcrowding, the end product is extremely satisfying. The richness and diversity of the collection, which now runs to some 37,500 volumes, reveal how attractive the topic of Africa has been in the publishing world. To find so much material readily available and to be able to draw on the expert help and advice of the Africana staff, which works so smoothly and efficiently under Africana's long-time curator, Mr. Hans Panofsky, attracts many scholars in addition to those from Northwestern. The great accomplishments in collecting this material, to which Professor Herskovits gave invaluable stimulus and help, have provided a magnificent base that all university libraries must envy, but the task and expense of keeping abreast of the mounting stream of publications is an ever-present strain.

Another by-product of the emphasis on scholarship was the establishment of an African Series by the Northwestern University Press. The basic financial support for this project has come from a small revolving fund (drawn from the ten-year Ford grant) which has been used to subsidize publications, with royalty returns flowing back into the fund. Although diminished, the revolving fund still continues to aid the publications of outstanding works to join the twenty already in the African Series and the fifty other books on Africa that are not part of the series because they were originally printed abroad.

The most striking reflection of the growth in the American scholarly interest in Africa, which has expanded so profusely in many universities, was the creation of the African Studies Association, which held its first annual meeting on the Evanston campus in 1958. Professor Herskovits was elected the first president, and the second was Professor Gwendolen M. Carter. Professor Paul Bohannan was President of the African Studies Association in 1965.

The untimely death of Professor Herskovits brought the first phase of Northwestern's African Studies Program to a close. He had worked hard in the cause of African scholarship, and the Program itself is a tribute to his concern and dedication. He perhaps overstrained himself in the leading role he took so successfully in the first Conference on Africanists held in Ghana in December, 1962, and he was intermittently ill in the remaining two months of his life. Professor Roland Young returned from leave in this emergency and served as Acting Director of the Program until Professor Gwendolen M. Carter took over in September, 1964, as Director and Melville J. Herskovits Professor of African Affairs, a new chair endowed by Ford Foundation funds.

In addition to this named chair, two other special marks of the great respect in which Professor Herskovits was held by his colleagues at home and abroad have been the transatlantic lecture series established on the initiative of Edinburgh University, and the annual book award through the African Studies Association. The Melville J. Herskovits Memorial Lecture series consists of formal lectures, subsequently printed in pamphlet form, that are presented alternately at Edinburgh University and at Northwestern University by faculty members associated with the other institution. The series was inaugurated in March, 1965, by Professor Carter with a lecture on "African Concepts of Nationalism in South Africa," and subsequent lectures from the Northwestern side have been given by Professor Alex Nekam on "Experiences in Customary Law" and Professor Robert W. Clower on "Mainsprings of African Economic Progress." From the Edinburgh side, Professor Kenneth Little lectured in Evanston on "Some Contemporary Trends in African Urbanization"; Professor George Shepperson on "Myth and Reality in Malawi"; and Professor R. Mansell Prothero on "Public Health, Pastoralism, and Politics in the Horn of Africa." The lecture series will continue to be given in alternate years.

The annual book award, similarly named for Professor Herskovits, is for the most outstanding scholarly work on Africa by an author resident in the United States. The prize, contributed to by American book publishers, including the Northwestern University Press, has been awarded so far to Professors Ruth Morganthau of Brandeis University, Leo Kuper of the University of California at Los Angeles, Jan Vansina of Wisconsin University, Crawford Young of the University of Wisconsin, and Herbert F. Weiss of New York University for their books, *Political Parties in French-Speaking Africa* (1964); *An African Bourgeoisie: Race, Class and Politics in South Africa* (1965); *Kingdoms of the Savanna* (1966); *Politics in the Congo* (1967); and *Political Protest in the Congo: The Parti Solidaire Africain during the Independence Struggle* (1967).

The impressive growth of the Program of African Studies in the second phase of its history is a tribute to the sound foundations and tradition Professor Herskovits established and the universal respect in which the Program is held in the United States and abroad. The ten-year Ford Foundation grant which he and Dean Simeon Leland cooperated to secure has provided the basic support for important faculty additions, graduate student fellowships, supplementary research grants, and the staff at Africa House. In 1967, Professor Ibrahim Abu-Lughod became Associate Director of the Program of African Studies, thereby enabling the Program to expand its competence to North Africa and to cope more adequately with an ever-increasing number of commitments.

In this period of American international responsibilities, the Program of African Studies can no longer confine its attention to advanced scholarship, vital as that will always continue to be. The number of undergraduate courses with African content at Northwestern has multiplied, and student enrollments do so also. While there is as yet no coordinated undergraduate program of African studies, the interest in Peace Corps service in Africa, Crossroads Africa, and Teachers for East and West Africa are additional stimuli to the developing concern for Africa. There is also growing understanding among academic institutions that an informed awareness of problems and potentialities in the developing countries is essential for intelligent citizenship.

The Program of African Studies has opened its weekly lecture series to the community and to the faculty members and students of nearby institutions so they may share the information and perspective brought by the outside speakers who visit the campus. Faculty members of other institutions are invited to the Program's faculty seminar, which was established in 1967–68. The Program is also assuming increasing responsibilities for training college and secondary school teachers, from whom come the earliest systematic introduction to the study of Africa.

In 1967, Professor Carter directed the Office of Education's eight-week summer seminar in Africa, arranging for university lectures and field experiences in Senegal, Ghana, Kenya, and Ethiopia for twenty-five American teachers, sixteen from high schools and nine from colleges and universities, situated in many parts of the United States. One of the basic requirements in selecting from the more than 400 applicants was three years of licensed teaching plus a commitment on the part of the institution from which the teacher came to make use of his or her widened experience and knowledge. In 1968,

Professor Abu-Lughod conducted an Office of Education–sponsored six-week seminar for thirty high school teachers on the Evanston campus, for which applications were equally numerous. This contribution to better teaching about Africa is being continued and is being joined by an additional summer institute for college teachers. In all these respects, the services provided by Northwestern's Program of African Studies are paralleled by those offered by other institutions, and the cumulative effect is considerable.

A unique contribution to the college curriculum on Africa has been made by an Office of Education–sponsored project to design basic material for an introductory interdepartmental course on Africa. In addition to the syllabus, the project includes an annotated bibliography adaptable to advanced computer techniques and a book of original essays designed for use with the syllabus. The major responsibilities in this project have been undertaken by Drs. Edward Soja and John Paden, and the Program staff as a whole has been associated as critics and contributors throughout its development and execution.

Looking ahead to the next twenty years, the Program of African Studies is equipped as never before for an expanding role of service to educational institutions throughout the country. It will not lose sight, however, of its major functions: to help to train African specialists, and to stimulate and, where feasible, coordinate research, not only among American scholars but also with our African and European colleagues. From the relatively small, but potent, beginnings of the Program of African Studies to the present, the overriding importance of working with Africans and contributing, where possible, to Africa has been kept to the fore. That African studies are now increasingly associated with Afro-American and Caribbean studies is part of the farsighted view that Professor Melville J. Herskovits always maintained.

CONFERENCE PROGRAM
September 10–13, 1968

Sept. 10	RECEPTION AND DINNER	President Roscoe Miller
		   Northwestern University
		Mrs. Melville J. Herskovits
		   Northwestern University
		Joseph H. Greenberg
		   Stanford University
		Akin L. Mabogunje
		   University of Ibadan

	OPENING SESSION	Paul Bohannan, Chairman Northwestern University

	S. Joshua L. Zake
	   Uganda Minister of
	   Education and Acting
	   Attorney-General
		Revision and Unification of
		African Legal Systems:
		The Uganda Experience

	Ali A. Mazrui
	   Makerere University
	   College
		Political Science and the
		Decline of African
		Nationalism

Sept. 11	PLENARY SESSION	Research Strategies for Studying Factors Affecting National Unity: Discussion by members of the faculty, Program of African Studies, Northwestern University Ibrahim Abu-Lughod, Chairman
	John N. Paden and Donald George Morrison	*National Integration and* *Stability in Africa*

	Remi Clignet	*Social Area Analysis of Douala and Yaounde*
	Edward W. Soja	*Transaction Flows and National Unity: The Nigerian Case*
	Jack Berry	*The Madina Project: Sociolinguistic Research in Ghana*
Sept. 11	SPECIALIST SESSION	Gus Liebenow, Chairman Indiana University
	Isaria N. Kimambo University College, Dar-es-Salaam	*Historical Research in Mainland Tanzania*
		Jean Herskovits, Discussant City College of New York
		Abeodu Jones, Discussant Liberian Department of Education
	James Fernandez Dartmouth College	*Contemporary African Religion: Confluents of Inquiry*
		Johannes Fabian, Discussant Northwestern University
		Robert Cameron Mitchell, Discussant Swarthmore College
Sept. 11	SPECIALIST SESSION	J. H. Kwabena Nketia, Chairman University of Ghana
	Joseph H. Greenberg Stanford University	*Dialogue on Sociolinguistics*
	Jack Berry Northwestern University	Gilbert Ansre, Discussant University of Ghana
		Abraham Demoz, Discussant Haile Selassie I University
Sept. 11	CONCERT	
	J. H. Kwabena Nketia University of Ghana	*Drum Performance*
	Seth Ladzekpo University of Ghana and Columbia University with Alfred Ladzekpo, Sviap Podstavski, and Joan Darby	*Illustrations of Traditional Styles of Drumming, Singing, and Dancing of the Ewe People of the Volta Region*

	Halim El-Dabh Howard University	*Performance of Nubian and Ethiopian Music*
Sept. 12	SPECIALIST SESSION	Robert A. Lystad, Chairman Johns Hopkins University
	Victor C. Uchendu Stanford University	*Priority Issues for Social Anthropological Research in Africa in the Next Two Decades*
		Igor Kopytoff, Discussant University of Pennsylvania
		Alvin W. Wolfe, Discussant University of Wisconsin, Milwaukee
	Marshall H. Segall Syracuse University	*The Growth of Psychology in African Studies*
		M. Brewster Smith, Discussant University of Chicago
		Douglas Price-Williams, Discussant Rice University
Sept. 12	SPECIALIST SESSION	Arrand Parsons, Chairman Northwestern University
	Klaus Wachsmann Northwestern University	*Ethnomusicology in African Studies: The Next Twenty Years*
		J. H. Kwabena Nketia, Discussant University of Ghana
		Halim El-Dabh, Discussant Howard University
		Norma McLeod, Discussant Tulane University
Sept. 12	SPECIALIST SESSION	Frank Willett, Chairman Northwestern University
	Robert Plant Armstrong Northwestern University	*The Arts in Human Cul- ture: Their Significance and Their Study*
		Justine Cordwell, Discussant Northwestern University
		Edward Callan, Discussant Western Michigan University

Daniel J. Crowley   *Traditional and Contem-*
University of California   *porary Art in Africa*
at Davis

                                        James Fernandez,
                                        Discussant
                                        Dartmouth College
                                        Joseph Okpaku,
                                        Discussant
                                        Journal of New African
                                        Literature and the Arts

Hamid Mowlana   *Communications Media in*
The American   *Africa: A Critique in Ret-*
University   *rospect and Prospect*
                                        Curtis MacDougall,
                                        Discussant
                                        Northwestern University

Sept. 12 SPECIALIST SESSION   Duane Marble, Chairman
                                        Northwestern University

Peter R. Gould   *Geography, Spatial Plan-*
Pennsylvania State   *ning, and Africa: The*
University   *Responsibility of the*
                                        Next Twenty Years
                                        Akin L. Mabogunje,
                                        Discussant
                                        University of Ibadan
                                        Robert H. Smith,
                                        Discussant
                                        University of Wisconsin

Harold K. Schneider   *A Formalist View of*
Lawrence University   *African Economic*
                                        Anthropology
                                        Simon Ottenberg,
                                        Discussant
                                        University of
                                        Washington
                                        Sheila van der Horst,
                                        Discussant
                                        South African Institute
                                        of Race Relations,
                                        University of Cape Town

Sept. 13 SPECIALIST SESSION   Joseph Harris, Chairman
                                        State University College,
                                        New York

Peter B. Hammond   *Afro-American Indians*
The Johns Hopkins   *and Afro-Asians: Cultural*
University   *Contacts between Africa*
                                        and the Peoples of Asia
                                        and Aboriginal America

		William Shack, Discussant University of Illinois
		Victor C. Uchendu, Discussant Stanford University
	Sterling Stuckey Northwestern University	*African and Afro-* *American Relationships:* *Research Possibilities*
		J. Congress Mbata, Discussant Northwestern University
		Mrs. Melville J. Herskovits, Discussant Northwestern University
Sept. 13	SPECIALIST SESSION	Robert Collins, Chairman University of California at Santa Barbara
	Kwamena Bentsi-Enchill University of Zambia	*Problems in the Construc-* *tion of Viable Consti-* *tutional Structures in* *Africa*
		S. Joshua L. Zake, Discussant Uganda Minister of Education
		Alexander Nekam, Discussant Northwestern University
Sept. 13	PLENARY SESSION	Gwendolen M. Carter, Chairman Northwestern University
	Nuradeen Alao, Robert Bunger, Jeff Donaldson, Susan Hanson, Joseph Kaufert, Erika King, Fay Leary, Barbara Lewis, Helaine Minkus, Femi Richards, William Schweer, Lance Sobel, Frank Stark, Phillips Stevens	Rapporteurs, summaries of specialist sessions and discussion from the floor.
Sept. 13	DINNER AND ADJOURNMENT	Vice-President Payson Wild Northwestern University
		Kwamena Bentsi-Enchill University of Zambia

Robert A. Lystad
  School of Advanced
  International Studies
  Johns Hopkins
  University
Victor Uchendu
  Stanford University
Sheila van der Horst
  South African Institute
  of Race Relations
  University of Cape Town
J. H. Kwabena Nketia
  University of Ghana
Douglas Price-Williams
  Rice University
S. Joshua L. Zake
  Uganda Minister of
  Education and Acting
  Attorney-General
Robert Collins
  University of California
  at Santa Barbara
Isaria N. Kimambo
  University College,
  Dar-es-Salaam
John Bainbridge
  International Legal
  Center, New York
Rene Wadlow
  Geneva Africa Institute
  Geneva, Switzerland

Gwendolen M. Carter, Director
Ann Moyal, Conference Coordinator

CONTRIBUTORS

Ibrahim Abu-Lughod

is Professor of Political Science at Northwestern University and Associate Director of the Program of African Studies.

Irma Adelman

is Professor of Economics at Northwestern University and is a member of the faculty of the Program of African Studies.

Robert Plant Armstrong

is Director of the Northwestern University Press and is associated with the Program of African Studies.

Kwamena Bentsi-Enchill

is a member of the faculty of the School of Law, University of Zambia, and has been a visiting professor at Northwestern University.

Jack Berry

is Chairman of the Department of Linguistics at Northwestern University, and is a member of the faculty of the Program of African Studies.

Edward Callan

is Professor of English at Western Michigan University.

Gwendolen M. Carter

is Professor of Political Science at Northwestern University and Director of the Program of African Studies.

Remi Clignet

is Associate Professor of Sociology at Northwestern University and is a member of the faculty of the Program of African Studies.

Daniel J. Crowley

received his Ph.D. from Northwestern University in 1956 and

is Chairman of the Department of Anthropology, University of California, Davis.

George Dalton

is Professor of Economics and Anthropology at Northwestern University and is a member of the faculty of the Program of African Studies.

James W. Fernandez

received his Ph.D. from Northwestern University in 1962 and is Associate Professor of Anthropology at Dartmouth College.

Peter R. Gould

received his Ph.D. from Northwestern University in 1960 and is Associate Professor of Geography at Pennsylvania State University.

Peter B. Hammond

received his Ph.D. from Northwestern University in 1962 and is Senior Post-Doctoral Fellow and Faculty Research Associate of the Institute of Southern History, the Johns Hopkins University.

Isaria N. Kimambo

received his Ph.D. from Northwestern University in 1967 and is Chairman of the Department of History, University College, Dar es Salaam, Tanzania.

Akin L. Mabogunje

is Professor of Geography at the University of Ibadan, Nigeria, and has been a visiting professor at Northwestern University.

Ali A. Mazrui

is Professor of Political Science and Dean of the Faculty of Liberal Arts at Makerere University College, Kampala, and has been a visiting professor at Northwestern University.

Robert Cameron Mitchell

is Assistant Professor of Sociology at Swarthmore College

and has been associated with the Program of African Studies.

Cynthia Taft Morris

is Associate Professor of Economics at the American University.

Donald George Morrison

is a Research Associate of the Council for Intersocietal Studies and a member of the Program of Applied Mathematics at Northwestern University.

Hamid Mowlana

received his Ph.D. from Northwestern University in 1963 and is Associate Professor of International Communication at the American University, Washington, D. C.

Alexander Nekam

is Professor of Law at Northwestern University Law School and is a member of the faculty of the Program of African Studies.

J. H. Kwabena Nketia

is Director of the Institute of African Studies at the University of Ghana and is Director of the Northwestern University–University of Ghana Summer Field Work Project.

Simon Ottenberg

received his Ph.D. from Northwestern University in 1957 and is Professor of Anthropology and Chairman of the Committee on African Studies at the University of Washington.

John N. Paden

is Assistant Professor of Political Science at Northwestern University and is a member of the faculty of the Program of African Studies.

Harold K. Schneider

received his Ph.D. from Northwestern University in 1953 and is Chairman of the Department of Anthropology at Lawrence University.

Marshall H. Segall

received his Ph.D. from Northwestern University in 1957 and is Professor of Psychology at Syracuse University.

Lance R. Sobel

is a member of the Department of Sociology at Northwestern University and is associated with the Program of African Studies.

Edward W. Soja

is Associate Professor of Geography at Northwestern University and is a member of the faculty of the Program of African Studies.

Sterling Stuckey

is a member of the Department of History at Atlanta University and has been associated with the Program of African Studies.

Victor C. Uchendu

received his Ph.D. from Northwestern University in 1966 and is Assistant Professor at the Food Research Institute, Stanford University.

Klaus Wachsmann

is Professor of Linguistics at Northwestern University and is a member of the faculty of the Program of African Studies.

Frank Willett

is a professor of African art and archaeology at Northwestern University and is a member of the faculty of the Program of African Studies.

Alvin W. Wolfe

received his Ph.D. from Northwestern University in 1957 and is Professor of Anthropology at the University of Wisconsin, Milwaukee.

S. Joshua L. Zake

received his Ph.D. from Northwestern University in 1962 and is Minister of Education and Acting Attorney-General of Uganda.